Contents Table

Welcome & What You'll Learn

Welcome to "TypeScript Made Easy: Elevate Your JavaScript Code"! If you're a JavaScript developer ready to unlock a new level of productivity, reliability, and scalability, you're in the right place. TypeScript, a superset of JavaScript, offers powerful tools that can transform how you build web applications and Node.js projects.

Why TypeScript? The JavaScript Evolution

JavaScript is the heart of modern web development, but it can also be a source of frustration. Large JavaScript projects can become difficult to manage, prone to subtle bugs, and challenging to maintain. TypeScript solves these problems by introducing a static type system, enhanced tooling, and features that make your code more readable, predictable, and robust.

What You'll Gain:

By the end of this book, you'll have a solid grasp of TypeScript's core concepts and practical skills to apply it effectively. Here's a glimpse of what you'll learn:

- **Strong Foundations:** You'll start by understanding why TypeScript is essential and how it complements JavaScript. You'll set up your development environment, explore the basics of TypeScript's type system (numbers, strings, arrays, etc.), and master TypeScript functions.
- **Advanced Concepts:** You'll dive into classes, generics, modules, and other powerful features that enable you to build well-structured, maintainable code. You'll explore enums, union types, and decorators to model complex data and enhance your code's capabilities.
- **Real-World Applications:** TypeScript shines in modern frameworks like React and Node.js. You'll learn how to leverage TypeScript to build responsive user interfaces with React and create scalable backend services with Node.js. You'll also tackle asynchronous programming, testing, and essential tooling to optimize your development workflow.
- **Beyond the Basics:** As you gain confidence, you'll explore advanced type manipulation techniques, strategies for integrating TypeScript into existing projects, and best practices to write clean, efficient TypeScript code.

Who This Book Is For

This book is designed for:

- **JavaScript Developers:** Whether you're a beginner or a seasoned JavaScript pro, if you're curious about TypeScript and want to elevate your skills, this book is for you.
- **Web Developers & Node.js Engineers:** If you build web applications, REST APIs, or server-side applications with Node.js, TypeScript can streamline your development and improve the quality of your code.
- **Anyone Seeking Reliable Code:** If you value catching errors early, reducing bugs, and making your codebase more maintainable, TypeScript is a valuable addition to your toolbox.

How to Use This Book

You can read this book from cover to cover or jump to the sections that most interest you. Each chapter builds on the knowledge from previous chapters, but you can also use it as a reference when you need to refresh specific concepts.

Are You Ready? Let's Get Started!

TypeScript is an exciting journey that empowers you to write code that's not just functional but also elegant and maintainable. Get ready to transform your JavaScript skills and build the next generation of web applications with confidence.

Let's embark on this TypeScript adventure together!

Section I:
TypeScript Fundamentals

Embracing TypeScript: Beyond JavaScript

Outline

- Understanding the Need for TypeScript
- JavaScript's Shortcomings
- Key Benefits of TypeScript
- When to Use (and Not Use) TypeScript
- Chapter Summary

Understanding the Need for TypeScript

JavaScript, with its flexibility and dynamic nature, has revolutionized web development. It allows for rapid prototyping, quick iterations, and the creation of interactive web experiences. However, as JavaScript projects grow in complexity, its dynamic nature can become a double-edged sword.

The Dynamic Nature of JavaScript

JavaScript's dynamic typing means that variables can hold values of any type, and their types can change at runtime. While this flexibility is great for quick development, it can lead to unexpected errors when types mismatch or change unexpectedly. Imagine a function expecting a number but receiving a string; this can cause your application to crash or behave erratically.

Challenges in Large Codebases

In large-scale applications with hundreds or thousands of lines of code, managing these type-related issues becomes a major headache. Refactoring code becomes risky, as seemingly small changes can have cascading effects due to hidden type dependencies. Debugging becomes more difficult because errors might not surface until runtime, often in production environments. Collaboration within teams also suffers, as developers need to rely on extensive documentation or conventions to understand how different parts of the code interact.

Enter TypeScript

TypeScript was born out of the need to address these challenges and bring the benefits of static typing to the JavaScript ecosystem. By adding a static type system to JavaScript, TypeScript empowers developers to catch errors during development, refactor code with confidence, and build more reliable and maintainable applications.

In essence, TypeScript is JavaScript with superpowers. It provides a layer of safety and predictability that helps you tame the dynamic nature of JavaScript while still leveraging its flexibility and expressive power. It's not a replacement for JavaScript; it's an enhancement that equips you with the tools to build better JavaScript projects.

JavaScript's Shortcomings

JavaScript's dynamic typing, while a boon for flexibility, introduces several challenges that can hinder development, especially as projects scale. TypeScript addresses these shortcomings head-on, improving code quality, maintainability, and the overall developer experience.

Type-Related Errors

Dynamic typing in JavaScript means that type mismatches often go unnoticed until runtime. Consider this example:

```
function calculateArea(width, height) { return width * height; } //
Accidentally passing a string: const area = calculateArea(10, "5");
console.log(area); // Output: NaN (Not a Number)
```

Since JavaScript doesn't enforce types upfront, this code runs without any complaints. The error only surfaces at runtime, potentially crashing the application or producing incorrect results. In contrast, TypeScript would catch this error during development:

```
function calculateArea(width: number, height: number): number { return width *
height; }
```

Now, TypeScript's type checker would flag the incorrect argument type, preventing the error before the code even runs.

Refactoring Challenges

Refactoring JavaScript code can be a minefield. Consider a function that processes user data:

```
function processUserData(user) { const name = user.name; const age = user.age;
// ... more logic }
```

If you decide to rename `user.name` to `user.fullName`, there's no guarantee that every usage of `name` in your codebase will be updated. TypeScript's type definitions provide a safety net. If you define an interface for `User`, TypeScript will alert you to any references that become broken due to refactoring.

Limited Tooling Support

Many modern IDE features rely on type information. Without it, features like code completion, type hints, and automated refactorings become less effective. TypeScript bridges this gap by providing rich type annotations that empower IDEs to offer a more productive development experience. For example, with TypeScript, your IDE can suggest valid properties and methods as you type, catch errors on the fly, and automatically update references during refactoring.

In summary, while JavaScript's flexibility is valuable, its shortcomings can lead to frustration and errors. TypeScript tackles these issues by introducing a type system, improving code quality, and enhancing the developer experience.

Key Benefits of TypeScript

TypeScript brings a wealth of advantages to the table that significantly enhance JavaScript development, resulting in more robust, maintainable, and developer-friendly code.

Static Typing

The heart of TypeScript lies in its static type system. This means that you explicitly define the types of variables, function parameters, and return values. This might seem like extra work upfront, but it pays off in several ways:

- **Early Error Detection:** TypeScript's compiler catches type-related errors during development, preventing them from causing issues in production. This leads to fewer bugs and a more stable codebase.
- **Safer Refactoring:** When you refactor TypeScript code, the compiler guides you, ensuring that changes don't inadvertently break existing functionality due to type mismatches.
- **Improved Maintainability:** TypeScript code is inherently self-documenting. Type annotations clearly convey the intended purpose of variables and functions, making it easier for you and other developers to understand and maintain the codebase in the long run.

Improved Developer Experience

TypeScript supercharges your development environment by enhancing the capabilities of your code editor or IDE:

- **Code Completion:** As you type, TypeScript can suggest relevant properties, methods, and even entire code snippets based on the types you've defined. This not only speeds up development but also reduces the chances of typos and errors.
- **Type Hints:** TypeScript provides helpful tooltips and inline documentation that display the types of variables and parameters, making it easier to navigate and understand complex code.
- **Navigation:** TypeScript's type system allows you to quickly jump to definitions of variables, functions, and classes, improving your workflow and understanding of the codebase.

Enhanced Readability and Maintainability

TypeScript's type annotations act as a form of documentation embedded directly within your code:

- **Self-Documenting Code:** Explicit types make the code's intent clear, reducing the need for extensive comments and making it easier for new developers to onboard.
- **Easier Collaboration:** When working in teams, TypeScript helps ensure that everyone adheres to the same type conventions, minimizing misunderstandings and conflicts.

Robust Codebase

By catching type-related errors early on, TypeScript significantly contributes to the robustness and reliability of your applications:

- **Fewer Bugs:** Type-related errors are a common source of bugs in JavaScript. TypeScript's static type checking dramatically reduces the likelihood of such errors making it to production.
- **Increased Confidence:** With TypeScript, you can deploy your code with greater confidence, knowing that it has passed rigorous type checks and is less likely to fail due to unexpected type issues.

In essence, TypeScript takes the best of JavaScript's flexibility and adds a layer of safety, structure, and tooling support that empowers you to build larger, more complex applications with ease.

When to Use (and Not Use) TypeScript

TypeScript offers substantial benefits, but it's not always the right tool for every job. Understanding when to embrace TypeScript and when to stick with plain JavaScript is crucial for making informed decisions.

When TypeScript Shines

TypeScript excels in the following scenarios:

- **Large Projects:** As projects grow in complexity, so does the potential for type-related errors. TypeScript's type system helps manage this complexity by catching errors early and providing a structured way to organize code. With a large codebase and multiple developers, the benefits of early error detection and improved maintainability become even more pronounced.
- **Collaborative Environments:** When teams work together, miscommunications and misunderstandings about code can easily lead to bugs. TypeScript's type annotations act as a shared language, clarifying the expectations and contracts within the codebase. This fosters better communication and reduces the likelihood of errors caused by incorrect assumptions.
- **Long-Term Maintenance:** Software projects often evolve over time. New features are added, existing ones are modified, and teams change. TypeScript's type definitions act as living documentation, making it easier for new developers to understand the codebase and make changes with confidence. This is especially valuable in projects with a long lifespan.
- **Desire for Confidence:** TypeScript's static type checking gives developers a sense of assurance. Knowing that many potential errors have been caught during development reduces the anxiety of unexpected runtime surprises. This boost in confidence can lead to faster development cycles and more reliable software.

When TypeScript Might Not Be Ideal

While TypeScript offers many advantages, there are cases where its benefits might not outweigh the costs:

- **Small, Simple Projects:** For small scripts, prototypes, or one-off tasks, the overhead of adding types might not be justified. JavaScript's flexibility can be beneficial for quickly getting things done without the need for strict type definitions.
- **Rapid Prototyping:** When you need to experiment and iterate rapidly, TypeScript's type system might feel like a constraint. JavaScript's dynamic nature allows for more flexibility and less upfront structure, which can be helpful in the early stages of development.
- **Teams Unfamiliar with TypeScript:** Adopting TypeScript involves a learning curve. If your team is primarily experienced in JavaScript and has limited time or resources for training, the transition might slow down development initially. It's essential to assess the team's willingness and ability to learn a new language before making the switch.

Ultimately, the decision to use TypeScript depends on the specific needs of your project and team. Weighing the benefits against the potential drawbacks will help you determine whether TypeScript is the right fit for your next JavaScript endeavor.

Chapter Summary

In this chapter, we explored the motivations behind TypeScript's creation and how it addresses the shortcomings of JavaScript in large-scale development. We delved into:

- **JavaScript's Dynamic Nature:** We discussed how JavaScript's flexibility, while advantageous for rapid development, can lead to challenges in maintaining large codebases.
- **TypeScript's Solution:** We introduced TypeScript as a statically typed superset of JavaScript that adds a layer of safety and predictability to your code.
- **Key Benefits:** We highlighted the core advantages of TypeScript, including early error detection, safer refactoring, improved developer experience, enhanced code readability, and a more robust codebase.

- **When to Choose TypeScript:** We explored scenarios where TypeScript shines, such as large projects, collaborative environments, and situations where long-term maintainability and code confidence are paramount.
- **When TypeScript Might Not Be Ideal:** We acknowledged situations where TypeScript's overhead might not be justified, such as small projects, rapid prototyping, or teams unfamiliar with the language.

By understanding the need for TypeScript and its unique benefits, you're now equipped to make informed decisions about when and how to leverage its power in your JavaScript projects. In the next chapter, we'll dive into setting up your TypeScript development environment and start exploring its core features.

Setting Up Your TypeScript Environment

Outline

- Installing Node.js and npm
- Installing TypeScript (Globally and Locally)
- Creating Your First TypeScript File
- Compiling TypeScript to JavaScript
- Understanding the tsconfig.json File
- Editor/IDE Integration (VS Code)
- Chapter Summary

Installing Node.js and npm

Before we dive into TypeScript, it's crucial to set up a solid foundation. Node.js and npm play a pivotal role in the TypeScript ecosystem, providing the runtime environment and package management capabilities necessary for efficient development.

Why Node.js and npm?

- **Node.js:** TypeScript is a superset of JavaScript, and Node.js allows you to execute JavaScript code outside of a web browser. This is essential for tasks like compiling TypeScript into JavaScript, running build tools, and managing dependencies. Node.js provides a robust runtime environment for your TypeScript projects.
- **npm:** The Node Package Manager (npm) is the default package manager for Node.js. It simplifies the process of installing, updating, and managing the various libraries and tools you'll need for TypeScript development. With npm, you can easily install TypeScript itself, along with popular frameworks, testing utilities, and other dependencies.

Installing Node.js and npm

The easiest way to install both Node.js and npm is to download the installer directly from the official Node.js website:

1. **Download:** Go to https://nodejs.org/ and download the appropriate installer for your operating system (Windows, macOS, or Linux).
2. **Install:**
   - **Windows/macOS:** Run the installer and follow the on-screen instructions. The installer will typically set up Node.js and npm in their default locations.
   - **Linux:** You can use package managers like `apt` (for Debian-based distributions) or `yum` (for Red Hat-based distributions). For example, on Ubuntu, you can run:
     `sudo apt install nodejs npm`
3. **Verify Installation:** Open your terminal or command prompt and run the following commands:
   `node -v npm -v`
   These commands should display the installed versions of Node.js and npm, respectively.

Additional Tips:

- **Consider nvm (Node Version Manager):** If you plan to work on multiple projects that require different versions of Node.js, using a version manager like nvm (Node Version Manager) can be incredibly helpful. It allows you to easily switch between different Node.js versions on your system.
- **Update npm:** After installing Node.js, it's a good practice to update npm to the latest version:
  `npm install -g npm`

With Node.js and npm installed, you have the foundation in place to start building your TypeScript development environment.

Installing TypeScript (Globally and Locally)

Now that we have Node.js and npm, we're ready to bring TypeScript into the picture. There are two primary ways to install TypeScript: globally and locally. Each approach has its own advantages and use cases.

Global Installation

A global installation makes the TypeScript compiler (`tsc`) accessible from anywhere on your system. This can be convenient for running TypeScript commands directly from the terminal, regardless of your project's location.

How to Install Globally

Open your terminal or command prompt and run the following command:

```
npm install -g typescript
```

This command uses npm to fetch the latest version of TypeScript from the npm registry and installs it globally. The `-g` flag indicates a global installation.

Local Installation

A local installation installs TypeScript as a dependency within your specific project. This approach is generally recommended for most projects, as it offers several benefits:

- **Project Isolation:** Each project has its own dedicated version of TypeScript, preventing conflicts that might arise if different projects rely on varying versions.
- **Version Control:** The TypeScript version is tracked in your project's `package.json` file, ensuring that all team members use the same version and making it easier to reproduce the project environment.
- **Cleaner Global Environment:** Avoids cluttering your global npm installation with project-specific dependencies.

How to Install Locally

Navigate to your project's root directory in the terminal and run the following command:

```
npm install --save-dev typescript
```

This command installs TypeScript as a development dependency, meaning it's only needed during development and won't be included in your final production code. The `--save-dev` flag automatically adds the dependency to the `devDependencies` section of your `package.json` file.

Which Approach Should You Choose?

In most cases, **local installations** are the preferred way to work with TypeScript. They provide better project management, version control, and isolation. However, if you frequently work with TypeScript outside of specific projects or prefer the convenience of global commands, a global installation might be suitable.

In this book, we'll primarily focus on using local installations, as they align with best practices for modern TypeScript development.

Creating Your First TypeScript File

Let's get our hands dirty with some TypeScript code! In this section, we'll create a simple TypeScript file, explore its basic syntax, and see how it differs from regular JavaScript.

Creating the File

1. **Open your code editor:** Choose your preferred code editor or IDE (we recommend Visual Studio Code).
2. **Create a new file:** Name it `hello.ts`. The `.ts` extension is the standard for TypeScript files.

Basic TypeScript Syntax

Here's the classic "Hello, world!" program in TypeScript:

```
const message: string = "Hello, world!"; console.log(message);
```

Let's break down what's happening:

- **`const message: string = "Hello, world!";`:**
  - **`const`:** This declares a constant variable named `message`. In TypeScript, you can also use `let` for variables that can be reassigned.
  - **`message`:** The name of your variable.
  - **`: string`:** This is a type annotation. It tells TypeScript that the `message` variable must hold a value of type `string`. This is the key difference from JavaScript, where types are not explicitly declared.
  - **`=`:** The assignment operator.
  - **`"Hello, world!"`:** The string value assigned to the `message` variable.
- **`console.log(message);`:** This line is identical to JavaScript. It logs the value of the `message` variable to the console.

How TypeScript Differs from JavaScript

The most significant difference you'll notice is the use of type annotations (`string` in our example). TypeScript uses these annotations to enforce type safety, meaning that it helps you catch errors related to mismatched types during development rather than at runtime.

Here are some other key differences:

- **Type Annotations:** TypeScript allows you to add type annotations to variables, function parameters, return values, and more. This makes your code more explicit and easier to understand.
- **Interfaces and Types:** TypeScript provides interfaces and type aliases to define complex types and structures, enhancing code organization and maintainability.
- **Classes:** TypeScript supports classes, which are a fundamental concept in object-oriented programming. Classes help you model real-world objects and create reusable code.
- **Generics:** TypeScript's generics enable you to write reusable code that can work with various types, promoting flexibility and type safety.
- **Modules:** TypeScript has a module system that helps you organize your code into logical units and avoid naming conflicts.

In the following chapters, we'll delve deeper into each of these TypeScript features and see how they empower you to write more reliable and maintainable code. But for now, savor the simplicity of this "Hello, world!" example, and get ready to unlock the full potential of TypeScript!

Compiling TypeScript to JavaScript

TypeScript, with its type annotations and advanced features, is not directly understood by web browsers or Node.js. That's where the TypeScript compiler (`tsc`) comes in. Its job is to translate your TypeScript code into plain JavaScript that can be executed.

The Role of the TypeScript Compiler

The `tsc` compiler acts as a bridge between your TypeScript source code and the JavaScript that runs in your environment. It performs several crucial tasks:

1. **Type Checking:** It scrutinizes your TypeScript code for any type-related errors. For example, if you accidentally try to assign a number to a variable declared as a string, `tsc` will raise a flag during compilation, preventing the error from causing problems at runtime.
2. **Transpilation:** It converts your TypeScript code into equivalent JavaScript code. This includes removing type annotations, converting modern JavaScript syntax to older versions (if configured to do so), and generating JavaScript files that can be executed by browsers or Node.js.
3. **Error Reporting:** If it finds any errors, `tsc` provides clear messages indicating the location and nature of the problems. This feedback loop is invaluable for quickly identifying and fixing issues in your code.

Compiling Your TypeScript File

Let's see how to compile the `hello.ts` file we created earlier:

1. **Open your terminal:** Navigate to the directory where your `hello.ts` file is located.
2. **Run the compiler:** Execute the following command:
   `tsc hello.ts`
3. **Check the output:** If your code is error-free, `tsc` will generate a `hello.js` file in the same directory. This JavaScript file is the result of the compilation process and can be executed directly.

Catching Errors Early

Let's introduce an intentional error into our `hello.ts` file:

```
const message: string = 123; // Error: Type 'number' is not assignable to type
'string'. console.log(message);
```

Now, when you try to compile it, `tsc` will immediately report the error:

hello.ts:1:15 - error TS2322: Type 'number' is not assignable to type 'string'.

1 const message: string = 123;
~

This early feedback loop allows you to correct the mistake before the code reaches runtime, where it could potentially cause problems. This is a major advantage of TypeScript's static type checking. It acts as a safety net, helping you catch and fix errors during development, leading to more robust and reliable applications.

Understanding the tsconfig.json File

In the world of TypeScript, the `tsconfig.json` file is your project's command center. It's a configuration file written in JSON format that tells the TypeScript compiler (`tsc`) how to behave and what options to use when transforming your TypeScript code into JavaScript.

Why a Configuration File?

Imagine you're working on a large project with multiple TypeScript files. You might want to:

- Specify which JavaScript version the output should be compatible with.
- Choose a module system (CommonJS, ES Modules, etc.).
- Define where the compiled JavaScript files should go.
- Control how strict TypeScript is when enforcing type rules.

The `tsconfig.json` file allows you to set these options and more in a centralized way, ensuring consistency across your project and making it easier to manage.

A Basic `tsconfig.json` Example

Here's a simple example of a `tsconfig.json` file:

```
{ "compilerOptions": { "target": "ES6", "module": "CommonJS", "outDir":
"./dist", "strict": true } }
```

Let's break down the key options within the `compilerOptions` section:

- **`target`:** This specifies the version of JavaScript that TypeScript should generate as output. For example, ES6 (also known as ECMAScript 2015) enables you to use modern JavaScript features like arrow functions, classes, and template literals. Choose a target that matches the level of browser or Node.js support you need.
- **`module`:** This determines the module system to use. Here are the most common options:
  - `CommonJS`: The traditional module system used in Node.js.
  - `ES Modules` (or `ESNext`): The newer standard module system supported by modern browsers and Node.js.
- **`outDir`:** This tells the compiler where to place the generated JavaScript files. In our example, they will be put in a `dist` folder within your project directory.
- **`strict`:** When set to `true`, TypeScript enables all strict type-checking options. This makes the compiler more rigorous in enforcing type rules, which can help catch potential errors early on.

Benefits of Using `strict` Mode

Enabling `strict` mode is highly recommended, especially for new projects. It enforces stricter rules around type inference, null and undefined values, and other potential pitfalls. While it might initially lead to more compiler errors, it ultimately helps you write safer, more predictable code in the long run.

Additional Options

The `tsconfig.json` file offers many more configuration options. We'll cover some of them in more detail later in this book. For now, you have the essential tools to set up your TypeScript projects and start compiling code.

Creating the `tsconfig.json` File

You can create the `tsconfig.json` file manually or use the TypeScript compiler to generate a basic configuration. Simply run this command in your terminal from your project's root directory:

```
tsc --init
```

This will create a `tsconfig.json` file with sensible default options, which you can then customize as needed.

Editor/IDE Integration (VS Code)

While you can technically write TypeScript code in any text editor, a code editor or Integrated Development Environment (IDE) with strong TypeScript support can significantly boost your productivity and make coding a more enjoyable experience.

Why a TypeScript-Aware Editor?

A specialized editor offers numerous benefits for TypeScript development:

- **Real-time Feedback:** It continuously checks your code for errors as you type, highlighting issues instantly and providing suggestions for fixes. This immediate feedback helps you catch errors early on, saving you time and frustration later.
- **Intelligent Code Completion:** It suggests relevant variables, functions, properties, and types as you type, reducing the need to look things up in documentation and helping you write code faster with fewer errors.
- **Refactoring Tools:** It simplifies refactoring tasks like renaming variables or functions, extracting code into separate functions, and more. This makes your codebase easier to maintain and evolve.
- **Debugging Support:** It provides integrated debugging tools to set breakpoints, inspect variables, and step through your code, making it easier to diagnose and fix issues.

Visual Studio Code: The Recommended Choice

Visual Studio Code (VS Code) has emerged as a favorite among TypeScript developers due to its excellent built-in TypeScript support, extensive customization options, and vibrant ecosystem of extensions.

Installing the TypeScript Extension

While VS Code has basic TypeScript support out of the box, installing the official TypeScript extension enhances its capabilities:

1. **Open the Extensions Marketplace:** Click on the Extensions icon in the sidebar or press `Ctrl+Shift+X` (or `Cmd+Shift+X` on macOS).
2. **Search for "TypeScript":** Type "TypeScript" in the search bar and look for the official Microsoft TypeScript extension.
3. **Install:** Click the "Install" button next to the extension.

VS Code Features in Action

Once installed, the TypeScript extension supercharges your VS Code experience:

- **Real-time Type Checking and Error Highlighting:** As you type, VS Code will underline any TypeScript errors in red squiggly lines, providing helpful error messages and often suggesting automatic fixes.

- **Intelligent Code Completion (IntelliSense):** When you start typing a variable or function name, VS Code will offer suggestions based on the available types and context. Press `Tab` to accept a suggestion and auto-complete your code.
- **Refactoring Tools:** Right-click on a variable, function, or class name and choose "Refactor" to access various refactoring options, such as renaming, extracting, or moving code.
- **Debugging:** VS Code provides a robust debugger for TypeScript. Set breakpoints, inspect variables, and step through your code to pinpoint and resolve issues.

Other Editors

While VS Code is highly recommended, other code editors like Sublime Text and WebStorm also offer solid TypeScript support through plugins or extensions. You can find instructions on setting them up by searching online or checking their official documentation.

Customization is Key

Remember, one of the strengths of code editors is their customizability. Take some time to explore the settings and preferences in your chosen editor. You can adjust themes, fonts, keyboard shortcuts, and other aspects to create a development environment that perfectly suits your workflow and preferences.

By harnessing the power of a TypeScript-aware editor or IDE, you'll be well-equipped to tackle even the most complex TypeScript projects with ease and efficiency.

Chapter Summary

In this chapter, we laid the groundwork for our TypeScript journey by setting up a robust development environment. We covered the following:

- **Node.js and npm:** We explained the importance of Node.js and npm as the runtime and package manager for TypeScript development and provided instructions for installing them.
- **TypeScript Installation:** We explored the differences between global and local TypeScript installations, demonstrating how to install TypeScript using npm.
- **First TypeScript File:** We created a simple "Hello, world!" program in TypeScript, highlighting the basic syntax and the use of type annotations.
- **Compilation with `tsc`:** We introduced the TypeScript compiler (`tsc`) and learned how to compile TypeScript code into JavaScript, emphasizing how TypeScript catches errors during compilation.
- **The `tsconfig.json` File:** We discussed the purpose and structure of the `tsconfig.json` configuration file, explaining key options like `target`, `module`, `outDir`, and `strict`.
- **Editor/IDE Integration:** We emphasized the importance of using a TypeScript-aware editor like Visual Studio Code (VS Code) and demonstrated how to install the TypeScript extension and utilize its features for enhanced productivity.

With your TypeScript environment ready to go, you're now prepared to delve deeper into the world of TypeScript and unlock its full potential for building robust and maintainable JavaScript applications. In the next chapter, we'll dive into the core building blocks of TypeScript: its type system.

Core Types: Building Blocks of TypeScript

Outline

- Number: Representing Numeric Values
- String: Working with Text
- Boolean: True or False Values
- Array: Collections of Data
- Tuple: Fixed-Length Arrays with Mixed Types
- Any: Flexible (But Use with Caution!)
- Void: Representing the Absence of a Value
- Never: Unreachable Code or Errors
- Unknown: Type-Safe Alternative to Any
- Type Inference: Let TypeScript Deduce the Types
- Type Assertions: Overriding Type Inference
- Chapter Summary

Number

In TypeScript, just like in JavaScript, the `number` type is your go-to for representing numeric data. Whether it's a whole number (integer) like `10` or a decimal value (floating-point) like `3.14`, TypeScript treats them all as `number`.

Declaring Number Variables and Constants

You can declare `number` variables using `let` (for variables that can be reassigned) or `const` (for constants that cannot be changed):

```
let age: number = 25; // Variable const pi: number = 3.14159; // Constant
```

Arithmetic Operations

TypeScript supports all the standard arithmetic operations you're familiar with from JavaScript:

```
let sum: number = 5 + 3; // Addition let difference: number = 12 - 7; //
Subtraction let product: number = 4 * 2; // Multiplication let quotient:
number = 20 / 5; // Division let remainder: number = 17 % 3; // Modulus
(remainder after division) // Increment and decrement age++; age--;
```

Math Functions

TypeScript, being a superset of JavaScript, gives you access to a wide range of math functions from the built-in `Math` object. Here are a few examples:

```
let roundedValue: number = Math.round(4.7); // Rounds to nearest integer (5)
let absoluteValue: number = Math.abs(-10); // Absolute value (10) let
squareRoot: number = Math.sqrt(16); // Square root (4) let power: number =
Math.pow(2, 3); // 2 raised to the power 3 (8)
```

Type Inference with Numbers

TypeScript is often smart enough to infer the type of a variable based on its initial value:

```
let num = 42; // TypeScript infers that 'num' is of type 'number'
```

Working with Numbers in TypeScript

You can use number variables and constants in expressions, functions, and other parts of your TypeScript code just like you would in JavaScript. TypeScript's type checking simply adds an extra layer of safety by ensuring that you're using numbers correctly and consistently throughout your codebase.

Important Considerations

- **NaN (Not a Number):** TypeScript uses the special `number` value `NaN` to represent the result of invalid mathematical operations (e.g., dividing by zero).
- **Infinity and -Infinity:** TypeScript also includes `Infinity` and `-Infinity` to represent positive and negative infinity, respectively.

With a solid understanding of the `number` type, you're ready to tackle a wide range of numerical computations and operations in your TypeScript projects.

String

In TypeScript, as in JavaScript, the `string` type is your trusty companion for handling text data. Whether it's a single character, a word, a sentence, or even an entire book, TypeScript treats it all as a `string`.

Declaring String Variables and Constants

You have three ways to enclose your text when declaring a `string` variable or constant in TypeScript:

```
let greeting: string = 'Hello'; // Single quotes let name: string = "Alice";
// Double quotes let message: string = `Welcome, ${name}!`; // Backticks
(template literal)
```

All three methods are valid, and the choice often comes down to personal preference or the specific needs of your code.

String Concatenation

To combine multiple strings, you can use the + operator:

```
let firstName: string = "John"; let lastName: string = "Doe"; let fullName:
string = firstName + " " + lastName; console.log(fullName); // Output: "John
Doe"
```

Template Literals

Template literals (strings enclosed in backticks) offer a more powerful way to work with strings. They allow for easy interpolation of variables and expressions:

```
let age: number = 30; let bio: string = `My name is ${name}, and I am ${age}
years old.`; console.log(bio); // Output: "My name is Alice, and I am 30 years
old."
```

Template literals also support multi-line strings and embedded expressions:

```
let multiLineString: string = `This is a multi-line string with an embedded
expression: ${2 + 2}`;
```

Common String Manipulation Methods

TypeScript inherits a wealth of string manipulation methods from JavaScript. Here are some of the most common ones:

```
let text: string = "TypeScript is awesome!"; let length: number = text.length;
// Length of the string let uppercaseText: string = text.toUpperCase(); //
Convert to uppercase let lowercaseText: string = text.toLowerCase(); //
Convert to lowercase let substring: string = text.substring(0, 10); // Extract
a portion of the string let replacedText: string = text.replace("awesome",
"amazing"); // Replace a substring
```

Type Inference with Strings

Similar to numbers, TypeScript can infer the type of a variable assigned a string value:

```
let city = "New York"; // TypeScript infers that 'city' is of type 'string'
```

Important Considerations

- **Immutability:** Strings in TypeScript (and JavaScript) are immutable, meaning you cannot change the individual characters within a string. Instead, you create new strings when performing modifications.
- **Unicode Support:** TypeScript strings are fully Unicode-compliant, allowing you to work with characters from a wide range of languages and scripts.

The `string` type is fundamental to handling text data in TypeScript. Mastering its declaration, manipulation, and interpolation techniques will enable you to build applications that effectively process and display textual information.

Boolean

The `boolean` type in TypeScript, just like in JavaScript, is the foundation of logical operations. It represents a binary state: `true` or `false`. Boolean values are essential for making decisions and controlling the flow of your programs.

Declaring Boolean Variables and Constants

Declaring a `boolean` variable or constant is straightforward:

```
let isLoggedIn: boolean = true; const isLoading: boolean = false;
```

You can use `let` for boolean variables that might change their value later and `const` for boolean values that remain constant throughout your code.

Boolean Values in Conditional Statements

The primary use of boolean values is in conditional statements (`if`, `else`) to control the execution path of your code:

```
let age: number = 18; if (age >= 18) { console.log("You are an adult."); }
else { console.log("You are a minor."); }
```

In this example, the condition `age >= 18` evaluates to a boolean value (`true` or `false`). Based on this value, either the first block (if true) or the second block (if false) is executed.

Logical Operators

TypeScript supports the following logical operators to work with boolean values:

- **AND (&&)**: Returns `true` if both operands are `true`.
- **OR (||)**: Returns `true` if at least one operand is `true`.
- **NOT (!)**: Reverses the boolean value of its operand (true becomes false, and false becomes true).

Here's how you can use logical operators:

```
let hasLicense: boolean = true; let hasCar: boolean = false; if (hasLicense &&
hasCar) { console.log("You can drive your car."); } if (hasLicense || hasCar)
{ console.log("You have either a license or a car."); } if (!hasCar) {
console.log("You don't have a car."); }
```

Type Inference with Booleans

As with numbers and strings, TypeScript can infer the `boolean` type when you assign a boolean value to a variable:

```
let isRaining = true; // TypeScript infers that 'isRaining' is of type
'boolean'
```

Boolean Values in Expressions

Boolean values are often the result of comparisons and other expressions:

```
let isEqual: boolean = 5 === 5; // true let isGreater: boolean = 10 > 3; //
true let isNotEmpty: boolean = "hello".length > 0; // true
```

Key Points to Remember

- Booleans are the backbone of logical decision-making in TypeScript.
- Use `if` and `else` statements to control program flow based on boolean conditions.
- Combine boolean values using logical operators (&&, ||, !) to create complex conditions.
- TypeScript can often infer the `boolean` type from the context, reducing the need for explicit annotations.

Understanding and using boolean values effectively is crucial for building robust and dynamic TypeScript applications that can respond intelligently to various conditions and inputs.

Array

In TypeScript, as in JavaScript, arrays are your trusty toolbox for organizing and managing collections of data. Whether it's a list of names, a series of numbers, or an assortment of objects, arrays provide a structured way to store multiple values.

Declaring Arrays

There are a couple of ways to declare an array in TypeScript:

```
// Using square brackets with type annotation let numbers: number[] = [1, 2, 3, 4, 5]; // Using the Array generic type let fruits: Array<string> = ['apple', 'banana', 'orange'];
```

In the first example, `number[]` indicates an array of numbers. In the second example, `Array<string>` also represents an array of strings.

Accessing Array Elements

You access individual elements in an array using their index (starting from 0):

```
console.log(numbers[0]); // Output: 1 console.log(fruits[2]); // Output: "orange"
```

Common Array Methods

TypeScript arrays come equipped with a rich set of methods inherited from JavaScript. Here are some of the most frequently used ones:

- **`push(element)`:** Adds an element to the end of the array.
- **`pop()`:** Removes and returns the last element of the array.
- **`map(callback)`:** Creates a new array by applying the `callback` function to each element.
- **`filter(callback)`:** Creates a new array containing only the elements that pass the `callback` function's test.
- **`reduce(callback, initialValue)`:** Reduces the array to a single value by applying the `callback` function to each element and accumulating the result.

Type Inference for Arrays

TypeScript's type inference shines when working with arrays. If you initialize an array with values of the same type, TypeScript automatically infers the array's type:

```
let colors = ['red', 'green', 'blue']; // TypeScript infers string[] let ages = [25, 30, 35]; // TypeScript infers number[]
```

Example: Using Array Methods

```
let numbers: number[] = [1, 2, 3, 4, 5]; // Adding elements numbers.push(6); // Transforming elements let doubledNumbers: number[] = numbers.map(num => num * 2); // Filtering elements let evenNumbers: number[] = numbers.filter(num => num % 2 === 0); // Reducing elements let sum: number = numbers.reduce((acc, num) => acc + num, 0);
```

Key Points to Remember

- Arrays are versatile tools for storing collections of data in TypeScript.
- You can declare arrays using square brackets or the `Array` generic type.
- Access elements by their index (0-based).
- Leverage a wide array of built-in methods for manipulating and transforming arrays.
- TypeScript's type inference often automatically determines the type of an array based on its elements.

By mastering arrays and their associated methods, you gain a powerful tool for working with structured data in your TypeScript projects.

Tuple

In addition to standard arrays, TypeScript offers a specialized type called a tuple. A tuple is essentially an array with a fixed number of elements, and importantly, each element can have a different type. This makes tuples a great tool for representing data where the order and types of elements are significant.

Defining Tuples

You define a tuple using square brackets [ ] and specifying the type of each element within the brackets:

```
let person: [string, number] = ['Alice', 30]; // Tuple with a string and a
number let coordinates: [number, number] = [10.5, -5.2]; // Tuple with two
numbers
```

In the examples above, `person` is a tuple that represents a person's name (string) and age (number). Similarly, `coordinates` is a tuple representing x and y coordinates.

Accessing Tuple Elements

You access tuple elements just like you do with regular arrays, using their index:

```
console.log(person[0]); // Output: "Alice" console.log(coordinates[1]); //
Output: -5.2
```

Use Cases for Tuples

Tuples are handy in several situations:

1. **Representing Data with Fixed Structure:** When you have a collection of values that represent a single entity with a specific order and types, tuples are a natural fit. For example, a tuple can represent a person's name and age, a color's RGB values, or a point's coordinates.
2. **Returning Multiple Values from Functions:** In JavaScript, functions can only return a single value. However, you can use tuples to return multiple values from a TypeScript function:
   ```
   function getPersonInfo(): [string, number] { return ['Bob', 45]; } const
   [name, age] = getPersonInfo();
   ```
3. **Destructuring Tuples:** You can easily destructure tuples to assign their elements to individual variables:
   ```
   let [firstName, lastName] = ['John', 'Smith'];
   ```

Important Considerations

- **Length is Fixed:** Once you define a tuple with a certain number of elements, you cannot change its length.

- **Type Safety:** TypeScript enforces type safety for each element within a tuple. You cannot assign a value of the wrong type to a specific position in the tuple.

When to Use Tuples (and When Not To)

Tuples are ideal for scenarios where you have a small, fixed number of elements with known types. If you need a more flexible data structure that can grow or shrink, a regular array is usually a better choice.

With tuples in your TypeScript arsenal, you gain a concise and type-safe way to represent structured data where the order and types of elements matter.

Any

The any type in TypeScript is a bit like a wild card. It signifies that a variable can hold a value of any data type: a number, a string, an object, or anything else. In this sense, it behaves very similarly to how variables work in regular JavaScript.

How to Use any

```
let data: any = "Hello"; data = 42; data = { name: "Alice" }; // All valid
assignments
```

The Trade-Off: Flexibility vs. Type Safety

While the any type offers flexibility, it comes at a cost: it sacrifices the type safety that TypeScript provides. When you use any, you're essentially telling the TypeScript compiler, "Trust me, I know what I'm doing." This means the compiler won't perform any type checking on variables or values annotated with any.

Consider this example:

```
let value: any = "some text"; let length = value.length; // No error, but
potential for runtime errors
```

TypeScript won't complain, even though `value` might not always be a string. If you later assign a number to `value`, the `length` property won't exist, leading to a runtime error.

When to Use any (Sparingly!)

There are legitimate use cases for the any type, but it's best to use it judiciously:

- **Interacting with Legacy JavaScript Code:** If you're working with existing JavaScript code that doesn't have type definitions, using any can be a pragmatic way to integrate it into your TypeScript project.
- **Dynamic Data from External Sources:** When you receive data from an external API or a data source where the structure isn't strictly defined, you might use any temporarily while you figure out the appropriate types.
- **Truly Unknown Types:** In rare cases where you genuinely don't know the type of a value, any can be a last resort. However, always strive to narrow down the type as soon as possible using type guards or type assertions.

Alternatives to any

In most cases, there are better alternatives to any:

- **unknown:** If you don't know the exact type of a value but want to maintain type safety, use `unknown`. You can then perform type checks to narrow down the type before using it.
- **Union Types:** If a value can be one of several known types, use a union type (e.g., `string | number`). This allows for more flexibility while still maintaining type safety.

Remember: The any type should be your last resort, not your first choice. TypeScript's power lies in its type system, and overusing any undermines that power. By using more specific types or alternatives like `unknown`, you can maximize the benefits of TypeScript's type safety and catch potential errors early in the development process.

Void

The `void` type in TypeScript is a bit like a silent partner. It signals that a function doesn't return a value, meaning it performs an action but doesn't produce any output to be used elsewhere in your code.

Declaring Functions That Return `void`

```
function greet(name: string): void { console.log(`Hello, ${name}!`); }
```

In the `greet` function above, the `void` type annotation after the parentheses indicates that the function doesn't return anything. It simply logs a greeting message to the console.

How TypeScript Handles `void`

TypeScript treats `void` as a type that can only be assigned the value `undefined` (or `null` if the `strictNullChecks` compiler option is disabled). This means you cannot assign the result of a `void` function to a variable:

```
let result = greet("Alice"); // Error: Type 'void' is not assignable to type
'let result'
```

The compiler correctly complains that the `result` variable cannot hold a value of type `void`.

Why Use `void`?

Using `void` explicitly for functions that don't return a value serves a few purposes:

- **Clarity:** It makes your code more self-documenting. By seeing `void`, other developers (or your future self) will instantly know that this function is primarily focused on side effects (e.g., logging to the console, modifying a variable, sending a network request) rather than producing a return value.
- **Error Prevention:** TypeScript helps you avoid mistakes by preventing you from accidentally using the result of a `void` function as if it had a meaningful value. This can prevent subtle bugs that might arise from incorrect assumptions about a function's behavior.

When `void` is Inferred

In many cases, you don't even need to explicitly specify `void` as the return type. TypeScript is intelligent enough to infer it if a function doesn't have a `return` statement:

```
function logMessage(message: string) { // Return type is implicitly 'void'
console.log(message); }
```

Key Points

- Use `void` to indicate that a function doesn't return a value.
- The result of a `void` function can only be assigned to `undefined` (or `null` if `strictNullChecks` is off).
- Explicitly using `void` improves code clarity and prevents errors.

By understanding the `void` type, you'll write more accurate function signatures, making your TypeScript code more self-explanatory and less prone to unexpected issues.

Never

The `never` type in TypeScript represents values that never occur. This might sound a bit unusual, but it serves a vital role in making your code safer and more predictable. Think of `never` as a signal to TypeScript that a particular code path is unreachable.

When `never` Comes into Play

The `never` type is used in the following scenarios:

1. **Functions That Always Throw Errors:** If you have a function that always throws an error (or terminates the program), its return type should be `never`. This is because the function never actually reaches a point where it would return a value.
   ```
   function raiseError(message: string): never { throw new Error(message); }
   ```
2. **Infinite Loops:** A function containing an infinite loop technically never returns, so its return type is also `never`.
   ```
   function infiniteLoop(): never { while (true) { // This loop will run forever } }
   ```

TypeScript's Use of `never` for Type Inference

TypeScript leverages the `never` type to improve its type inference and error detection capabilities. Consider this example:

```
function processValue(value: string | number): string { if (typeof value === 'string') { return value.toUpperCase(); } else if (typeof value === 'number') { return value.toString(); // This line will be inferred as returning 'never' } }
```

In this function, if the `value` is a number, it tries to call `toUpperCase()` on it, which is invalid. TypeScript recognizes this and infers that this branch of the `if` statement will never return a value. Therefore, it assigns the `never` type to the return statement, leading to a compiler error. This early detection prevents a runtime error that might have been difficult to diagnose.

Benefits of Using `never`

- **Enhanced Type Safety:** By explicitly marking functions that should never return, you prevent accidental misuse of their results, making your code more robust.
- **Improved Code Analysis:** TypeScript's ability to infer `never` helps it identify potential issues in your code, leading to better error detection and a more reliable codebase.

- **Clearer Intent:** Using `never` makes your code more self-documenting. It signals to other developers that a function has a specific behavior: either it always throws an error or it never terminates.

Key Points

- The `never` type represents values that never occur.
- Use `never` for functions that always throw errors or have infinite loops.
- TypeScript uses `never` for better type inference and error detection.

The `never` type might seem a bit unconventional at first, but its role in ensuring type safety and improving code quality is invaluable. By understanding how TypeScript uses `never`, you can write more predictable and error-resistant code.

Unknown

The unknown type, introduced in TypeScript 3.0, is a powerful addition to the type system. Like any, it can hold values of any type, making it useful for handling data whose structure isn't fully known at compile time. However, unlike any, unknown is type-safe. It forces you to perform checks before you can use an unknown value, preventing potential runtime errors.

How to Use unknown

```
let data: unknown = "Hello"; data = 42; data = { name: "Alice" }; // All valid assignments
```

Type Safety with unknown

The key difference between unknown and any is that you cannot directly perform operations on a variable of type unknown:

```
let value: unknown = "some text"; let length = value.length; // Error: Object is of type 'unknown'.
```

TypeScript correctly complains because it doesn't know if `value` has a `length` property. This is where type checks come in.

Type Guards and Type Assertions

There are two primary ways to work with unknown values:

1. **Type Guards:** Use conditional statements (`if`, `switch`) and type checking operators (like `typeof`, `instanceof`, or custom type guards) to narrow down the type of the unknown variable.
   ```
   if (typeof value === 'string') { length = value.length; // Now valid because 'value' is narrowed to 'string' }
   ```
2. **Type Assertions:** If you're confident about the type of an unknown value, you can use type assertions (`as` keyword or angle bracket syntax `<type>`) to tell TypeScript to treat it as a specific type.
   ```
   length = (value as string).length; // Type assertion (use with caution!)
   ```

Example: Fetching Data from an API

```
function fetchData(): unknown { // ... (fetch data from an API) ... return response.data; // Data type is unknown at this point } const data = fetchData(); if (typeof data === 'object' && data !== null) { console.log(data.message); // Accessing 'message' property after type check }
```

In this example, `fetchData` returns data of an unknown type. We use a type guard (`typeof data === 'object' && data !== null`) to ensure that `data` is an object before accessing its properties.

Benefits of Using unknown

- **Enhanced Type Safety:** unknown forces you to be explicit about type checks, reducing the risk of runtime errors caused by unexpected types.
- **Improved Code Reliability:** By narrowing down types, you can write more predictable and maintainable code.
- **Gradual Adoption:** If you're migrating a JavaScript codebase to TypeScript, using `unknown` can be a stepping stone towards adding more specific types.

Remember: The unknown type strikes a balance between flexibility and type safety. It allows you to work with dynamic data while still leveraging TypeScript's type checking capabilities to catch errors early on.

Type Inference

One of TypeScript's most convenient features is its ability to infer types. Type inference means that TypeScript can automatically deduce the type of a variable based on how you use it. This saves you from having to write explicit type annotations everywhere, making your code cleaner and easier to read.

Type Inference in Action

Let's see some examples:

```
let message = "Hello, world!"; // TypeScript infers type 'string' let age = 30; // TypeScript infers type 'number' let isActive = true; // TypeScript infers type 'boolean' let numbers = [1, 2, 3]; // TypeScript infers type 'number[]' let person = { name: "Alice", age: 25 }; // TypeScript infers type '{ name: string; age: number; }'
```

In each case, TypeScript looks at the initial value assigned to the variable and figures out its type. This is called *contextual typing.*

Type Inference in Function Arguments and Return Values

TypeScript can also infer types in function arguments and return values:

```
function add(x, y) { // TypeScript infers that x and y are of type 'number' return x + y; // TypeScript infers that the return type is 'number' }
```

In this example, TypeScript infers that both x and y are of type `number` because they're used in an arithmetic operation. It also infers that the function returns a `number` because of the `x + y` expression.

Benefits of Type Inference

- **Concise Code:** Type inference reduces the need for repetitive type annotations, making your code cleaner and more focused on the logic.
- **Less Verbosity:** You don't have to explicitly specify types for every variable and function, saving you keystrokes and reducing clutter.
- **Refactoring Safety:** TypeScript's type checker still ensures type safety even with inferred types. If you change the type of a value in one place, TypeScript will alert you to any potential errors caused by that change in other parts of your code.

When Type Inference Might Not Be Enough

There are cases where TypeScript might not be able to infer a type or where you might want to be more explicit:

- **Ambiguous Types:** If a variable can potentially hold values of different types, TypeScript might not be able to determine a single type.
- **Complex Types:** For intricate types or when you want to clearly document the intended type, it's often better to provide explicit type annotations.
- **Return Types of Functions:** While TypeScript can infer the return type of simple functions, it's considered good practice to explicitly annotate the return type, especially for functions that are part of a public API.

Remember: Type inference is a powerful tool, but it's not always perfect. When in doubt, it's better to be explicit with your type annotations to ensure type safety and clarity in your TypeScript code.

Type Assertions

Type assertions in TypeScript are like a gentle nudge to the compiler, saying, "Hey, I know more about this value's type than you do, so trust me on this one." They allow you to override TypeScript's type inference when you have additional information that the compiler might not be aware of.

Two Ways to Assert Types

TypeScript offers two syntaxes for type assertions:

1. **as Keyword:**
   `let data: unknown = "Hello, world!"; let message = data as string;`
   Here, we tell TypeScript to treat `data` as a `string`, even though it was initially declared as `unknown`.
2. **Angle Bracket Syntax (<>)**
   `let data: unknown = 42; let num = <number>data;`
   In this case, we use angle brackets to assert that `data` is a `number`.

When to Use Type Assertions

Type assertions are helpful in situations where:

- **Narrowing Types:** You might use type assertions after performing type guards (as discussed in the unknown section) to work with the narrowed-down type.
- **Working with Libraries:** Some libraries or APIs might not provide complete type definitions. Type assertions can be used to bridge the gap and provide type information to TypeScript.
- **Overriding Inaccurate Inference:** In some cases, TypeScript's type inference might be too broad or inaccurate. Type assertions can help you provide more specific type information.

Caution: Use with Care

While type assertions are powerful, they come with a risk. If you assert an incorrect type, TypeScript won't be able to catch the error, and you might introduce runtime issues. For example:

```
let data: unknown = { name: "Alice" }; let num = data as number; // Incorrect
assertion! console.log(num + 5); // Runtime error: Cannot add 5 to an object
```

In this case, the assertion is wrong. `data` is an object, not a number. This error won't be caught during compilation, but it will cause a problem when the code runs.

Best Practices for Type Assertions

- **Use Sparingly:** Only use type assertions when you are absolutely certain about the type of a value.
- **Prefer Type Guards:** When possible, use type guards to narrow down types in a safe and controlled way.
- **Double-Check:** Always verify your assertions to avoid introducing runtime errors.
- **Document:** If you use a type assertion, consider adding a comment explaining why it's necessary and what you expect the type to be.

Key Points

- Type assertions let you override TypeScript's type inference.
- Use the `as` keyword or angle bracket syntax (`<>`) for type assertions.
- Be cautious when using type assertions to avoid runtime errors.
- Prioritize type guards over type assertions whenever possible.

By using type assertions judiciously and following best practices, you can leverage this feature to write more expressive and flexible TypeScript code while still maintaining type safety and preventing bugs.

Chapter Summary

In this chapter, we explored the core types that form the foundation of TypeScript's type system. We covered the following:

- **Number:** We learned how TypeScript uses a single `number` type to represent all numeric values, including integers and floating-point numbers. We discussed arithmetic operations and common math functions.
- **String:** We explored how to declare and work with strings using single quotes, double quotes, and template literals. We also discussed string concatenation, interpolation, and common string manipulation methods.
- **Boolean:** We learned that boolean values (`true` or `false`) are used for logical operations and demonstrated their use in conditional statements and with logical operators.
- **Array:** We covered arrays as collections of values and how to declare, access, and manipulate them using various methods. We also saw how TypeScript infers array types based on their elements.
- **Tuple:** We introduced tuples as a special kind of array with a fixed length and potentially different types for each element, highlighting their use cases for representing structured data.
- **Any, Void, Never, Unknown:** We explored the `any`, `void`, `never`, and `unknown` types, discussing their roles and when to use them (or avoid them) for maintaining type safety and clarity in your code.
- **Type Inference and Assertions:** We learned how TypeScript can automatically infer types based on context and how type assertions allow you to override that inference when necessary.

By mastering these core types, you've taken a significant step towards writing robust and predictable TypeScript code. In the next chapter, we'll shift our focus to TypeScript functions and how they empower you to create reusable blocks of logic with well-defined inputs and outputs.

Mastering TypeScript Functions

Outline

- Function Basics: Declaring and Calling Functions
- Function Parameters and Return Types
- Optional and Default Parameters
- Rest Parameters
- Function Overloads
- Arrow Functions: Concise Syntax for Functions
- Callback Functions: Passing Functions as Arguments
- Function Types: Defining Function Signatures
- this Keyword in Functions
- Function Scoping and Closures
- Chapter Summary

Function Basics: Declaring and Calling Functions

Functions are the building blocks of any TypeScript (and JavaScript) program. They encapsulate reusable blocks of code that perform specific tasks. In this section, we'll cover the fundamentals of declaring and using functions in TypeScript.

Declaring Functions

You declare a function in TypeScript using the `function` keyword, followed by the function's name, a list of parameters (if any) enclosed in parentheses, and the function's body enclosed in curly braces `{}`. Here's the basic syntax:

```
function functionName(parameter1: type, parameter2: type, ...): returnType {
// Function body: Code to be executed }
```

- **`functionName`:** A descriptive name for your function.
- **`parameter1`, `parameter2`, etc.:** Names of parameters (inputs) the function accepts, along with their types.
- **`returnType`:** The type of value the function returns (if any).

Examples

Let's look at a few examples:

```
// Function with no parameters or return value function greet() {
console.log("Hello!"); } // Function with parameters and a return value
function add(x: number, y: number): number { return x + y; } // Function with
a string parameter and a string return value function greetByName(name:
string): string { return "Hello, " + name + "!"; }
```

Calling Functions

To execute the code inside a function, you call it by its name, followed by parentheses containing any required arguments:

```
greet(); // Output: "Hello!" let sum = add(5, 3); // sum = 8 let message =
greetByName("Alice"); // message = "Hello, Alice!"
```

Using Return Values

If a function has a return type other than `void`, you can use the value it returns in your code. In the `add` and `greetByName` examples, we assign the return values to variables (`sum` and `message`, respectively) and can then use those variables elsewhere.

Key Points

- Functions are reusable blocks of code that perform specific tasks.
- Use the `function` keyword to declare functions.
- Functions can have parameters (inputs) and return values (outputs).
- Type annotations for parameters and return values help TypeScript enforce type safety.
- Call functions by their name followed by parentheses and any required arguments.

Understanding the basics of function declaration and usage is essential for building organized and maintainable TypeScript code. As we progress through this book, we'll explore more advanced function concepts like optional parameters, rest parameters, and function overloads.

Function Parameters and Return Types

In TypeScript, you can make your functions much more powerful and predictable by adding type annotations to their parameters and return values. These annotations tell TypeScript what types of data a function expects as input and what type of data it will produce as output. This is a key aspect of TypeScript's type safety system.

Type Annotations for Parameters

To specify the types of parameters in a function, you add a colon (`:`) followed by the type name after each parameter:

```
function greet(name: string) { console.log(`Hello, ${name}!`); }
```

In this example, the `greet` function expects a single parameter called `name`, which must be of type `string`. If you try to call `greet` with a number or another type, TypeScript will raise a type error.

Type Annotations for Return Values

To specify the return type of a function, you add a colon (`:`) followed by the type name after the parameter list:

```
function add(x: number, y: number): number { return x + y; }
```

Here, the `add` function expects two parameters, `x` and `y`, both of type `number`. It also indicates that the function will return a value of type `number`.

TypeScript's Type Safety Enforcement

When you provide type annotations for function parameters and return values, TypeScript's compiler becomes your vigilant guardian. It ensures that:

- **Correct Arguments:** You pass the right types of values to the function. If you try to pass a `string` where a `number` is expected, TypeScript will immediately flag it as an error.
- **Consistent Return Values:** The function always returns a value of the specified type. This prevents unexpected surprises when using the function's result.

Examples of Functions with Different Types

```
// Function with a string parameter and a number return value function calculateLength(text: string): number { return text.length; } // Function with a boolean parameter and a boolean return value function isEven(num: number): boolean { return num % 2 === 0; } // Function with multiple parameters and a string return value function formatDate(year: number, month: number, day: number): string { return `${year}-${month}-${day}`; }
```

Benefits of Type Annotations

- **Early Error Detection:** TypeScript catches type-related errors during development, preventing them from causing problems at runtime.
- **Self-Documenting Code:** Type annotations make your code more readable and understandable. They serve as inline documentation, clarifying the expected types of inputs and outputs.
- **Safer Refactoring:** When you modify your code, TypeScript helps you ensure that your changes don't break existing functionality due to type mismatches.
- **Improved Tooling:** IDEs and code editors with TypeScript support can provide better autocompletion, type hints, and refactoring tools based on type annotations.

By diligently adding type annotations to your function parameters and return values, you harness the full power of TypeScript's type system, leading to code that is more robust, maintainable, and easier to reason about.

Optional and Default Parameters

TypeScript gives you the power to create functions that are more flexible and adaptable to different scenarios by using optional parameters and default values. This means you can design functions that work seamlessly whether the caller provides all arguments or just some.

Optional Parameters

An optional parameter is a parameter that may or may not be provided when calling a function. You mark a parameter as optional by adding a question mark (?) after its name:

```
function greet(name: string, greeting?: string) { if (greeting) { console.log(`${greeting}, ${name}!`); } else { console.log(`Hello, ${name}!`); } } greet("Alice"); // Output: "Hello, Alice!" greet("Bob", "Good morning"); // Output: "Good morning, Bob!"
```

In this example, the `greeting` parameter is optional. If it's not provided, the function uses the default greeting "Hello."

Default Parameters

You can take flexibility a step further by providing a default value for an optional parameter. If the caller doesn't provide a value for the parameter, the default value kicks in:

```
function greet(name: string, greeting: string = "Hello") {
console.log(`${greeting}, ${name}!`); } greet("Alice"); // Output: "Hello,
Alice!" greet("Bob", "Good morning"); // Output: "Good morning, Bob!"
```

Now, the `greeting` parameter has a default value of "Hello." You can still override it by providing a different greeting when calling the function.

Benefits of Optional and Default Parameters

- **Flexibility:** Your functions can handle a wider range of inputs, making them more versatile and easier to use in different contexts.
- **Readability:** Default values make your code more self-explanatory. It's clear what value a parameter will have if the caller doesn't provide one.
- **Less Error Handling:** You don't need to write as much code to check for missing arguments, leading to cleaner and more concise functions.

Important Considerations

- **Optional Parameters at the End:** Optional parameters should always be placed at the end of the parameter list. If you place a required parameter after an optional one, TypeScript will complain.
- **Type Safety:** Even with optional parameters, TypeScript still enforces type safety. If you provide an argument for an optional parameter, it must be of the correct type.

Example: A More Flexible Calculation Function

```
function calculateTotal(price: number, quantity: number = 1, discount?:
number): number { let total = price * quantity; if (discount) { total -=
discount; } return total; } calculateTotal(10); // Output: 10 (quantity
defaults to 1, no discount) calculateTotal(10, 3); // Output: 30
calculateTotal(10, 3, 5); // Output: 25 (discount applied)
```

By embracing optional parameters and default values, you can write functions that gracefully adapt to different input scenarios, enhancing the usability and versatility of your TypeScript code.

Rest Parameters

TypeScript, like JavaScript, allows you to create functions that accept a variable number of arguments using a feature called *rest parameters*. This is particularly useful when you don't know in advance how many arguments a function might receive.

Syntax

You define a rest parameter using the spread syntax (`...`) followed by the parameter name and its type:

```
function functionName(...parameterName: type[]): returnType { // Function body
}
```

The type of the rest parameter is always an array, and it gathers all the remaining arguments passed to the function into that array.

Example: Calculating the Sum of Numbers

```
function calculateSum(...numbers: number[]): number { let sum = 0; for (let
num of numbers) { sum += num; } return sum; } console.log(calculateSum(1, 2,
3)); // Output: 6 console.log(calculateSum(5, 10, 15, 20)); // Output: 50
```

In this example, `...numbers` is the rest parameter. It collects all the numbers passed to the `calculateSum` function into an array called `numbers`. The function then iterates over this array and calculates the sum.

Example: Logging Multiple Values

```
function logValues(...values: any[]): void { for (let value of values) {
console.log(value); } } logValues("Hello", 42, true, { name: "Alice" });
```

Here, `...values` captures any number of arguments of any type (thanks to the any type) and logs them to the console.

Key Points

- A function can have only **one** rest parameter.
- The rest parameter must be the **last** parameter in the function's parameter list.
- The rest parameter is always an **array**.
- TypeScript infers the array element type based on the type annotation you provide for the rest parameter.

Benefits of Rest Parameters

- **Flexibility:** Rest parameters allow you to create functions that can handle a variable number of arguments.
- **Readability:** They make your code more concise and expressive compared to using the `arguments` object (which is available in plain JavaScript but not recommended in TypeScript).

When to Use Rest Parameters

Rest parameters are ideal when:

- You don't know the exact number of arguments a function will receive.
- You want to collect multiple arguments into an array for processing.

By incorporating rest parameters into your TypeScript toolbox, you gain a flexible and elegant way to create functions that can adapt to varying input scenarios.

Function Overloads

Function overloading is a powerful concept in TypeScript that allows you to define a function with multiple signatures. Each signature can have different parameter types or a different number of parameters, but they all share the same function name. This gives you flexibility while maintaining type safety.

How Function Overloads Work

1. **Declaration:** You declare multiple versions of the function, each with a distinct signature. These declarations serve as the "overloads."
2. **Implementation:** You provide a single implementation of the function. This implementation must be compatible with all the overload signatures.

3. **Type Checking:** When you call the overloaded function, TypeScript analyzes the arguments you provide. It then selects the most specific overload signature that matches the argument types and uses the corresponding type information for type checking.

Declaring Function Overloads

Here's how you declare function overloads:

```
function greet(person: string): string; function greet(people: string[]): string[]; function greet(person: any): any { if (typeof person === "string") { return `Hello, ${person}!`; } else if (Array.isArray(people)) { return people.map((person) => `Hello, ${person}!`); } }
```

In this example, we have two overload signatures for the `greet` function:

- The first signature accepts a single `string` parameter and returns a `string`.
- The second signature accepts an array of `string` values (`string[]`) and returns an array of `string` values.

The actual implementation of the function handles both cases.

Calling Overloaded Functions

```
let message1: string = greet("Alice"); // Calls the first overload let message2: string[] = greet(["Bob", "Eve"]); // Calls the second overload
```

TypeScript correctly infers the return type based on the arguments you pass.

Benefits of Function Overloads

- **Flexibility:** You can design a single function to handle different types of input.
- **Type Safety:** TypeScript ensures that you call the function with the correct argument types and receive the expected return type.
- **Readability:** Function overloads make it clear how a function can be used in different ways.

Key Points

- Function overloads provide multiple signatures for the same function.
- Each overload signature must have different parameter types or a different number of parameters.
- The implementation of the function must be compatible with all overload signatures.
- TypeScript uses the most specific matching overload signature for type checking.

Example: A Versatile Area Calculation Function

```
function calculateArea(sideLength: number): number; // For squares function calculateArea(length: number, width: number): number; // For rectangles function calculateArea(radius: number): number; // For circles function calculateArea(shape: any, dimension2?: number): number { if (typeof shape === 'number' && !dimension2) { return shape * shape; // Square } else if (typeof shape === 'number' && typeof dimension2 === 'number') { return shape * dimension2; // Rectangle } else if (typeof shape === 'number') { return Math.PI * shape * shape; // Circle } } calculateArea(5); // Output: 25
```

```
(square) calculateArea(4, 6); // Output: 24 (rectangle) calculateArea(3); //
Output: 28.27... (circle)
```

By mastering function overloads, you unlock a new level of expressiveness and flexibility in your TypeScript code, allowing you to create functions that are both versatile and type-safe.

Arrow Functions: Concise Syntax for Functions

Arrow functions, introduced in ES6, provide a streamlined and often more readable way to write functions in TypeScript (and JavaScript). They offer a concise syntax and some unique behavior compared to traditional function declarations.

Arrow Function Syntax

The basic syntax of an arrow function looks like this:

```
(parameter1: type, parameter2: type, ...) => expression;
```

Here's a breakdown of the elements:

- **Parameters (Optional):** A comma-separated list of parameters enclosed in parentheses. If there's only one parameter, you can omit the parentheses.
- **Arrow (=>)**: The fat arrow symbol indicates that you're defining an arrow function.
- **Expression:** The code to be executed by the function. If it's a single-line expression, the return value is implicit. For multi-line expressions, you'll need to use an explicit `return` statement.

Examples

```
// Function with no parameters const greet = () => console.log("Hello!"); //
Function with one parameter const double = (x: number) => x * 2; // Function
with multiple parameters and an explicit return const add = (x: number, y:
number): number => { return x + y; };
```

Differences from Regular Functions

Arrow functions have a few key differences from regular functions:

1. **Concise Syntax:** They are often shorter and more expressive, especially for simple functions.
2. **Implicit Return:** If the function body is a single expression, the return value is implicit (no need for the `return` keyword).
3. **`this` Binding:** Arrow functions don't have their own `this` binding. They inherit the `this` value from the surrounding scope (the context in which the arrow function is defined). This can be a major advantage, as it eliminates many of the `this`-related issues that arise in regular functions.

Example: `this` in Arrow Functions

```
const person = { name: "Alice", greet: function () { setTimeout(function () {
console.log(this.name); // Output: undefined (in a regular function, 'this'
refers to the global object) }, 1000); }, greetArrow: function () {
setTimeout(() => { console.log(this.name); // Output: "Alice" (arrow function
captures 'this' from surrounding scope) }, 1000); } }; person.greet(); //
undefined person.greetArrow(); // Alice
```

When to Use Arrow Functions

Arrow functions are a great choice when:

- You want a more concise and expressive syntax.
- You need to preserve the `this` value from the surrounding scope.
- You're working with higher-order functions (functions that take other functions as arguments).

Remember: Arrow functions aren't always the best fit. For instance, you might prefer regular functions when you need to use the `this` keyword to refer to the function itself, or when you want to use the `arguments` object (which is not available in arrow functions). Choose the right tool for the job based on the specific requirements of your code.

Callback Functions: Passing Functions as Arguments

In TypeScript, as in JavaScript, functions are not just blocks of code; they are values that can be assigned to variables, passed as arguments to other functions, and even returned from functions. This ability to treat functions as first-class citizens opens up a world of possibilities for creating flexible and reusable code. A key concept in this realm is the **callback function**.

What is a Callback Function?

A callback function is simply a function that is passed as an argument to another function. The function receiving the callback is often called a *higher-order function*. The purpose of a callback is to allow the higher-order function to execute the callback at a specific time or under certain conditions.

Why Use Callback Functions?

Callback functions enable you to:

- **Customize Behavior:** A higher-order function can delegate specific tasks to a callback, allowing you to tailor its behavior without modifying its core logic.
- **Handle Asynchronous Operations:** In asynchronous programming, callbacks are often used to handle events or responses that might happen at an unknown time in the future (e.g., when a network request completes).
- **Improve Code Reusability:** By extracting common logic into higher-order functions and providing callbacks, you can create more modular and reusable code.

Example: Sorting with a Custom Comparison Function

```
function sortArray(arr: number[], compareFn: (a: number, b: number) =>
number): number[] { // ... (Sorting logic using compareFn) ... } function
ascendingOrder(a: number, b: number): number { return a - b; } function
descendingOrder(a: number, b: number): number { return b - a; } let numbers =
[5, 2, 8, 1, 4]; let sortedAscending = sortArray(numbers, ascendingOrder); //
[1, 2, 4, 5, 8] let sortedDescending = sortArray(numbers, descendingOrder); //
[8, 5, 4, 2, 1]
```

In this example, `sortArray` is a higher-order function that takes an array of numbers and a callback function `compareFn`. The `compareFn` callback defines how to compare two numbers, allowing you to sort the array in either ascending or descending order.

Example: Event Handling

```
function handleClick(event: MouseEvent) { console.log("Button clicked!"); }
document.getElementById("myButton").addEventListener("click", handleClick);
```

Here, `handleClick` is a callback function that gets executed when the "myButton" element is clicked.

Important Points

- A callback function can be named or anonymous (using arrow function syntax).
- Type annotations are crucial for ensuring type safety when working with callbacks.
- Callback functions are often used in conjunction with interfaces to define more complex function types.

Asynchronous Programming and Callbacks

Callback functions have historically been the primary way to handle asynchronous operations in JavaScript. While modern TypeScript often favors Promises and `async/await`, understanding callbacks is still important for working with older libraries or APIs.

By mastering the concept of callback functions, you gain a powerful technique for writing flexible, adaptable, and reusable code in TypeScript. They are a fundamental building block for many advanced programming patterns, including event handling, asynchronous programming, and functional programming.

Function Types: Defining Function Signatures

In TypeScript, function types are a way to describe the structure of a function, specifying its parameter types and return type. This is akin to defining a blueprint for how a function should look and behave.

Defining Function Types

The syntax for defining a function type in TypeScript is simple and elegant:

```
(parameter1: type, parameter2: type, ...) => returnType;
```

It closely resembles the arrow function syntax but without the actual function body. Let's break it down:

- **Parentheses:** Enclose the list of parameters, each with its name and type, separated by commas.
- **Fat Arrow (=>)**: Indicates a function type.
- **`returnType`:** Specifies the type of value the function returns.

Examples

```
let greet: (name: string) => void; let add: (x: number, y: number) => number;
let isEven: (num: number) => boolean;
```

In these examples:

- `greet` is a function type that takes a `string` argument and returns `void` (nothing).
- `add` is a function type that takes two `number` arguments and returns a `number`.
- `isEven` is a function type that takes a `number` argument and returns a `boolean`.

Using Function Types

1. **Typing Variables:** You can use function types to declare variables that will hold functions:
   `let greetFunction: (name: string) => void; greetFunction = (name: string)`

```
=> { console.log(`Hello, ${name}!`); }; greetFunction("Alice"); // Output: "Hello, Alice!"
```

2. **Creating Higher-Order Functions:** Function types are especially valuable for creating higher-order functions—functions that take other functions as arguments or return functions.
```
function applyOperation(x: number, y: number, operation: (a: number, b: number) => number): number { return operation(x, y); } const addResult = applyOperation(5, 3, add); // Output: 8 const multiplyResult = applyOperation(5, 3, (a, b) => a * b); // Output: 15
```

Here, `applyOperation` takes three arguments: two numbers and a function of type `(a: number, b: number) => number`. This function type ensures that the passed `operation` function has the correct parameters and return type.

Benefits of Function Types

- **Explicit Contracts:** Function types clearly define the expected input and output of a function, making your code more self-documenting and easier to understand.
- **Enhanced Type Safety:** TypeScript checks whether functions passed as arguments or assigned to variables adhere to the defined function types, catching potential errors early on.
- **Improved Reusability:** Function types promote the creation of reusable functions that can operate on a variety of data types, enhancing code flexibility and modularity.

Key Points to Remember

- Function types describe the structure of a function (parameters and return type).
- Use function types to type variables that hold functions.
- Function types are crucial for creating type-safe higher-order functions.

By mastering function types, you'll write more reliable, flexible, and reusable code in TypeScript. They provide a powerful way to express the contracts between functions and the rest of your code, ensuring that your functions are used correctly and consistently.

this Keyword in Functions

The `this` keyword in JavaScript and TypeScript is a powerful but sometimes confusing mechanism. It refers to the execution context of a function – essentially, the object that "owns" the function at the time it's called. The behavior of `this` varies between regular functions and arrow functions, and understanding this difference is crucial for avoiding unexpected results.

this in Regular Functions

In regular functions, the value of `this` is determined by how the function is called, not where it's defined:

- **Method Call:** When a function is called as a method on an object, `this` refers to that object.
- **Simple Call:** When a function is called without an object context (e.g., `myFunction()`), `this` refers to the global object (usually `window` in browsers or `global` in Node.js).
- **Call and Apply:** You can explicitly set the value of `this` using the `call` or `apply` methods.
- **Constructor Call:** When a function is called with the new keyword (to create an object), `this` refers to the newly created object.

Example:

```
function sayHello() { console.log("Hello, " + this.name); } const person = { name: "Alice", sayHi: sayHello }; sayHello(); // Output: "Hello, undefined" (or "Hello, window/global") person.sayHi(); // Output: "Hello, Alice"
```

this in Arrow Functions

Arrow functions have a different behavior for `this`. They inherit the `this` value from the surrounding scope (the lexical context) where they are defined. This means they don't have their own `this` binding.

Example:

```
const person = { name: "Bob", greet: () => { console.log("Hello, " + this.name); } }; person.greet(); // Output: "Hello, undefined" (or "Hello, window/global")
```

In this case, the arrow function `greet` inherits `this` from the surrounding global scope, not from the `person` object.

Accessing Object Properties with this

To access properties and methods of an object context using `this`, make sure the function is called as a method on that object. Here's how you can fix the previous example:

```
const person = { name: "Bob", greet() { // Regular function declaration as a method console.log("Hello, " + this.name); } }; person.greet(); // Output: "Hello, Bob"
```

Key Points

- The value of `this` in regular functions depends on how the function is called.
- Arrow functions inherit `this` from the surrounding scope (lexical binding).
- To access properties and methods of an object with `this`, call the function as a method on that object.

Understanding the nuances of `this` is crucial for writing predictable and reliable TypeScript (and JavaScript) code. By choosing the right type of function and paying attention to how it's called, you can avoid common pitfalls and harness the power of `this` for effective object-oriented programming.

Function Scoping and Closures

Understanding how variables are scoped and how functions interact with their surrounding context is fundamental for writing well-structured and predictable TypeScript code. Let's delve into the concepts of function scope and closures.

Function Scope

In TypeScript (and JavaScript), variables declared within a function have function scope. This means they are only accessible within the function itself and are not visible outside of it.

Example:

```
function greet(name: string): void { let message = `Hello, ${name}!`; // 'message' is only accessible within this function console.log(message); } greet("Alice"); console.log(message); // Error: 'message' is not defined
```

In this example, trying to access the `message` variable outside the `greet` function results in an error because `message` exists only within the function's scope.

Closures

Closures are a powerful feature that arises from the combination of function scope and the ability of functions to be treated as values. A closure is essentially the ability of a function to "remember" and access variables from its surrounding scope, even after the outer function has finished executing.

Example:

```
function outerFunction(name: string): () => string { let message = `Hello, ${name}!`; function innerFunction(): string { return message; } return innerFunction; } let myFunction = outerFunction("Bob"); console.log(myFunction()); // Output: "Hello, Bob!"
```

Here's what's happening:

1. `outerFunction` is called with the argument "Bob."
2. Inside `outerFunction`, a variable `message` is created, and `innerFunction` is defined.
3. `innerFunction` has access to the `message` variable from its surrounding scope.
4. `outerFunction` returns `innerFunction`.
5. `myFunction` now holds a reference to the `innerFunction`.
6. When `myFunction` is called, it accesses and returns the `message` variable, even though `outerFunction` has already finished executing.

The `innerFunction` forms a closure – it encloses the `message` variable from its lexical scope and retains access to it.

Using Closures: Private Variables

Closures can be used to create private variables within JavaScript and TypeScript. Here's an example:

```
function counter(): () => number { let count = 0; return () => { count++; return count; }; } let myCounter = counter(); console.log(myCounter()); // Output: 1 console.log(myCounter()); // Output: 2
```

In this code, the `count` variable is private to the closure created by `counter()`. The returned function acts as a getter/incrementer for `count`, providing controlled access to the variable.

Encapsulating State

Closures are also instrumental in encapsulating state within objects or modules. By returning functions from a "constructor" function, you can create objects with private data and methods that operate on that data:

```
function createPerson(name: string): { getName: () => string } { let privateName = name; return { getName: () => privateName }; } let person = createPerson("Alice"); console.log(person.getName()); // Output: "Alice"
```

In this example, the `privateName` variable is only accessible through the `getName` method, effectively encapsulating the person's name.

Key Points

- **Function Scope:** Variables within a function are only accessible within that function.
- **Closures:** Functions "remember" and access variables from their surrounding scope, even after the outer function finishes.
- **Private Variables:** Closures enable you to create private variables in JavaScript/TypeScript.
- **Encapsulation:** Closures facilitate encapsulation of state within objects and modules.

Understanding closures is key to writing more sophisticated TypeScript code. They allow you to create more modular, reusable, and maintainable code by controlling variable access and managing state effectively.

Chapter Summary

In this chapter, we delved into the world of functions, the workhorses of TypeScript. We covered:

- **Function Basics:** We started with how to declare and call functions, highlighting the importance of type annotations for parameters and return values.
- **Optional and Default Parameters:** We explored how to make functions more flexible by allowing optional parameters and providing default values.
- **Rest Parameters:** We learned how to capture a variable number of arguments into an array using rest parameters, making functions more versatile.
- **Function Overloads:** We discovered how to define multiple signatures for the same function name, allowing for different parameter types and return values while maintaining type safety.
- **Arrow Functions:** We introduced the concise syntax of arrow functions and discussed their unique behavior with the `this` keyword.
- **Callback Functions:** We explored how to pass functions as arguments to other functions (higher-order functions), a powerful technique for customization and asynchronous operations.
- **Function Types:** We learned how to define function types to describe the shape of functions and ensure type safety when working with functions as values.
- **`this` Keyword:** We demystified the `this` keyword and its behavior in both regular and arrow functions, explaining how it depends on the context in which a function is called.
- **Function Scope and Closures:** We covered the concept of function scope and how closures allow functions to "remember" their lexical environment, leading to powerful patterns like private variables and state encapsulation.

By mastering these function concepts, you've significantly expanded your TypeScript toolkit. You can now create well-structured, reusable, and type-safe functions that form the backbone of your TypeScript applications. In the next chapter, we'll move on to another essential aspect of TypeScript: interfaces and type aliases, which provide a way to define contracts for objects and create more organized and maintainable code.

Interfaces and Type Aliases: Contracts and Flexibility

Outline

- Introduction to Interfaces
  - Describing Object Shapes with Interfaces
  - Optional Properties
  - Readonly Properties
- Working with Interfaces
  - Implementing Interfaces with Classes
  - Type Checking with Interfaces
  - Extending Interfaces
- Type Aliases
  - Creating Reusable Type Definitions
  - Union Types with Type Aliases
  - Intersection Types with Type Aliases
- When to Use Interfaces vs. Type Aliases
- Best Practices and Tips
- Chapter Summary

Introduction to Interfaces

In the world of TypeScript, **interfaces** are your blueprint for defining the structure and behavior of objects. Think of them as contracts that specify the required properties (data members) and methods (functions) that an object must adhere to. Interfaces don't create actual objects; they simply define the *shape* those objects should have.

Why Use Interfaces?

Interfaces bring several benefits to your TypeScript code:

- **Type Safety:** Interfaces ensure that objects used in your code have the expected properties and methods. TypeScript's compiler will raise errors if an object doesn't match the structure defined by its interface. This helps catch errors early in development.
- **Readability and Maintainability:** Interfaces make your code more self-documenting. By looking at an interface, you (or other developers) can quickly understand what an object is supposed to represent and what it can do. This makes code easier to reason about and maintain.
- **Enforcing Contracts:** Interfaces help establish clear agreements about the shape of data between different parts of your code. They act as a communication tool, ensuring that functions and modules interact with objects in a consistent way.

The Contract Analogy

Imagine an interface as a contract between a restaurant and a customer. The contract might specify that the restaurant will provide a certain menu with specific dishes. If the restaurant doesn't fulfill the terms of the contract, the customer has a reason to complain.

Similarly, in TypeScript, an object that is supposed to adhere to an interface must provide the properties and methods outlined in that interface. If the object doesn't, the TypeScript compiler will raise an error, indicating that the "contract" has been violated.

Example: Defining a `Person` Interface

```
interface Person { name: string; age: number; greet(message: string): void; }
```

This interface defines a contract for objects representing people. It specifies that a `Person` object must have a `name` (string), an `age` (number), and a `greet` method that takes a `string` argument and returns `void`.

Interfaces are Everywhere

Interfaces are pervasive in TypeScript. They are used to define the structure of:

- Objects used as parameters or return values in functions
- Classes (which we'll cover in a later chapter)
- Data structures like arrays and dictionaries
- APIs and libraries

By defining and using interfaces, you create a clear structure for your code, improve type safety, and make your TypeScript projects easier to understand and maintain.

Describing Object Shapes with Interfaces

Think of an interface as a blueprint for an object. It outlines the specific properties (data) and methods (functions) that an object should have, along with their types. This blueprint provides a clear structure that any object claiming to be of that type must adhere to.

Syntax

You define an interface using the `interface` keyword, followed by the interface name and a block of code enclosed in curly braces `{}`:

```
interface InterfaceName { // Properties and methods }
```

Inside the curly braces, you declare the properties and methods of the interface:

- **Properties:** Property declarations look similar to variable declarations, but without the actual value assignment. You specify the property name followed by a colon `:`, then the data type.
- **Methods:** Method declarations look similar to function declarations, specifying the method name, parameter list (with types), and the return type.

Example: `Person` Interface

```
interface Person { name: string; // Property: name (string) age: number; // Property: age (number) greet(message: string): void; // Method: greet that takes a string argument and returns nothing }
```

Example: `Product` Interface

```
interface Product { id: number; name: string; price: number; description?: string; // Optional property (marked with '?') inStock: boolean; }
```

Example: Book Interface

```
interface Book { title: string; author: string; isbn: string; pageCount: number; isAvailable(): boolean; // Method that returns a boolean }
```

Key Points

- Interfaces define the *shape* of an object, not the actual object itself.
- You can specify property types (string, number, boolean, etc.) and method signatures (parameter types and return type).
- Optional properties are marked with a ? symbol.
- You can use `readonly` to define properties that cannot be changed after an object is created.

By creating well-defined interfaces, you establish clear expectations for how objects should look and behave in your TypeScript code. This enhances type safety, code readability, and maintainability.

Important Note: TypeScript interfaces are purely a design-time concept. They are not transpiled into JavaScript. Their primary purpose is to provide type checking and improve the developer experience during development.

Optional Properties

In TypeScript, interfaces can define optional properties. This means that an object implementing the interface doesn't have to provide a value for every single property defined in the interface. Optional properties add flexibility to your code, allowing you to model objects that may or may not have certain attributes.

Syntax

To mark a property as optional in an interface, simply add a question mark (?) after the property name:

```
interface Address { street: string; city: string; state: string; zipCode:
string; country?: string; // Optional property }
```

In this example, the `country` property is optional. An object implementing the `Address` interface can have a `country` property, but it's not mandatory.

Using Optional Properties

When working with objects that implement interfaces with optional properties, you'll need to be mindful of the possibility that a property might not be present. Here's how you can handle it:

```
function printAddress(address: Address) { console.log(address.street);
console.log(address.city); console.log(address.state);
console.log(address.zipCode); if (address.country) { // Check if the optional
property exists console.log(address.country); } else { console.log("Country
not specified"); } } let myAddress: Address = { street: "123 Main St", city:
"Anytown", state: "CA", zipCode: "12345" }; printAddress(myAddress); //
Country not specified
```

Benefits of Optional Properties

- **Flexibility:** Optional properties allow you to model real-world scenarios where certain data might not always be available. For instance, not every user in your application might provide a middle name, or not every product might have a detailed description.
- **Reduced Boilerplate:** You don't have to initialize every property of an object with a placeholder value (like `null` or an empty string) if it's not required.

- **Smoother Integration:** Optional properties are especially useful when working with external data sources (like APIs) where the response structure might not be entirely predictable.

Important Considerations

- **Type Safety:** Even though a property is optional, if it is provided, TypeScript will still enforce its type. In the `Address` example, if you assign a number to the `country` property, you'll get a type error.
- **Nullish Coalescing:** You can use the nullish coalescing operator (??) to provide a default value for an optional property if it's missing or `null`/`undefined`. (e.g., `console.log(address.country ?? "Unknown")`)

By utilizing optional properties, you can make your interfaces more adaptable and better represent real-world data structures, leading to more accurate and expressive TypeScript code.

Readonly Properties

In TypeScript, interfaces can also include `readonly` properties. As the name suggests, a readonly property's value cannot be changed after an object is initially created. This provides a valuable layer of immutability, helping you prevent accidental or unintended modifications to important data.

Syntax

To declare a readonly property within an interface, simply add the `readonly` keyword before the property name:

```
interface Point { readonly x: number; readonly y: number; }
```

In this example, both the x and y properties of a `Point` object are readonly.

How Readonly Properties Work

Once an object is created that implements an interface with readonly properties, you cannot directly reassign values to those properties.

```
let p1: Point = { x: 5, y: 10 }; p1.x = 20; // Error: Cannot assign to 'x'
because it is a read-only property.
```

Benefits of Readonly Properties

- **Immutability:** Readonly properties promote immutability, which can lead to more predictable code and fewer bugs. When you know that certain values cannot change, it simplifies reasoning about your code.
- **Data Protection:** They help protect critical data from accidental modifications. For example, in a financial application, you might make an account's balance readonly to prevent unauthorized changes.
- **Compiler Assistance:** The TypeScript compiler will enforce readonly restrictions, catching any attempts to modify readonly properties and alerting you to potential errors.

Important Considerations

- **Initialization:** Readonly properties must be initialized either when the object is created or within the constructor of a class that implements the interface.
- **Nested Objects:** If a readonly property refers to an object, you can still modify the *properties* of that object, but you cannot replace the object itself.

- **`ReadonlyArray`:** TypeScript also offers a `ReadonlyArray` type, which is similar to a regular array but prevents modifications like adding or removing elements.

Example: Using Readonly Properties

```
interface Circle { readonly center: Point; radius: number; } let circle: Circle = { center: { x: 0, y: 0 }, radius: 5 }; circle.radius = 10; // Valid (radius is not readonly) circle.center.x = 15; // Error: Cannot assign to 'x' because it is a read-only property. circle.center = {x: 15, y: 20}; // Error: Cannot assign to 'center' because it is a read-only property.
```

By incorporating readonly properties into your interfaces, you gain a valuable tool for expressing the immutability of certain aspects of your data models, making your code more robust and easier to reason about.

Working with Interfaces

Implementing Interfaces with Classes

While interfaces define a blueprint for objects, classes are the tools you use to actually create those objects. In TypeScript, a class can *implement* one or more interfaces, meaning it promises to adhere to the structure and behavior specified by those interfaces.

Syntax

To indicate that a class implements an interface, you use the `implements` keyword after the class name, followed by the names of the interfaces it implements (separated by commas):

```
class MyClass implements Interface1, Interface2 { // Class properties and methods }
```

Contract Fulfillment

The key rule for implementing interfaces is that a class must provide concrete implementations for all the properties and methods declared in the interfaces it implements. This includes:

- Defining properties with matching names and types.
- Implementing methods with the correct parameter types and return type.

Example: Implementing the `Person` Interface

Let's revisit the `Person` interface we defined earlier:

```
interface Person { name: string; age: number; greet(message: string): void; }
```

Here's how you could implement this interface with a `Person` class:

```
class Person implements Person { name: string; age: number; constructor(name: string, age: number) { this.name = name; this.age = age; } greet(message: string): void { console.log(`${message}, my name is ${this.name} and I'm ${this.age} years old.`); } } const alice = new Person("Alice", 30);
```

```
alice.greet("Hello"); // Output: "Hello, my name is Alice and I'm 30 years old."
```

Key Points

- A class can implement multiple interfaces.
- The class must provide concrete implementations for all properties and methods defined in the interfaces.
- The TypeScript compiler will enforce this contract and raise errors if the class doesn't fulfill the requirements of the interfaces.

Benefits of Implementing Interfaces

- **Strong Typing:** Implementing interfaces ensures that your objects have the correct structure and behavior, leading to more reliable code.
- **Code Reuse:** Interfaces promote code reusability by defining a common structure that multiple classes can implement.
- **Flexibility:** You can change the implementation details of a class without affecting how it's used as long as it continues to adhere to its interfaces.
- **Polymorphism:** Objects of different classes that implement the same interface can be used interchangeably, promoting flexibility and modularity in your code.

By understanding how to implement interfaces with classes, you unlock a powerful mechanism for creating well-structured, type-safe, and reusable code in TypeScript.

Type Checking with Interfaces

One of the most powerful features of TypeScript interfaces is their role in type checking. When you assign an object to a variable or parameter that has an interface type, TypeScript's compiler meticulously examines the object to ensure it adheres to the interface's contract.

How TypeScript Checks Objects Against Interfaces

TypeScript doesn't care about whether an object was explicitly created from a class that implements an interface. It focuses solely on the *shape* of the object – does it have the required properties and methods with the correct types? If so, the object is considered compatible with the interface.

Example:

```
interface Person { name: string; age: number; greet(message: string): void; } // Object literal that conforms to the Person interface let alice = { name: "Alice", age: 30, greet(message: string) { console.log(message + ", I'm Alice!"); } }; // Variable with the Person interface type let person: Person; // Valid assignment (object matches the interface) person = alice; // Invalid assignment (missing 'greet' method) // person = { name: "Bob", age: 40 }; // Error: Property 'greet' is missing // Invalid assignment (incorrect type for 'age') // person = { name: "Carol", age: "thirty" }; // Error: Type 'string' is not assignable to type 'number'
```

In this example, the `alice` object is compatible with the `Person` interface because it has all the required properties (`name`, `age`) and the `greet` method with the correct signature. TypeScript allows us to assign it to the `person` variable, which is declared with the `Person` type.

However, TypeScript prevents us from assigning objects that don't match the interface. This is how interfaces enforce type safety, ensuring that objects used in different parts of your code adhere to the expected structure.

Benefits of Type Checking with Interfaces

- **Early Error Detection:** TypeScript catches inconsistencies between objects and interfaces during development, preventing potential runtime errors.
- **Code Confidence:** You can be confident that objects used in your code conform to the expected structure, leading to more reliable and predictable behavior.
- **Enhanced Tooling:** IDEs leverage interface information to provide intelligent code completion, type hints, and refactoring assistance.

Key Points

- TypeScript checks the *shape* of an object, not its origin, to determine if it's compatible with an interface.
- Interfaces provide strong type checking, ensuring objects have the correct properties and methods.
- Type checking with interfaces helps catch errors early and improves code reliability.

By leveraging the power of interfaces for type checking, you create a safety net that protects your TypeScript code from unexpected type-related issues, ultimately leading to more robust and maintainable applications.

Extending Interfaces

In TypeScript, you can extend existing interfaces to create new interfaces that inherit all the properties and methods of the original interface. This is similar to inheritance in object-oriented programming, where a subclass inherits properties and methods from its parent class. Interface extension is a powerful way to build hierarchies of related types and promote code reusability.

Syntax

To extend an interface, you use the `extends` keyword followed by the name of the base interface:

```
interface Animal { name: string; makeSound(): void; } interface Dog extends
Animal { breed: string; fetch(): void; }
```

In this example, the Dog interface extends the `Animal` interface. This means that any object that conforms to the Dog interface must have all the properties and methods of both `Animal` (name and `makeSound`) and Dog (breed and `fetch`).

Example:

```
let myDog: Dog = { name: "Buddy", breed: "Golden Retriever", makeSound() {
console.log("Woof!"); }, fetch() { console.log("Fetching the ball..."); } };
myDog.makeSound(); // Output: "Woof!" (inherited from Animal) myDog.fetch();
// Output: "Fetching the ball..."
```

Benefits of Interface Extension

- **Code Reusability:** You can avoid repeating common properties and methods across multiple interfaces. The child interface automatically inherits the members of its parent interface.
- **Type Hierarchy:** You can create a hierarchy of interfaces that reflect real-world relationships between objects. For example, a `Dog` is an `Animal`, and a `Cat` is also an `Animal`.

- **Stronger Type Checking:** TypeScript can ensure that objects assigned to an interface type adhere to the complete contract defined by the entire interface hierarchy.
- **Flexibility:** You can extend multiple interfaces to create a new interface that combines their features:
```
interface Swimmable { swim(): void; } interface Flyable { fly(): void; }
interface Duck extends Animal, Swimmable, Flyable { quack(): void; }
```
- **Liskov Substitution Principle:** TypeScript's type system encourages you to follow the Liskov Substitution Principle, which states that objects of a child type should be usable wherever an object of the parent type is expected. This promotes code that is more flexible and easier to maintain.

Key Points

- Use `extends` to create new interfaces that inherit from existing ones.
- Child interfaces inherit all properties and methods from their parent interface(s).
- Interface extension promotes code reusability, type safety, and flexibility.

By mastering interface extension, you can model complex relationships between objects, create reusable type definitions, and build a solid foundation for your TypeScript applications.

Type Aliases

In TypeScript, **type aliases** provide a way to create alternative names for existing types or to define new, complex types. They are essentially a shorthand for referring to a type that might be long, cumbersome, or used frequently in your code.

Defining Type Aliases

You create a type alias using the `type` keyword, followed by the new name you want to give to the type, an equals sign =, and the type definition itself:

```
type NewTypeName = ExistingType;
```

Examples

Here are some examples of type aliases:

```
type ID = number; type Name = string; type Coordinates = [number, number];
type StringOrNumber = string | number;
```

In these examples:

- `ID` is an alias for `number`.
- `Name` is an alias for `string`.
- `Coordinates` is an alias for a tuple of two numbers.
- `StringOrNumber` is a union type representing either a string or a number.

Using Type Aliases

You can use type aliases anywhere you would normally use a type:

```
let userId: ID = 12345; let userName: Name = "Alice"; let location:
Coordinates = [40.7128, -74.0060]; // New York City coordinates let data:
StringOrNumber = "Hello" // or 42;
```

Benefits of Type Aliases

- **Readability:** Type aliases make your code more self-explanatory by providing descriptive names for types.
- **Code Reuse:** You can avoid repeating complex type definitions throughout your code.
- **Refactoring:** If the underlying type changes, you only need to update it in one place – the type alias definition.

Key Points

- Type aliases are purely a TypeScript concept and do not affect the generated JavaScript code.
- Type aliases can represent primitive types, object types, union types, intersection types, and even other type aliases.
- Use type aliases judiciously to improve code clarity and maintainability.

By incorporating type aliases into your TypeScript toolkit, you gain a convenient and powerful way to manage complex types and make your code more concise, reusable, and expressive.

Creating Reusable Type Definitions

Type aliases truly shine when dealing with complex types that occur frequently in your codebase. By assigning a meaningful name to a complex type, you create a reusable building block that enhances code readability, maintainability, and overall organization.

Type Aliases for Data Structures

Let's consider a few common scenarios where type aliases can streamline your code:

1. **`Coordinate`:** When working with 2D coordinates (x, y), you can define a type alias:
   ```
   type Coordinate = [number, number]; function distance(point1: Coordinate, point2: Coordinate): number { // ... (Distance calculation logic) }
   ```
   Now, instead of writing `[number, number]` repeatedly, you can simply use `Coordinate`, making your code more concise and self-explanatory.
2. **`Dimension`:** For width and height values:
   ```
   type Dimension = { width: number; height: number }; function calculateArea(dimensions: Dimension): number { return dimensions.width * dimensions.height; }
   ```
   The `Dimension` alias encapsulates the concept of width and height, making your code more expressive.
3. **`User`:** For representing user data:
   ```
   type User = { id: number; name: string; email: string; }; function greetUser(user: User): void { console.log(`Hello, ${user.name}!`); }
   ```
   The `User` type alias encapsulates the properties associated with a user, providing a clear structure for your user data.

Type Aliases for Function Types

Type aliases are incredibly useful for defining function types:

1. **`Callback`:**
   ```
   type Callback = (data: any) => void; function fetchData(url: string, callback: Callback): void { // ... (Fetch data and call the callback with the result) }
   ```
   Here, the `Callback` alias defines the expected signature of a callback function: it takes an

argument of any type (`data`) and doesn't return a value (`void`). This makes it clear what kind of function you need to pass to `fetchData`.

2. **`EventHandler`:**
   ```
   type EventHandler = (event: Event) => void;
   ```

Key Advantages

- **Improved Readability:** Descriptive type aliases make your code more self-documenting and easier for others (and yourself) to understand.
- **Code Reuse:** You avoid repetition by centralizing the definition of a complex type.
- **Refactoring:** If the structure of your data or function types needs to change, you only have to modify the type alias definition.
- **Enhanced Type Safety:** Type aliases, when combined with TypeScript's type checking, help prevent errors by ensuring that values used in your code match the expected types.

By strategically using type aliases, you can significantly improve the clarity, maintainability, and robustness of your TypeScript projects.

Union Types with Type Aliases

In TypeScript, union types allow you to express that a value can be one of several types. This is incredibly useful when dealing with situations where data can come in different forms. Type aliases make working with union types even more convenient by giving them meaningful names.

Defining Union Types with Type Aliases

The syntax for defining a union type using a type alias is straightforward:

```
type UnionTypeName = Type1 | Type2 | ... | TypeN;
```

You list the possible types, separated by vertical bars (`|`). This means that a value of the `UnionTypeName` can be of `Type1`, `Type2`, and so on, up to `TypeN`.

Example: `StringOrNumber` Type Alias

```
type StringOrNumber = string | number; let data: StringOrNumber; data = "Hello, world!"; // Valid data = 42; // Valid data = true; // Error: Type 'boolean' is not assignable to type 'StringOrNumber'.
```

In this example, `data` can hold either a `string` or a `number`. Trying to assign a `boolean` value will result in a type error because it doesn't match the union type.

Use Cases for Union Types

Union types are versatile and have a wide range of applications:

- **Flexible Function Parameters:** You can create functions that accept arguments of different types:
  ```
  function logValue(value: StringOrNumber) { console.log(value); }
  ```
- **Modeling Varied Data:** Represent data that can have different shapes:
  ```
  type Shape = | { kind: "circle"; radius: number } | { kind: "rectangle"; width: number; height: number };
  ```
- **Optional Properties:** Combine a type with `undefined` to indicate an optional value:
  ```
  type UserInfo = { name: string; email?: string; // Equivalent to `email: string | undefined` };
  ```

Working with Union Types

When working with union types, you'll often need to narrow down the type to perform specific operations. You can use type guards (like `typeof` or `instanceof`) or type assertions to achieve this.

Example:

```
function displayValue(value: StringOrNumber) { if (typeof value === "string")
{ console.log(value.toUpperCase()); } else { console.log(value * 2); } }
```

In this case, we use `typeof` to check whether `value` is a string or a number before performing the appropriate operation.

Key Points

- Union types represent values that can be of multiple types.
- Type aliases simplify the definition and use of union types.
- Use union types for flexibility in function parameters, modeling varied data, and representing optional values.
- Use type guards or type assertions to narrow down the type of a union type value before using it.

By understanding and using union types with type aliases, you unlock a powerful tool for modeling real-world data and building flexible and type-safe TypeScript code.

Intersection Types with Type Aliases

In contrast to union types (where a value can be one of several types), intersection types in TypeScript allow you to combine multiple types into a single, more specific type. This new type inherits all the properties and methods of the original types, creating a composite type that meets a stricter set of requirements.

Defining Intersection Types with Type Aliases

The syntax for defining an intersection type using a type alias is as follows:

```
type IntersectionTypeName = Type1 & Type2 & ... & TypeN;
```

The ampersand (&) symbol is used to combine types. This means that a value of the `IntersectionTypeName` must simultaneously satisfy all the requirements of `Type1`, `Type2`, and so on, up to `TypeN`.

Example: Combining Interfaces

```
interface Printable { print(): void; } interface Savable { save(): void; }
type Document = Printable & Savable; function processDocument(doc: Document) {
doc.print(); doc.save(); }
```

In this example, the `Document` type alias represents objects that must implement both the `Printable` and `Savable` interfaces. This means a `Document` object must have both a `print` and a `save` method. The `processDocument` function can safely operate on any object that satisfies this combined type.

Use Cases for Intersection Types

Intersection types are handy in several situations:

- **Adding Capabilities:** You can use intersection types to add capabilities to existing types without creating new classes. For example, you might have an interface `User` and want to create a type `AdminUser` that has additional administrative methods.
- **Mixing Functionality:** Combine types from different libraries or modules to create custom types that fit your specific needs.
- **Type Narrowing:** In some cases, TypeScript's type inference can be improved by using intersection types to explicitly express constraints on a type.

Important Considerations

- **Conflicts:** If the types being combined have properties or methods with the same name but different types, TypeScript will raise an error.
- **Order Independence:** The order of the types in an intersection type doesn't matter. `Type1 & Type2` is equivalent to `Type2 & Type1`.

Example: Creating a Custom Type

```
type NamedEntity = { name: string } & { id: number }; let employee:
NamedEntity = { name: "John Doe", id: 12345 };
```

The `NamedEntity` type combines two anonymous object types, creating a type that requires both a `name` (string) and an `id` (number) property.

By mastering intersection types and type aliases, you can create powerful and flexible type definitions that model complex data structures and relationships, while also promoting code reusability and type safety.

When to Use Interfaces vs. Type Aliases

In TypeScript, interfaces and type aliases share the common purpose of defining custom types, but they have nuanced differences that make them better suited for specific scenarios. Understanding these differences will help you make informed decisions when choosing between them.

Key Differences

Feature	Interface	Type Alias
Declaration	`interface` keyword	`type` keyword
Object Type Definition	Primary use case	Can also define object types, but interfaces are more common for this purpose
Extension	Supports `extends` for inheritance	Supports intersection (&) for combining types
Declaration Merging	Interfaces with the same name are automatically merged	No declaration merging
Brand New Types	Creates a named type that appears in error messages	Doesn't create a new type, just an alias

When to Use Interfaces

- **Object Type Definitions:** Interfaces are primarily designed for defining the shape of objects. This includes properties, methods, and even index signatures.

- **Inheritance:** When you want to create a hierarchy of types where child types inherit from parent types, interfaces with `extends` are the way to go.
- **Declaration Merging:** If you need to define an interface in multiple places (e.g., in different modules) and have TypeScript automatically merge those declarations, interfaces are the only option.

When to Use Type Aliases

- **Primitive Types, Unions, and Intersections:** Type aliases are more flexible and can be used to define simpler types like primitives (string, number, boolean) as well as complex union and intersection types.
- **Function Types:** Type aliases are commonly used to define function types, especially when working with higher-order functions.
- **Tuples:** Type aliases are the preferred way to define tuple types.
- **When You Don't Need a Named Type:** If you simply need a shorthand for a type and don't need it to appear in error messages or be extended, a type alias is often simpler.

General Recommendations

- **Start with Interfaces:** For defining object types, start with interfaces unless you have a specific reason to use a type alias. Interfaces tend to be more idiomatic for this purpose.
- **Prefer Type Aliases for Other Cases:** For primitive types, unions, intersections, function types, and tuples, type aliases are often a more natural choice.
- **Consider Readability:** Choose the option that makes your code the most clear and self-explanatory.
- **Flexibility:** Remember that you can often use either interfaces or type aliases to achieve similar results. The choice ultimately comes down to your personal preference and the specific requirements of your project.

By understanding the nuances and trade-offs between interfaces and type aliases, you can leverage the full power of TypeScript's type system to create well-organized, flexible, and type-safe code.

Best Practices and Tips

While interfaces and type aliases are powerful tools for managing types in TypeScript, following best practices can help you use them more effectively and avoid potential pitfalls. Here's a collection of tips and recommendations:

Naming Conventions

- **Interfaces:** Use PascalCase (e.g., `Person`, `Product`, `MyInterface`) for interface names. This aligns with the convention for class names in TypeScript.
- **Type Aliases:** Use PascalCase for object types (e.g., `UserType`, `ConfigOptions`) and camelCase for other types (e.g., `userId`, `coordinate`, `myCallback`).

Organization

- **Separate Files:** For larger projects, consider organizing interfaces and type aliases into separate files (e.g., `types.ts` or `interfaces.ts`). This keeps your codebase tidy and improves maintainability.
- **Module-Based Organization:** Group related interfaces and type aliases into modules to avoid naming collisions and make your code more modular.

Using Interfaces and Type Aliases

- **Interfaces for Object Shapes:** Prefer interfaces when defining object types. They offer features like extension and declaration merging that are not available for type aliases.
- **Type Aliases for Other Types:** Use type aliases for primitive types, union types, intersection types, function types, and tuples.
- **Readability Over Brevity:** While type aliases can make your code concise, prioritize readability. Choose meaningful and descriptive names that accurately convey the purpose of your types.
- **Avoid Overuse of any:** Limit the use of the `any` type, as it undermines type safety. Instead, use more specific types or `unknown` when necessary.
- **Leverage Type Inference:** Let TypeScript infer types whenever possible to reduce unnecessary type annotations.
- **Document Complex Types:** If a type alias or interface is particularly complex or used in multiple places, consider adding comments to explain its purpose and structure.

Avoiding Pitfalls

- **Circular References:** Be mindful of circular references between types, where two or more types depend on each other. This can lead to compilation errors.
- **Overly Complex Types:** Avoid creating excessively complex type definitions. If a type becomes too convoluted, consider breaking it down into smaller, more manageable types.

Additional Tips

- **Use Type Parameters (Generics):** For creating reusable types that can work with different data types, explore using type parameters (generics). We'll cover generics in depth in a later chapter.
- **Leverage TypeScript Tooling:** Utilize your IDE's TypeScript support for features like code navigation, type hints, and refactoring tools to improve your workflow and catch errors early on.
- **Stay Up-to-Date:** TypeScript is a constantly evolving language. Keep up with new features and best practices to make the most of its capabilities.

By following these best practices and staying aware of potential pitfalls, you'll be well on your way to becoming a TypeScript expert and writing cleaner, safer, and more maintainable code.

Chapter Summary

In this chapter, we explored two powerful tools for defining custom types in TypeScript: interfaces and type aliases. We covered the following:

- **Interfaces:** We learned how interfaces act as blueprints for objects, specifying the properties, methods, and their types that an object must have. We discussed optional and readonly properties and demonstrated how classes can implement interfaces.
- **Type Checking:** We saw how TypeScript uses interfaces to enforce type safety, ensuring that objects adhere to the contract defined by an interface.
- **Extending Interfaces:** We explored how to build hierarchies of related types by extending interfaces, promoting code reuse and maintainability.
- **Type Aliases:** We introduced type aliases as a way to create alternative names for existing types or complex type definitions. We saw how they can enhance readability and maintainability by providing concise names for frequently used types.
- **Union and Intersection Types:** We delved into how type aliases can be used to define union types (where a value can be one of several types) and intersection types (where a value must satisfy multiple types simultaneously).
- **Interfaces vs. Type Aliases:** We discussed the key differences and trade-offs between interfaces and type aliases, providing guidance on when to use each one.
- **Best Practices:** We offered tips on naming conventions, organization, and usage for interfaces and type aliases, helping you write cleaner, more reliable, and more expressive TypeScript code.

By understanding and applying the concepts covered in this chapter, you have a solid foundation for defining custom types in TypeScript and leveraging the power of its type system to build well-structured, maintainable, and type-safe applications.

In the next section of this book, we'll move on to more advanced TypeScript concepts, starting with classes – the fundamental building blocks of object-oriented programming in TypeScript.

Section II:
Advanced TypeScript Concepts

Classes: Building with Object-Oriented Power

Outline

- Introduction to Classes
    - Why Use Classes in TypeScript?
    - Basic Class Syntax
    - Constructors
- Class Members
    - Properties
    - Methods
- Access Modifiers
    - Public, Private, and Protected
    - Getters and Setters
- Inheritance
    - Extending Classes
    - Overriding Methods and Properties
    - The `super` Keyword
- Abstract Classes
- Static Members
- Classes vs. Interfaces
- Best Practices and Tips
- Chapter Summary

Introduction to Classes

Classes are the cornerstone of object-oriented programming (OOP) in TypeScript, and by extension, in JavaScript. They provide a structured way to organize code, model real-world entities, and create reusable blueprints for objects. Let's dive into the world of classes and explore the power they bring to your TypeScript projects.

Object-Oriented Programming (OOP) Fundamentals

Before we get into the specifics of TypeScript classes, let's briefly review the core principles of OOP:

1. **Encapsulation:** The idea of bundling data (properties) and the functions (methods) that operate on that data into a single unit, called an object. This helps organize code and protect data by controlling access to it.
2. **Inheritance:** The ability to create new classes (child classes) that inherit properties and methods from existing classes (parent classes). This promotes code reuse and allows you to build hierarchies of related objects.
3. **Polymorphism:** The ability of objects of different classes to be treated as if they belong to a common superclass. This enables you to write more flexible and generic code.

Classes in TypeScript

In TypeScript, a class is like a template or blueprint for creating objects. It defines the properties (attributes) and methods (behaviors) that objects of that class will possess. Here's the basic syntax:

```
class ClassName { // Properties // Methods }
```

Think of a class as a cookie cutter, and objects as the cookies you create from that cutter. Each cookie (object) has the same basic shape and ingredients (properties) as defined by the cutter (class), but they can have unique variations (different property values).

Benefits of Using Classes

TypeScript classes offer several advantages:

- **Code Organization:** Classes provide a clear structure for grouping related data and functionality. This makes your code more organized and easier to understand.
- **Object Modeling:** Classes allow you to model real-world entities in your code. For example, you could create classes for `Customer`, `Product`, `Order`, or any other concept relevant to your application.
- **Reusability:** By defining common properties and methods in a parent class, you can avoid code duplication and create specialized child classes that inherit those members.
- **Type Safety:** TypeScript's type system enhances the safety of your code by ensuring that objects are used correctly according to their class definitions.
- **Readability:** Class-based code is often more readable and easier to reason about than code based solely on functions and prototypes.

Classes vs. JavaScript's Prototypes

While JavaScript has classes, they are essentially syntactic sugar on top of its prototype-based inheritance model. TypeScript classes provide a more familiar syntax for developers coming from other object-oriented languages, while still leveraging the power of JavaScript prototypes.

Key Points

- Classes are blueprints for creating objects.
- Classes encapsulate data and behavior.
- Classes support inheritance, allowing you to create hierarchies of related objects.
- TypeScript classes enhance JavaScript's prototype-based inheritance.

By understanding and using classes effectively, you can harness the power of object-oriented programming in TypeScript, leading to code that is more organized, reusable, and easier to maintain.

Why Use Classes in TypeScript?

TypeScript's classes enhance the way you work with objects in JavaScript. While JavaScript itself has a prototype-based inheritance system, TypeScript's class syntax provides a more structured, familiar, and type-safe approach to object-oriented programming.

Structure and Clarity

In vanilla JavaScript, creating objects often involves working with prototypes and constructor functions. While powerful, this can lead to code that's less intuitive and harder to follow, especially for developers accustomed to class-based languages like Java or C#. TypeScript classes provide a clear and concise syntax for defining objects, their properties, and their methods, all in one place.

Consider this JavaScript example:

```
function Person(name, age) { this.name = name; this.age = age; }
Person.prototype.greet = function() { console.log("Hello, I'm " + this.name);
};
```

Compare that to the equivalent TypeScript class:

```
class Person { constructor(public name: string, public age: number) {} greet()
{ console.log("Hello, I'm " + this.name); } }
```

The TypeScript class is more self-explanatory. You immediately see the properties (`name`, `age`) and the method (`greet`), making it easier to grasp the object's structure and capabilities.

Type Safety

TypeScript's type system truly shines when working with classes. You can define precise types for your class properties and method parameters, ensuring that objects are used correctly throughout your code. This helps catch errors early, before they lead to runtime problems.

In the TypeScript example above, the constructor clearly defines that `name` must be a string and `age` must be a number. If you accidentally try to create a `Person` object with a numerical name or a string age, TypeScript will raise a type error during compilation.

Maintainability in Large Projects

As JavaScript projects grow larger, the benefits of classes become even more apparent. With classes, you can create well-organized modules and libraries, encapsulate logic within objects, and easily reuse code through inheritance. This leads to a codebase that is easier to reason about, maintain, and extend over time.

Key Points

- TypeScript classes provide a more familiar and structured syntax for defining objects compared to JavaScript's prototypes.
- Classes enhance code readability and clarity by grouping related data and behavior.
- TypeScript's type system adds a layer of safety to classes by enforcing type checks for properties and methods.
- Classes promote code reusability through inheritance.
- In large projects, classes improve maintainability and make the codebase more manageable.

If you're coming from a background in object-oriented languages or simply prefer a more structured approach to organizing your code, TypeScript classes offer a natural and powerful way to work with objects in JavaScript. They combine the flexibility of JavaScript with the benefits of type safety and object-oriented design principles.

Basic Class Syntax

In TypeScript, you create a class using the `class` keyword. Let's break down the essential components of a class:

```
class ClassName { // Constructor (optional) constructor(parameters: types) {
// Initialization logic } // Properties (data members) propertyName: type; //
...other properties // Methods (functions) methodName(parameters: types):
returnType { // Method logic } // ...other methods }
```

- **`ClassName`:** The name you give to your class. It's convention to use PascalCase (e.g., `Car`, `Person`, `BankAccount`).
- **Constructor (Optional):** A special method called when you create a new object of the class. It's used to initialize the object's properties. The `constructor` keyword is followed by parentheses containing any parameters you want to pass in when creating the object.
- **Properties:** Variables that store data associated with an object of the class. Each property has a name and a type.
- **Methods:** Functions that define the actions or behaviors of an object. Methods can have parameters and return values, just like regular functions.

Example: `Car` Class

```
class Car { make: string; model: string; year: number; constructor(make: string, model: string, year: number) { this.make = make; this.model = model; this.year = year; } startEngine(): void { console.log("Vroom! The engine is starting."); } }
```

In this example:

- We define a class named `Car`.
- The constructor takes three parameters: `make`, `model`, and `year`.
- It initializes the corresponding properties using the `this` keyword.
- The `startEngine` method simulates starting the car's engine.

Creating Objects

To create an object from a class, you use the new keyword:

```
let myCar = new Car("Toyota", "Camry", 2023); myCar.startEngine(); // Output: "Vroom! The engine is starting."
```

Other Example Classes

- **`Animal`:** Could have properties like `name`, `species`, and `age`, and methods like `makeSound` and `move`.
- **`BankAccount`:** Could have properties like `accountNumber`, `balance`, and `owner`, and methods like `deposit`, `withdraw`, and `getBalance`.

Feel free to experiment with creating your own classes to model different objects and concepts!

Constructors

Constructors are special methods in TypeScript classes that are automatically called when you create a new instance (object) of that class using the new keyword. Their primary purpose is to initialize the object's state by assigning initial values to its properties.

Defining a Constructor

To define a constructor within a class, you use the `constructor` keyword followed by parentheses () that may contain parameters. The body of the constructor contains the logic to set up the initial state of the object:

```
class Person { name: string; age: number; constructor(name: string, age: number) { this.name = name; this.age = age; } // ... other methods ... }
```

In this example, the `Person` class has a constructor that takes two parameters: `name` and `age`. Inside the constructor, we use the `this` keyword to refer to the current object being created. We then assign the values of the `name` and `age` parameters to the corresponding properties of the object.

Calling the Constructor

When you create a new `Person` object using `new`, the constructor is automatically invoked, and the values you pass as arguments are used to initialize the object's properties:

```
let alice = new Person("Alice", 30); console.log(alice.name); // Output: "Alice" console.log(alice.age); // Output: 30
```

Constructors with Default Values

You can also provide default values for constructor parameters:

```
class Book { title: string; author: string; pageCount: number; constructor(title: string, author: string, pageCount: number = 100) { // Default value for pageCount this.title = title; this.author = author; this.pageCount = pageCount; } } let book1 = new Book("The Hitchhiker's Guide to the Galaxy", "Douglas Adams"); console.log(book1.pageCount); // Output: 100 (default value used) let book2 = new Book("Pride and Prejudice", "Jane Austen", 367); console.log(book2.pageCount); // Output: 367 (provided value overrides default)
```

Key Points

- Constructors are special methods used to initialize objects.
- Use the `constructor` keyword to define a constructor within a class.
- Constructors can accept parameters to set initial values for properties.
- The `this` keyword is used to refer to the current object being created.
- You can provide default values for constructor parameters.

Best Practice

It's generally a good practice to define a constructor for your classes to ensure that objects are properly initialized with valid values. This helps prevent errors and makes your code more reliable.

Class Members

Properties

Properties are the backbone of objects in TypeScript. They represent the data or state associated with an object, defining its characteristics and attributes. In a class, properties act as variables that hold values specific to each instance of the class.

Declaring Properties

You declare properties within a class just like you would declare variables, by specifying a name followed by a type annotation:

```
class Person { name: string; age: number; }
```

In this example, name and age are properties of the Person class.

Instance Properties

Most properties you'll work with are instance properties. These properties are unique to each object created from a class. Each Person object you create will have its own name and age.

```
const alice = new Person(); alice.name = "Alice"; alice.age = 30; const bob = new Person(); bob.name = "Bob"; bob.age = 45; console.log(alice.name); // Output: "Alice" console.log(bob.name); // Output: "Bob"
```

Static Properties

Static properties, in contrast, belong to the class itself rather than to individual instances of the class. They are shared among all objects created from that class. You declare a static property using the `static` keyword:

```
class Counter { static count: number = 0; // Static property constructor() { Counter.count++; } } const counter1 = new Counter(); const counter2 = new Counter(); console.log(Counter.count); // Output: 2
```

In this example, `count` is a static property that keeps track of the total number of `Counter` objects created. It's accessed using the class name (`Counter.count`), not through instances.

Initializing Properties

You can initialize properties in a few ways:

1. **Directly in the Class:**
   `class Rectangle { width: number = 10; height: number = 5; }`
2. **In the Constructor:** (Common for properties that need initial values)
   `class Circle { radius: number; constructor(radius: number) { this.radius = radius; } }`
3. **Using Parameter Properties (Shorthand):**
   `class Person { constructor(public name: string, public age: number) {} // Automatically creates name and age properties }`

Key Points

- Properties represent data associated with an object.
- Instance properties are unique to each object.
- Static properties are shared among all objects of a class.
- You can initialize properties directly in the class, in the constructor, or using parameter properties.

By understanding how to declare, initialize, and use both instance and static properties, you can effectively model and manipulate the state of objects in your TypeScript applications.

Methods

While properties define the *state* of an object, methods define its *behavior* – the actions it can perform. In TypeScript classes, methods are essentially functions associated with objects of that class. They encapsulate the logic that operates on the object's data (its properties).

Defining Methods

You define methods within a class similar to how you define regular functions. However, methods have access to the object's properties through the `this` keyword. Here's the basic syntax:

```
class ClassName { // ... properties ... methodName(parameter1: type,
parameter2: type, ...): returnType { // Method logic } // ... other methods
... }
```

Let's break down the components of a method declaration:

- **`methodName`:** A descriptive name for your method (e.g., `startEngine`, `calculateBalance`, `bark`). It's common to use camelCase for method names.
- **`parameter1`, `parameter2`, etc.:** Parameters (inputs) the method accepts, along with their types. These are similar to function parameters.
- **`returnType`:** The type of value the method returns (if any). If a method doesn't return a value, you can use the `void` type.

Example: `Animal` Class

```
class Animal { name: string; species: string; constructor(name: string,
species: string) { this.name = name; this.species = species; } makeSound():
void { // Method with no parameters, returns void console.log("Generic animal
sound!"); } move(distance: number): void { // Method with a parameter
console.log(`${this.name} moved ${distance} meters.`); } } const myDog = new
Animal("Fido", "Dog"); myDog.makeSound(); // Output: "Generic animal sound!"
myDog.move(10); // Output: "Fido moved 10 meters."
```

In this example:

- The `Animal` class has two methods: `makeSound` and `move`.
- `makeSound` takes no parameters and doesn't return a value (it just logs a message).
- `move` takes a `number` parameter (`distance`) and also doesn't return a value.
- Both methods use `this.name` to access the `name` property of the current `Animal` object.

Key Points

- Methods define the actions that an object can perform.
- Methods can have parameters and return values.
- Methods use the `this` keyword to access the object's properties.

Example: BankAccount Class

```
class BankAccount { balance: number; constructor(initialBalance: number) {
this.balance = initialBalance; } deposit(amount: number): void { this.balance
+= amount; } withdraw(amount: number): void { if (amount <= this.balance) {
```

```
this.balance -= amount; } else { console.log("Insufficient funds!"); } }
getBalance(): number { return this.balance; } }
```

By defining methods within your classes, you create objects that can interact with each other and perform meaningful actions, bringing your TypeScript code to life.

Access Modifiers

Access modifiers are keywords in TypeScript (and many other object-oriented languages) that determine the visibility and accessibility of class members (properties and methods). They play a crucial role in encapsulation, a fundamental principle of object-oriented programming.

`public`, `private`, and `protected`

TypeScript offers three access modifiers:

1. **`public` (Default):** Members declared as `public` are accessible from anywhere – both within the class itself and from outside the class. This is the default access level if you don't specify any modifier.
2. **`private`:** Members declared as `private` are only accessible from within the class where they are defined. They are not visible to the outside world, including subclasses.
3. **`protected`:** Members declared as `protected` are accessible within the class itself and within its subclasses (through inheritance). However, they are not accessible from outside the class hierarchy.

Encapsulation and Access Modifiers

Encapsulation is the practice of bundling data (properties) and the functions (methods) that operate on that data into a single unit (the class). This promotes modularity, information hiding, and code maintainability.

Access modifiers help you enforce encapsulation by controlling which parts of your class are exposed to the outside world. By making certain members private, you protect them from accidental or unauthorized modification. This allows you to change the internal implementation details of your class without affecting how other parts of your code interact with it.

Examples

```
class BankAccount { private balance: number; constructor(initialBalance:
number) { this.balance = initialBalance; } deposit(amount: number): void {
this.balance += amount; } public withdraw(amount: number): void { // Public
method (accessible from outside) if (amount <= this.balance) { this.balance -=
amount; } else { console.log("Insufficient funds!"); } } getBalance(): number
{ // No access modifier (implicitly public) return this.balance; } } const
myAccount = new BankAccount(1000); myAccount.deposit(500);
myAccount.withdraw(200); console.log(myAccount.getBalance()); // Output: 1300
//myAccount.balance = 5000; // Error: Property 'balance' is private and only
accessible within class 'BankAccount'.
```

In this example:

- The `balance` property is `private`, so it can only be accessed and modified within the `BankAccount` class. This protects the balance from being changed arbitrarily from the outside.
- The `deposit` and `withdraw` methods are `public`, so they can be called from outside the class to manage the account.
- The `getBalance` method doesn't have an access modifier, which means it's implicitly `public`.

Key Points

- Access modifiers control the visibility and accessibility of class members.
- `public` members are accessible from anywhere.
- `private` members are only accessible within the class itself.
- `protected` members are accessible within the class and its subclasses.
- Encapsulation is a core OOP principle that promotes code organization and information hiding.
- Access modifiers help you achieve encapsulation by controlling access to class members.

By using access modifiers thoughtfully, you can create well-encapsulated classes with clear boundaries between their internal implementation and their external interface. This leads to code that is easier to maintain, more reliable, and less prone to unexpected side effects.

Getters and Setters

Getters and setters are special methods in TypeScript classes that allow you to control how properties are accessed and modified. They act as intermediaries between the outside world and your object's internal state, providing a layer of abstraction and enabling you to add custom logic whenever a property is read or written.

Syntax

- **Getters:** Defined using the `get` keyword followed by the property name and parentheses `()`. They must return a value of the same type as the property.
- **Setters:** Defined using the `set` keyword followed by the property name and parentheses containing a single parameter of the same type as the property.

```
class Rectangle { private _width: number; // Private property (accessible only within the class) private _height: number; constructor(width: number, height: number) { this._width = width; this._height = height; } get width(): number { // Getter for width return this._width; } set width(value: number) { // Setter for width if (value <= 0) { throw new Error("Width must be positive."); } this._width = value; } // ... similar getter and setter for height ... }
```

Using Getters and Setters

You access getters and setters just like regular properties:

```
let rect = new Rectangle(10, 5); console.log(rect.width); // Output: 10 (calls the getter) rect.width = 20; // Calls the setter //rect.width = -5; // Error: Width must be positive. (setter throws an error)
```

Use Cases

Getters and setters are valuable for several reasons:

1. **Validation:** You can add validation logic in setters to ensure that values assigned to properties meet certain criteria. In the `Rectangle` example, the setter prevents negative widths.
2. **Derived Properties:** Getters can calculate and return values derived from other properties. `get area(): number { return this._width * this._height; }`
3. **Side Effects:** Setters can trigger additional actions when a property is changed. For example, you could recalculate other values or update the UI when a property is set.
4. **Encapsulation:** Getters and setters help encapsulate the internal representation of data within an object. You can change how a property is stored internally without affecting the way it's used externally.

Key Points

- Getters and setters provide controlled access to properties.
- Use `get` and `set` keywords to define them.
- Getters must return a value of the property's type.
- Setters take a single parameter of the property's type.
- Use cases include validation, derived properties, side effects, and encapsulation.

Example: Converting Temperature

```
class Temperature { private _celsius: number; constructor(celsius: number) {
this._celsius = celsius; } get celsius(): number { return this._celsius; } set
celsius(value: number) { this._celsius = value; } get fahrenheit(): number {
return (this._celsius * 9) / 5 + 32; } set fahrenheit(value: number) {
this._celsius = ((value - 32) * 5) / 9; } }
```

By incorporating getters and setters into your TypeScript classes, you enhance your control over object properties, add a layer of protection, and create more expressive and maintainable code.

Inheritance

Inheritance is a cornerstone of object-oriented programming. It allows you to create new classes (child classes) that automatically inherit properties and methods from existing classes (parent classes). This promotes code reusability and helps you establish clear relationships between different types of objects.

Extending Classes

In TypeScript, you use the `extends` keyword to create a child class that inherits from a parent class:

```
class Animal { // Parent (or base) class name: string; species: string;
constructor(name: string, species: string) { this.name = name; this.species =
species; } makeSound(): void { console.log("Generic animal sound!"); } } class
Dog extends Animal { // Child (or derived) class breed: string;
constructor(name: string, breed: string) { super(name, "Dog"); // Call the
parent class constructor this.breed = breed; } bark(): void {
console.log("Woof!"); } }
```

In this example:

1. `Animal` is the parent class. It defines common properties (`name`, `species`) and a method (`makeSound`).

2. Dog is the child class. It extends `Animal`, inheriting its properties and methods.
3. Dog adds a specific property (`breed`) and a specific method (`bark`).
4. The `super` keyword in the Dog constructor calls the parent class's (`Animal`) constructor to initialize the inherited properties (`name`, `species`).

Parent vs. Child Classes

- **Parent (Base) Class:** The class from which another class inherits properties and methods. It provides a foundation for common characteristics.
- **Child (Derived) Class:** The class that inherits from a parent class. It can add its own unique properties and methods while also having access to those from the parent class.

Using Inherited Members

Objects created from a child class have access to both their own members and the inherited members from the parent class:

```
const myDog = new Dog("Buddy", "Golden Retriever"); myDog.makeSound(); //
Output: "Generic animal sound!" (Inherited from Animal) myDog.bark(); //
Output: "Woof!" console.log(myDog.name); // Output: "Buddy"
console.log(myDog.breed); // Output: "Golden Retriever"
```

Key Points

- Inheritance allows you to create hierarchical relationships between classes.
- Use the `extends` keyword to make a class inherit from another class.
- Child classes inherit properties and methods from their parent class.
- Child classes can add their own unique members and override inherited ones.
- Use `super` to call the parent class constructor and access its members.

By understanding inheritance, you can model complex relationships between objects, avoid code duplication, and build more structured and maintainable TypeScript applications.

Overriding Methods and Properties

Inheritance provides a powerful way to reuse code, but sometimes you need to customize the behavior of a child class. That's where method and property overriding come into play. Overriding allows you to provide a different implementation for a method or property in a child class, tailoring it to the specific needs of that class while still benefiting from the inherited structure.

Method Overriding

To override a method in a child class, you simply define a method with the same name and signature (parameter types and return type) as the method in the parent class. The child class's implementation will then take precedence when you call the method on an object of the child class.

Example:

```
class Animal { makeSound(): void { console.log("Generic animal sound!"); } }
class Dog extends Animal { makeSound(): void { console.log("Woof!"); } } const
myDog = new Dog("Buddy", "Golden Retriever"); myDog.makeSound(); // Output:
"Woof!" (Overridden method in Dog)
```

Property Overriding

Property overriding is similar. You declare a property in the child class with the same name and type as the property in the parent class. The child class's property value will then be used instead of the parent's.

The `super` Keyword

The `super` keyword is a special reference that allows you to access the parent class's implementation of a method or property within the overridden method or property of a child class.

Example: Using `super` in a Method

```
class Dog extends Animal { makeSound(): void { super.makeSound(); // Call the parent's makeSound() method console.log("and wagging tail!"); } }
```

In this modified example, the Dog class's `makeSound` method first calls the `Animal` class's `makeSound` method (using `super`) to get the generic animal sound, and then adds a dog-specific behavior.

Key Points

- Method overriding allows you to provide a specialized implementation of an inherited method.
- Property overriding lets you provide a different value for an inherited property.
- Use the `super` keyword to access the parent class's implementation from within a child class.
- Overriding is a fundamental concept in inheritance that enables you to tailor the behavior of child classes while still benefiting from the structure and functionality provided by the parent class.

By mastering method and property overriding, along with the `super` keyword, you unlock the full power of inheritance in TypeScript, enabling you to create flexible and adaptable object hierarchies.

The `super` Keyword: Bridging the Inheritance Gap

In TypeScript, the `super` keyword is your bridge between a child class and its parent class. It serves two primary purposes:

1. **Calling the Parent Constructor:** When a child class has its own constructor, you often need to call the constructor of the parent class to properly initialize the inherited properties. The `super` keyword allows you to do this. It must be the first statement within the child class constructor.
2. **Accessing Parent Members:** If a child class overrides a method or property from its parent, you can still access the parent's original implementation using `super`. This enables you to reuse or extend existing functionality.

Calling the Parent Constructor

```
class Animal { constructor(public name: string) {} } class Dog extends Animal { constructor(name: string, public breed: string) { super(name); // Call the parent's constructor } } const myDog = new Dog("Buddy", "Golden Retriever"); console.log(myDog.name); // Output: "Buddy"
```

In this example, the Dog constructor uses `super(name)` to pass the `name` argument to the `Animal` constructor. This ensures that the `name` property is correctly initialized in the Dog object.

Accessing Parent Methods and Properties

```
class Animal { makeSound() { console.log("Generic animal sound!"); } } class Cat extends Animal { makeSound() { super.makeSound(); // Call the parent's
```

```
makeSound() console.log("Meow!"); } } const myCat = new Cat("Whiskers");
myCat.makeSound(); // Output: "Generic animal sound!\nMeow!"
```

In this modified example, the `Cat` class overrides the `makeSound` method. However, it still uses `super.makeSound()` to invoke the parent's implementation before adding its own "Meow!" sound.

Key Points

- `super` is used in child classes to access the parent class.
- Use `super()` within a child class constructor to call the parent constructor (and pass any necessary arguments).
- Use `super.methodName()` or `super.propertyName` to access overridden methods or properties from the parent class.
- The `super` keyword must be used within the context of a child class, as it refers to the parent of that class.

By understanding and using the `super` keyword effectively, you can create well-structured class hierarchies where child classes can leverage the functionality of their parent classes while adding their own unique capabilities. This leads to code that is more organized, reusable, and easier to maintain.

Abstract Classes

In TypeScript, abstract classes serve as blueprints or templates for other classes. Unlike regular classes, you cannot create instances (objects) directly from an abstract class. Their primary purpose is to define a common structure and set of behaviors that their subclasses must adhere to.

Abstract Methods

The defining feature of an abstract class is the ability to declare *abstract methods*. These are methods that have a signature (name, parameters, and return type) but no implementation. It's the responsibility of any concrete subclass that extends the abstract class to provide the actual implementation for these methods.

```
abstract class Animal { // Abstract class name: string; constructor(name:
string) { this.name = name; } abstract makeSound(): void; // Abstract method
(no implementation) }
```

In this example, the `Animal` class is abstract (denoted by the `abstract` keyword). It has a concrete property `name` and an abstract method `makeSound`. Any class that extends `Animal` *must* provide a concrete implementation for the `makeSound` method.

```
class Dog extends Animal { makeSound(): void { console.log("Woof!"); } } class
Cat extends Animal { makeSound(): void { console.log("Meow!"); } }
```

Why Use Abstract Classes?

- **Enforcing Structure:** Abstract classes ensure that all subclasses share a common set of methods, even if the implementations differ. This is useful for defining a standardized interface for a family of related classes.
- **Preventing Direct Instantiation:** Abstract classes prevent you from accidentally creating objects of a generic type that might not be fully functional. You're forced to create specialized subclasses that provide the necessary implementation details.

- **Code Reusability:** Concrete properties and methods defined in an abstract class can be reused by all its subclasses, reducing code duplication.
- **Polymorphism:** Abstract classes facilitate polymorphism, allowing you to work with objects of different subclasses through a common interface (the abstract class).

Abstract Classes vs. Interfaces

While both abstract classes and interfaces can define contracts, there are key differences:

Feature	Abstract Class	Interface
Instantiation	Cannot be instantiated	Cannot be instantiated
Members	Can have both concrete (with implementation) and abstract members	All members are implicitly abstract (no implementation in the interface itself)
Inheritance	Can be extended by subclasses using `extends`	Can be implemented by classes using `implements` or extended by other interfaces
Relationships	Defines an "is-a" relationship (e.g., Dog "is-a" Animal)	Defines a "can-do" relationship (e.g., a class "can-do" printing)

When to Use Abstract Classes

Abstract classes are a good fit when:

- You want to create a base class that provides some shared functionality but cannot be instantiated on its own.
- You need to enforce that all subclasses have a specific set of methods, even if the implementations differ.
- You want to create a type hierarchy that represents a common abstraction.

By mastering abstract classes, you'll be able to design more robust and flexible class hierarchies in TypeScript. They provide a powerful way to combine the benefits of interfaces (defining contracts) with the ability to share implementation details between classes.

Static Members

In TypeScript, classes can have both instance members (properties and methods that belong to individual objects) and static members. Static members are associated with the class itself, not with any specific instance of the class. They act as shared resources that are accessible across all instances of the class.

Declaring Static Members

You declare static members using the `static` keyword before the member's name:

```
class MyClass { static staticProperty: string = "Hello"; // Static property
static staticMethod(): void { // Static method console.log("This is a static
method."); } }
```

Using Static Members

Unlike instance members, which are accessed through objects (e.g., `myObject.instanceProperty`), static members are accessed directly through the class name:

```
console.log(MyClass.staticProperty); // Output: "Hello"
MyClass.staticMethod(); // Output: "This is a static method."
```

Example: `Math` Class

A classic example of static members is the built-in `Math` class in JavaScript and TypeScript. Its properties (like `PI`) and methods (like `random()`, `sqrt()`, etc.) are all static because they don't depend on any specific instance of the `Math` class. They provide general-purpose mathematical utilities.

```
console.log(Math.PI); // Output: 3.14159... let randomNumber = Math.random();
// Generate a random number
```

Use Cases for Static Members

- **Utility Functions:** Static methods are often used to create utility functions that operate on data related to the class but don't require an object instance. For example, a `Math.random()` function doesn't need to know about any specific number; it just generates a random value.
- **Factory Methods:** Static methods can be used to create instances of a class in a controlled way. For example, a `Date.now()` method returns the current timestamp without needing a `Date` object to be created beforehand.
- **Shared State:** Static properties can be used to store data that is shared among all instances of the class. For example, you could use a static property to keep track of the total number of objects created from a class.

Key Points

- Static members belong to the class itself, not to instances of the class.
- Use the `static` keyword to declare static properties and methods.
- Access static members using the class name (e.g., `MyClass.staticProperty`).

By utilizing static members effectively, you can create well-organized and efficient classes that encapsulate both object-specific data and behavior as well as class-level functionality and shared state.

Classes vs. Interfaces

Classes and interfaces are both powerful constructs in TypeScript, but they serve distinct purposes and have different capabilities. Understanding their differences is key to making informed decisions about which to use in various scenarios.

Key Differences

Feature	Classes	Interfaces
Purpose	Blueprint for creating objects. Defines properties, methods, and constructors.	Defines a contract for the structure of objects (properties and methods).
Instantiation	Can be instantiated using the new keyword.	Cannot be instantiated.

Implementation	Contains the actual implementation of methods and optional initial values for properties.	Only declares method signatures and property types, not their implementation.
Inheritance	Supports inheritance using the `extends` keyword.	Can be extended by other interfaces or implemented by classes.
Declaration Merging	No declaration merging.	Allows merging multiple declarations of the same interface.
Runtime Existence	Exists at runtime as JavaScript objects.	Erased during compilation and not present in the generated JavaScript.
Type vs. Value	Represents both a type and a value (the object instance).	Represents only a type.

When to Use Classes

- **Creating Objects:** When you need to create multiple objects with the same structure and behavior, classes are the way to go. They encapsulate data and functions and provide a mechanism for creating instances.
- **Inheritance:** If you want to create a hierarchy of objects where child objects inherit properties and methods from parent objects, classes and the `extends` keyword are ideal.
- **Shared Behavior:** If you have complex logic or behavior that needs to be shared among multiple objects, encapsulating it within a class makes sense.

When to Use Interfaces

- **Defining Contracts:** Interfaces are best used for defining the shape or contract that objects should adhere to. This is useful for type checking, ensuring that objects used in different parts of your code have the expected structure.
- **Type Checking Function Parameters/Return Values:** Interfaces are often used to describe the types of arguments and return values in functions.
- **Duck Typing:** TypeScript's structural type system allows you to treat objects as compatible with an interface as long as they have the required properties and methods, regardless of whether they explicitly implement that interface. This is known as duck typing ("If it walks like a duck and quacks like a duck, then it must be a duck").

Classes and Interfaces Working Together

The most common way classes and interfaces interact is through implementation. A class can `implement` one or more interfaces, promising to provide concrete implementations for all the members defined in those interfaces.

```
interface Printable { print(): void; } class Document implements Printable {
// ... properties and other methods ... print(): void { console.log("Printing
document..."); } }
```

In this example, the `Document` class implements the `Printable` interface, ensuring that it has a `print` method.

Key Points

- Classes create objects; interfaces define contracts for objects.
- Classes contain implementations; interfaces only declare signatures.
- Classes can inherit from other classes; interfaces can extend other interfaces or be implemented by classes.
- Use classes when you need to create objects with state and behavior.
- Use interfaces to define contracts, enable duck typing, and improve type checking.

By understanding the distinct roles of classes and interfaces and how they can work together, you can create well-organized, flexible, and type-safe TypeScript code.

Best Practices and Tips

TypeScript classes empower you to create well-structured, maintainable, and reusable code. To maximize the benefits of classes, consider these best practices and tips:

Naming Conventions

- **Classes:** Use PascalCase (e.g., `Customer`, `Product`, `OrderService`). This improves readability and distinguishes classes from other types.
- **Properties and Methods:** Use camelCase (e.g., `firstName`, `calculatePrice`, `isValid`). This is the standard convention for JavaScript/TypeScript identifiers.
- **Private Members:** Consider prefixing private properties and methods with an underscore (_) (e.g., `_name`, `_calculateDiscount`). This signals that they are internal to the class and shouldn't be accessed directly from outside.

Organization

- **Modules:** Organize your classes into modules. This helps avoid naming collisions, improves code structure, and makes it easier to manage dependencies. Use the `export` keyword to make classes accessible from other modules, and `import` to use classes from other modules.
- **Single Responsibility Principle (SRP):** Strive to make each class responsible for a single, well-defined purpose. This makes your classes easier to understand, test, and maintain.

Composition over Inheritance

While inheritance is a powerful tool, it can sometimes lead to tightly coupled and inflexible code. When possible, consider using composition (having objects contain references to other objects) to achieve code reuse and flexibility.

Access Modifiers

- **Encapsulation:** Use access modifiers (`public`, `private`, `protected`) to control access to class members and enforce encapsulation. This helps protect data and internal implementation details.
- **Data Hiding:** Make properties private and provide access to them through public methods (getters and setters). This allows you to add validation or other logic when getting or setting property values.

Interfaces and Classes

- **Prefer Interfaces for Contracts:** When defining the shape or contract of an object, use interfaces. This promotes flexibility and allows for multiple implementations.
- **Classes for Implementation:** Use classes to provide the concrete implementation of the interface. This keeps your code organized and separates the “what” (interface) from the “how” (class).

Inheritance (Judicious Use)

- **"Is-a" Relationship:** Use inheritance when there's a clear "is-a" relationship between classes (e.g., `Dog` is a `Animal`, `SavingsAccount` is a `BankAccount`).
- **Avoid Deep Hierarchies:** Be cautious of creating overly deep inheritance hierarchies, as they can become difficult to manage and understand.

Abstract Classes

- **Common Interface:** Use abstract classes to define common interfaces and enforce a certain structure for a group of related classes.
- **Partial Implementation:** Abstract classes can provide some concrete implementations for methods while leaving others as abstract to be implemented by subclasses.

Static Members

- **Class-Level Data and Behavior:** Use static members for properties and methods that belong to the class itself rather than to individual instances. This is useful for utility functions, factory methods, and shared state.

By adhering to these best practices, you'll be well on your way to writing clean, efficient, and maintainable TypeScript classes that form a solid foundation for your applications.

Chapter Summary

In this chapter, we explored the world of classes in TypeScript, a cornerstone of object-oriented programming. We covered the following key concepts:

- **OOP Fundamentals:** We briefly reviewed the core principles of OOP: encapsulation, inheritance, and polymorphism.
- **Why Classes in TypeScript:** We discussed how TypeScript classes enhance JavaScript's prototype-based inheritance model by providing a more structured, type-safe, and readable approach.
- **Basic Class Syntax:** We learned the fundamental syntax of defining classes, including their names, constructors, properties, and methods.
- **Constructors:** We explored the role of constructors in initializing object properties and how to use the `this` keyword within them.
- **Class Members:** We delved into properties (representing object data) and methods (defining object behavior), differentiating between instance and static members.
- **Access Modifiers:** We introduced `public`, `private`, and `protected` access modifiers and discussed their role in encapsulation and controlling access to class members.
- **Getters and Setters:** We explored how getters and setters provide controlled access to class properties, allowing for validation, derived properties, and side effects.
- **Inheritance:** We learned how to create hierarchies of classes using the `extends` keyword, allowing child classes to inherit properties and methods from parent classes.
- **Overriding:** We discussed how to override inherited methods and properties in child classes and how to use the `super` keyword to access the parent class's implementation.
- **Abstract Classes:** We introduced abstract classes as blueprints for other classes, emphasizing their use for defining common interfaces and enforcing structure in class hierarchies.
- **Static Members:** We explored how to define and use static properties and methods that belong to the class itself rather than to instances.
- **Classes vs. Interfaces:** We summarized the key differences between classes and interfaces, clarifying when to use each one.

- **Best Practices:** We offered guidance on naming conventions, organization, composition over inheritance, encapsulation, interface usage, and the judicious use of inheritance, abstract classes, and static members.

By mastering these concepts, you have gained the knowledge and skills to leverage classes effectively in your TypeScript projects. You can now create well-organized, reusable, and type-safe code that models real-world objects and relationships, ultimately leading to more maintainable and robust applications.

Generics: Reusable Code with Type Safety

Outline

- Introduction to Generics
  - The Problem of Code Duplication
  - What Are Generics?
  - Type Parameters
- Generic Functions
  - Writing Generic Functions
  - Type Inference with Generic Functions
  - Multiple Type Parameters
  - Constraints on Type Parameters
- Generic Classes
  - Creating Generic Classes
  - Generic Constraints in Classes
- Generic Interfaces
  - Defining Generic Interfaces
  - Using Generic Interfaces
- Generic Types and Arrays
- Common Use Cases for Generics
- When (and When Not) to Use Generics
- Chapter Summary

Introduction to Generics

The Problem of Code Duplication

In the world of programming, we strive for efficiency and reusability. However, there are times when we encounter a roadblock: the need to write very similar code to handle different data types. Let's consider a common example: finding the largest element in an array.

The Non-Generic Approach

Imagine you want to write a function called `findLargest` to find the largest number in an array of numbers:

```
function findLargestNumber(numbers: number[]): number { let largest =
numbers[0]; for (let num of numbers) { if (num > largest) { largest = num; } }
return largest; } const numbers = [3, 8, 1, 6, 2]; const largestNumber =
findLargestNumber(numbers); console.log(largestNumber); // Output: 8
```

This works perfectly for numbers. But what if you also need to find the largest string (based on alphabetical order) in an array of strings? You might end up writing another function:

```
function findLargestString(strings: string[]): string { let largest =
strings[0]; for (let str of strings) { if (str > largest) { largest = str; } }
return largest; } const strings = ["apple", "banana", "orange"]; const
largestString = findLargestString(strings); console.log(largestString); //
Output: "orange"
```

Notice how these two functions have nearly identical logic, except for the type of data they handle (numbers vs. strings). This is a classic case of code duplication.

Why Code Duplication is a Problem

- **Maintenance Headache:** If you need to change the logic of how you find the largest element, you'll have to update multiple functions, increasing the chance of introducing errors.
- **Increased Code Size:** Duplicate code bloats your project, making it harder to manage and understand.
- **Less Elegant Code:** Repetitive code violates the DRY (Don't Repeat Yourself) principle and doesn't feel as elegant or well-designed.

Generics to the Rescue

Generics in TypeScript offer an elegant solution to this problem. They allow you to write functions, classes, or interfaces that work with multiple types, eliminating the need for code duplication. By using generics, you can create a single `findLargest` function that can handle both numbers and strings, or even other data types!

We'll dive into the details of how generics work shortly. But for now, keep in mind that they are your secret weapon for writing more concise, reusable, and type-safe TypeScript code.

What Are Generics?

In essence, generics in TypeScript are like **type variables**. They allow you to write code that can work with various types without sacrificing type safety. Think of them as placeholders for types that get filled in later when you actually use the code.

How Generics Work

Let's use an analogy to understand generics better. Imagine you have a cookie cutter. You can use this cutter to create different types of cookies: chocolate chip, oatmeal raisin, peanut butter, and so on. The cutter itself doesn't care about the specific type of cookie; it just defines the shape.

Generics work in a similar way. They define the structure and behavior of a function, class, or interface, but they leave the specific types as placeholders. When you use the generic code, you provide the actual types you want to work with, and TypeScript "fills in" those placeholders, tailoring the code to your specific needs.

The Power of Reusability

Generics are all about reusability. Instead of writing separate functions for each data type, you can write a single generic function that can handle multiple types. This not only reduces code duplication but also makes your code more adaptable and easier to maintain.

Type Safety with Generics

One of the most important aspects of generics is that they maintain type safety. When you use a generic function or class, TypeScript checks to ensure that the types you provide are consistent throughout the code. This helps prevent errors and bugs that can arise from mismatched types.

Example: A Generic Identity Function

```
function identity<T>(value: T): T { return value; }
```

In this example:

- The <T> after the function name is a *type parameter*. It's like a placeholder for any type.
- The function takes an argument `value` of type T and returns a value of the same type T.

Here's how you can use it:

```
let num = identity<number>(10); // num is of type 'number' let str =
identity<string>("Hi"); // str is of type 'string'
```

TypeScript automatically infers that num is a `number` and `str` is a `string` based on the arguments passed to the `identity` function.

Key Points

- Generics enable you to write reusable code that can work with multiple types.
- Type parameters are placeholders for types in generic definitions.
- Generics provide type safety by ensuring type consistency.
- TypeScript often infers type arguments for generic functions and classes.

Type Parameters

Type parameters are the essence of generics in TypeScript. They act as placeholders for types, allowing you to write code that is flexible and adaptable to different data types without sacrificing type safety.

Syntax

Type parameters are defined using angle brackets (<>) after the name of the generic function, class, or interface. You can have one or more type parameters, separated by commas.

```
function genericFunction<T>(arg: T): T { // ... } class GenericClass<T> { //
... } interface GenericInterface<T> { // ... }
```

Naming Conventions

While you can name type parameters anything you want, it's customary to use single uppercase letters to make them easily distinguishable. Here are some common conventions:

- **T:** A general-purpose type parameter.
- **K:** Used for keys in key-value pairs (e.g., in dictionaries).
- **V:** Used for values in key-value pairs.
- **U, V, etc.:** Used for additional type parameters when you have more than one.

How Type Parameters Work

Type parameters act as variables that hold types. When you use a generic function, class, or interface, you provide the actual types you want to use as arguments for these type parameters. TypeScript then substitutes those types wherever the type parameters appear in the definition.

Example: Generic Identity Function

Let's revisit the `identity` function from the previous section:

```
function identity<T>(value: T): T { return value; }
```

In this function, T is a type parameter. When you call the function, you can specify the actual type you want to use:

```
let num = identity<number>(10); // T is now 'number' let str =
identity<string>("Hi"); // T is now 'string'
```

TypeScript replaces T with the specific type you provide, ensuring type safety while allowing for flexibility.

Key Points

- Type parameters are placeholders for types in generic definitions.
- Use angle brackets (<>) to define type parameters.
- Follow common naming conventions (e.g., T, K, V).
- Type parameters are like type variables that get substituted with concrete types when the generic code is used.
- Type parameters enable you to write reusable code that can work with various types while maintaining type safety.

Generic Functions

Writing Generic Functions

Now that you understand the concept of type parameters, let's see how to put them into action by creating generic functions. Generic functions allow you to write reusable code that can operate on different types of data while maintaining type safety.

Example 1: Finding the Largest Element in an Array

```
function findLargest<T>(arr: T[]): T { let largest = arr[0]; for (let item of
arr) { if (item > largest) { // Assumes that '>' is defined for the type T
largest = item; } } return largest; }
```

In this example, the <T> type parameter acts as a placeholder for the type of elements in the array. The function then uses the > operator to compare elements. This function works for any type T as long as the > operator is defined for that type (e.g., numbers, strings, dates).

Example 2: Identity Function

```
function identity<T>(value: T): T { return value; }
```

The identity function simply returns the value passed to it. By making it generic, you can use it with any type of data.

Example 3: Creating an Array from a Single Value

```
function createArray<T>(value: T): T[] { return [value]; }
```

This function takes a value of any type and returns an array containing that single value.

Example 4: Swapping Values

```
function swap<T, U>(pair: [T, U]): [U, T] { const [first, second] = pair;
return [second, first]; }
```

This function takes a tuple (an array with a fixed number of elements of potentially different types) and returns a new tuple with the elements swapped. It uses two type parameters (T and U) to represent the types of the first and second elements, respectively.

Key Points

- Generic functions provide a template for working with different data types.
- Type parameters act as placeholders for types.
- TypeScript can often infer the type arguments for generic functions, making them easier to use.
- Constraints can be added to type parameters to restrict the types that can be used.

By embracing generic functions, you can write more flexible and reusable code in TypeScript while still enjoying the benefits of strong type checking and improved developer experience.

Type Inference with Generic Functions

One of the beauties of TypeScript is that it often eliminates the need to explicitly specify type arguments when using generic functions. TypeScript's powerful type inference engine can automatically deduce the correct types based on the context, making your code cleaner and more concise.

How Type Inference Works

When you call a generic function, TypeScript analyzes the types of the arguments you provide. If it can determine the appropriate type for the type parameter (or parameters) based on those arguments, it will do so automatically. This means you can often omit the angle brackets (<>) and type arguments when calling the function.

Example: Identity Function

```
function identity<T>(value: T): T { return value; } let num = identity(10); // Inferred as number let str = identity("hello"); // Inferred as string
```

In this case, TypeScript infers that `num` should be of type `number` because the argument passed to `identity` is `10`, which is a number. Similarly, it infers `str` as a `string`. You don't need to explicitly write `<number>` or `<string>` when calling the function.

Example: Creating an Array

```
function createArray<T>(value: T): T[] { return [value]; } let numbers = createArray(42); // Inferred as number[] let words = createArray("word"); // Inferred as string[]
```

TypeScript infers that `numbers` should be an array of numbers (`number[]`) and `words` should be an array of strings (`string[]`).

Example: Finding the Largest Element

```
function findLargest<T>(arr: T[]): T { // ... (implementation from previous section) } let biggestNumber = findLargest([3, 8, 1, 6, 2]); // Inferred as number let longestString = findLargest(["apple", "banana", "kiwi"]); // Inferred as string
```

TypeScript infers the types of the return values (`biggestNumber` and `longestString`) based on the types of the elements in the input arrays.

When Type Inference Might Not Work

There are cases where TypeScript might not be able to infer the type arguments for a generic function. For example:

- **No Arguments:** If a generic function has no arguments, TypeScript has no information to base its inference on. You'll need to explicitly specify the type arguments in this case.
- **Ambiguous Types:** If the arguments could potentially match multiple type parameters, TypeScript might not be able to determine the correct types without your guidance.

Benefits of Type Inference

- **Conciseness:** You can write less code when TypeScript can infer types for you.
- **Readability:** Your code becomes less cluttered and easier to read without redundant type annotations.
- **Developer Experience:** Type inference makes working with generics more intuitive and less verbose.

By leveraging TypeScript's type inference capabilities, you can write generic functions that are both flexible and easy to use, while still maintaining the benefits of type safety.

Multiple Type Parameters

TypeScript allows you to define generic functions with more than one type parameter, opening up even greater possibilities for reusable code. This is especially useful when you need to work with multiple types simultaneously, each potentially having different characteristics or behaviors.

Syntax

To define a generic function with multiple type parameters, simply list them within the angle brackets, separated by commas:

```
function genericFunction<T, U, V>(arg1: T, arg2: U, arg3: V): [T, U, V] { //
... }
```

In this example, T, U, and V are all type parameters that can be replaced with specific types when you call the function.

Example: Combining Arrays

Let's create a generic function called `combineArrays` that takes two arrays of potentially different types and returns a single array containing the elements of both:

```
function combineArrays<T, U>(arr1: T[], arr2: U[]): (T | U)[] { return
[...arr1, ...arr2]; // Use the spread syntax to concatenate arrays }
```

Here's how you would use it:

```
const numbers = [1, 2, 3]; const strings = ["a", "b", "c"]; const combined =
combineArrays(numbers, strings); console.log(combined); // Output: [1, 2, 3,
"a", "b", "c"]
```

In this example, T is inferred as `number` and U is inferred as `string`, so the return type becomes `(number | string)[]`, which represents an array that can hold both numbers and strings.

Example: Creating a Key-Value Pair

```
function createPair<K, V>(key: K, value: V): [K, V] { return [key, value]; }
let pair = createPair("name", "Alice"); // Inferred as [string, string]
```

Here, `createPair` takes a key (K) and a value (V) of potentially different types and returns a tuple `[K, V]` where the types are preserved.

Example: Generic Reducer

```
function customReducer<T, U>(arr: T[], initialValue: U, reducer: (acc: U, curr: T) => U): U { let accumulator = initialValue; for (let elem of arr) { accumulator = reducer(accumulator, elem); } return accumulator; }
```

This generic reducer function takes an array, an initial value, and a reducer function. It allows you to reduce an array of type T to a single value of type U, providing flexibility and type safety for custom reduction operations.

Key Points

- Generic functions can have multiple type parameters.
- Each type parameter can be independent and represent different types.
- Type inference can often deduce multiple type arguments based on the arguments you pass.
- You can use multiple type parameters to create highly flexible and reusable functions.

By mastering multiple type parameters in generic functions, you unlock a new dimension of versatility in your TypeScript code. You can create functions that operate seamlessly on diverse data types, leading to more concise, adaptable, and type-safe solutions.

Constraints on Type Parameters

While the flexibility of generics is a powerful tool, there are times when you might want to limit the types that can be used as type arguments. This is where generic constraints come in handy. They allow you to specify that a type parameter must meet certain criteria, such as having specific properties or extending a particular interface.

Using the `extends` Keyword

To add a constraint to a type parameter, you use the `extends` keyword followed by the type or interface that the type parameter must extend:

```
function myGenericFunction<T extends SomeType>(arg: T): T { // ... }
```

In this example, the type parameter T is constrained to types that extend `SomeType`. This means you can only call `myGenericFunction` with types that are compatible with `SomeType`.

Examples of Constraints

1. **Properties:** You can require a type parameter to have specific properties:
   ```
   interface HasName { name: string; } function greet<T extends HasName>(obj: T) { console.log(`Hello, ${obj.name}!`); }
   ```
   Here, `greet` can only be called with objects that have a `name` property of type `string`.
2. **Methods:** You can require a type parameter to have specific methods:
   ```
   interface Printable { print(): void; } function printObject<T extends Printable>(obj: T) { obj.print(); }
   ```
   Here, `printObject` can only be called with objects that have a `print` method.

3. **Extending a Class:** You can also constrain a type parameter to be a subclass of a specific class:
```
class Animal { /* ... */ } class Dog extends Animal { /* ... */ }
function makeAnimalSound<T extends Animal>(animal: T) {
animal.makeSound(); } makeAnimalSound(new Dog()); // Valid
//makeAnimalSound("not an animal"); // Error: Argument of type 'string'
is not assignable to parameter of type 'Animal'.
```

Key Points

- Generic constraints restrict the types that can be used as type arguments.
- Use the `extends` keyword to specify constraints.
- Constraints can require properties, methods, or class inheritance.
- Constraints improve type safety by catching errors early.
- Constraints make your code more predictable and easier to understand.

By using constraints on type parameters, you strike a balance between flexibility and safety. You can write generic functions and classes that are versatile enough to work with different types, while also ensuring that those types meet certain criteria, preventing potential errors and enhancing the robustness of your TypeScript code.

Generic Classes

Generic classes in TypeScript, just like generic functions, enable you to create reusable classes that can work with various data types while preserving type safety. They allow you to parameterize the types used within the class, making it adaptable to different scenarios.

Creating Generic Classes

To create a generic class, you place type parameters in angle brackets (<>) after the class name:

```
class GenericClassName<T> { // Class members using the type parameter T }
```

The type parameter T acts as a placeholder for the actual type that will be specified when the class is used. You can use the type parameter T throughout your class definition to represent the type of properties, method parameters, and return values.

Example 1: `Stack<T>` **Class**

```
class Stack<T> { private items: T[] = []; // Array to hold the items (of type
T) push(item: T): void { this.items.push(item); } pop(): T | undefined {
return this.items.pop(); } } const numberStack = new Stack<number>();
numberStack.push(10); numberStack.push(20); const stringStack = new
Stack<string>(); stringStack.push("hello"); stringStack.push("world");
```

In this example:

- `Stack<T>` is a generic class with a type parameter T.
- `items` is a private property that holds an array of elements of type T.
- The `push` method takes an argument of type T and adds it to the stack.
- The `pop` method removes and returns the top element of the stack, which is also of type T.

We can create stacks to hold numbers (`numberStack`) or strings (`stringStack`). TypeScript ensures that each stack can only hold values of its specified type.

Example 2: `Result<T>` Class

```
class Result<T> { isSuccess: boolean; value?: T; error?: string;
constructor(isSuccess: boolean, value?: T, error?: string) { this.isSuccess =
isSuccess; this.value = value; this.error = error; } } const successResult =
new Result<number>(true, 42); const errorResult = new Result<string>(false,
undefined, "Something went wrong");
```

The `Result<T>` class represents the outcome of an operation. It can be either a success (with a `value` of type T) or a failure (with an `error` message).

Key Points

- Generic classes allow you to create reusable classes that can work with various data types.
- Type parameters are placeholders for types that are specified when the class is used.
- You can use the type parameter(s) throughout the class definition.
- Generic classes provide type safety by enforcing that the types used are consistent.

By utilizing generic classes, you empower yourself to create flexible and adaptable code that can be applied to a wide range of scenarios, all while maintaining the integrity of your TypeScript types.

Show how to create generic classes by adding type parameters to class definitions. Provide examples of generic classes like:

- A `Stack` class that can hold values of any type
- A `Result` class to represent success/failure results with a value of a specific type

Generic Constraints in Classes

Generic classes offer a high degree of flexibility, but sometimes you need to ensure that the types used with a generic class meet specific requirements. Generic constraints allow you to do just that. They restrict the types that can be used as type arguments for your generic class, ensuring that those types have certain properties or methods.

Applying Constraints with the `extends` Keyword

Just as with generic functions, you use the `extends` keyword to apply constraints to type parameters in generic classes. The syntax is similar:

```
class MyClass<T extends SomeType> { // Class members using the type parameter
T }
```

In this case, the type parameter T must extend or implement `SomeType`. `SomeType` can be another class, an interface, or even another type alias.

Example: Constraining to an Interface

Let's enhance our `Stack` example from the previous section. We'll add a `peek` method that returns the top element of the stack without removing it. However, we only want this method to be available if the stack elements have a `name` property:

```
interface NamedItem { name: string; } class Stack<T extends NamedItem> { //
Constraint: T must extend NamedItem private items: T[] = []; push(item: T):
void { this.items.push(item); } pop(): T | undefined { return
```

```
this.items.pop(); } peek(): T | undefined { return this.items[this.items.length - 1]; } } const personStack = new Stack<NamedItem>(); // Valid personStack.push({ name: "Alice" }); const numberStack = new Stack<number>(); // Error: Type 'number' does not satisfy the constraint 'NamedItem'.
```

Now, you can only create a `Stack` of objects that have a `name` property, thanks to the constraint.

Example: Constraining to a Class

You can also constrain a type parameter to be a subclass of a specific class:

```
class Animal { makeSound(): void { /* ... */ } } class Dog extends Animal { /* ... */ } class Kennel<T extends Animal> { animals: T[] = []; } const dogKennel = new Kennel<Dog>(); // Valid
```

Benefits of Constraints

- **Enhanced Type Safety:** Constraints prevent you from accidentally using the wrong types with a generic class, leading to fewer runtime errors.
- **Improved Code Expressiveness:** Constraints clearly communicate the requirements for types that can be used with the class.
- **Access to Specific Members:** Constraints allow you to access properties and methods of the constrained types within the generic class.

Key Points

- Generic constraints restrict the types that can be used as type arguments for classes.
- Use the `extends` keyword to apply constraints.
- Constraints can require types to have specific properties, methods, or inherit from certain classes or interfaces.

By using constraints in your generic classes, you add an extra layer of type safety and expressiveness to your TypeScript code. This helps you build more reliable and predictable software, ensuring that your generic classes are used correctly and consistently.

Generic Interfaces

Generic interfaces, similar to generic functions and classes, allow you to create flexible type definitions that can work with a variety of data types. They provide a blueprint for objects, but with the added flexibility of allowing the specific types of properties or methods to be determined later.

Defining Generic Interfaces

The syntax for defining a generic interface is similar to that of generic functions or classes:

```
interface GenericInterfaceName<T> { // Properties and methods using the type parameter T }
```

The type parameter T acts as a placeholder for the actual type that will be provided when the interface is implemented.

Example 1: `Comparator<T>` Interface

Let's create a generic interface called `Comparator` that defines a method for comparing two objects of the same type:

```
interface Comparator<T> { compare(a: T, b: T): number; }
```

The `compare` method takes two arguments of type T and returns a number indicating their order:

- Negative number if a is less than b
- Zero if a is equal to b
- Positive number if a is greater than b

This interface is generic, meaning it can be used to compare numbers, strings, dates, or any other type that can be ordered.

Example 2: `KeyValue<K, V>` Interface

Now, let's define a generic interface called `KeyValue` to represent key-value pairs where the key and value types can vary:

```
interface KeyValue<K, V> { key: K; value: V; }
```

Here, we have two type parameters:

- K: Represents the type of the key.
- V: Represents the type of the value.

This interface can be used to create objects that associate keys of one type with values of potentially another type.

Key Points

- Generic interfaces are like reusable templates for defining object structures.
- Type parameters allow you to customize the types used within the interface.
- Generic interfaces can be implemented by classes, providing a way to ensure type safety for objects that adhere to the interface contract.

Using Generic Interfaces (Example)

```
function sortByKey<K, V>( items: KeyValue<K, V>[], comparator: Comparator<K>
): KeyValue<K, V>[] { // ... (Sorting logic using the comparator) ... }
```

In this example, the `sortByKey` function takes an array of `KeyValue` objects and a `Comparator` function that knows how to compare keys of type K. The function then sorts the `KeyValue` objects based on their keys using the provided comparator.

By mastering generic interfaces, you unlock the power to define versatile contracts that can be implemented by a wide range of types, making your TypeScript code more adaptable and reusable.

Using Generic Interfaces

Generic interfaces, as blueprints with flexible types, are most powerful when combined with classes and used as type constraints for variables and functions. Let's see how this works in practice.

1. Implementing Generic Interfaces with Classes

To implement a generic interface, a class must provide concrete types for the interface's type parameters. This effectively specializes the generic interface for a particular use case.

Example: Implementing `Comparator<T>`

```
interface Comparator<T> { compare(a: T, b: T): number; } class NumberComparator implements Comparator<number> { compare(a: number, b: number): number { return a - b; // Compare numbers } } class StringComparator implements Comparator<string> { compare(a: string, b: string): number { return a.localeCompare(b); // Compare strings } }
```

In this example:

- `NumberComparator` implements `Comparator<number>`, providing a comparison method specific to numbers.
- `StringComparator` implements `Comparator<string>`, offering a way to compare strings.

2. Using Generic Interfaces as Types

Generic interfaces can be used as types for variables, function parameters, and return values. This ensures type safety and allows functions to operate on a wide range of objects that adhere to the interface's contract.

Example: `sortByKey` Function (Revisited)

```
interface KeyValue<K, V> { key: K; value: V; } function sortByKey<K, V>(items: KeyValue<K, V>[], comparator: Comparator<K>): KeyValue<K, V>[] { // ... (Sorting logic) }
```

The `sortByKey` function is generic, taking an array of `KeyValue` objects where the key type is K and the value type is V. It also accepts a `Comparator` for comparing keys of type K. This flexibility allows you to sort arrays of key-value pairs with different key types (e.g., numbers, strings, dates).

Example: Generic Data Storage

```
interface DataStore<T> { add(item: T): void; remove(item: T): void; getAll(): T[]; } class InMemoryDataStore<T> implements DataStore<T> { // ... (implementation for storing data in memory) } const numberStore = new InMemoryDataStore<number>(); numberStore.add(10); const stringStore = new InMemoryDataStore<string>(); stringStore.add("hello");
```

The `DataStore` interface provides a generic contract for storing data, while the `InMemoryDataStore` class provides a concrete implementation. You can create instances of `InMemoryDataStore` to store different data types (like numbers or strings).

Benefits of Using Generic Interfaces

- **Enhanced Type Safety:** Ensures that the objects you work with have the expected structure and methods, as defined by the interface.
- **Flexibility:** Allows you to write code that can work with various types, promoting reusability and reducing code duplication.

- **Clear Contracts:** Generic interfaces act as clear contracts, making your code more self-documenting and easier to understand.

By mastering the use of generic interfaces, you can build more robust and flexible TypeScript applications that leverage the power of polymorphism and type safety.

Generic Types and Arrays

Generic types and arrays are a match made in TypeScript heaven. They work seamlessly together to provide a flexible and type-safe way to represent collections of data. Let's explore their harmonious relationship.

`Array<T>`: The Generic Array Type

In TypeScript, `Array<T>` is a generic type that represents an array where all elements are of type T. The type parameter T acts as a placeholder for the actual element type, which is determined when you create an instance of the array.

This is equivalent to the shorthand syntax `T[]`:

```
let numbers: Array<number> = [1, 2, 3]; // Array of numbers let strings:
string[] = ["a", "b", "c"]; // Array of strings
```

Both `Array<number>` and `number[]` represent the same type: an array that can only hold numbers. Similarly, `Array<string>` and `string[]` both represent arrays of strings.

Why Use `Array<T>`?

The `Array<T>` syntax is particularly useful in the following scenarios:

1. **Clarity with Complex Types:** When dealing with complex types like interfaces or type aliases, using `Array<T>` can make your code more readable:
   `interface Product { /* ... */ } let products: Array<Product> = [];`
2. **Consistency with Generics:** When working with generic functions or classes, using `Array<T>` can make your type annotations more consistent and easier to understand.
3. **Compatibility with Other Languages:** The `Array<T>` syntax is similar to the generic syntax used in other languages like Java or C#, making it easier for developers with diverse backgrounds to understand your code.

Type Inference with Arrays

As we've seen before, TypeScript's type inference works exceptionally well with arrays. If you initialize an array with values of the same type, TypeScript will automatically infer the type of the array:

```
let colors = ["red", "green", "blue"]; // Inferred as string[] let ages = [25,
30, 35]; // Inferred as number[]
```

Arrays and Generic Functions

Generic types and arrays naturally complement each other when used with generic functions. Consider our `findLargest` function from earlier:

```
function findLargest<T>(arr: T[]): T { // ... }
```

Here, the `arr` parameter is of type `T[]`, meaning it's an array of elements of type T. This allows the function to work with arrays of any type.

Key Points

- `Array<T>` is a generic type that represents an array of elements of type T.
- `T[]` is shorthand for `Array<T>`.
- TypeScript can often infer the type of an array based on its elements.
- Generic types and arrays are often used together in generic functions and classes.

By understanding the relationship between generic types and arrays, you unlock a powerful way to work with collections of data in a type-safe and flexible manner. You can create reusable functions and classes that operate on arrays of various types, making your TypeScript code more adaptable and efficient.

Common Use Cases for Generics

Generics are a powerful tool in TypeScript, enabling you to write code that is both flexible and type-safe. They find applications in various domains, enhancing the reusability and maintainability of your codebase. Here are some common scenarios where generics shine:

Data Structures

- **Arrays:** The `Array<T>` type (or its shorthand `T[]`) is perhaps the most common use of generics. It allows you to create arrays that hold elements of a specific type, ensuring type safety when accessing and manipulating those elements.
- **Lists, Stacks, Queues:** These linear data structures can be easily generalized using generics to hold elements of any desired type.
- **Trees and Graphs:** More complex data structures like trees and graphs can also benefit from generics. You can define generic nodes and edges that can store data of different types, making your implementations adaptable to various use cases.

Utility Functions

- **Sorting:** Generic functions like `sort` can be applied to arrays of different types, as long as a comparison function is provided that works for the specific type of elements.
- **Filtering and Mapping:** Generic functions like `filter` and `map` allow you to transform arrays in a type-safe way, ensuring that the output array maintains the correct type.
- **Searching:** Generic search algorithms can be written to find elements in various data structures, regardless of the specific type of data they contain.

Libraries and APIs

- **Reusable Components:** Generics are essential for building reusable components, both in UI frameworks (like React) and in general libraries. You can create components that accept and render data of different types without needing to write separate versions for each type.
- **Type-Safe APIs:** When designing libraries or APIs, generics allow you to create type-safe interfaces that can be used with a wide range of types, improving the developer experience for users of your code.
- **Error Handling:** Generic types like `Result<T>` (as shown earlier) provide a standardized way to represent success or failure results, making error handling more consistent and predictable.

Additional Use Cases

Generics can be applied to many other scenarios, including:

- **Promises:** The `Promise<T>` type represents a value that will be available in the future and is of type T.
- **Observables:** In reactive programming, generics are used to define the types of values emitted by observables.
- **Caching:** Generic cache implementations can store and retrieve values of any type.
- **Plugins and Extensions:** Generics enable you to create extensible systems where plugins or extensions can work with a variety of data types.

By recognizing these common use cases and applying generics strategically, you can write more versatile, adaptable, and type-safe TypeScript code that is easier to maintain and reuse across different parts of your applications.

When (and When Not) to Use Generics

Generics are a powerful tool in your TypeScript arsenal, but like any tool, they are best used in the right situations. Understanding when to leverage generics and when to consider simpler alternatives is crucial for writing clean, maintainable, and efficient code.

When Generics Shine

Consider using generics when:

- **Reusability:** You need to write code that can work with multiple types, avoiding code duplication.
- **Type Safety:** You want to maintain strong type checking even when dealing with unknown types.
- **Flexibility:** You require functions or classes that can adapt to various types of data.
- **Abstraction:** You want to create generic algorithms or data structures that can be applied to different contexts.
- **Libraries and APIs:** You're developing reusable components or libraries that need to work with a wide range of types.

When Simpler Alternatives Might Be Suitable

Generics might not be the best fit in the following scenarios:

- **Simple Types:** If you're only dealing with a few specific types and don't need extensive reusability, explicit type annotations might be simpler.
- **Overly Complex Types:** If your generic type definitions become overly complex, they might make your code harder to understand and maintain. In such cases, it might be better to break down the problem into smaller, more manageable types.
- **Performance Critical Code:** In some highly performance-critical scenarios, the overhead of generics might be a concern. However, in most cases, the performance impact of generics is negligible.

Trade-offs: Reusability vs. Complexity

The main trade-off with generics is between reusability and complexity. While generics promote code reuse, they can also introduce a level of abstraction that might make the code harder to grasp for developers unfamiliar with generics.

It's important to strike a balance between these two factors. If the added complexity of generics doesn't significantly improve code reusability or type safety, then a simpler approach might be preferable.

Tips for Deciding When to Use Generics

1. **Identify Patterns:** Look for patterns in your code where you're repeating similar logic for different types. This is often a good indicator that generics could be beneficial.
2. **Consider Future Use:** Think about how your code might evolve. Will you need to handle additional types in the future? If so, generics can provide a flexible solution.
3. **Keep it Simple:** Start with simple generic use cases and gradually introduce more complex scenarios as you gain experience and confidence.
4. **Don't Overuse:** Don't feel compelled to use generics everywhere. Sometimes, simple type annotations are sufficient and easier to understand.
5. **Readability Matters:** Strive for code that is not only reusable but also readable and maintainable. If generics make your code significantly harder to understand, consider alternative approaches.

By carefully considering the benefits and drawbacks of generics and applying them judiciously, you can harness their power to create elegant, efficient, and type-safe TypeScript code.

Chapter Summary

In this chapter, we delved into the power of generics in TypeScript, a tool for creating reusable code that can adapt to various data types while preserving type safety. Here's a recap of what we covered:

- **The Problem of Code Duplication:** We started by highlighting the challenges of writing repetitive code to handle different types and how generics offer a solution.
- **What Are Generics?** We introduced generics as placeholders for types, allowing you to create flexible "templates" for functions, classes, and interfaces.
- **Type Parameters:** We explored the syntax of type parameters using angle brackets (<>) and common naming conventions.
- **Generic Functions:** We demonstrated how to write generic functions, showcasing examples for common operations like finding the largest element in an array, creating arrays, and swapping values.
- **Type Inference with Generics:** We explained how TypeScript can often infer the type arguments for generic functions, making them easier to use.
- **Multiple Type Parameters:** We showed how to create generic functions with multiple type parameters to handle diverse types of data.
- **Generic Constraints:** We introduced the concept of constraining type parameters using the `extends` keyword, allowing you to define requirements for the types used with generics.
- **Generic Classes:** We demonstrated how to create generic classes, providing examples like a `Stack` class and a `Result` class.
- **Generic Interfaces:** We explored how to define and use generic interfaces, showcasing examples like a `Comparator` interface and a `KeyValue` interface.
- **Generics and Arrays:** We discussed the relationship between generic types and arrays, explaining the `Array<T>` type.
- **Common Use Cases:** We summarized common scenarios where generics are beneficial, including data structures, utility functions, and libraries.
- **When (and When Not) to Use Generics:** We provided guidance on when generics are the right tool for the job, highlighting the trade-off between reusability and complexity.

By mastering generics, you've unlocked a new level of flexibility and power in TypeScript. You can now write code that is more adaptable, reusable, and type-safe, leading to cleaner, more maintainable projects. The ability to create generic functions, classes, and interfaces will be invaluable as you continue your TypeScript journey.

Modules: Organizing and Sharing Your Code

Outline

- What are Modules?
    - Why Modules Matter
    - Namespaces vs. Modules
- Module Syntax
    - Exporting from Modules
    - Importing into Modules
- Module Resolution Strategies
    - Relative vs. Non-Relative Paths
    - Module Resolution in Node.js
    - Module Resolution in the Browser
- Working with Modules
    - Organizing Code with Modules
    - Creating and Consuming Libraries
- CommonJS vs. ES Modules
    - Understanding the Differences
    - Choosing the Right Module System
- Chapter Summary

What Are Modules?

Why Modules Matter

In the realm of software development, **modules** are your organizational superheroes. They empower you to break down your code into smaller, manageable pieces, each residing in its own file or unit. Think of modules as self-contained building blocks that work together to form your complete application. But why are modules so essential, and how do they benefit your TypeScript projects?

Managing Complexity

As your projects grow, the lines of code multiply, and the complexity escalates. Modules offer a way to tame this complexity by providing a logical structure for your code. Instead of having everything crammed into a single, monolithic file, you can divide your code into modules, each responsible for a specific feature or area of functionality.

This modular approach makes your codebase more manageable, easier to navigate, and less overwhelming. You can focus on one module at a time, knowing that its internal workings won't interfere with other parts of your application.

Avoiding Naming Collisions

In large projects, it's easy to accidentally use the same name for different variables, functions, or classes. This can lead to conflicts and unpredictable behavior. Modules provide a solution by creating separate namespaces for each module. This means that names within one module don't conflict with names in other modules, even if they are the same.

Improved Code Reusability

Modules encourage you to write more reusable code. By encapsulating specific functionality within a module, you can easily import and use it in different parts of your application or even in other projects.

This reduces redundancy and saves you from having to reinvent the wheel every time you need a particular feature.

Enhanced Maintainability

When your code is organized into modules, it becomes easier to maintain. If you need to fix a bug or add a new feature, you can often isolate the changes to a specific module, reducing the risk of unintended consequences in other parts of your application. Modules also make it easier to test and debug individual pieces of code.

Example: A Modular Project Structure

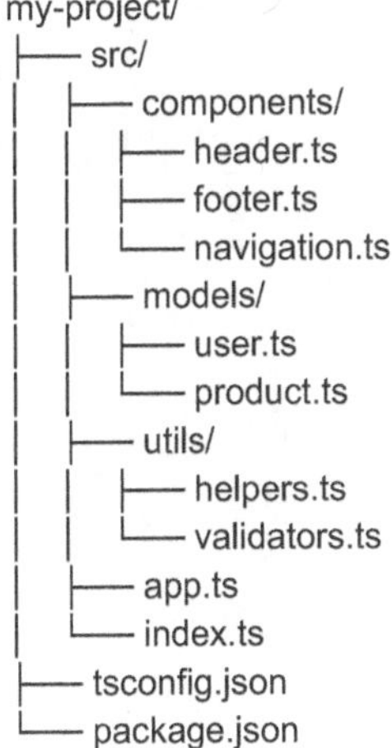

```
my-project/
├── src/
│   ├── components/
│   │   ├── header.ts
│   │   ├── footer.ts
│   │   └── navigation.ts
│   ├── models/
│   │   ├── user.ts
│   │   └── product.ts
│   ├── utils/
│   │   ├── helpers.ts
│   │   └── validators.ts
│   ├── app.ts
│   └── index.ts
├── tsconfig.json
└── package.json
```

In this hypothetical project:

- The `components` module contains UI components.
- The `models` module defines data models.
- The `utils` module holds utility functions.
- The `app.ts` and `index.ts` files might handle the overall application logic and entry point.

Each of these modules can be developed and tested independently, promoting a cleaner and more maintainable codebase.

Key Points

- Modules are the foundation of code organization in TypeScript (and JavaScript).
- They help manage complexity, prevent naming collisions, and improve code reusability.
- Modules make your codebase more maintainable and easier to evolve over time.

By embracing modules, you'll be well on your way to writing cleaner, more organized, and more scalable TypeScript code.

Namespaces vs. Modules

In the early days of TypeScript, *namespaces* were the primary way to organize code into logical groups. They provided a way to encapsulate related types, functions, and classes within a named container. However, as TypeScript matured and aligned more closely with JavaScript's module system, *modules* emerged as the preferred approach to code organization.

Namespaces: A Legacy Approach

Namespaces are essentially just nested objects in the global scope. They provide a hierarchical way to group related code, but they don't offer the same level of isolation and flexibility as modules.

Here's a quick example of a namespace:

```
namespace MyNamespace { export class MyClass { /* ... */ } export function
myFunction() { /* ... */ } }
```

To use members of the namespace, you would prefix them with the namespace name:

```
const myObject = new MyNamespace.MyClass(); MyNamespace.myFunction();
```

Modules: The Modern Standard

Modules, on the other hand, are self-contained units of code that can be imported and exported using the `import` and `export` keywords. They are aligned with the JavaScript module system and offer a more standardized and robust way to organize your code.

Here's the same example using modules:

```
// myModule.ts export class MyClass { /* ... */ } export function myFunction()
{ /* ... */ } // main.ts import { MyClass, myFunction } from './myModule';
```

Why Modules are Preferred

- **Standardized:** Modules are aligned with the ECMAScript standard for modules, making your TypeScript code more interoperable with other JavaScript projects.
- **Better Encapsulation:** Modules provide better encapsulation and isolation than namespaces. Members of a module are only accessible if explicitly exported.
- **Improved Tooling Support:** Modern build tools and IDEs are designed to work seamlessly with modules, offering features like code navigation, autocompletion, and refactoring.
- **Tree-Shaking:** Modules support tree-shaking, which means that unused exports can be eliminated during the build process, leading to smaller bundle sizes.

Recommendation: Use Modules

While namespaces still technically work in TypeScript, they are now discouraged in favor of modules. The TypeScript team recommends using modules as the standard way to organize and structure your code.

Throughout the rest of this book, we'll focus exclusively on modules, as they represent the best practice for building maintainable and scalable TypeScript applications.

Module Syntax

Modules in TypeScript are self-contained units of code. To make the elements within a module (like functions, classes, variables) accessible to other modules, you need to export them. Similarly, to use elements from other modules, you need to import them.

Exporting from Modules

The `export` keyword is your key to sharing code between modules. There are two primary ways to export:

1. **Named Exports:** You can export multiple members (functions, classes, variables, interfaces, or types) from a module by prefixing each declaration with the `export` keyword.

```
// mathUtils.ts export const PI = 3.14159; export function square(x: number): number { return x * x; } export class Circle { // ... } export interface Shape { // ... } export type Area = number;
```

Each of these members can be individually imported into other modules.

2. **Default Exports:** You can export a single value (usually a function or a class) as the default export of a module.

```
// myClass.ts class MyClass { // ... } export default MyClass;
```

The default export can be imported without curly braces `{}`.

Choosing Between Named and Default Exports

- **Named Exports:** Use named exports when you want to export multiple values from a module and give consumers the flexibility to choose which ones to import.
- **Default Exports:** Use default exports when you have a single, primary value (like a component or a library) that you want to export from a module. This makes importing easier for consumers.

Example: Exporting from a Module

Let's create a module called `stringUtils.ts` that exports some string utility functions:

```
// stringUtils.ts export function capitalize(str: string): string { return str.charAt(0).toUpperCase() + str.slice(1); } export function reverseString(str: string): string { return str.split('').reverse().join(''); }
```

Now we have a module called `stringUtils.ts` in which we have exported two functions `capitalize()` and `reverseString()` to use them in another module.

Key Points

- Use `export` to make members of a module accessible to other modules.
- Named exports allow you to export multiple values.
- Default exports allow you to export a single primary value.

By mastering the `export` keyword, you can effectively share and reuse your TypeScript code, creating well-organized and modular applications.

Importing into Modules: Bringing in External Code

After exporting members from a module, you can easily bring them into other parts of your TypeScript code using the `import` keyword. This allows you to utilize functions, classes, interfaces, or other values defined elsewhere.

Syntax

The `import` statement has a few variations depending on what and how you want to import:

1. **Importing Named Exports:** When a module exports multiple named members, you can import specific ones using curly braces `{}`.

```
import { capitalize, reverseString } from "./stringUtils";
```

This imports the `capitalize` and `reverseString` functions from the `stringUtils` module. You can now use them in the current module.

2. **Importing Default Exports:** If a module has a default export, you import it directly without curly braces.

```
import MyClass from "./myClass";
```

This imports the default export (the `MyClass` class in this case) from the `myClass` module.

3. **Renaming Imports:** You can use the `as` keyword to give an imported member a different name within the current module.

```
import { capitalize as cap } from "./stringUtils"; let capitalizedName = cap("john doe");
```

Here, we import the `capitalize` function and rename it to `cap` for use in the current module.

Example: Using Imported Functions

```
// main.ts (assuming stringUtils.ts is in the same directory) import { capitalize, reverseString } from "./stringUtils"; const name = "alice"; const capitalizedName = capitalize(name); const reversedName = reverseString(name); console.log(capitalizedName); // Output: "Alice" console.log(reversedName); // Output: "ecila"
```

Important Considerations

- **File Paths:** The path you specify in the `import` statement should be relative to the current module's location. You can use `./` for files in the same directory, `../` to go up a directory, or specify a deeper path if needed.
- **Module Resolution:** TypeScript follows specific rules to determine how to resolve module imports. This involves looking in the `node_modules` folder for external dependencies or following relative paths for local modules. We'll discuss module resolution strategies in more detail in the next section.
- **Import Types:** You can also import types (interfaces, type aliases) using the same syntax: `import { Shape } from "./shapes";`

By mastering the `import` keyword and understanding how TypeScript resolves modules, you'll be able to efficiently bring in code from other modules and leverage the benefits of modularity in your TypeScript projects.

Module Resolution Strategies

Relative vs. Non-Relative Paths

In TypeScript, the way you specify the path to a module in your `import` statement plays a crucial role in how the compiler locates that module. Let's dive into the distinction between relative and non-relative paths.

Relative Paths

A relative path starts with `./` or `../`, indicating that the module you're importing is located relative to the current file.

- `./`: Denotes the current directory.
- `../`: Denotes the parent directory.

Example:

```
// File: /src/app.ts import { myFunction } from './utils/helpers';
```

In this example, TypeScript will look for the `helpers` module within a `utils` folder in the same directory as `app.ts`.

Non-Relative Paths

A non-relative path doesn't start with `./` or `../`. This typically signifies that the module you're importing is an external library or package (like Lodash or React) installed in your project's `node_modules` directory.

Example:

```
import * as _ from 'lodash'; // Importing the Lodash library
```

Here, TypeScript will search for the `lodash` module within the `node_modules` folder at the root of your project or in any of its parent directories.

When to Use Relative vs. Non-Relative Paths

- **Relative Paths:** Use relative paths when importing modules that are part of your own project's codebase. This ensures that the import paths remain valid even if you move or rename files within your project.
- **Non-Relative Paths:** Use non-relative paths when importing external libraries or packages that are installed as dependencies in your project. This helps keep your code cleaner and avoids the need to specify long relative paths that might change depending on your project's structure.

How TypeScript Resolves Module Imports

The process of finding the actual file corresponding to a module import is called module resolution. TypeScript uses different strategies depending on whether you're using relative or non-relative paths and whether you're working in a Node.js or browser environment.

- **Relative Paths (Node.js and Browser):** TypeScript resolves relative paths by starting at the directory of the current file and following the path you specify.
- **Non-Relative Paths (Node.js):** TypeScript follows the Node.js module resolution algorithm, which involves searching for the module in the `node_modules` folder at the current directory level and then moving up the directory tree until it finds a match.
- **Non-Relative Paths (Browser):** The browser environment doesn't have a built-in module resolution mechanism like Node.js. You typically need a module loader (like RequireJS) or a bundler (like webpack or Parcel) to handle module resolution and bundling in the browser.

By understanding these concepts, you can write more robust and portable TypeScript code that works seamlessly in different environments.

Module Resolution in Node.js

Node.js has its own specific way of resolving module imports, which is deeply intertwined with the `node_modules` directory and the `package.json` file. Understanding how this process works is crucial for working effectively with modules in your Node.js and TypeScript projects.

The `node_modules` Directory

When you install a package using npm (Node Package Manager), it gets placed inside the `node_modules` directory. This directory acts as a central repository for all your project's external dependencies. Each package you install has its own subdirectory within `node_modules`.

The `package.json` File

The `package.json` file, located at the root of your Node.js project, contains metadata about your project, including its dependencies. The `"main"` field in this file usually points to the entry point of your package – the main file that should be loaded when someone imports your module.

Module Resolution Algorithm

When you import a module in your Node.js code, Node.js follows this algorithm:

1. **Core Modules:** If the module name refers to a core Node.js module (like `fs` for file system operations or `http` for creating servers), Node.js locates and loads it directly from its internal module cache.
2. **Relative Paths:** If the module name starts with `./` or `../`, Node.js treats it as a relative path and searches for the file relative to the current module's location.
3. **Non-Relative Paths:** If the module name is not a core module and doesn't start with `./` or `../`, Node.js assumes it's an external dependency. It then performs the following steps:
   - **Current Directory:** It looks for a `node_modules` folder in the same directory as the current module and tries to find the module there. If found, it loads it.
   - **Parent Directories:** If not found, it moves up one directory and repeats the search in the parent directory's `node_modules` folder. This process continues recursively, traversing up the directory tree until either the module is found or the root of the file system is reached.

The Role of `package.json`

When Node.js finds a matching module in the `node_modules` folder, it looks for a `package.json` file within that module's directory. If found, it checks the `"main"` field to determine the main entry point of the module. By default, if the `"main"` field is not specified, Node.js looks for a file named `index.js` or `index.json`.

Example

Let's say you have a project structure like this:

```
my-project/
├── node_modules/
│   └── lodash/
│       ├── package.json  (with "main": "lodash.js")
│       └── lodash.js
├── src/
│   └── app.ts
└── package.json
```

In your `app.ts` file, you write:

```
import * as _ from 'lodash'; // Non-relative path
```

Node.js will follow these steps:

1. `lodash` is not a core module.
2. `lodash` doesn't start with `./` or `../`.
3. It looks for a `node_modules` folder in the same directory as `app.ts`. It finds it.
4. It finds the `lodash` module inside the `node_modules` folder.
5. It checks the `package.json` file in the `lodash` directory and finds the `"main"` field pointing to `lodash.js`.

6. It loads `lodash.js`.

Key Points

- Node.js uses the `node_modules` directory to store external dependencies.
- The `package.json` file's `"main"` field specifies the entry point of a module.
- Node.js uses a specific algorithm to resolve module imports, searching for modules in the `node_modules` folder and its parent directories.
- Understanding module resolution is crucial for managing dependencies and organizing your Node.js/TypeScript projects effectively.

Module Resolution in the Browser

In contrast to Node.js, the browser environment doesn't have a built-in mechanism for understanding and resolving modules out of the box. Historically, JavaScript code in browsers was loaded as a single, monolithic file, making it difficult to organize code into modules. However, with the advent of ES Modules and the help of module loaders and bundlers, modern browsers are now capable of working with modular code.

ES Modules in the Browser

Modern browsers natively support the ES Modules standard, which defines the syntax for importing and exporting modules using the `import` and `export` keywords. However, there are some key differences compared to Node.js:

- **Strict Mode:** ES Modules are always executed in strict mode. This means that certain coding practices that are allowed in non-strict mode JavaScript (like using undeclared variables) will throw errors in ES Modules.
- **`import.meta`:** Browsers provide the `import.meta` object, which contains information about the current module, such as its URL.
- **Module Scripts:** To indicate that a script tag loads an ES Module, you need to add the `type="module"` attribute:
  `<script type="module" src="./myModule.js"></script>`

Module Loaders and Bundlers

While browsers can now understand ES Modules, there are still challenges when dealing with larger projects:

- **Multiple Network Requests:** If your project has many modules, each import statement could result in a separate network request, potentially slowing down your application.
- **Browser Compatibility:** Older browsers might not fully support ES Modules.

To overcome these challenges, developers often use module loaders and bundlers:

- **Module Loaders (e.g., RequireJS):** These tools handle the dynamic loading of modules at runtime. They can manage dependencies, resolve relative paths, and ensure that modules are loaded in the correct order.
- **Bundlers (e.g., webpack, Parcel):** These tools analyze your code, resolve module imports, and combine multiple modules into a single bundle file. This reduces the number of network requests and improves performance. Bundlers can also transform your code (e.g., transpile TypeScript to JavaScript) and optimize it for production.

The Role of Module Loaders/Bundlers

In the context of TypeScript, module loaders and bundlers play a crucial role:

1. **Module Resolution:** They take care of resolving module imports, even if you use non-relative paths.
2. **Transpilation and Bundling:** They transpile your TypeScript code into JavaScript that browsers can understand and bundle it together with its dependencies.
3. **Compatibility:** They can generate code that is compatible with older browsers that don't fully support ES Modules.

Example: Using webpack

You can configure webpack to bundle your TypeScript project for the browser. Here's a simplified example of a webpack configuration file (`webpack.config.js`):

```
module.exports = { entry: './src/index.ts', // Entry point of your application
output: { filename: 'bundle.js', // Output bundle file path: __dirname +
'/dist' }, resolve: { extensions: ['.ts', '.js'] // Allow importing TypeScript
files without extensions }, module: { rules: [ { test: /\.ts$/, // Apply the
loader to TypeScript files use: 'ts-loader' // Use the ts-loader to transpile
TypeScript } ] } };
```

This configuration tells webpack to:

1. Start at the `src/index.ts` file.
2. Transpile TypeScript files using `ts-loader`.
3. Bundle the output into `dist/bundle.js`.

Key Points

- Browsers don't have built-in module resolution like Node.js.
- Modern browsers support ES Modules natively.
- Module loaders and bundlers are essential for managing module imports and optimizing code for the browser.
- They handle module resolution, transpilation, bundling, and compatibility issues.

By understanding the differences between module resolution in Node.js and the browser, you'll be better equipped to write TypeScript code that works seamlessly in both environments.

Working with Modules

Organizing Code with Modules

Modules are not just about importing and exporting; they're your primary tool for organizing your TypeScript projects into a well-structured, maintainable, and scalable codebase. Let's explore how to use modules effectively to create a clear and logical architecture for your applications.

Project Structure: Folders and Modules

A well-organized TypeScript project typically uses a combination of folders and modules to group related code. Here's a common structure:

```
my-project/
├── src/
│   ├── components/  # Reusable UI components
│   ├── models/      # Data models or entities
│   ├── services/    # Business logic and data access
```

```
│   ├── utils/        # Utility functions and helpers
│   ├── index.ts      # Main entry point (optional)
│   └── ...           # Other modules as needed
├── tests/            # Unit and integration tests
├── tsconfig.json
└── package.json
```

- **`src`:** The main source code directory.
- **`components`:** Holds reusable UI components (if your project has a frontend).
- **`models`:** Defines the data models or entities that your application works with.
- **`services`:** Contains the logic for interacting with data sources (APIs, databases) and performing business operations.
- **`utils`:** Houses utility functions, helper classes, or constants that are used across your project.
- **`index.ts` (Optional):** Can be used as the main entry point for your application or library.
- **`tests`:** Contains your test files.
- **`tsconfig.json`:** The TypeScript configuration file for your project.
- **`package.json`:** The Node.js package file for your project.

Organizing Modules Within Folders

Within each folder, you'll typically have multiple TypeScript files, each representing a module. For example, your `components` folder might contain files like `button.ts`, `card.ts`, and `modal.ts`, each exporting a UI component.

Defining Clear Boundaries

One of the core principles of modular architecture is to create clear boundaries between modules. Each module should have a well-defined responsibility and avoid depending too heavily on other modules.

Here are some tips for defining clear boundaries:

- **Single Responsibility Principle (SRP):** Ensure each module focuses on a single aspect of functionality. Avoid creating modules that do too much.
- **Interface-Based Communication:** If modules need to interact, define clear interfaces for communication. This establishes a contract that helps prevent tight coupling and makes it easier to modify or replace modules.
- **Minimizing Dependencies:** Avoid creating circular dependencies between modules. Instead, design your modules to depend on more stable and fundamental modules.
- **Cohesion:** Group related code together within a module. This makes it easier to understand and maintain the module.

Best Practices

- **Meaningful Names:** Choose descriptive names for your modules and files that accurately reflect their purpose.
- **Flat vs. Deep:** In general, prefer a flatter module structure over a deeply nested one. This makes it easier to find and import modules.
- **Exports:** Be deliberate about what you export from a module. Only export what's necessary for other modules to use, keeping the interface as small as possible.
- **`index.ts` Files:** Consider using `index.ts` files within folders to re-export multiple modules, creating a simpler interface for consumers.

Example: Using `index.ts`

```
// components/index.ts export * from './button'; export * from './card';
export * from './modal';
```

Now, you can import components like this:

```
import { Button, Card, Modal } from './components'; // Cleaner import
statement
```

By following these guidelines and establishing a well-organized module structure, you'll create a solid foundation for your TypeScript projects, making them easier to manage, understand, and scale as they grow.

Creating and Consuming Libraries

Modules aren't just for organizing code within a project; they're also the foundation for building and sharing reusable libraries. In this section, we'll explore how to create your own TypeScript libraries and publish them to npm, the Node Package Manager, making them accessible to the wider development community.

Creating a TypeScript Library

1. **Project Structure:** Organize your library code into modules within a dedicated project folder. You'll likely have modules for different features or components, each with its own TypeScript files.
2. **Entry Point:** Decide on a main entry point for your library. This is typically an `index.ts` file that exports the core functionality you want users to access.
3. **`package.json`:** Create a `package.json` file at the root of your project. This file is essential for defining your library's metadata (name, version, description), dependencies, and scripts for building and publishing.
   ```
   { "name": "my-awesome-library", "version": "1.0.0", "description": "A
   description of your library", "main": "dist/index.js", // Entry point for
   your library (compiled JavaScript) "scripts": { "build": "tsc" },
   "devDependencies": { "typescript": "^4.9.3" // Or your preferred
   TypeScript version } }
   ```
4. **tsconfig.json:** Configure your TypeScript compiler options in the `tsconfig.json` file. Typically, you'll want to set options like:
   ```
   { "compilerOptions": { "target": "ES6", // Or a suitable target "module":
   "CommonJS", // Or "ESNext" for ES Modules "declaration": true, //
   Generate TypeScript declaration files (.d.ts) "outDir": "dist" // Output
   directory for compiled JavaScript and declaration files } }
   ```
5. **Build Your Library:** Run the build command (e.g., `npm run build`) to compile your TypeScript code into JavaScript. This will typically generate JavaScript files and TypeScript declaration files (`.d.ts`) in the `dist` directory.

Publishing to npm

1. **Create an npm Account:** If you don't have one already, create a free account on the npm website.
2. **Login to npm:** In your terminal, run `npm login` and enter your credentials.
3. **Publish:** From your project's root directory, run `npm publish`. This will upload your compiled library code and package metadata to the npm registry.

Consuming a TypeScript Library

Once your library is published on npm, other developers can easily install it as a dependency:

```
npm install my-awesome-library
```

They can then import and use your library's exported members in their TypeScript code:

```
import { myFunction } from 'my-awesome-library';
```

TypeScript will automatically look for the type definitions (`.d.ts` files) within the library's `node_modules` folder to provide type checking and autocompletion.

Key Points

- Modules form the basis for creating reusable TypeScript libraries.
- The `package.json` and `tsconfig.json` files are essential for configuring and building your library.
- Publish your library to npm to make it accessible to the wider community.
- Consumers of your library can install it via npm and use its exported members with type safety.

By understanding how to create and consume TypeScript libraries, you can leverage the power of modules to build a collection of reusable components, utilities, and even full-fledged frameworks, contributing to the thriving TypeScript ecosystem.

CommonJS vs. ES Modules

TypeScript supports both CommonJS and ES Modules, two distinct systems for organizing and sharing code. Understanding their differences is key for making informed decisions about which to use in your projects.

Understanding the Differences

Feature	CommonJS	ES Modules (ESM)
Syntax	`module.exports` for exporting, `require()` for importing	`export` for exporting, `import` for importing
Loading	Dynamic (at runtime)	Static (analyzed at compile time)
Exports	Object-based (mutable exports)	Value-based (immutable exports)
Top-Level `await`	Not supported	Supported (within an `async` function or module)
Compatibility	The default for Node.js (prior to version 14)	Standard for modern JavaScript and newer Node.js versions
Circular Dependencies	Supported, but can lead to issues	More strict, requires careful management
Dynamic Imports	Supported with `require.resolve` and `require.cache`	Supported with `import()`
Live Bindings	Exports are live references	Exports are static values

Syntax Differences

The most obvious difference lies in the syntax. CommonJS uses `module.exports` to export and `require()` to import, while ES Modules use `export` and `import`.

CommonJS:

```
// myModule.js module.exports.myFunction = function() { /* ... */ };
module.exports.myVariable = 42; // main.js const myModule =
require('./myModule'); myModule.myFunction();
console.log(myModule.myVariable);
```

ES Modules:

```
// myModule.ts export function myFunction() { /* ... */ }; export const
myVariable = 42; // main.ts import { myFunction, myVariable } from
'./myModule';
```

Dynamic vs. Static Imports

CommonJS modules are loaded dynamically at runtime. When you use `require()`, the module is evaluated and loaded when that line of code is executed.

ES Modules, on the other hand, are statically analyzed during compilation. The `import` statements are resolved at compile time, not at runtime. This enables better optimization by tools like bundlers.

Live Bindings vs. Static Values

In CommonJS, exports are live references. This means that if you modify a value within a module after it has been exported, the change will be reflected in the imported object.

In ES Modules, exports are static values. Once a value is exported, it becomes immutable. Any changes made to the original value within the module won't affect the imported value.

Other Differences

ES Modules offer features like top-level `await` (awaiting Promises outside of `async` functions) and a more straightforward syntax for dynamic imports (`import()`). CommonJS has more relaxed rules around circular dependencies, while ES Modules enforce stricter checks.

In general, ES Modules are the future of JavaScript modularity, offering better performance, stricter type checking, and wider compatibility with modern tooling. However, CommonJS is still relevant in some cases, particularly when working with older Node.js projects or libraries that haven't yet migrated to ES Modules.

Choosing the Right Module System

While both CommonJS (CJS) and ES Modules (ESM) serve the purpose of modularity, their differences can significantly impact your development experience and the compatibility of your code. Let's consider the factors that influence the decision between the two.

Target Environment

- **Node.js:** Node.js has historically been the realm of CommonJS. However, since Node.js version 13.2+, it has full support for ES Modules. If you're starting a new Node.js project and don't have legacy dependencies that require CommonJS, ES Modules are the way to go.
- **Browser:** Modern browsers fully support ES Modules natively. If you're building a frontend application targeting modern browsers, ES Modules are the default choice.

Project Type

- **Libraries:** If you're creating a library, it's generally best to publish it as an ES Module to maximize compatibility with both Node.js and browsers. You can still provide a CommonJS version for older Node.js users if necessary.
- **Applications:** For applications, the choice depends on your environment and dependencies. However, leaning towards ES Modules is a good future-proofing strategy.

Compatibility with Other Libraries

- **Check Dependencies:** Before choosing a module system, check if your project's dependencies have any restrictions. Some older libraries might only work with CommonJS, while newer ones might have adopted ES Modules.
- **Interop:** If you need to mix CommonJS and ES Modules within a project, there are ways to achieve interoperability, but it might introduce some complexity.

Additional Considerations

- **Performance:** ES Modules are generally considered to have better performance due to their static nature, allowing for optimizations like tree-shaking.
- **Dynamic Imports:** If you need dynamic imports (loading modules on demand), both CommonJS and ES Modules support this, but the syntax is slightly different.
- **`__dirname` and `__filename`:** These Node.js global variables are available in CommonJS modules but not in ES Modules. You can work around this limitation using `import.meta.url`.

Recommendations

- **New Projects:** If you're starting a new project, strongly consider using ES Modules as the default, especially if you're targeting modern browsers or newer Node.js versions. This aligns with the current direction of the JavaScript ecosystem.
- **Existing Projects:** If you have a legacy project that heavily relies on CommonJS, migrating to ES Modules might require some effort. Assess the benefits and drawbacks before making the switch.
- **Mixed Environments:** If you absolutely need to use both CommonJS and ES Modules within a project, carefully research and implement the necessary interoperability techniques.
- **Tooling:** Be aware that some tools might require specific configurations to work with ES Modules. Consult the documentation for your build tools and IDEs for guidance.

By carefully evaluating these factors and considering your project's specific needs, you can make an informed decision about which module system is the best fit for your TypeScript code.

Chapter Summary

In this chapter, we explored modules, the fundamental units of organization in TypeScript projects. We covered the following key points:

- **What Are Modules?** We defined modules as self-contained blocks of code that promote organization, reusability, and maintainability. We discussed how they help manage complexity and avoid naming conflicts.

- **Namespaces vs. Modules:** We briefly touched upon the older concept of namespaces and explained why modules are now the preferred approach for code organization in TypeScript.
- **Module Syntax (Exporting):** We learned how to use the `export` keyword to make functions, classes, interfaces, variables, and types accessible from other modules. We explored both named exports and default exports.
- **Module Syntax (Importing):** We demonstrated how to use the `import` keyword to bring in exported members from other modules, covering named imports, default imports, and renaming imports.
- **Module Resolution Strategies:** We discussed the difference between relative and non-relative paths in module imports and explained how TypeScript resolves module imports in both Node.js and browser environments.
- **Node.js Module Resolution:** We delved into how Node.js resolves modules using the `node_modules` directory and the `package.json` file's "main" field.
- **Browser Module Resolution:** We explored how module resolution in the browser differs from Node.js and discussed the role of module loaders and bundlers (like webpack) in handling module imports in the browser.
- **Organizing Code with Modules:** We provided guidance on structuring TypeScript projects using modules, emphasizing the importance of clear boundaries, single responsibility, and cohesion.
- **Creating and Consuming Libraries:** We explained how modules can be used to create reusable libraries and published to npm for sharing with other developers.
- **CommonJS vs. ES Modules:** We discussed the key differences between the two module systems, including syntax, loading behavior, exports, compatibility, and circular dependencies. We also offered recommendations on when to choose each system.

With a solid understanding of modules, you can now build well-structured, maintainable, and scalable TypeScript projects. You can confidently organize your code into logical units, reuse modules across your projects, and leverage the vast ecosystem of TypeScript libraries available on npm.

In the next chapter, we'll dive into another important aspect of TypeScript's type system: enums and union types, which provide powerful ways to model different options and states in your code.

Enums and Union Types: Modeling Options

Outline

- Enums: Enumerated Types
  - Basic Enum Syntax
  - Numeric and String Enums
  - Computed and Constant Members
  - Reverse Mapping
- Union Types: Flexible Type Combinations
  - Defining Union Types
  - Type Guards and Narrowing
  - Using Union Types in Functions
- Combining Enums and Union Types
- Best Practices and Considerations
- Chapter Summary

Enums: Enumerated Types

In TypeScript, enums (short for "enumerations") provide a way to define a set of named constants. They make your code more readable, maintainable, and less error-prone by using descriptive names for a group of related values.

Basic Enum Syntax

The syntax for declaring an enum is simple:

```
enum EnumName { Member1, Member2, Member3, // ... }
```

Let's break down the key elements:

- **`enum`:** The keyword used to declare an enum.
- **`EnumName`:** The name you choose for your enum (e.g., `DaysOfWeek`, `Colors`, `OrderStatus`).
- **`Member1`, `Member2`, etc.:** The names of the members (or constants) within the enum. These members should be descriptive and represent the possible values of the enum.

Example: `DaysOfWeek` Enum

```
enum DaysOfWeek { Monday, Tuesday, Wednesday, Thursday, Friday, Saturday,
Sunday }
```

In this example, we define an enum called `DaysOfWeek` with members representing each day of the week.

Using Enum Members

You can access enum members using the enum name followed by a dot and the member name:

```
let today: DaysOfWeek = DaysOfWeek.Friday; console.log(today); // Output: 5
if(today === DaysOfWeek.Friday){ console.log("It's Friday!"); // Output: "It's
Friday!" }
```

Notice that by default, the first enum member (`Monday`) is assigned the value 0, and subsequent members are automatically assigned incrementing values (1, 2, 3, etc.). This is often convenient when you don't care about the specific numeric values but just want to represent a set of distinct options.

Example: `Colors` Enum

```
enum Colors { Red, Green, Blue }
```

This enum represents different colors. You can use it like this:

```
let favoriteColor: Colors = Colors.Green;
```

Key Points

- Enums provide a way to define a set of named constants.
- Use the `enum` keyword to declare an enum.
- Enum members are accessed using dot notation (e.g., `EnumName.Member1`).
- By default, numeric enums start with 0 and increment for each member.

Enums are a powerful tool for modeling fixed sets of options or states in your TypeScript code. By using enums, you improve code readability, make your intentions clearer, and ensure type safety.

Numeric and String Enums

TypeScript offers two distinct flavors of enums: numeric enums and string enums. Each type has its own characteristics and use cases. Let's explore them in detail.

Numeric Enums

Numeric enums are the default in TypeScript. When you define an enum without explicitly assigning values to its members, TypeScript automatically assigns them numeric values starting from 0 and incrementing by 1 for each subsequent member.

Example:

```
enum Direction { Up, // 0 Down, // 1 Left, // 2 Right // 3 }
```

You can also explicitly assign numeric values to some or all of the members:

```
enum StatusCode { Ok = 200, BadRequest = 400, Unauthorized = 401, NotFound =
404 }
```

String Enums

In string enums, each member is explicitly assigned a string value.

Example:

```
enum MediaType { Image = "image", Video = "video", Audio = "audio" }
```

When to Use Each Type

- **Numeric Enums:**
  - Ideal when you primarily care about the distinctness of values and not the specific numeric representation.
  - Useful when the values are used in comparisons or calculations.
  - Often used for representing states, options, or flags.

    - More compact in memory.
    - Can be used in conjunction with bitwise operators.
- **String Enums:**
    - Ideal when you want more descriptive and self-documenting member names.
    - Helpful when the string values themselves have inherent meaning.
    - Can be more robust in case of future code changes where you might need to rearrange or add enum members (since the numeric values won't change).

Choosing the Right Enum Type

The choice between numeric and string enums often comes down to personal preference and the specific requirements of your project. Here's a quick guideline:

- If the values primarily serve as distinct identifiers and you don't need human-readable labels, numeric enums are a good option.
- If the values themselves have inherent meaning and you want them to be self-explanatory, go for string enums.

Example: Combining Numeric and String Enums

You can even combine both types in a single enum:

```
enum LogLevel { Error = "ERROR", Warn = "WARN", Info = "INFO", Debug =
"DEBUG", Trace = 5 // Numeric value }
```

In this case, the first four members have explicit string values, while the last member (`Trace`) has an automatic numeric value of 5.

By understanding the nuances of numeric and string enums, you can choose the most appropriate type for your specific use case, making your TypeScript code more expressive and easier to understand.

Computed and Constant Members

Enum members in TypeScript can be classified into two categories based on how their values are determined:

1. **Constant Members:** These members have values that are known and fixed at compile time. They are typically simple numeric or string literals.
2. **Computed Members:** These members have values that are calculated based on expressions. The expressions can involve other enum members or even external values.

Constant Members

```
enum Direction { Up = 1, Down = 2, Left = 3, Right = 4 }
```

In this example, all members are constant. Their values (1, 2, 3, 4) are fixed and known at compile time.

Advantages:

- **Predictability:** The values of constant members are always the same, making them easier to reason about.
- **Performance:** Since the values are known at compile time, there's no need for runtime computation.

Disadvantages:

- **Less Flexibility:** You cannot dynamically calculate values based on other data.

Computed Members

```
enum FileAccess { Read = 1 << 1, // 2 (bitwise left shift) Write = 1 << 2, //
4 ReadWrite = Read | Write, // 6 (bitwise OR) }
```

In this example, the members Read and `Write` use bitwise operations to calculate their values. The `ReadWrite` member is computed by combining Read and `Write` using the bitwise OR operator.

Advantages:

- **Dynamic Values:** You can calculate enum member values based on other data or expressions.
- **Flexibility:** This allows for more dynamic and adaptable enums.

Disadvantages:

- **Less Predictability:** The values of computed members might not be immediately obvious, requiring you to understand the expressions used to calculate them.
- **Potential Runtime Overhead:** If the expressions are complex, calculating the values at runtime could have a slight performance impact.

Choosing Between Computed and Constant Members

The choice between computed and constant members depends on your specific use case:

- If you need fixed, unchanging values that are easy to understand, use constant members.
- If you need to calculate values dynamically based on other data, use computed members.

It's important to note that you can mix both constant and computed members within the same enum, allowing you to leverage the benefits of both approaches. However, currently, computed members are only allowed in numeric enums.

Example: Combining Constant and Computed Members

```
enum Weekday { Monday = 1, // Constant Tuesday, Wednesday, Thursday, Friday,
Weekend = Monday + 5 // Computed } console.log(Weekday.Weekend); // Output: 6
```

By understanding the nuances of computed and constant members, you can design enums that are both flexible and predictable, striking the right balance between dynamic behavior and compile-time safety.

Reverse Mapping

String enums in TypeScript offer a handy feature called *reverse mapping*. This means that TypeScript automatically creates a mapping not only from enum names to their string values but also from string values back to their corresponding names. This bi-directional relationship can be a powerful tool for making your code more expressive and easier to maintain.

How Reverse Mapping Works

When you define a string enum, TypeScript generates an object behind the scenes that stores both the forward mapping (name -> value) and the reverse mapping (value -> name).

```
enum LogLevel { Error = "ERROR", Warn = "WARN", Info = "INFO", }
console.log(LogLevel.Error); // Output: "ERROR"
console.log(LogLevel["ERROR"]); // Output: LogLevel.Error
```

In this example, you can access the enum member value using `LogLevel.Error`, as expected. But you can also use the string value `"ERROR"` as a key to retrieve the corresponding enum member (`LogLevel.Error`). This is possible due to the reverse mapping that TypeScript creates.

Enhancing Readability and Maintainability

Reverse mapping can be particularly helpful when you receive a string value (e.g., from an API response or a configuration file) and need to match it to a corresponding enum member.

```
function logMessage(message: string, level: LogLevel) {
console.log(`[${LogLevel[level]}] ${message}`); } logMessage("An error
occurred", "ERROR"); // Output: "[LogLevel.Error] An error occurred"
```

In this example, the `logMessage` function takes a string value for the `level` parameter. By using `LogLevel[level]`, we can easily retrieve the human-readable enum member name (e.g., "Error", "Warn", "Info") for logging purposes. This makes the log messages clearer and more informative.

Important Notes

- **String Enums Only:** Reverse mapping only works for string enums. Numeric enums don't have this feature because their values are automatically assigned and might not be unique.
- **Type Safety:** While reverse mapping is convenient, be cautious when using it with values that might not be valid enum members. TypeScript will not raise an error if you access a non-existent member, and you might end up with `undefined` as the result.

Best Practice: Consider adding a validation step to ensure that the string value you're using is a valid enum member before accessing the reverse mapping to avoid unexpected results.

By leveraging the reverse mapping feature of string enums, you can write more expressive, self-documenting code that is easier to understand and maintain.

Union Types: Flexible Type Combinations

In the real world, data doesn't always fit neatly into a single category. Sometimes a value can be a number *or* a string, or maybe an object *or* null. Union types in TypeScript provide a way to express this flexibility, allowing you to define a type that can represent values of different types.

Defining Union Types

The syntax for union types is remarkably simple: you use the pipe symbol (|) to separate the possible types.

```
type ID = number | string;
```

In this example, `ID` is a union type that can represent either a `number` or a `string`. This means you can assign a number or a string to a variable of type `ID`:

```
let userId: ID = 12345; // Valid (number) userId = "user-54321"; // Valid
(string)
```

More Examples

```
type Status = "success" | "error" | "pending"; type Point = { x: number; y:
number } | [number, number]; type MaybeNumber = number | undefined;
```

In these examples:

- `Status` can be one of three string literals: "success", "error", or "pending".
- `Point` can be either an object with x and y properties or a tuple of two numbers.
- `MaybeNumber` can be either a number or `undefined`.

Why Use Union Types?

Union types offer several benefits:

- **Flexibility:** They allow you to model real-world scenarios where data can take on different forms.
- **Type Safety:** TypeScript still enforces type checking for each possible type within the union, preventing you from accidentally performing operations that are not valid for all types.
- **Reduced Code Duplication:** You can write functions or interfaces that can handle multiple types, avoiding the need to write separate versions for each type.

Key Points

- Union types represent values that can be of multiple types.
- The | symbol is used to separate the possible types.
- Use union types when you need to express flexibility in the types a variable, function parameter, or return value can accept.

We'll shortly explore how to work with union types effectively using type guards, type narrowing, and other techniques. By mastering union types, you'll be equipped to handle the diversity of data that you'll encounter in your TypeScript projects.

Type Guards and Narrowing

Union types give you flexibility by allowing a variable to hold values of different types. However, to perform actions specific to a particular type within that union, you need a way to narrow down the possibilities. That's where type guards and the concept of type narrowing come into play.

Type Narrowing

Type narrowing is the process of refining a variable's type from a broader union type to a more specific type. This is typically done within a conditional block (e.g., `if` statement) based on some runtime checks.

Type Guards

Type guards are expressions that perform runtime checks to determine the type of a variable. TypeScript recognizes certain patterns as type guards, allowing it to narrow down the type within the guarded block of code.

Common Type Guards

1. **`typeof` Operator:** Use the `typeof` operator to check the type of a variable against primitive types (like `string`, `number`, `boolean`, `symbol`, etc.).
   ```
   function logValue(value: string | number) { if (typeof value ===
   "string") { console.log(value.toUpperCase()); // value is narrowed to
   string } else { console.log(value.toFixed(2)); // value is narrowed to
   number } }
   ```
2. **`instanceof` Operator:** Use the `instanceof` operator to check if an object is an instance of a specific class.
   ```
   class Dog { /* ... */ } class Cat { /* ... */ } function
   makeSound(animal: Dog | Cat) { if (animal instanceof Dog) {
   ```

```
console.log("Woof!"); // animal is narrowed to Dog } else {
console.log("Meow!"); // animal is narrowed to Cat } }
```

3. **User-Defined Type Guards:** You can create custom type guards using functions that return a type predicate. A type predicate has the form `parameterName is Type`.
```
function isFish(pet: Fish | Bird): pet is Fish { return (pet as
Fish).swim !== undefined; }
```

How Type Guards Enable Type Narrowing

Within the `if` block of a type guard, TypeScript's compiler knows the type of the variable has been narrowed down. This allows you to safely access properties or methods specific to that type without getting type errors.

Example: Type Narrowing with Multiple Type Guards

```
type Shape = | { kind: "circle"; radius: number } | { kind: "rectangle";
width: number; height: number }; function getArea(shape: Shape) { if
(shape.kind === "circle") { return Math.PI * shape.radius ** 2; // shape is
narrowed to { kind: "circle"; radius: number } } else { return shape.width *
shape.height; // shape is narrowed to { kind: "rectangle"; width: number;
height: number } } }
```

In this example, we use two type guards to narrow down the `shape` variable's type before calculating the area.

Key Points

- Type narrowing refines a union type to a more specific type within a conditional block.
- Type guards are expressions that perform runtime checks to determine a variable's type.
- Common type guards include `typeof`, `instanceof`, and user-defined type guards.
- Type guards enable TypeScript to safely narrow down types within conditional blocks.

By using type guards and type narrowing, you can write more flexible and expressive TypeScript code that handles values of different types in a type-safe manner.

Using Union Types in Functions

Union types shine when you want to create functions that can gracefully handle different types of input or produce different types of output. TypeScript's type system, along with type guards and other techniques, helps you work with these functions safely and efficiently.

1. Union Types as Function Parameters

You can define functions that accept parameters of a union type. This means the caller can provide a value of any of the allowed types:

```
function displayValue(value: string | number): void { if (typeof value ===
"string") { console.log(value.toUpperCase()); } else {
console.log(value.toFixed(2)); // Assuming value is a number } }
displayValue("hello"); // Output: "HELLO" displayValue(3.14159); // Output:
"3.14"
```

In this example, the `displayValue` function accepts either a `string` or a `number`. Inside the function, we use a type guard (`typeof value === "string"`) to determine the actual type of the `value` and then perform the appropriate action.

2. Union Types as Return Values

Functions can also return a union type, indicating that the result can be of multiple possible types:

```
function getRandomValue(): string | number { if (Math.random() < 0.5) { return
"heads"; } else { return 42; } } let result = getRandomValue(); if (typeof
result === "string") { console.log(result.length); // result is narrowed to
string } else { console.log(result * 2); // result is narrowed to number }
```

The `getRandomValue` function returns either a string ("heads") or a number (42). To work with the returned value, you'll again need to use type guards to determine its actual type at runtime.

3. Union Types with Object Literals

You can use union types with object literals to define functions that accept objects with different sets of properties:

```
type Circle = { kind: "circle"; radius: number }; type Rectangle = { kind:
"rectangle"; width: number; height: number }; type Shape = Circle | Rectangle;
function calculateArea(shape: Shape): number { if (shape.kind === "circle") {
return Math.PI * shape.radius ** 2; } else { return shape.width *
shape.height; } }
```

In this example, the `Shape` type is a union of `Circle` and `Rectangle` types. The `calculateArea` function can accept objects of either shape, using the `kind` property to determine which calculation to perform.

Key Points

- Union types can be used as parameters or return types of functions.
- Type guards are essential for working with union types safely within functions.
- You can use `typeof`, `instanceof`, or custom type guards to narrow down union types.

By mastering the use of union types in functions, you can create flexible, adaptable, and type-safe functions that can handle a variety of input and output scenarios, making your TypeScript code more robust and expressive.

Combining Enums and Union Types: A Powerful Duo

Enums and union types are often used in tandem in TypeScript to create expressive and type-safe representations of states, options, or values that can belong to distinct categories. Let's explore how this combination works and why it's so valuable.

Enums as Members of Union Types

The core idea is simple: you can include enum members within a union type to represent the different possible values that a variable or function parameter can accept. This provides a clear and structured way to model situations where a value can fall into one of several well-defined categories.

Example: Representing Shapes

```
enum ShapeType { Circle, Rectangle, Triangle } type Shape = | { type:
ShapeType.Circle; radius: number } | { type: ShapeType.Rectangle; width:
number; height: number } | { type: ShapeType.Triangle; base: number; height:
number };
```

In this example:

1. We define an enum `ShapeType` to represent the possible types of shapes.
2. We create a union type `Shape` that can be one of three object types:
    - A circle (with a `radius`).
    - A rectangle (with `width` and `height`).
    - A triangle (with `base` and `height`).
3. Each object type in the union has a `type` property whose value is a member of the `ShapeType` enum. This property is called a *discriminant* (or *tag*), and it allows you to distinguish between the different types within the union.

Benefits of Combining Enums and Union Types

- **Clear and Descriptive:** Enums provide descriptive names for the different possible values, making your code more self-explanatory.
- **Type Safety:** TypeScript's type checker ensures that you only use valid enum members within the union type.
- **State Modeling:** This combination is ideal for modeling state machines or objects that can have different states with different properties (e.g., a button that can be in a "loading", "success", or "error" state).
- **Extensibility:** You can easily add new enum members to represent additional states or options without breaking existing code.

Working with Combined Enums and Union Types

To work with a variable of this `Shape` type, you'll typically use a type guard (e.g., `switch` statement) to narrow down the type before accessing its specific properties:

```
function calculateArea(shape: Shape): number { switch (shape.type) { case
ShapeType.Circle: return Math.PI * shape.radius ** 2; case
ShapeType.Rectangle: return shape.width * shape.height; case
ShapeType.Triangle: return (shape.base * shape.height) / 2; } }
```

Key Points

- Combining enums and union types is a powerful pattern for representing different states, options, or categories.
- Use an enum to define the possible values and a union type to represent the objects that can have those values.
- Use a discriminant property to distinguish between the different types within the union.
- Use type guards (e.g., `switch`) to narrow down the type before accessing specific properties.

By mastering this combination, you'll be equipped to model complex data structures and scenarios in a type-safe and expressive way, making your TypeScript code more robust and maintainable

Best Practices and Considerations for Enums and Union Types

Enums and union types are valuable tools in your TypeScript arsenal, but like any tool, they're best used with intention and care. Let's explore some best practices and considerations to help you leverage their power effectively.

Enums

- **Naming Conventions:** Use PascalCase (e.g., `DaysOfWeek`, `LogLevel`, `OrderStatus`) for enum names to distinguish them from other types (variables, functions).
- **String vs. Numeric Enums:**
  - Favor string enums for better readability and maintainability, as they provide more descriptive values.
  - Use numeric enums when you need specific numeric values for calculations or bitwise operations.
- **Computed vs. Constant Members:**
  - Prefer constant members when the values are fixed and known at compile time.
  - Use computed members only when you need to calculate values dynamically.
- **Explicit Initialization:** Initialize the first enum member to a value (usually 0 or 1) to avoid unexpected behavior.
- **Consider Const Enums (if applicable):** In some cases, using `const enum` can provide a slight performance advantage, as the enum values are inlined during compilation. However, this also removes the ability to perform reverse mapping.

Union Types

- **Type Guards:** Always use type guards (like `typeof`, `instanceof`, or custom type guards) to narrow down union types before accessing properties or methods specific to a particular type. This ensures type safety and prevents runtime errors.
- **Avoid Excessive Use:** Don't overuse union types. While they offer flexibility, they can also make code harder to reason about if overused. Consider if a more specific type or an interface would be a better fit.
- **Discriminated Unions:** When defining union types for objects, use a discriminant property (like `kind` or `type`) to easily distinguish between the different types within the union.
- **Readability:** Prioritize code clarity when using union types. Ensure that the potential types within a union are logically related and that the type names are descriptive.

General Considerations

- **Code Readability:** Always keep code readability in mind. Your goal is to make your code easy for yourself and others to understand. Avoid overcomplicating your types.
- **Performance:** In most cases, the performance impact of enums and union types is negligible. However, be aware of potential overhead when using computed enum members or complex type guards with large union types.
- **Tooling:** Utilize the power of your IDE's TypeScript support. Features like code completion, type hints, and refactoring tools can significantly improve your development experience when working with enums and union types.

The Right Tool for the Job

Remember, enums and union types are just tools. There's no one-size-fits-all answer to when you should use them. Consider the specific requirements of your project, the trade-offs involved, and the overall maintainability and readability of your code.

By using enums and union types judiciously and following best practices, you can write expressive, flexible, and type-safe TypeScript code that is both robust and easy to understand.

Chapter Summary

In this chapter, we explored two powerful tools in TypeScript's type system: enums and union types. We covered the following key concepts:

- **Enums:** We learned how enums provide a way to define sets of named constants, making our code more readable and self-documenting. We explored both numeric and string enums, discussed computed and constant members, and highlighted the benefits of reverse mapping in string enums.
- **Union Types:** We learned how union types allow variables or parameters to hold values of multiple different types, providing flexibility in our type definitions. We used the `|` symbol to define union types and discussed their various use cases.
- **Type Guards and Narrowing:** We explored the concept of type narrowing, which allows us to refine a union type to a more specific type within a conditional block. We saw how type guards like `typeof`, `instanceof`, and user-defined type guards are used to achieve this narrowing, ensuring type safety when working with union types.
- **Combining Enums and Union Types:** We demonstrated how to use enum members within union types to represent different possible values, particularly in scenarios where we need to model states or options.
- **Best Practices:** We offered guidance on best practices for using enums and union types, including naming conventions, choosing the right enum type, using type guards effectively, and avoiding overuse of union types.

By mastering enums and union types, you've gained valuable tools for modeling a wide range of data and scenarios in TypeScript. You can now write more expressive, adaptable, and type-safe code that clearly communicates your intentions and helps prevent errors.

In the next chapter, we'll delve into another advanced TypeScript concept: decorators, which provide a way to modify or enhance the behavior of classes, methods, and properties.

Decorators: Enhancing Your Code

Outline

- What are Decorators?
  - The Essence of Decorators
  - Decorators as Functions
  - Why Use Decorators?
- Decorator Types
  - Class Decorators
  - Method Decorators
  - Property Decorators
  - Parameter Decorators
- Creating Custom Decorators
  - Decorator Factories
  - Composition of Decorators
- Common Use Cases for Decorators
  - Logging and Debugging
  - Validation
  - Dependency Injection
  - Authorization
- Decorators in Popular Frameworks
  - Angular
  - NestJS
- Considerations and Limitations
- Chapter Summary

What are Decorators?

Decorators in TypeScript are like elegant accessories that you can attach to your code to enhance its functionality or add metadata. They are a form of metaprogramming, allowing you to modify or extend the behavior of classes, methods, properties, or even parameters without directly altering their source code.

The Essence of Decorators

Think of decorators as annotations that you apply using the @ symbol followed by the decorator's name, just before the declaration of the class, method, property, or parameter.

Example:

```
@Component({ selector: 'app-my-component', template: `<h1>Hello, world!</h1>`,
}) class MyComponent { // ... }
```

In this example, `@Component` is a decorator from the Angular framework. It adds metadata to the `MyComponent` class, indicating that it's an Angular component with specific properties (`selector`, `template`).

Decorators as Functions

Behind the scenes, decorators are simply functions that receive information about the decorated element and can perform various actions:

1. **Introspection:** A decorator can examine the structure of the class, method, or property it's applied to. It can access names, types, metadata, and other details.
2. **Modification:** A decorator can change the behavior of the decorated element. For example, it could add new properties, methods, or change the existing ones.
3. **Metadata Addition:** A decorator can attach metadata to the decorated element. This metadata can be used by other parts of your application or by frameworks like Angular.

Key Reasons to use Decorators

Decorators offer several compelling benefits:

- **Separation of Concerns:** Decorators allow you to keep cross-cutting concerns (like logging, validation, or authentication) separate from your core business logic. This leads to cleaner and more maintainable code.
- **Code Reusability:** Decorators can be applied to multiple elements, making it easy to reuse common functionality across your codebase.
- **Extensibility:** Decorators provide a way to extend the behavior of classes, methods, and properties without having to modify their original source code directly.
- **Framework Integration:** Many popular frameworks like Angular and NestJS heavily rely on decorators to simplify common tasks like component creation, dependency injection, routing, and more.
- **Declarative Style:** Decorators offer a declarative way to enhance your code. Instead of writing imperative code to achieve a certain behavior, you simply apply a decorator, making your code more concise and expressive.

Decorators open up a world of possibilities for customizing and extending the behavior of your TypeScript code in a clean and modular way.

Decorators as Functions

While the syntax of decorators with the `@` symbol might seem magical, under the hood, they are simply functions. Let's unravel this magic and see how decorators work as functions.

The Decorator Function Signature

A decorator function typically takes the following parameters:

- **`target`:** The constructor of the class (for class decorators), the prototype of the class (for method and property decorators), or the property descriptor (for property decorators).
- **`propertyKey` (Optional):** The name of the method or property being decorated (for method and property decorators).
- **`descriptor` (Optional):** A property descriptor object (for method and property decorators) that contains information about the decorated member.

Decorator Return Value

A decorator can optionally return a value:

- **Class Decorators:** Can return a new constructor function to replace the original class constructor.
- **Method and Property Decorators:** Can return a new property descriptor object to modify the behavior of the method or property.
- **Parameter Decorators:** Don't return anything.

Example: A Simple Method Decorator

```
function log(target: any, propertyKey: string, descriptor: PropertyDescriptor)
{ const originalMethod = descriptor.value; descriptor.value = function
(...args: any[]) { console.log(`Calling ${propertyKey} with arguments:`,
args); const result = originalMethod.apply(this, args); console.log(`Result:`,
result); return result; }; return descriptor; }
```

In this example:

1. `log` is a decorator function that takes the standard parameters.
2. It saves the original method (`descriptor.value`).
3. It replaces `descriptor.value` with a new function that logs the method name and arguments before calling the original method and logging the result.
4. It returns the modified descriptor.

Applying the Decorator

```
class Calculator { @log add(x: number, y: number): number { return x + y; } }
const calculator = new Calculator(); calculator.add(2, 3);
```

Output:

Calling add with arguments: [2, 3]
Result: 5

Key Points

- Decorators are functions that accept information about the decorated element.
- They can modify or replace the decorated element or its behavior.
- Decorators can be used to add metadata to elements.
- Decorator factories are functions that return decorators.

By understanding the function-based nature of decorators, you can create powerful and flexible tools to enhance your TypeScript code in a variety of ways, from logging and validation to dependency injection and beyond.

Why Use Decorators?

Decorators offer a powerful and elegant way to enhance your TypeScript code. Let's delve into the key advantages that make them a valuable addition to your development toolkit.

Separation of Concerns

One of the core principles of software design is the separation of concerns (SoC). It advocates for breaking down a complex application into distinct modules, each responsible for a specific aspect of functionality. Decorators excel at this by allowing you to isolate cross-cutting concerns—features that span multiple parts of your codebase—into reusable decorators.

Consider logging, a common cross-cutting concern. Instead of cluttering your business logic with logging statements, you can create a `@log` decorator that automatically logs method calls, parameters, and return values. This keeps your main code focused on its core purpose while the decorator handles logging.

Similarly, you can use decorators for validation, authentication, error handling, and other aspects that are orthogonal to your core logic.

Readability

Decorators often lead to more expressive and concise code. Instead of writing repetitive boilerplate code to implement cross-cutting concerns, you can simply apply a decorator to the relevant class, method, or property. This declutters your code and makes it easier to grasp the intent behind each element.

For instance, consider a validation decorator:

```
@validateEmail email: string;
```

This is far more succinct and clearer than writing manual validation logic within your class.

Flexibility

Decorators offer a non-invasive way to modify the behavior of existing code. You can add functionality, alter existing functionality, or even replace the implementation entirely without directly touching the original code. This is particularly useful when you want to enhance a third-party library or framework without forking or modifying its source code.

For instance, imagine you have a class with a method that performs a time-consuming operation. You could use a decorator to add caching to that method, optimizing its performance without changing its core logic.

Additional Advantages

- **Aspect-Oriented Programming (AOP):** Decorators facilitate AOP, a programming paradigm that focuses on modularizing cross-cutting concerns.
- **Framework Integration:** Many popular TypeScript frameworks (like Angular and NestJS) rely heavily on decorators for features like component definition, dependency injection, and routing. Understanding decorators is crucial for working effectively with these frameworks.

Key Points

- Decorators are functions that you apply to classes, methods, properties, or parameters using the `@` symbol.
- They allow you to separate cross-cutting concerns from your core logic, improving code organization.
- Decorators make your code more readable and expressive by reducing boilerplate.
- They offer a flexible way to modify or extend existing code without direct modification.

By leveraging decorators, you can elevate your TypeScript code to a new level of modularity, maintainability, and expressiveness. However, it's important to use them judiciously and avoid excessive or overly complex decorators that could hinder code readability.

Decorator Types

Class Decorators

Class decorators are a special kind of decorator that are applied to the constructor of a class. They allow you to intercept and modify the class definition itself, adding new properties, methods, or metadata. This can be incredibly powerful for implementing cross-cutting concerns or extending the behavior of existing classes.

How Class Decorators Work

A class decorator is a function that receives a single argument: the constructor of the class it decorates. The decorator can then modify the constructor or the class prototype (which defines the shared methods and properties for all instances of the class).

Syntax

```
function ClassDecorator(constructor: Function) { // Decorator logic }
@ClassDecorator class MyClass { // ... }
```

In this example, the `@ClassDecorator` syntax is applied to the `MyClass` declaration. Behind the scenes, TypeScript calls the `ClassDecorator` function, passing the `MyClass` constructor as its argument.

Example: Logging Class Creation

Let's create a simple class decorator that logs a message whenever a new instance of the decorated class is created:

```
function logged(constructor: Function) { console.log("New instance created:",
constructor.name); } @logged class Person { constructor(public name: string)
{} } let alice = new Person("Alice"); // Output: "New instance created:
Person"
```

Example: Adding Metadata

Here's a class decorator that adds a custom metadata property to the decorated class:

```
function addMetadata(metadataKey: string, metadataValue: string) { return
function (constructor: Function) { Reflect.defineMetadata(metadataKey,
metadataValue, constructor); }; } @addMetadata("api-version", "1.0.0") class
MyApiService { // ... } const version = Reflect.getMetadata("api-version",
MyApiService); console.log(version); // Output: "1.0.0"
```

Important Considerations

- **Timing:** Class decorators are executed when the class is *declared*, not when an instance is created. This means that the decorator can modify the class definition itself but not the individual objects created from it.
- **Return Value:** A class decorator can optionally return a new constructor function to replace the original constructor of the class. This allows you to completely alter how the class is created.
- **Experimental:** Class decorators are still considered an experimental feature in JavaScript. They are supported in TypeScript by enabling the `experimentalDecorators` compiler option.

Key Points

- Class decorators modify the class definition itself.
- They receive the class constructor as an argument.
- They can be used to add properties, methods, or metadata to the class.
- They can optionally return a new constructor function to replace the original.

Class decorators are a powerful tool for metaprogramming in TypeScript. They allow you to add behavior to your classes in a modular and reusable way, leading to cleaner and more maintainable code.

Method Decorators

Method decorators are applied to the methods within a class, allowing you to intercept and modify their behavior before, during, or after their execution. This opens up possibilities for adding cross-cutting concerns like logging, performance tracking, caching, and more.

How Method Decorators Work

A method decorator is a function that receives three arguments:

1. `target`: The prototype of the class that contains the method.
2. `propertyKey`: The name of the method being decorated (a string).
3. `descriptor`: A `PropertyDescriptor` object that describes the method's attributes (like `value`, `writable`, `enumerable`, `configurable`).

The decorator can then modify the `descriptor` object or replace the original method with a new function that wraps around it, adding additional behavior.

Syntax

```
function MethodDecorator( target: any, propertyKey: string, descriptor:
PropertyDescriptor ): PropertyDescriptor { // Decorator logic } class MyClass
{ @MethodDecorator myMethod() { // ... } }
```

Example 1: Logging Method Calls

Let's create a `logMethod` decorator that logs a message whenever a decorated method is called:

```
function logMethod(target: any, propertyKey: string, descriptor:
PropertyDescriptor) { const originalMethod = descriptor.value;
descriptor.value = function (...args: any[]) { console.log(`Calling
${propertyKey} with arguments: ${args}`); const result =
originalMethod.apply(this, args); console.log(`Result: ${result}`); return
result; }; } class Calculator { @logMethod add(x: number, y: number): number {
return x + y; } } const calculator = new Calculator(); calculator.add(2, 3);
// Output: "Calling add with arguments: 2,3\nResult: 5"
```

Example 2: Measuring Execution Time

```
function measureTime(target: any, propertyKey: string, descriptor:
PropertyDescriptor) { const originalMethod = descriptor.value;
descriptor.value = function (...args: any[]) { const start =
performance.now(); const result = originalMethod.apply(this, args); const end
= performance.now(); console.log(`${propertyKey} took ${end - start}
milliseconds`); return result; }; }
```

Example 3: Basic Caching

```
function cache(target: any, propertyKey: string, descriptor:
PropertyDescriptor) { const originalMethod = descriptor.value; const cacheMap
= new Map(); descriptor.value = function (...args: any[]) { const cacheKey =
```

```
JSON.stringify(args); if (cacheMap.has(cacheKey)) { return
cacheMap.get(cacheKey); } else { const result = originalMethod.apply(this,
args); cacheMap.set(cacheKey, result); return result; } }; }
```

Key Points

- Method decorators modify the behavior of methods within a class.
- They can be used for logging, performance measurement, caching, and more.
- Decorator functions receive the target, property key, and descriptor as arguments.
- They can modify the descriptor to alter the method's behavior.

By using method decorators, you can add cross-cutting concerns to your classes in a clean, reusable, and declarative way, keeping your core logic focused and easy to maintain.

Property Decorators

Property decorators in TypeScript are a powerful tool for adding metadata or modifying the behavior of class properties. They give you fine-grained control over how properties are accessed and manipulated, allowing you to implement validation, formatting, logging, and other custom logic.

How Property Decorators Work

A property decorator is a function that receives two arguments:

1. `target`: The prototype of the class that contains the property or the constructor function if the property is static.
2. `propertyKey`: The name of the property being decorated (a string).

The decorator can then modify the property's behavior by defining a getter and/or a setter.

Syntax

```
function PropertyDecorator(target: any, propertyKey: string) { // Decorator
logic (typically defining a getter/setter) } class MyClass {
@PropertyDecorator myProperty: string; }
```

Example 1: Validation

Let's create a `validate` decorator that ensures a property's value meets certain criteria:

```
function positiveNumber(target: any, propertyKey: string) { let value: number;
const getter = () => value; const setter = (newVal: number) => { if (newVal <=
0) { throw new Error("Value must be positive"); } value = newVal; };
Object.defineProperty(target, propertyKey, { get: getter, set: setter, }); }
class Example { @positiveNumber myNumber: number; constructor(myNumber:
number) { this.myNumber = myNumber; } } const example = new Example(5);
console.log(example.myNumber); // 5 //example.myNumber = -2; // Error: Value
must be positive
```

Example 2: Formatting

```
function formatDate(target: any, propertyKey: string) { let value: Date; const
getter = () => value.toLocaleDateString(); const setter = (newVal: Date) => {
```

```
value = newVal; }; Object.defineProperty(target, propertyKey, { get: getter,
set: setter, }); } class Transaction { @formatDate dateCreated: Date;
constructor(dateCreated: Date) { this.dateCreated = dateCreated; } }
```

Example 3: Observability

```
function observable(target: any, propertyKey: string) { let value: any; const
getter = () => value; const setter = (newVal: any) => { value = newVal;
console.log(`Property ${propertyKey} changed to: ${newVal}`); };
Object.defineProperty(target, propertyKey, { get: getter, set: setter, }); }
```

Key Points

- Property decorators modify the behavior of properties within a class.
- They can be used for validation, formatting, logging property changes, and more.
- Decorator functions receive the target and property key as arguments.
- They typically define getters and setters to customize property access.

By using property decorators, you can add sophisticated features to your classes without cluttering their implementation. They provide a clean and reusable way to enhance the functionality of your data attributes, making your TypeScript code more robust and maintainable.

Parameter Decorators

Parameter decorators, as the name suggests, are decorators applied to parameters within the method definitions of a class. While they don't directly modify the behavior of the method itself, they provide a way to intercept, validate, or transform the arguments passed to the method.

How Parameter Decorators Work

A parameter decorator is a function that receives three arguments:

1. `target`: Either the constructor function of the class (for static members) or the prototype of the class (for instance members).
2. `propertyKey`: The name of the method (a string).
3. `parameterIndex`: The index of the parameter being decorated (a number).

Unlike other decorator types, parameter decorators do not have a return value. Their primary purpose is to observe or modify the metadata associated with the parameter.

Syntax

```
function ParameterDecorator(target: any, propertyKey: string, parameterIndex:
number) { // Decorator logic } class MyClass { myMethod(@ParameterDecorator
param1: string, param2: number) { // ... } }
```

Use Cases

While parameter decorators are not as widely used as class or method decorators, they can be handy in several scenarios:

1. **Validation:** You can create decorators to validate parameter values before they are passed to the method. For example, you could write a decorator that checks if a string argument is a valid email address or if a number argument is within a certain range.

2. **Type Transformation:** Parameter decorators can be used to transform the types of arguments. For example, you might have a decorator that converts a string representing a date into a `Date` object.
3. **Logging:** While you can use method decorators for logging, parameter decorators can be more fine-grained, allowing you to log specific arguments or their types.

Example: Validation Decorator

```
function required(target: Object, propertyKey: string, parameterIndex: number)
{ const existingRequiredParameters: number[] =
Reflect.getOwnMetadata('required_parameters', target, propertyKey) || [];
existingRequiredParameters.push(parameterIndex);
Reflect.defineMetadata('required_parameters', existingRequiredParameters,
target, propertyKey); } function validate(target: any, propertyName: string,
descriptor: TypedPropertyDescriptor<Function>) { let method =
descriptor.value!; descriptor.value = function (...args: any[]) { let
requiredParameters: number[] = Reflect.getOwnMetadata('required_parameters',
target, propertyName); if (requiredParameters) { for (let parameterIndex of
requiredParameters) { if (parameterIndex >= args.length ||
args[parameterIndex] === undefined) { throw new Error("Missing required
argument."); } } } return method.apply(this, args); } } class Greeter {
@validate greet(@required name: string) { return "Hello " + name; } } const
greeter = new Greeter(); console.log(greeter.greet("John")); // Output: "Hello
John" //console.log(greeter.greet()); // Error: Missing required argument.
```

Note: In the above example, the `reflect-metadata` library is used to store and retrieve metadata associated with the parameters. You'll need to install and import it to use this functionality.

Key Points

- Parameter decorators can be used to observe, validate, or transform method arguments.
- They are often used in conjunction with metadata to attach additional information to parameters.
- Use parameter decorators to create more robust and self-documenting code.

By understanding parameter decorators, you gain another tool for fine-tuning the behavior of your TypeScript functions and improving the overall structure and maintainability of your codebase.

Creating Custom Decorators

Decorator Factories

Decorator factories are a powerful mechanism for creating more versatile and customizable decorators. They are simply functions that return decorators, allowing you to parameterize the behavior of the decorator based on the arguments passed to the factory function.

Why Use Decorator Factories?

- **Configuration:** Decorator factories allow you to create decorators that can be configured with different options. For example, you could create a logging decorator that allows you to specify the logging level or the destination for the logs.

- **Additional Arguments:** Decorator factories can accept additional arguments beyond the standard `target`, `propertyKey`, and `descriptor` parameters that are passed to a regular decorator. This gives you more flexibility to tailor the decorator's behavior.

Syntax

```
function DecoratorFactory(...factoryArgs: any[]): (target: any, propertyKey?: string, descriptor?: PropertyDescriptor) => PropertyDescriptor { return function (target: any, propertyKey?: string, descriptor?: PropertyDescriptor) { // Decorator logic (using factoryArgs) }; }
```

Let's break it down:

1. **`DecoratorFactory`:** The outer function that acts as the factory. It can accept any number of arguments (`factoryArgs`) that you want to use to configure the decorator.
2. **Inner Function:** The factory function returns another function, which is the actual decorator. This inner function receives the standard decorator arguments (`target`, `propertyKey`, `descriptor`).
3. **Decorator Logic:** Inside the inner function, you can use the `factoryArgs` to customize the behavior of the decorator.

Example: Configurable Logging Decorator

```
function Log(level: "info" | "warn" | "error") { return function (target: any, propertyKey: string, descriptor: PropertyDescriptor) { const originalMethod = descriptor.value; descriptor.value = function (...args: any[]) { console[level](`Calling%20${propertyKey}%20with%20arguments:%20${args}`); const result = originalMethod.apply(this, args); console[level](`Result:%20${result}`); return result; }; }; } class Calculator { @Log("info") // Configure logging level add(x: number, y: number): number { return x + y; } @Log("error") divide(x: number, y: number): number { if (y === 0) { throw new Error("Division by zero!"); } return x / y; } }
```

In this example:

- Log is a decorator factory that takes a `level` argument to determine the logging level (info, warn, or error).
- It returns a method decorator that logs messages to the console using the specified level.
- We apply the `@Log` decorator to the `add` and `divide` methods of the `Calculator` class, configuring different logging levels for each.

Key Points

- Decorator factories are functions that return decorators.
- They allow you to create decorators with configurable behavior.
- They can accept additional arguments beyond the standard decorator parameters.
- They are a powerful way to create reusable decorators that can be tailored to different scenarios.

By mastering decorator factories, you'll be able to write more flexible and reusable decorators that can adapt to the specific needs of your TypeScript projects.

Composition of Decorators

One of the most powerful aspects of decorators in TypeScript is the ability to compose them – that is, apply multiple decorators to the same class, method, or property. This allows you to combine different functionalities seamlessly, creating a modular and extensible way to enhance your code.

Applying Multiple Decorators

To apply multiple decorators, you simply stack them one above the other, each preceded by the `@` symbol:

```
@decorator1 @decorator2 class MyClass { @decorator3 @decorator4 myMethod() {
// ... } }
```

In this example, `MyClass` is decorated with `decorator1` and `decorator2`, while the `myMethod` method is decorated with `decorator3` and `decorator4`.

Decorator Execution Order

The order of execution for multiple decorators is crucial. They are executed from **top to bottom** during the definition phase, but the resulting functions that they return are invoked from **bottom to top** during the runtime.

Here's a visual representation:

```
Definition Order:   @decorator1 -> @decorator2 -> Class/Method/Property
Execution Order:     decorator2() -> decorator1()
```

Example: Combining Decorators

Let's combine the `logMethod` and `measureTime` decorators from the previous section:

```
class Calculator { @measureTime @logMethod add(x: number, y: number): number {
return x + y; } }
```

In this case:

1. During definition, `measureTime` is applied first, wrapping the `add` method.
2. Then, `logMethod` is applied, wrapping the result of `measureTime`.
3. At runtime, when `add` is called, the `logMethod` wrapper is executed first, logging the function call and arguments.
4. Then, the `measureTime` wrapper is executed, measuring the execution time and logging it.
5. Finally, the original `add` method is executed, and its result is returned.

Key Points

- You can apply multiple decorators to the same class, method, or property.
- Decorators are executed in top-to-bottom order during definition.
- The resulting decorator functions are invoked in bottom-to-top order at runtime.

Real-World Applications

Decorator composition is widely used in frameworks like Angular and NestJS. You might combine decorators for dependency injection, logging, authorization, validation, and other cross-cutting concerns to create complex, yet maintainable, application logic.

By mastering decorator composition, you unlock a powerful way to layer functionality and customize the behavior of your TypeScript code in a clean and modular fashion.

Common Use Cases for Decorators

Logging and Debugging

Decorators are indispensable for adding logging and debugging capabilities to your TypeScript code. They allow you to effortlessly track function calls, monitor arguments, and observe changes to properties, making it easier to pinpoint issues and understand how your application flows.

Logging Method Calls

Let's revisit the `logMethod` decorator we created earlier:

```
function logMethod(target: any, propertyKey: string, descriptor:
PropertyDescriptor) { const originalMethod = descriptor.value;
descriptor.value = function (...args: any[]) { console.log(`Calling
${propertyKey} with arguments:`, args); // Log method call const result =
originalMethod.apply(this, args); console.log(`Result:`, result); // Log
method result return result; }; return descriptor; }
```

This decorator neatly encapsulates the logging logic, allowing you to focus on your core functionality. You can simply add the `@logMethod` decorator to any method you want to track.

Logging Property Changes

```
function logProperty(target: any, propertyKey: string) { let value =
target[propertyKey]; const getter = () => value; const setter = (newValue:
any) => { console.log(`Property ${propertyKey} changed from ${value} to
${newValue}`); value = newValue; }; Object.defineProperty(target, propertyKey,
{ get: getter, set: setter, enumerable: true, configurable: true, }); } class
Person { @logProperty public name: string; constructor(name: string) {
this.name = name; } } const person = new Person('Alice'); person.name = 'Bob';
// Output: "Property name changed from Alice to Bob"
```

This `logProperty` decorator adds logging to both the getter and setter of the property, providing visibility into when and how the property's value changes.

Benefits of Logging Decorators

- **Reduced Boilerplate:** You don't need to manually write logging code within every method or property.
- **Centralized Logic:** Logging behavior is encapsulated within the decorator, making it easier to manage and modify.
- **Debugging Aid:** Logs provide a trail of information that can be invaluable for tracking down bugs and understanding program flow.
- **Performance Profiling:** You can use similar decorators to measure execution times of methods, helping you identify performance bottlenecks.

Customizing Logging

You can further customize these decorators to log to files, remote servers, or structured logging systems. You can also add conditional logging based on log levels, filtering, or other criteria.

Debugging with Decorators

Decorators can aid in debugging beyond simple logging. For example, you could create a decorator that automatically sets breakpoints within a method or prints stack traces when errors occur.

Key Points

- Decorators are a convenient way to add logging and debugging functionality to your TypeScript code.
- Use method decorators to log method calls and results.
- Use property decorators to track changes to property values.
- Customize your decorators to fit your specific logging and debugging needs.

By strategically using decorators for logging and debugging, you'll gain better insight into your application's behavior, streamline the debugging process, and create more robust and maintainable TypeScript code.

Validation

Decorators are a fantastic tool for implementing validation logic in TypeScript. By encapsulating validation rules within decorators, you can centralize your validation code, making it more reusable and easier to manage. This leads to cleaner and more robust applications where data integrity is enforced consistently.

Validation Decorators for Properties

Let's start by creating a property decorator called `validateEmail` that ensures the value of a decorated property is a valid email address:

```
function validateEmail(target: any, propertyKey: string) { let value: string;
const getter = () => value; const setter = (newValue: string) => { if
(!validateEmailFormat(newValue)) { throw new Error(`Invalid email format for
${propertyKey}`); } value = newValue; }; Object.defineProperty(target,
propertyKey, { get: getter, set: setter, enumerable: true, configurable: true,
}); } function validateEmailFormat(email: string): boolean { // Implement your
email validation logic here (using regular expressions or other methods) //
... return true; // Replace with your actual validation logic } class User {
@validateEmail email: string; constructor(email: string) { this.email = email;
} }
```

In this example:

1. The `validateEmail` decorator takes the `target` object and the `propertyKey` as arguments.
2. It defines a getter that simply returns the property's value.
3. It defines a setter that performs the email validation. If the validation fails, it throws an error; otherwise, it assigns the new value to the property.
4. We use `Object.defineProperty` to replace the original property with this getter and setter.

Now, whenever the `email` property of a `User` object is set, the validation logic will be automatically applied.

Validation Decorators for Parameters

We can also create parameter decorators for validating function arguments:

```
function validateNumberRange(min: number, max: number) { return function (target: any, propertyKey: string, parameterIndex: number) { // Get the existing parameter validators or create an empty array let existingValidators: any[] = Reflect.getOwnMetadata('validators', target, propertyKey) || []; // Add a new validator function for the current parameter existingValidators[parameterIndex] = (value: number) => { if (value < min || value > max) { throw new Error(`Parameter at index ${parameterIndex} must be between ${min} and ${max}`); } }; // Store the updated validators using reflect-metadata Reflect.defineMetadata('validators', existingValidators, target, propertyKey); }; } function validateParams(target: any, propertyKey: string, descriptor: TypedPropertyDescriptor<Function>) { let method = descriptor.value!; descriptor.value = function (...args: any[]) { let validators: ((value: any) => void)[] = Reflect.getOwnMetadata('validators', target, propertyKey); if (validators) { for (let i = 0; i < args.length; i++) { if (validators[i]) { validators[i](args[i]); // call the validator function on the corresponding argument } } } return method.apply(this, args); } } class MathUtils { @validateParams add(@validateNumberRange(0, 10) x: number, @validateNumberRange(0, 10) y: number): number { return x + y; } }
```

Benefits of Validation Decorators

- **Centralized Logic:** Validation rules are defined in one place (the decorator), making them easier to maintain and update.
- **Code Reusability:** Decorators can be reused for different properties or parameters, promoting DRY (Don't Repeat Yourself) principles.
- **Improved Readability:** Your class definitions become cleaner, as validation logic is separated from the core business logic.

Additional Considerations

- **Error Handling:** Think about how you want to handle validation errors. You can throw exceptions (as shown in the examples), return a validation result object, or use other error reporting mechanisms.
- **Customizable Decorators:** Create decorator factories to allow users to configure validation rules (e.g., minimum/maximum values, regular expressions).
- **Framework Integration:** If you're using a framework like Angular or NestJS, explore their built-in validation decorators and how they can simplify your validation process.

By incorporating validation decorators into your TypeScript workflow, you'll be well on your way to building more robust applications with clean, reusable, and well-organized validation logic.

Dependency Injection

Dependency injection (DI) is a powerful design pattern that promotes loose coupling and easier testing in software development. Instead of objects creating their own dependencies, a DI system provides them with the necessary dependencies, often at the time of object creation. Think of it as a way to build your application like a Lego set, where each piece (object) fits together seamlessly without being rigidly connected.

How Decorators Facilitate Dependency Injection

In TypeScript, decorators play a key role in implementing dependency injection, especially within frameworks like Angular and NestJS. Decorators are used to mark classes as *injectable* and to specify the dependencies a class requires.

Example: Angular Dependency Injection

```
import { Injectable, Inject } from '@angular/core'; import { HttpClient } from '@angular/common/http'; @Injectable() // Mark the class as injectable class ProductService { constructor(@Inject(HttpClient) private http: HttpClient) {} // Inject HttpClient getProducts(): Observable<Product[]> { return this.http.get<Product[]>('/api/products'); } }
```

In this Angular example:

1. The `@Injectable` decorator tells Angular that the `ProductService` class can be injected into other components or services.
2. The `@Inject(HttpClient)` decorator indicates that the `ProductService` constructor requires an `HttpClient` dependency.
3. Angular's DI system automatically provides an instance of `HttpClient` when creating an instance of `ProductService`.

Benefits of Decorator-Based DI

- **Declarative:** The decorators clearly express the dependencies a class requires, making the code more self-documenting.
- **Loose Coupling:** Classes don't directly create their dependencies, making them easier to test in isolation.
- **Flexibility:** The DI system can easily manage different implementations of dependencies, promoting modularity and testability.

Dependency Injection Beyond Angular

While the previous example showcased Angular's specific DI mechanism, the concept of using decorators to facilitate dependency injection is applicable in other frameworks and libraries as well. The exact syntax and implementation details might vary, but the core principle remains the same: decorators are used to mark classes as injectable and declare their dependencies.

Key Points

- Dependency injection (DI) is a design pattern that provides objects with their dependencies.
- Decorators play a crucial role in implementing DI in TypeScript frameworks.
- Decorators mark classes as injectable and specify their dependencies.
- DI promotes loose coupling, testability, and flexibility.

By understanding how decorators and dependency injection work together, you can build TypeScript applications that are more modular, maintainable, and easier to test. The ability to manage dependencies effectively is a hallmark of well-designed software, and decorators provide a powerful tool for achieving this in the TypeScript world.

Authorization

Decorators are a convenient way to implement authorization checks in your TypeScript applications. By encapsulating authorization logic within decorators, you can create reusable security mechanisms that protect sensitive operations and data.

Authorization Decorator for Methods

Let's create a simple decorator called `authorize` that checks if a user has the required role to access a method:

```
function authorize(allowedRoles: string[]) { return function (target: any,
propertyKey: string, descriptor: PropertyDescriptor) { const originalMethod =
descriptor.value; descriptor.value = function (...args: any[]) { // Get the
user's role (replace with your actual logic) const userRole =
getCurrentUserRole(); // Assume this function exists if
(allowedRoles.includes(userRole)) { // User is authorized, call the original
method return originalMethod.apply(this, args); } else { // User is not
authorized, throw an error or take other action throw new Error("Unauthorized
access"); } }; }; }
```

In this example:

1. The `authorize` decorator is a factory function that takes an array of `allowedRoles`.
2. It returns a method decorator that intercepts the method call.
3. Inside the decorator, we get the current user's role (using a hypothetical `getCurrentUserRole` function).
4. We check if the user's role is included in the `allowedRoles`.
   - If authorized, we call the original method.
   - If not authorized, we throw an "Unauthorized access" error.

Using the `authorize` Decorator

```
class AdminPanel { @authorize(["admin"]) getSensitiveData() { // ... retrieve
sensitive data ... } @authorize(["admin", "manager"]) generateReport() { //
... generate a report ... } }
```

In this class, the `getSensitiveData` method can only be accessed by users with the "admin" role, while the `generateReport` method can be accessed by either "admin" or "manager" roles.

Authorization Decorator for Classes

You can also apply an authorization decorator to an entire class, making all its methods subject to the authorization check:

```
@authorize(["admin"]) class AdminController { // All methods in this class are
now restricted to users with the "admin" role }
```

Streamlining Security

Authorization decorators significantly streamline the implementation of security mechanisms in your code:

- **Centralized Authorization Logic:** You define the authorization rules in one place (the decorator), avoiding code duplication.
- **Declarative Syntax:** Decorators make authorization checks more explicit and easier to understand, as you simply decorate the relevant methods or classes.
- **Easier Maintenance:** If your authorization rules change, you only need to update the decorator, not every method or class individually.

Additional Considerations

- **Complex Authorization:** For more intricate authorization scenarios, you can create custom decorators that check for multiple roles, permissions, or even specific user attributes.
- **Integration with Authentication:** Ensure your authorization decorators work seamlessly with your authentication system to correctly identify the current user and their roles.
- **Error Handling:** Carefully consider how to handle unauthorized access. You might throw errors, redirect the user to a login page, or display an error message.

By incorporating authorization decorators into your TypeScript toolkit, you'll enhance the security of your applications, protect sensitive data, and create a more secure and controlled user experience.

Decorators in Popular Frameworks

Angular

Angular is a prime example of a framework that leverages decorators to streamline development and enhance code organization. Decorators are at the heart of Angular, playing a pivotal role in defining components, services, directives, pipes, and managing various aspects of the application lifecycle.

Component Definition with `@Component`

The `@Component` decorator is the most fundamental decorator in Angular. It's used to mark a class as an Angular component, providing metadata that defines its template, styles, and how it interacts with the rest of the application.

```
import { Component } from '@angular/core'; @Component({ selector: 'app-my-component', // HTML tag to use for the component template: '<h1>Hello, {{name}}!</h1>', // HTML template styles: ['h1 { color: blue; }'] // CSS styles }) export class MyComponent { name = 'Angular'; }
```

Dependency Injection with `@Injectable`

The `@Injectable` decorator marks a class as a service that can be injected into other components or services. This facilitates dependency injection, a core principle of Angular architecture that promotes loose coupling and testability.

```
import { Injectable } from '@angular/core'; @Injectable({ providedIn: 'root' // Make the service available globally }) export class DataService { // ... }
```

Input and Output Properties with `@Input` and `@Output`

The `@Input` and `@Output` decorators enable communication between parent and child components.

- `@Input`: Marks a property as an input, allowing the parent component to pass data to the child component.
- `@Output`: Marks a property as an output, allowing the child component to emit events to the parent component.

Other Common Angular Decorators

- **`@Directive`:** Used to create custom directives that add behavior to HTML elements.
- **`@Pipe`:** Used to create custom pipes for transforming data in templates.

- **`@NgModule`:** Used to define Angular modules, which group related components, directives, and pipes.
- **`@HostListener`:** Used to listen for DOM events on the host element of a component or directive.

Key Points

- Angular heavily relies on decorators to define components, services, directives, pipes, and other elements.
- Decorators in Angular provide a declarative way to configure and add behavior to your code.
- Common decorators like `@Component`, `@Injectable`, `@Input`, and `@Output` are essential for building Angular applications.

By understanding how Angular leverages decorators, you'll be well-equipped to build well-structured, maintainable, and testable Angular applications that follow best practices for code organization and reusability.

NestJS

NestJS is a powerful framework built on top of Node.js and Express (or optionally Fastify) that makes heavy use of decorators to streamline the creation of scalable and well-structured server-side applications. Inspired by Angular, NestJS adopts a similar decorator-driven approach, providing a familiar development experience for developers coming from frontend frameworks.

Key Decorators in NestJS

- **`@Controller`:** Used to define a controller class, which is responsible for handling incoming requests and sending responses. You can specify a route prefix for the controller's endpoints.

  ```
  @Controller('products') // Handles requests starting with '/products'
  class ProductsController { // ... }
  ```

- **`@Get, @Post, @Put, @Delete`:** These decorators are used to define HTTP method handlers for specific routes within a controller.

  ```
  @Controller('products') class ProductsController { @Get(':id')
  getProduct(@Param('id') id: string) { // ... get a product by ID ... }
  @Post() createProduct(@Body() createProductDto: CreateProductDto) { //
  ... create a new product ... } }
  ```

- **`@Module`:** Used to define a module, which is a container for a group of related controllers, providers (services), and other modules. Modules help organize the structure of your application.

  ```
  @Module({ controllers: [ProductsController], providers:
  [ProductsService], }) export class ProductsModule {}
  ```

Additional NestJS Decorators

NestJS offers a rich set of decorators for various purposes:

- **Request Handling:** `@Body`, `@Query`, `@Param`, `@Headers`, etc., for accessing request data.
- **Response Handling:** `@Res`, `@HttpCode`, `@Redirect`, etc., for managing responses.
- **Exception Filters:** `@Catch` for handling exceptions globally or for specific controllers/methods.
- **Pipes:** `@UsePipes` for transforming and validating input data.

- **Guards:** `@UseGuards` for implementing authentication and authorization checks.
- **Interceptors:** `@UseInterceptors` for modifying requests or responses globally or for specific controllers/methods.

Benefits of Decorators in NestJS

- **Declarative Syntax:** Decorators provide a clean and concise way to define routes, controllers, and other aspects of your application.
- **Code Organization:** Modules help structure your application into logical units, making it more maintainable.
- **Dependency Injection:** NestJS comes with a built-in dependency injection system that works seamlessly with decorators, promoting loose coupling and testability.
- **Flexibility:** You can easily customize the behavior of your application using NestJS's extensive collection of decorators.

Key Points

- NestJS is a framework designed for building efficient and scalable server-side applications.
- It utilizes decorators to define controllers, routes, modules, and other aspects of your application.
- NestJS provides a rich set of decorators for handling requests, responses, validation, authorization, and more.
- Decorators in NestJS promote a declarative style of programming, improving code readability and maintainability.

By understanding how NestJS leverages decorators, you can create well-structured, modular, and scalable server-side applications with ease. Decorators, combined with NestJS's other features, make it a compelling choice for building robust and efficient backends for your TypeScript projects.

Considerations and Limitations

While decorators offer a powerful way to enhance TypeScript code, it's important to be mindful of their potential drawbacks and use them judiciously.

Potential for Overuse

Decorators can easily become addictive. Their concise syntax and ability to add behavior to code might tempt you to sprinkle them everywhere. However, excessive use of decorators can make your codebase more complex and harder to understand, especially for developers who are not familiar with them.

Remember, decorators are not a silver bullet for every problem. Sometimes, plain old functions or methods might be a simpler and more straightforward solution. Always consider whether a decorator truly adds value to your code or if it's just syntactic sugar.

Learning Curve

Decorators have a unique syntax and behavior that might take some time for developers to fully grasp. The concept of metaprogramming and function composition can be challenging for newcomers.

It's important to invest time in understanding decorators thoroughly before using them extensively in your projects. Start with simple examples and gradually progress to more complex scenarios. Ensure that everyone on your team has a good understanding of decorators to avoid confusion and maintainability issues.

Experimental Feature in JavaScript

While TypeScript has fully embraced decorators, they are still considered an experimental feature in JavaScript. This means that the syntax and behavior of decorators might change in future versions of JavaScript.

If you're writing TypeScript code that you intend to transpile to JavaScript, be aware of this potential for future incompatibility. Keep an eye on the ECMAScript proposals related to decorators and be prepared to adapt your code if necessary.

Responsible Use of Decorators

To use decorators effectively, follow these recommendations:

- **Use Case First:** Always start by identifying a clear use case for a decorator. Don't just use decorators for the sake of using them.
- **Single Responsibility:** Each decorator should ideally focus on a single responsibility. Avoid creating overly complex decorators that do too much.
- **Naming:** Choose descriptive and meaningful names for your decorators that clearly convey their purpose.
- **Testing:** Write unit tests for your decorators to ensure they function correctly and don't introduce unexpected side effects.
- **Documentation:** Clearly document the purpose and usage of your decorators so that other developers (or your future self) can easily understand them.
- **Moderation:** Use decorators judiciously. Don't overload your code with them. Use them when they truly add value in terms of code organization, clarity, or reusability.

Key Points

- Decorators are a powerful but potentially complex feature.
- Overuse of decorators can lead to code that is difficult to understand and maintain.
- Decorators are still an experimental feature in JavaScript.
- Use decorators thoughtfully and responsibly to enhance your code without sacrificing readability or maintainability.

By understanding the benefits and limitations of decorators and using them wisely, you can leverage their power to create elegant, flexible, and well-structured TypeScript code.

Chapter Summary

In this chapter, we explored the world of decorators in TypeScript, a powerful mechanism for metaprogramming and enhancing code functionality. Here's a recap of what we covered:

- **What Are Decorators?** We introduced decorators as functions that modify or add metadata to classes, methods, properties, or parameters. We discussed their essence as annotations and their role in separating concerns, improving readability, and providing flexibility.
- **Decorators as Functions:** We delved into the inner workings of decorators, exploring their function signatures, parameters, and return values. We demonstrated how decorators can intercept and modify the behavior of the elements they decorate.
- **Why Use Decorators?** We discussed the advantages of decorators, including separation of concerns, improved code readability, flexibility in modifying existing code, and their integral role in frameworks like Angular and NestJS.
- **Decorator Types:** We explored different types of decorators:
    - **Class decorators:** Applied to the constructor of a class to modify its definition.
    - **Method decorators:** Applied to methods to alter their behavior.
    - **Property decorators:** Applied to properties to add metadata or change getter/setter behavior.

    - **Parameter decorators:** Applied to parameters to validate or transform input.
- **Creating Custom Decorators:** We learned how to create our own decorators using decorator factories, which allow for configurable behavior and additional parameters. We also discussed decorator composition, where multiple decorators can be applied to the same element.
- **Common Use Cases:** We explored practical examples of decorators for logging and debugging, validation, dependency injection, and authorization, demonstrating how they can streamline common tasks and improve code quality.
- **Decorators in Popular Frameworks:** We touched upon the prominent use of decorators in Angular and NestJS, highlighting their role in defining components, services, routes, and other aspects of application development.
- **Considerations and Limitations:** We discussed potential drawbacks of decorators, such as overuse leading to complexity, their unique syntax requiring a learning curve, and their experimental status in JavaScript. We emphasized the importance of using decorators responsibly to maintain code readability and future compatibility.

By mastering decorators, you've gained a valuable skill for building sophisticated and well-structured TypeScript applications. You can now leverage decorators to separate concerns, enhance code readability, and add powerful functionality to your classes, methods, and properties in a modular and reusable way.

Section III:
TypeScript in the Real World

TypeScript with React: Building Modern User Interfaces

Outline

- Introduction
  - Why TypeScript and React Are a Perfect Match
  - Benefits of Using TypeScript with React
- Setting Up a TypeScript React Project
  - Create React App with TypeScript
  - Manual Project Setup
- TypeScript in React Components
  - Function Components
  - Class Components
  - Props and State
- TypeScript with JSX
  - Typing JSX Elements
  - Intrinsic Elements
  - Custom Components
- React Hooks
  - useState
  - useEffect
  - useContext
  - Custom Hooks
- TypeScript with React Router
  - Defining Routes and Links
  - Type Safety with Route Parameters
- Advanced Topics
  - Context API with TypeScript
  - Redux with TypeScript
  - TypeScript and React Testing
- Chapter Summary

Introduction

Why TypeScript and React Are a Perfect Match

React, with its component-based architecture, has revolutionized the way we build user interfaces. It promotes reusability, maintainability, and a declarative style of programming. However, as React applications grow in complexity, managing the types of data flowing through components and props can become challenging. This is where TypeScript steps in as a perfect companion, enhancing React's strengths and mitigating its weaknesses.

The Synergy

- **Component-Based Architecture:** React's core philosophy revolves around building reusable components. Each component is a self-contained unit with its own props (inputs) and state (internal data). TypeScript's interfaces and type aliases are ideal for defining the shape of these props and state, ensuring type safety at the component level.
- **Static Typing vs. Dynamic Nature:** JavaScript, the language of React, is dynamically typed, which can lead to unexpected errors at runtime. TypeScript's static type system brings predictability and early error detection to React, catching type-related issues during development rather than in production.
- **Large-Scale Applications:** As React projects grow, the complexity of managing component interactions and data flow increases. TypeScript's strong typing helps prevent errors, making refactoring safer and ensuring that your application remains robust as it scales.

Concrete Benefits

Let's delve into the specific benefits of combining TypeScript and React:

1. **Early Error Detection:** TypeScript's compiler catches type mismatches, incorrect prop types, and other errors during development, saving you from debugging headaches later on.
2. **Improved Developer Experience:** TypeScript-aware editors provide enhanced code completion, type hints, and refactoring tools, making your React development workflow smoother and more efficient.
3. **Self-Documenting Code:** TypeScript's type annotations act as living documentation, making it easier for you and your team to understand the expected types of props and the structure of components.
4. **Robust Refactoring:** When you make changes to your React codebase, TypeScript's type checker acts as a safety net, alerting you if your modifications introduce type inconsistencies.
5. **Reduced Bugs:** By catching errors early and ensuring type safety, TypeScript significantly reduces the likelihood of bugs in your React applications.
6. **Community and Ecosystem:** TypeScript has a vibrant community and a vast ecosystem of libraries and tools built specifically for React. You'll find type definitions for most popular React libraries, making integration seamless.

Example: Type-Safe Props

```
interface ProductProps { id: number; name: string; price: number;
description?: string; // Optional property } function Product({ id, name,
price, description }: ProductProps) { // ... }
```

By defining the types of the product component in the props interface, TypeScript will highlight any discrepancies in the data types. **In Summary**

The combination of TypeScript and React is a powerful one. TypeScript's static type system perfectly complements React's component-based architecture, providing a robust foundation for building modern, scalable, and maintainable user interfaces. Whether you're starting a new project or adding TypeScript to an existing React codebase, you'll quickly appreciate the benefits it brings to your development workflow and the overall quality of your applications.

Benefits of Using TypeScript with React

TypeScript's synergy with React extends beyond a simple pairing; it's a powerful combination that unlocks numerous advantages, elevating your development process and the quality of your code. Let's explore these benefits in detail:

1. **Early Error Detection:**
   TypeScript's static type system acts as an early warning system for your React code. By defining types for props, state, and other variables, you enable the TypeScript compiler to catch type-related errors during development, long before they manifest as runtime bugs in your application.
   Imagine you have a component that expects a `number` as a prop, but you accidentally pass a `string`. In JavaScript, this might lead to cryptic errors or unexpected behavior at runtime. In TypeScript, the compiler would immediately flag this as an error, saving you time and frustration during debugging.
2. **Improved Developer Experience:**
   TypeScript-aware code editors, such as Visual Studio Code, offer a significant boost to your React development workflow. These editors leverage TypeScript's type information to provide:
   - **Intelligent Code Completion (IntelliSense):** As you type, your editor suggests relevant components, props, methods, and even entire code snippets, making you more productive and reducing typos.
   - **Type Hints:** Hovering over variables or function calls reveals their types, providing instant documentation and aiding in understanding complex code.
   - **Refactoring Tools:** Renaming variables, extracting components, or moving code around becomes safer and more efficient with TypeScript's assistance.
3. **Enhanced Code Readability:**
   By explicitly defining types for props, state, and other components, your React code becomes more self-documenting. Type annotations act as clear signposts, communicating the expected data structures and interfaces. This not only makes it easier for you to understand your own code but also helps other developers quickly grasp the structure and purpose of your components.
4. **Scalability:**
   As your React projects grow in size and complexity, maintaining a consistent structure and preventing errors become increasingly challenging. TypeScript's strong typing acts as a guiding force, helping you catch potential issues early on and maintain a well-organized codebase. This makes it easier to scale your applications without sacrificing quality or maintainability.
5. **Maintainability:**
   Refactoring large JavaScript codebases can be a daunting task due to the risk of introducing subtle bugs. TypeScript's type system provides a safety net. It alerts you to any type inconsistencies that might arise from your changes, ensuring that your codebase remains robust and reliable as it evolves over time.

In summary, the combination of TypeScript and React offers a powerful way to build modern user interfaces. TypeScript's static type system complements React's component-based architecture, providing early error detection, improved developer experience, enhanced code readability, scalability, and long-term maintainability. Whether you're a seasoned React developer or just starting your journey, incorporating TypeScript into your workflow can significantly elevate your React skills and the quality of your applications.

Setting Up a TypeScript React Project

Create React App with TypeScript

Create React App (CRA) is a popular command-line tool maintained by Facebook that simplifies the process of bootstrapping new React projects. The beauty of CRA lies in its streamlined setup and built-in support for TypeScript, making it the preferred method for many developers to get started with TypeScript and React.

Benefits of Using Create React App

- **Zero Configuration:** CRA takes care of all the initial setup, including installing dependencies, configuring the TypeScript compiler, and setting up a development server. This allows you to focus on writing code rather than wrestling with configuration details.
- **Best Practices:** CRA incorporates industry-standard best practices for project structure, linting, testing, and building, ensuring that your project starts on the right foot.
- **Community Support:** CRA is widely used and has a large community of developers, making it easy to find help and resources if you encounter issues.

Step-by-Step Instructions

1. **Prerequisites:**
   - Ensure you have Node.js and npm (or yarn) installed on your system (see Chapter 2).
2. **Create the Project:** Open your terminal and run the following command:
   ```
   npx create-react-app my-app --template typescript
   ```
   Replace "my-app" with your desired project name. The `--template typescript` flag tells CRA to use the TypeScript template.
3. **Navigate to the Project Directory:**
   ```
   cd my-app
   ```
4. **Start the Development Server:**
   ```
   npm start // or yarn start
   ```
   CRA will start a development server, and your default browser should automatically open to display the initial React app.

What's Included

CRA with the TypeScript template sets up a fully functional TypeScript React project, including:

- **`tsconfig.json`:** The TypeScript configuration file with sensible defaults.
- **React and ReactDOM:** The core React libraries for building user interfaces.
- **TypeScript and Type Definitions:** TypeScript is pre-installed, along with type definitions for React (`@types/react`) and ReactDOM (`@types/react-dom`).
- **Testing Setup:** A basic testing environment is set up using Jest, a popular JavaScript testing framework.
- **Linting:** ESLint is included to help you maintain code quality and consistency.
- **Build Scripts:** Scripts for building your application for production (`npm run build` or `yarn build`) are also provided.

Customizing Your Project

Once your project is up and running, you can customize it to your needs:

- **Ejecting:** If you want complete control over your project's configuration and tooling, you can eject from CRA using `npm run eject` or `yarn eject`. This will expose the underlying configuration files, but it's a one-way operation and cannot be undone.
- **Configuration:** You can modify the `tsconfig.json` file to adjust TypeScript compiler options or add other configurations to suit your project's requirements.

By leveraging the power of Create React App with TypeScript, you can quickly and effortlessly get started with building modern and type-safe React applications.

Manual Project Setup

While Create React App offers a convenient way to start, some developers prefer a more hands-on approach with greater control over their project setup. If you fall into this category, here's a guide to setting up a TypeScript React project from scratch.

1. Project Initialization

- Create a new project directory (e.g., `my-react-app`).
- Open your terminal and navigate to the project directory.
- Initialize the project with npm or yarn:
  `npm init -y # or yarn init -y`
  This will create a `package.json` file to manage project dependencies.

2. Install Essential Dependencies

Install the core React and TypeScript dependencies:

```
npm install react react-dom typescript @types/react @types/react-dom # or yarn
add react react-dom typescript @types/react @types/react-dom
```

Here's what these packages do:

- **`react` and `react-dom`:** The core React libraries for building user interfaces.
- **`typescript`:** The TypeScript compiler.
- **`@types/react` and `@types/react-dom`:** TypeScript type definitions for React and ReactDOM.

3. Create TypeScript Configuration (`tsconfig.json`)

Create a `tsconfig.json` file at the root of your project to configure the TypeScript compiler. Here's a basic configuration:

```
{ "compilerOptions": { "target": "ES6", "module": "ESNext", // Or "CommonJS"
if you prefer "jsx": "react-jsx", // Enable JSX support "strict": true, //
Enable strict mode for better type checking "esModuleInterop": true, // Allows
interoperability between CommonJS and ES Modules "skipLibCheck": true, //
Skips type checking of declaration files (e.g., from node_modules)
"forceConsistentCasingInFileNames": true, // Helps avoid case-sensitivity
issues with imports "moduleResolution": "node" // Use Node.js style module
resolution }, "include": ["src"] // Include all TypeScript files in the src
directory }
```

Feel free to customize these options to match your project's requirements.

4. Set Up a Build Process

You'll need a way to compile your TypeScript code into JavaScript for the browser. You can use a bundler like webpack, Parcel, or Rollup. Here's how to set up a basic build with webpack:

- Install webpack and its CLI: `npm install --save-dev webpack webpack-cli`
- Create a `webpack.config.js` file for webpack configuration (see example in previous section on "Module Resolution in the Browser").
- Add a build script to your `package.json`:
  `"scripts": { "build": "webpack" }`
  Now you can run `npm run build` to compile your TypeScript code.

5. Create React Components

Start building your React components in TypeScript files within the `src` directory. Make sure to give your files the `.tsx` extension (for TypeScript with JSX).

```
// src/App.tsx import React from "react"; function App() { return <h1>Hello, world!</h1>; } export default App;
```

6. Run Your Application

You'll typically need to use a local development server to run your React app. You can use tools like webpack-dev-server or create a custom server using Express or other libraries.

Key Points

- Manual setup gives you more control over your project's configuration and tooling.
- You need to install essential dependencies like React, ReactDOM, and TypeScript.
- Configure the TypeScript compiler using `tsconfig.json`.
- Set up a build process (e.g., using webpack) to compile TypeScript to JavaScript.
- Create your React components in TypeScript files with the `.tsx` extension.

While manual project setup requires more initial steps, it empowers you to tailor your development environment to your exact preferences and needs.

TypeScript in React Components

Function Components

Function components are the most common way to build components in modern React. They're simple, concise, and offer excellent performance characteristics. Let's see how TypeScript seamlessly integrates with function components, bringing the benefits of type safety and improved developer experience.

Typing Function Components

The core idea is to define an interface or type alias to describe the shape of your component's props (inputs). You then use this type annotation for the function component's parameter.

Using Interfaces

```
interface GreetingProps { name: string; message?: string; // Optional property } function Greeting(props: GreetingProps) { return ( <div> <h1>{props.message || "Hello"}, {props.name}!</h1> </div> ); }
```

In this example:

1. We define an interface `GreetingProps` that describes the expected props:
   - `name` (string): The name to be greeted.
   - `message` (string, optional): A custom greeting message (defaults to "Hello" if not provided).
2. The `Greeting` function component accepts an argument `props` that is explicitly typed as `GreetingProps`. TypeScript will then enforce that you pass the correct props to this component.

Using Type Aliases

You can achieve the same result using a type alias:

```
type GreetingProps = { name: string; message?: string; };
```

The rest of the code remains the same.

Typing the Return Value (JSX)

TypeScript automatically infers that the return value of a function component is a JSX element (`JSX.Element` or a more specific type if you're using TypeScript 4.1 or later). You can explicitly annotate it if you prefer, but it's usually not necessary:

```
function Greeting(props: GreetingProps): JSX.Element { // ... (rest of the
component code) }
```

Accessing Props

You can access the individual props within the component using either dot notation (`props.name`) or destructuring:

```
function Greeting({ name, message = "Hello" }: GreetingProps) { //
Destructuring return ( <div> <h1>{message}, {name}!</h1> </div> ); }
```

Default Props

You can also define default props using a static property on the function component:

```
Greeting.defaultProps = { message: "Hello" };
```

Key Points

- Function components are the most common way to build components in React.
- Use interfaces or type aliases to define the shape of your component's props.
- Annotate the function component's parameter with the props type.
- TypeScript infers the return type of a function component as JSX.
- Access props using dot notation or destructuring.
- Define default props using the `defaultProps` static property.

By embracing TypeScript with your React function components, you'll enhance code readability, catch potential errors early, and enjoy a smoother development experience with the help of your editor's autocompletion and type checking features.

Class Components

While function components are the current trend in React, class components still hold relevance, especially in legacy projects or when you need more advanced features like error boundaries. Let's explore how TypeScript brings its type-safety benefits to React class components.

Defining Class Components with TypeScript

To create a class component, you extend the `React.Component` class and provide type parameters for the component's props and state:

```
import React from "react"; interface CounterProps { initialCount: number; }
interface CounterState { count: number; } class Counter extends
React.Component<CounterProps, CounterState> { // ... }
```

In this example:

1. We define `CounterProps` to specify the type of props the `Counter` component accepts.
2. We define `CounterState` to describe the shape of the component's internal state.
3. The `Counter` class extends `React.Component`, and we provide the type parameters `CounterProps` and `CounterState` to explicitly define the types of props and state.

Typing Props and State

As shown above, you use interfaces or type aliases to define the structure of props and state for your class components. This allows TypeScript to check that you're using props and state correctly throughout your component's lifecycle.

Lifecycle Methods

TypeScript provides type definitions for React's lifecycle methods. When you override these methods in your class component, TypeScript ensures that you use the correct signatures:

```
class Counter extends React.Component<CounterProps, CounterState> {
componentDidMount() { // This method is called after the component is mounted
} componentDidUpdate(prevProps: CounterProps, prevState: CounterState) { //
This method is called after the component updates } }
```

Event Handlers

Event handlers in class components are typically defined as methods. TypeScript provides type definitions for React events (e.g., `React.MouseEvent`, `React.KeyboardEvent`), allowing you to accurately type your event handlers:

```
class Button extends React.Component { handleClick(event:
React.MouseEvent<HTMLButtonElement>) { // ... event handling logic ... }
render() { return <button onClick={this.handleClick}>Click me!</button>; } }
```

In this example, the handleClick method takes a `React.MouseEvent<HTMLButtonElement>` argument, which gives you type-safe access to the mouse event object and the button element that was clicked.

Key Points

- Class components extend the `React.Component` class with type parameters for props and state.
- Use interfaces or type aliases to define the types for props and state.
- TypeScript provides type definitions for React's lifecycle methods and events.

Note: Class components are becoming less common in React, but they still have their place in certain situations. If you're working with a legacy codebase or need specific features like error boundaries, understanding how to use class components with TypeScript is still valuable.

Props and State

In React, components manage two types of data: props (external input) and state (internal data). TypeScript helps you ensure the integrity of this data by allowing you to define precise types for both props and state. Let's explore the best practices for typing props and state in both function and class components.

Function Components

1. Interfaces:

Interfaces are the most common way to define the shape of your component's props.

```
interface ProductProps { id: number; name: string; price: number;
description?: string; } function Product({ id, name, price, description }:
ProductProps) { // ... }
```

In this example, the `ProductProps` interface defines the properties that the `Product` component expects to receive.

2. Type Aliases:

You can also use type aliases to achieve the same result:

```
type ProductProps = { id: number; name: string; price: number; description?:
string; };
```

The choice between interfaces and type aliases is often a matter of preference.

3. Generic Components:

Generics come in handy when you want to create reusable components that can work with different types of data.

```
interface DataProps<T> { data: T; } function DataComponent<T>({ data }:
DataProps<T>) { // ... }
```

In this example, the `DataComponent` is generic, allowing it to accept data of any type.

Class Components

Class components require you to specify types for both props and state when extending the `React.Component` class.

1. Interfaces or Type Aliases:

```
interface CounterProps { /* ... */ } interface CounterState { /* ... */ }
class Counter extends React.Component<CounterProps, CounterState> { // ... }
```

2. Initializing State in the Constructor:

You'll often initialize your component's state within the constructor:

```
class Counter extends React.Component<CounterProps, CounterState> {
constructor(props: CounterProps) { super(props); this.state = { count:
props.initialCount }; } // ... }
```

Best Practices

- **Be Explicit:** Always define types for your props and state, even if TypeScript can infer them. This makes your code more self-documenting and helps catch potential errors early.
- **Use Interfaces or Type Aliases:** Both interfaces and type aliases work well for defining prop types. Choose the one that suits your style and project conventions.

- **Leverage Generics:** Consider using generics for reusable components that can handle different data types.
- **Optional Properties:** Mark props as optional using the ? symbol if they might not always be provided.
- **Default Props:** Define default props using the `defaultProps` static property (for function components) or in the constructor (for class components).
- **Readonly Props:** Use the `readonly` modifier for props that should not be modified within the component.

Example: Complete Type Definitions

```
interface ProductProps { id: number; name: string; price: number;
description?: string; onAddToCart: (productId: number) => void; // Function
prop } function Product({ id, name, price, description, onAddToCart }:
ProductProps) { // ... (component logic) ... }
```

In this example, we define the `Product` component with types for all props, including a function prop (`onAddToCart`) that is called when the "Add to Cart" button is clicked.

By diligently typing your props and state, you'll unlock the full power of TypeScript's type checking and inference, leading to React components that are not only more reliable and maintainable but also a joy to work with.

TypeScript with JSX

Typing JSX Elements

JSX (JavaScript XML) is a syntax extension that allows you to write HTML-like code within your JavaScript or TypeScript files. TypeScript understands and provides type checking for JSX, ensuring that you use elements and attributes correctly.

Intrinsic Elements and Their Interfaces

In JSX, intrinsic elements are the standard HTML elements you're familiar with, such as `div`, `button`, `span`, `input`, `h1`, etc. TypeScript defines interfaces for each of these intrinsic elements, specifying the valid attributes (props) and their types.

Example:

```
import React from "react"; function MyComponent() { const name: string =
"Alice"; const age: number = 30; return ( <div> <h1 className="heading">Hello,
{name}!</h1> <p>You are {age} years old.</p> <button onClick={() =>
alert("Clicked!")}>Click me</button> </div> ); }
```

In this example:

- TypeScript recognizes the intrinsic elements (`div`, `h1`, `p`, `button`).
- It infers the types of the `className` and `onClick` attributes based on the corresponding intrinsic element interfaces (e.g., `HTMLDivElement`, `HTMLButtonElement`).
- It type-checks the values you provide for these attributes (e.g., `className` must be a string, `onClick` must be a function).

- It ensures that you don't use invalid attributes for a given element (e.g., you can't use `onClick` on an h1 element).

Defining Types for JSX Props

For more complex prop types or to customize attributes, you can use interfaces or type aliases:

```
interface ButtonProps { label: string; onClick: () => void; disabled?:
boolean; } function MyButton(props: ButtonProps) { return <button
onClick={props.onClick} disabled={props.disabled}>{props.label}</button>; }
```

By utilizing these typing features, TypeScript ensures that you use the correct attributes and provide valid values, improving your code's robustness.

Key Points

- TypeScript provides type checking for JSX.
- Intrinsic elements have corresponding interfaces that define their valid attributes (props) and types.
- You can use interfaces or type aliases to define custom types for your JSX element props.

By combining the power of TypeScript with the expressive syntax of JSX, you can create type-safe and maintainable React components that are a pleasure to develop and work with.

Intrinsic Elements

TypeScript provides a comprehensive set of interfaces that correspond to the standard HTML elements you use in JSX. These interfaces define the valid attributes (props) and their types for each element, ensuring type safety when you work with JSX in your TypeScript code.

Where to Find Intrinsic Element Interfaces

You can find the complete list of intrinsic element interfaces in the official TypeScript documentation:

JSX in the TypeScript Handbook: https://www.typescriptlang.org/docs/handbook/jsx.html

This section of the handbook provides a detailed explanation of how TypeScript handles JSX and lists all the available intrinsic element interfaces.

`JSX.IntrinsicElements` Interface

The `JSX.IntrinsicElements` interface acts as a namespace for all the intrinsic element interfaces. For example, if you want to know the valid props for an `input` element, you can refer to `JSX.IntrinsicElements["input"]`.

Example:

```
import React from "react"; function MyComponent() { return ( <div> <input
type="text" placeholder="Enter your name" /> </div> ); }
```

If you need more information for this you can visit the TypeScript documentation linked above for more detailed information on the specific types and properties of each element.

Custom Components

While React's intrinsic elements (like `div` and `button`) have their own built-in TypeScript definitions, you'll likely create your own custom components to encapsulate reusable UI logic. Let's explore how TypeScript helps you define and use these custom components in a type-safe manner.

Typing Custom Component Props

The same principles we used for typing function components apply to custom components as well. You'll typically use an interface or a type alias to define the structure of your component's props.

Example: `Button` Component

```
interface ButtonProps { label: string; onClick?: () => void; disabled?:
boolean; } function Button({ label, onClick, disabled }: ButtonProps) { return
( <button onClick={onClick} disabled={disabled}> {label} </button> ); }
```

In this example, the `ButtonProps` interface clearly defines the expected props for the `Button` component. TypeScript will then ensure that you use the component correctly by passing in props of the right types.

Typing Children (Optional)

If your component accepts children, you can use the `ReactNode` type to represent any valid React child (elements, strings, numbers, etc.):

```
interface CardProps { title: string; children: React.ReactNode; } function
Card({ title, children }: CardProps) { return ( <div className="card">
<h2>{title}</h2> {children} </div> ); }
```

Generic Components for Flexibility

If you need to create a component that can accept different types of children or props, you can leverage generics:

```
interface ListProps<T> { items: T[]; renderItem: (item: T) => React.ReactNode;
} function List<T>({ items, renderItem }: ListProps<T>) { return ( <ul>
{items.map((item, index) => ( <li key={index}>{renderItem(item)}</li> ))}
</ul> ); }
```

The `List` component in this example can be used to render lists of any data type, as long as you provide a `renderItem` function that knows how to render individual items of that type.

The Importance of Type-Safe Component Libraries

Creating reusable, type-safe components is a core aspect of building maintainable React applications. By defining clear interfaces for your components' props, you establish a contract that ensures they are used correctly.

Here's why it matters:

- **Easier Collaboration:** When working in teams, type-safe components provide clarity about how to use and interact with them. This reduces misunderstandings and makes collaboration smoother.
- **Reduced Errors:** TypeScript catches errors related to incorrect prop types during development, preventing them from causing runtime failures.

- **Improved Refactoring:** Changing the props of a component becomes safer with TypeScript, as it will alert you to any breaking changes in other parts of your code that use that component.
- **Better Documentation:** Type annotations act as a form of documentation, making your components more self-explanatory and easier for other developers to understand.

By investing time in creating type-safe component libraries, you create a foundation for building scalable, maintainable, and reliable React applications in TypeScript.

React Hooks

useState

The `useState` hook is a cornerstone of state management in React function components. TypeScript enhances its capabilities by allowing you to explicitly define types for the state variable and the function used to update it. This ensures type safety and prevents errors that could arise from accidental type mismatches.

Basic Usage

The general syntax for using `useState` with TypeScript is:

```
const [state, setState] = useState<Type>(initialValue);
```

Here's how it breaks down:

- **`state`:** The current state value. Its type is inferred from the `initialValue` or explicitly specified with the type argument <Type>.
- **`setState`:** A function to update the state. TypeScript infers its type based on the <Type> you provide.
- **`useState<Type>(initialValue)`:** The `useState` hook call. You provide:
    - **<Type> (Optional):** The explicit type of your state.
    - **`initialValue`:** The initial value for the state.

Example: Counter Component

```
import React, { useState } from 'react'; function Counter() { const [count,
setCount] = useState<number>(0); // State is explicitly typed as number const
increment = () => { setCount(count + 1); }; return ( <div> <p>Count:
{count}</p> <button onClick={increment}>Increment</button> </div> ); }
```

In this example:

- `count` is a state variable of type `number`, initialized to 0.
- `setCount` is a function that updates the `count` state. TypeScript infers its type as `React.Dispatch<React.SetStateAction<number>>`.
- The `increment` function correctly calls `setCount` with a number, ensuring type safety.

Type Inference vs. Explicit Types

TypeScript is often smart enough to infer the type of your state based on the initial value. However, it's generally considered a best practice to explicitly provide the type argument to `useState`. This makes your code more self-documenting and can prevent issues when the initial value doesn't fully convey the type (e.g., when the initial value is `null` or `undefined`).

Example: State as an Object

```
interface User { name: string; email: string; } function Profile() { const [user, setUser] = useState<User>({ name: "", email: "" }); // ... }
```

Here, the `user` state is explicitly typed as the `User` interface, ensuring that it always has the correct properties and types.

Key Points

- Use the `useState` hook to manage state in function components.
- Explicitly provide the type argument to `useState` for better type safety and documentation.
- TypeScript infers the setter function's type based on the state type.
- You can use interfaces, type aliases, or even primitive types to define your state.

By leveraging TypeScript's type system with `useState`, you ensure that your state variables and updates are type-safe, leading to more reliable and easier-to-maintain React components.

useEffect

The `useEffect` hook is your tool for handling side effects in React function components. Side effects are operations that interact with the outside world, such as fetching data, updating the DOM, or setting up subscriptions. Let's explore how to use `useEffect` effectively with TypeScript while ensuring type safety and avoiding unnecessary re-renders.

Basic Usage

The general syntax of `useEffect` in TypeScript is:

```
useEffect(() => { // Side effect logic here }, [dependencies]); // Dependency array (optional)
```

Here's a breakdown:

1. **Effect Function:** The first argument to `useEffect` is a function that contains your side effect logic. This function is called after the component renders.
2. **Dependency Array (Optional):** The second argument is an array that lists the variables (dependencies) that the effect depends on. When any of these dependencies change, React will re-execute the effect function. If you omit the dependency array, the effect will run after every render.

Example: Fetching Data

```
import React, { useState, useEffect } from 'react'; function DataFetcher() { const [data, setData] = useState<string | null>(null); useEffect(() => { fetch('/api/data') .then(response => response.text()) .then(setData); }, []); // Empty dependency array: runs only once after initial render return <div>{data}</div>; }
```

In this example, the effect fetches data from an API and updates the `data` state. The empty dependency array [ ] ensures that the effect only runs once, after the initial render.

Typing the Dependency Array

TypeScript requires the dependency array to be an array of values that are used within the effect function. This helps prevent bugs where dependencies are accidentally omitted, leading to unexpected behavior.

```
let someExternalValue = "initial value"; useEffect(() => {
console.log(someExternalValue); }, [someExternalValue]); // Correct typing
```

Avoiding Unnecessary Re-renders

Carefully consider which values you include in the dependency array. Adding unnecessary dependencies will cause the effect to re-execute more often than needed, potentially impacting performance.

```
let counter = 0; function MyComponent() { useEffect(() => { const timer =
setInterval(() => { counter++; // Incorrect: this will create an infinite
re-render loop }, 1000); return () => clearInterval(timer); }, []); // Empty
dependency array is appropriate here }
```

In this example, `counter` is not a dependency of the effect, as the effect is only concerned with setting up and clearing the interval. Including `counter` in the dependency array would lead to an infinite loop of re-renders.

Key Points

- Use `useEffect` for handling side effects in function components.
- The first argument is a function that contains the side effect logic.
- The second (optional) argument is a dependency array that controls when the effect re-runs.
- An empty array (`[]`) means the effect runs only once after the initial render.
- Be mindful of which values you include in the dependency array to avoid unnecessary re-renders.
- TypeScript helps ensure type safety by requiring the dependency array to match the types used within the effect.

By understanding how to use `useEffect` effectively with TypeScript, you can manage side effects in your React components while maintaining type safety and optimizing performance.

useContext

The `useContext` hook in React is a convenient way to share data across components without manually passing props through multiple levels of the component tree. TypeScript adds a layer of type safety to this process, ensuring that you access context values with the correct types.

1. Defining the Context

First, you create a context object using `React.createContext`. You provide a default value for the context, which is used when a component doesn't have a matching provider above it.

```
import React, { createContext, useContext } from "react"; interface
ThemeContextProps { theme: string; toggleTheme: () => void; } const
ThemeContext = createContext<ThemeContextProps>({ theme: "light", // Default
value toggleTheme: () => {}, // Default no-op function });
```

Here, we create a `ThemeContext` that defines its properties (`theme` and `toggleTheme`) along with their types.

2. Providing the Context

Next, you use the ThemeContext.Provider component to wrap the parts of your component tree that need access to the context values. You pass the actual context values as the value prop of the Provider.

```
function App() { const [theme, setTheme] = useState<string>("light"); const
toggleTheme = () => { setTheme(theme === "light" ? "dark" : "light"); };
return ( <ThemeContext.Provider value={{ theme, toggleTheme }}> {/* Your
component tree goes here */} </ThemeContext.Provider> ); }
```

In this example:

- We use the useState hook to manage the theme state within the App component.
- The toggleTheme function updates the theme when called.
- The ThemeContext.Provider component wraps the rest of the application, making the theme and toggleTheme values available to any child component that uses the useContext hook.

3. Consuming the Context

Finally, you use the useContext hook within any child component to access the context values:

```
function Button() { const { theme, toggleTheme } = useContext(ThemeContext);
// Get context values return <button onClick={toggleTheme}>{theme === "light"
? "Dark Mode" : "Light Mode"}</button>; }
```

By passing in ThemeContext to the useContext hook we can directly access the context values (theme and toggleTheme) within this function component. **Type Safety with useContext**

The magic of TypeScript shines here:

- TypeScript infers the types of theme and toggleTheme based on the type you provided when creating the ThemeContext.
- If you try to use these values in ways that don't match their types, TypeScript will raise a type error.

Key Points

- Use React.createContext to create a context object with a default value.
- Use Context.Provider to wrap the components that need access to the context.
- Use the useContext hook to access the context values within your components.
- TypeScript ensures type safety by inferring types from the context definition.

By understanding how to use useContext with TypeScript, you can create well-organized React applications where data is shared efficiently and type-safely across components. This leads to a more predictable and maintainable codebase.

Custom Hooks

Custom hooks are a powerful feature in React that let you extract component logic into reusable functions. TypeScript complements this functionality by ensuring that your custom hooks are type-safe, making them easier to use and maintain.

Creating Custom Hooks

A custom hook is simply a JavaScript function whose name starts with "use". Inside this function, you can use other React hooks (like `useState`, `useEffect`, or `useContext`) to manage state, side effects, or access context.

Example: `useCounter` Hook

```
import { useState } from "react"; function useCounter(initialValue: number = 0): [number, () => void, () => void] { const [count, setCount] = useState(initialValue); const increment = () => setCount(count + 1); const decrement = () => setCount(count - 1); return [count, increment, decrement]; }
```

In this example:

- The `useCounter` hook takes an optional `initialValue` (defaulting to 0).
- It uses the `useState` hook to manage a `count` state variable.
- It defines two functions, `increment` and `decrement`, to update the count.
- It returns an array containing the current `count`, the `increment` function, and the `decrement` function.

Using the `useCounter` Hook

```
function MyComponent() { const [count, increment, decrement] = useCounter(10); // Initial value of 10 return ( <div> <p>Count: {count}</p> <button onClick={decrement}>Decrement</button> <button onClick={increment}>Increment</button> </div> ); }
```

Typing Custom Hooks

To ensure type safety, it's crucial to type your custom hook's arguments and return values:

- **Arguments:** Define an interface or type alias for the arguments.
- **Return Value:** Specify the type of the value(s) that your hook returns. This could be a single value, an array, an object, or even a function.

Best Practices

- **Naming:** Follow the "use" prefix convention (e.g., `useFetchData`, `useLocalStorage`).
- **Single Responsibility:** Each custom hook should ideally focus on a single piece of logic or functionality.
- **Type Safety:** Always provide type annotations for your hook's arguments and return value.
- **Testing:** Write tests for your custom hooks to ensure their correctness and reliability.
- **Documentation:** Clearly document your custom hooks, explaining their purpose, usage, and any potential caveats.

Example: `useFetch` Hook

```
import { useState, useEffect } from "react"; interface FetchDataResult<T> { data: T | null; isLoading: boolean; error: Error | null; } function useFetch<T>(url: string): FetchDataResult<T> { const [data, setData] = useState<T | null>(null); const [isLoading, setIsLoading] = useState(true); const [error, setError] = useState<Error | null>(null); useEffect(() => { fetch(url) .then(res => res.json()) .then(setData) .catch(setError)
```

```
.finally(() => setIsLoading(false)); }, [url]); return { data, isLoading, error }; }
```

This useFetch hook fetches data from a URL and returns an object with the fetched data, a loading state, and an error state. It is type-safe, allowing you to specify the expected type of the data.

By following these best practices and leveraging TypeScript's type system, you can create custom hooks that are not only reusable and powerful but also safe and predictable. This will greatly enhance your React development experience and the quality of your applications.

TypeScript with React Router

Defining Routes and Links

React Router is the go-to library for implementing navigation and routing in React applications. TypeScript enhances the React Router experience by providing type safety for your routes and links, ensuring that you navigate to valid locations and access route parameters with the correct types.

Setting Up React Router

Before you start, make sure you have React Router and its type definitions installed in your project:

```
npm install react-router-dom @types/react-router-dom
```

Defining Routes with `Route`

The `Route` component is the heart of React Router. It renders a component when the current location matches the specified path.

```
import { BrowserRouter, Routes, Route } from 'react-router-dom'; function App() { return ( <BrowserRouter> <Routes> <Route path="/" element={<Home />} /> <Route path="/about" element={<About />} /> <Route path="/products/:id" element={<ProductDetail />} /> </Routes> </BrowserRouter> ); }
```

In this example:

- We use `BrowserRouter` to enable routing within our app.
- The `Routes` component acts as a container for all the `Route` components.
- We define three routes:
    - `/`: Renders the `Home` component.
    - `/about`: Renders the `About` component.
    - `/products/:id`: Renders the `ProductDetail` component and captures the product ID as a route parameter.

Creating Links with `Link`

The `Link` component is used to create navigational links in your application. When clicked, it changes the current location and triggers the rendering of the corresponding `Route` component.

```
import { Link } from 'react-router-dom'; function Navigation() { return ( <nav> <Link to="/">Home</Link> <Link to="/about">About</Link> </nav> ); }
```

Type Safety with React Router

TypeScript and React Router work together seamlessly to provide type safety:

- **Route Props:** TypeScript can infer the types of props passed to the `element` prop of a `Route` component based on the component's type definition. This ensures that you pass the correct data to your route components.
- **Link Props:** TypeScript enforces that the `to` prop of a `Link` component is a valid route path, preventing you from linking to non-existent routes.

Additional Tips

- **Nested Routes:** React Router allows you to create nested routes using the `Outlet` component. This enables you to build more complex navigation structures.
- **Dynamic Routing:** You can create dynamic routes that match patterns using wildcards or parameters. We'll cover this in more detail in the next section.
- **Navigation Guards:** You can use React Router hooks like `useNavigate` and `useLocation` to programmatically navigate and access location information within your components.

By combining React Router's routing capabilities with TypeScript's type safety, you can build robust and user-friendly navigation experiences for your React applications.

Type Safety with Route Parameters

React Router's dynamic segments allow you to capture values from the URL and use them as parameters in your components. TypeScript provides tools to ensure that you access these route parameters with the correct types, preventing unexpected errors and enhancing your development experience.

1. Typing Route Parameters with `useParams` Hook

The `useParams` hook from React Router returns an object of key/value pairs representing the dynamic params from the current URL. You can provide a type argument to `useParams` to define the expected shape of this object.

Example:

```
import { useParams } from 'react-router-dom'; interface ProductDetailParams {
id: string; } function ProductDetail() { const { id } =
useParams<ProductDetailParams>(); // Now TypeScript knows that 'id' is a
string // ... (fetch product data using id) }
```

In this example, the `ProductDetailParams` interface defines that the `id` parameter should be a string. By passing this interface to `useParams`, TypeScript ensures that you use the `id` parameter correctly within your component.

2. Generics for More Flexibility

If you have multiple routes with different parameter types, you can create a generic `Route` component to handle them:

```
interface RouteParams { [key: string]: string; // Allow any string parameters
} const TypedRoute = <T extends RouteParams>({ ...props }: RouteProps<T>) =>
<Route {...props} />;
```

Now you can use the `TypedRoute` component to define your routes with type safety:

```
<TypedRoute path="/products/:id" element={<ProductDetail />} /> <TypedRoute
path="/users/:username" element={<UserProfile />} />
```

3. String Literal Types for Exact Path Matching

If you want to enforce that a route parameter matches a specific set of values, you can use string literal types:

```
type ValidCategories = 'electronics' | 'clothing' | 'books'; function
CategoryPage() { const { category } = useParams<{ category: ValidCategories
}>(); // 'category' is now restricted to the values "electronics", "clothing",
or "books" }
```

Error Prevention and Improved Development Experience

By adding type safety to your route parameters, you gain several benefits:

- **Early Error Detection:** TypeScript will catch any attempts to access a parameter that doesn't exist or use it with the wrong type.
- **Improved Code Completion:** Your editor can provide suggestions for valid parameter names and types based on your route definitions.
- **Refactoring Safety:** If you change the parameter name or type in a route, TypeScript will help you update all references throughout your code.

Key Points

- Use the `useParams` hook to access route parameters in function components.
- Provide a type argument to `useParams` to define the expected shape of the parameter object.
- Use generics to create reusable route components that handle different parameter types.
- Utilize string literal types to restrict route parameters to a specific set of valid values.

By embracing these TypeScript techniques, you ensure that your React Router routes and parameters are handled in a type-safe manner, leading to more reliable and easier-to-maintain applications.

Advanced Topics

Context API with TypeScript

The Context API in React provides a convenient way to share data across your component tree without the need to pass props through every level. When combined with TypeScript, you can add type safety to your context, ensuring that your components access the correct data types and preventing potential errors.

1. Creating a Context Object

```
import React, { createContext, useContext } from "react"; interface
AuthContextValue { isAuthenticated: boolean; login: () => void; logout: () =>
void; } const AuthContext = createContext<AuthContextValue |
undefined>(undefined);
```

In this example, we define an interface `AuthContextValue` that describes the shape of the context data:

- `isAuthenticated`: A boolean indicating if the user is authenticated.
- `login` and `logout`: Functions for managing authentication state.

We then create the context object `AuthContext` using `createContext`. Notice that we provide an initial default value of `undefined`. This is important because, unlike props, context values are not always guaranteed to be available when a component renders. We can use this default value as a fallback until the context provider is rendered.

2. Context Provider

The `AuthContext.Provider` component is responsible for making the context values available to its descendants. You typically place it near the top of your component tree, wrapping the components that need access to the context data.

```
function App() { const [isAuthenticated, setIsAuthenticated] =
useState(false); const login = () => setIsAuthenticated(true); const logout =
() => setIsAuthenticated(false); return ( <AuthContext.Provider value={{
isAuthenticated, login, logout }}> {/* The rest of your app components */}
</AuthContext.Provider> ); }
```

In this simplified example, we manage the `isAuthenticated` state within the App component and pass the relevant values (`isAuthenticated`, `login`, `logout`) to the context provider.

3. Consuming the Context

Inside any component that needs to access the context values, you use the `useContext` hook:

```
function Profile() { const { isAuthenticated, login, logout } =
useContext(AuthContext)!; // Non-null assertion // Since the default value is
undefined, we need to provide a non-null assertion operator // ... use
isAuthenticated, login, and logout ... }
```

Type Safety in Action

TypeScript's type system enhances the Context API in several ways:

- **Strong Typing of Context Values:** The `AuthContextValue` interface clearly defines the types of the context data, so TypeScript will flag any errors if you try to use them incorrectly.
- **Type Inference with `useContext`:** TypeScript automatically infers the types of the values returned by `useContext`, eliminating the need for manual type annotations in most cases.
- **Avoiding "Prop Drilling":** Context helps you avoid passing props through multiple layers of components, improving code organization and maintainability.

Key Points

- Use `React.createContext` with a type parameter to define a type-safe context.
- Wrap the relevant parts of your app with `Context.Provider` to provide context values.
- Use `useContext` to access the context values within your components.
- TypeScript ensures type safety throughout the context API usage.

By embracing the Context API with TypeScript's type safety, you can effectively manage global state in your React applications while maintaining a high level of code quality and predictability.

Redux with TypeScript

Redux is a widely used state management library for JavaScript applications, including those built with React. While Redux itself doesn't enforce types, integrating it with TypeScript brings a host of benefits, enhancing your development experience and ensuring type safety throughout your Redux workflow.

Why Use TypeScript with Redux?

- **Predictability:** Defining types for your Redux state, actions, and reducers makes your code more predictable and less error-prone. TypeScript can catch type-related issues at compile time, preventing runtime errors.
- **Developer Experience:** TypeScript-aware editors provide autocompletion, type hints, and refactoring tools that significantly improve your productivity when working with Redux.
- **Self-Documenting Code:** Type annotations in your Redux code act as documentation, making it easier to understand the structure of your state, the types of actions, and the logic within your reducers.
- **Maintainability:** As your Redux codebase grows, TypeScript's type system helps you maintain consistency and prevents regressions when refactoring or adding new features.

Setting Up Redux with TypeScript

To integrate Redux with TypeScript, you'll typically follow these steps:

1. **Install Redux Toolkit:** Redux Toolkit is the recommended way to write modern Redux applications. It simplifies setup and provides convenient utilities for working with Redux.

```
npm install @reduxjs/toolkit react-redux
```

2. **Define Types:** Create TypeScript interfaces or type aliases to represent your Redux state, actions, and reducers.

```
// Example state interface interface RootState { counter: number; todos:
Todo[]; } // Example action interface interface IncrementAction { type:
'counter/increment'; payload: number; // Optional payload }
```

3. **Create a Slice:** Use the `createSlice` function from Redux Toolkit to define a "slice" of your state. A slice is a collection of reducer logic and actions for a specific feature or part of your application.

```
import { createSlice, PayloadAction } from '@reduxjs/toolkit'; const
counterSlice = createSlice({ name: 'counter', initialState: { value: 0 },
reducers: { increment(state, action: PayloadAction<number>) { state.value
+= action.payload; }, decrement(state) { state.value -= 1; }, }, });
```

- Here the slice creates an initial state, and two reducer functions.

4. **Configure the Store:** Create your Redux store using the `configureStore` function from Redux Toolkit.

```
import { configureStore } from '@reduxjs/toolkit'; import counterReducer
from './features/counter/counterSlice'; export const store =
configureStore({ reducer: { counter: counterReducer, // ...other reducers
}, });
```

- Combine the reducers into one place, then pass it to the `configureStore` function.

5. **Typing the Store and Dispatch:** Use the `RootState` and `AppDispatch` types from Redux Toolkit to get type-safe access to your store and the `dispatch` function.

```
import { TypedUseSelectorHook, useDispatch, useSelector } from
'react-redux'; import type { RootState, AppDispatch } from './store'; //
Use throughout your app instead of plain `useDispatch` and `useSelector`
export const useAppDispatch = () => useDispatch<AppDispatch>(); export
const useAppSelector: TypedUseSelectorHook<RootState> = useSelector;
```

6. **Connect with React Components:** Use the `Provider` component from `react-redux` to make the store available to your React components. Then, use the `useSelector` and `useDispatch` hooks to interact with the store.

```
import React from 'react'; import ReactDOM from 'react-dom/client';
import { Provider } from 'react-redux'; import { store } from './store';
import App from './App'; const root =
ReactDOM.createRoot(document.getElementById('root') as HTMLElement);
root.render( <React.StrictMode> <Provider store={store}> <App />
</Provider> </React.StrictMode> );
```

Key Points:

- Use TypeScript interfaces or type aliases to model your Redux state, actions, and reducers.
- Leverage Redux Toolkit's `createSlice` function to simplify slice creation.
- Use the `configureStore` function to create a typed Redux store.
- Use `useAppDispatch` and `useAppSelector` to ensure type safety when interacting with the store and dispatching actions in your React components.
- Use `Provider` from `react-redux` to make the Redux store available to your React component tree.

By integrating Redux with TypeScript, you gain a more reliable, predictable, and enjoyable state management experience for your React applications.

TypeScript and React Testing

Testing is a crucial part of any software development process, and React applications are no exception. TypeScript's static type system can greatly enhance your React testing experience by catching errors early and providing a safety net when refactoring code. Let's explore how TypeScript seamlessly integrates with popular React testing libraries.

Popular React Testing Libraries

1. **Jest:** A comprehensive JavaScript testing framework developed by Facebook. It's known for its speed, ease of use, and rich set of features, including mocking, snapshot testing, and code coverage reporting. Jest is often the default choice for testing React applications.
2. **React Testing Library (RTL):** A lightweight library focused on testing components from the user's perspective. It encourages testing practices that closely resemble how users interact with your application, leading to more reliable and user-centric tests.

Writing Type-Safe React Tests with TypeScript

Here's a breakdown of how to write type-safe tests for your React components using TypeScript and either Jest or React Testing Library:

1. **Type Definitions:** Ensure that your component props and state are properly typed using interfaces or type aliases. This allows TypeScript to check that you're passing the correct types to your components in your tests.
2. **Test Data:** Create type-safe test data that adheres to the defined prop types. This ensures that your tests accurately reflect how the component would be used in your application.
3. **Render and Assertions:** Use the testing library's functions (e.g., `render`, `screen.getByText` from RTL or `render`, `expect` from Jest) to render your component and make assertions about its output. TypeScript's type checking will help you catch errors if you try to interact with elements that don't exist or use them in unexpected ways.
4. **Mocking:** If your component interacts with external dependencies (like API calls or browser events), you can use mocking to simulate their behavior in a controlled way. TypeScript can help you type the mock objects and functions to ensure type safety in your tests.

Example: Testing a Button Component (using React Testing Library)

```
import React from "react"; import { render, fireEvent, screen } from
"@testing-library/react"; import Button from "./Button"; // Your Button
component import { ButtonProps } from "./types/components"; test("Button
renders with correct label and calls onClick when clicked", () => { const
onClickMock = jest.fn(); render(<Button label="Click Me" onClick={onClickMock}
/>); // Type-safe rendering const buttonElement = screen.getByText("Click
Me"); // Get the button by its text expect(buttonElement).toBeInTheDocument();
fireEvent.click(buttonElement); expect(onClickMock).toHaveBeenCalledTimes(1);
// Check if onClick was called });
```

- In this example, we define an interface `ButtonProps` to describe the types for the button component, and use it when we call the `render` function.

Key Points

- TypeScript enhances React testing by providing type safety for props, state, and other elements.
- Use TypeScript's type definitions to ensure that your test data and interactions with components are correct.
- Choose a testing library (like Jest or React Testing Library) that works well with TypeScript.
- Use mocking to simulate external dependencies and ensure type safety in your tests.

By incorporating TypeScript into your React testing workflow, you create a robust safety net that catches errors early on and gives you confidence that your components are working as expected. This leads to higher quality React applications that are easier to maintain and extend.

Chapter Summary

In this chapter, we explored the powerful synergy between TypeScript and React, discovering how to build type-safe and maintainable user interfaces. Here's a recap of the key points:

- **Why TypeScript and React are a Perfect Match:** We discussed how TypeScript's static type system complements React's component-based architecture, leading to improved code quality, developer experience, and maintainability.
- **Setting Up a TypeScript React Project:** We covered two approaches:

- **Create React App with TypeScript:** A streamlined way to bootstrap a new project with built-in TypeScript support.
- **Manual Setup:** For those seeking more control, we outlined the steps involved in configuring a project from scratch, including installing dependencies and setting up the TypeScript compiler and build process.

- **TypeScript in React Components:** We delved into how to write both function and class components with TypeScript, covering:
    - **Typing Props and State:** Using interfaces, type aliases, and generics to define the shape of your component's data.
    - **Lifecycle Methods and Event Handlers:** Ensuring type safety for these methods with TypeScript's type definitions for React events.
- **TypeScript with JSX:** We explained how TypeScript handles JSX elements, including intrinsic elements and custom components. We discussed how to define types for JSX props and children.
- **React Hooks:** We showed how to use popular React hooks like `useState`, `useEffect`, and `useContext` in a type-safe manner, ensuring that state variables and effects are handled correctly. We also provided a guide on creating custom hooks with proper TypeScript typing.
- **TypeScript with React Router:** We demonstrated how to define routes and links using React Router with TypeScript, emphasizing how type safety applies to route parameters and navigation.
- **Advanced Topics:** We briefly touched upon using the Context API and Redux with TypeScript for state management, as well as how to write type-safe tests for your React components.

By following the practices and techniques outlined in this chapter, you are now equipped to build React applications that are not only robust and scalable but also enjoyable to develop thanks to the power of TypeScript's type system. The combination of React's component-based architecture and TypeScript's static typing enables you to create modern user interfaces with confidence, knowing that your code is more predictable, maintainable, and less error-prone.

As you continue your TypeScript journey, you'll discover even more advanced techniques and patterns for building sophisticated React applications. Embrace the type safety and tooling support that TypeScript offers, and watch your productivity and code quality soar to new heights.

TypeScript with Node.js: Building Robust Backends

Outline

- Introduction
    - Node.js: The JavaScript Runtime for the Server
    - Why TypeScript is Ideal for Node.js Development
- Setting Up a TypeScript Node.js Project
    - Project Initialization
    - Installing Dependencies
    - Configuring TypeScript
- Building a Simple API
    - Express.js: The Web Framework
    - Defining Routes and Controllers
    - Handling Requests and Responses
- Type Safety in Node.js with TypeScript
    - Request and Response Types
    - Middleware with TypeScript
    - Error Handling
- Working with Databases
    - Connecting to MongoDB with Mongoose
    - Defining Data Models and Schemas
- Authentication and Authorization
    - Implementing Authentication Middleware
    - Protecting Routes
- Advanced Topics
    - WebSockets with Socket.IO and TypeScript
    - GraphQL APIs with TypeScript
    - Serverless Functions with TypeScript
- Chapter Summary

Introduction

Node.js: The JavaScript Runtime for the Server

In the early days of the web, JavaScript was confined to the browser, where it primarily enhanced user interfaces and added interactivity to web pages. Node.js revolutionized this landscape by bringing JavaScript to the server-side, opening up a whole new world of possibilities for backend development.

What is Node.js?

At its core, Node.js is a runtime environment that allows you to execute JavaScript code outside of a web browser. This means you can now use JavaScript to build a wide range of server-side applications, including:

- **Web Servers:** Node.js can handle incoming HTTP requests, serve web pages, and manage server-side logic.
- **APIs (Application Programming Interfaces):** Node.js is well-suited for building RESTful APIs that provide data and services to other applications.

- **Microservices:** Node.js's lightweight and scalable nature makes it an excellent choice for building microservices architectures.
- **Real-time Applications:** With its event-driven model and support for WebSockets, Node.js excels at creating real-time applications like chat apps, collaborative tools, and live dashboards.
- **Command-Line Tools:** Node.js can be used to build powerful command-line tools for automating tasks, managing projects, or interacting with APIs.

Event-Driven, Non-Blocking Architecture

The secret sauce behind Node.js's efficiency is its event-driven, non-blocking architecture. Unlike traditional server-side technologies that might create a new thread for each incoming request, Node.js uses a single thread to handle multiple requests concurrently.

Here's how it works:

1. **Event Loop:** Node.js has an event loop that constantly listens for events (like incoming requests, timers, or file system operations).
2. **Callback Functions:** When an event occurs, Node.js calls the associated callback function to handle the event.
3. **Non-Blocking Operations:** For operations that take time (like network requests or file I/O), Node.js doesn't wait for them to complete. It registers a callback and moves on to the next event. When the operation finishes, its callback is added to the event queue, and the event loop eventually picks it up and executes it.

This non-blocking approach allows Node.js to handle a large number of concurrent connections with high efficiency, making it ideal for applications that require real-time responsiveness and scalability.

Popularity of Node.js

Node.js has gained immense popularity due to several factors:

- **JavaScript Everywhere:** It allows developers to use the same language (JavaScript) for both frontend and backend development, streamlining the development process and improving team collaboration.
- **High Performance:** Its event-driven architecture makes it incredibly efficient at handling concurrent requests.
- **Vast Ecosystem:** Node.js boasts a massive ecosystem of packages and libraries (available through npm) that cover a wide range of functionalities, making it easy to build complex applications quickly.
- **Active Community:** It has a large and active community of developers who contribute to its growth and provide support.

In the following sections, we'll see how TypeScript seamlessly integrates with Node.js, bringing the benefits of type safety and improved tooling to server-side development. Get ready to build robust, scalable, and type-safe backend applications with TypeScript and Node.js!

Why TypeScript is Ideal for Node.js Development

While Node.js empowers you to leverage JavaScript's versatility on the server, TypeScript supercharges this experience by addressing some of JavaScript's inherent weaknesses. Let's delve into why TypeScript has become the preferred choice for many Node.js developers.

1. Type Safety: Your Early Warning System

JavaScript's dynamic nature, where variables can hold values of any type, can lead to runtime errors that are often difficult to track down. TypeScript's static type system acts as an early warning system, catching type-related errors during development.

Imagine a function that expects a numeric ID but receives a string. In JavaScript, this might silently fail or cause unexpected behavior at runtime. With TypeScript, the compiler would immediately flag this as an error, saving you from debugging nightmares and potential crashes in production.

2. Enhanced Tooling: Your Productivity Booster

Modern code editors and IDEs (Integrated Development Environments) with TypeScript support provide a wealth of features that enhance your Node.js development workflow:

- **Intelligent Code Completion (IntelliSense):** Get suggestions for variables, functions, classes, and their types as you type, reducing typos and speeding up development.
- **Type Hints:** Hover over variables or function calls to see their types, making your code self-documenting and easier to understand.
- **Refactoring Tools:** Rename variables, extract functions, and perform other refactorings with confidence, as TypeScript helps you identify and update all references throughout your code.
- **Go-to Definition:** Quickly jump to the definition of a variable, function, or class, even in large codebases, saving you valuable time navigating through files.

3. Scalability: Taming the Complexity

As your Node.js projects grow in size and complexity, managing the codebase can become a daunting task. TypeScript's type system helps you impose structure and order on your code, making it easier to reason about, maintain, and extend.

With TypeScript, you can define clear interfaces and types for your data models, API responses, and other components of your application. This helps prevent inconsistencies and ensures that different parts of your code work together seamlessly.

4. Maintainability: Building for the Future

TypeScript code is inherently more self-documenting than plain JavaScript. The presence of type annotations clarifies the expected data types for variables, function arguments, and return values. This makes it easier for new developers to understand your code and for you to revisit it after a long time.

Moreover, TypeScript's type system acts as a safety net when refactoring or making changes. If your modifications introduce type inconsistencies, the compiler will alert you, preventing errors and regressions.

Example: Type-Safe API Endpoint

```
import express from "express"; const app = express(); app.get("/users/:id",
(req, res) => { const userId: number = parseInt(req.params.id); // Explicitly
parse the ID as a number // ... (fetch user data from database using userId)
});
```

In this example, by explicitly defining the type of `userId` as `number` and using `parseInt` to convert the string parameter from the request, we ensure type safety and prevent errors that might arise if the ID is used as a string in database queries or other operations.

Key Points

- TypeScript provides type safety, catching errors during development and leading to more reliable Node.js applications.
- TypeScript-aware editors offer enhanced tooling support, improving developer productivity.
- TypeScript helps manage the complexity of large-scale Node.js projects.
- TypeScript code is more self-documenting and maintainable due to explicit type annotations.

By combining the power and flexibility of Node.js with the type safety and structure of TypeScript, you create a winning formula for building robust, scalable, and maintainable backend applications.

Setting Up a TypeScript Node.js Project

Project Initialization

Before we dive into building the backend, let's get your TypeScript Node.js project off the ground. You can use either npm (Node Package Manager) or yarn as your package manager for this process.

Using npm

1. **Create a Project Directory:** Open your terminal or command prompt and create a new directory for your project:
   `mkdir my-nodejs-app # Replace 'my-nodejs-app' with your desired project name cd my-nodejs-app`
2. **Initialize the Project:** Run the following command to initialize a new Node.js project:
   `npm init -y`
   The `-y` flag accepts all the default options, quickly creating a `package.json` file that will store your project's metadata and dependencies.

Using yarn

1. **Create a Project Directory:** (Same as step 1 for npm)
2. **Initialize the Project:**
   `yarn init -y`
   Similar to npm, this command initializes the project and creates a `package.json` file.

What's in the `package.json` File?

The `package.json` file contains important information about your project, such as:

- **`name`:** The name of your project.
- **`version`:** The current version of your project.
- **`description`:** A brief description of your project.
- **`main`:** The entry point file for your project (usually `index.js` or similar).
- **`scripts`:** Commands that you can run to perform tasks like starting the server, building your project, or running tests.
- **`dependencies`:** Packages that your project needs to run in production.
- **`devDependencies`:** Packages that are only needed during development (e.g., TypeScript compiler, testing frameworks).

Key Points

- You can use either npm or yarn to initialize and manage your Node.js projects.
- The `npm init -y` or `yarn init -y` commands create a `package.json` file that stores project metadata and dependencies.
- This `package.json` file will be crucial for installing TypeScript and other dependencies later.

Now that your project is initialized, you're ready to take the next step: installing the essential dependencies for your TypeScript Node.js backend.

Installing Dependencies

Now that you have a Node.js project initialized, let's equip it with the essential tools and libraries you'll need for your TypeScript Node.js backend.

1. TypeScript (`typescript`)

The heart of our backend is, of course, TypeScript itself. Since you already have Node.js and npm (or yarn) installed, installing TypeScript is a breeze:

```
npm install --save-dev typescript # or yarn add --dev typescript
```

The `--save-dev` flag indicates that TypeScript is a development dependency, meaning it's used for compiling your code but isn't needed in the production environment.

2. Node.js Type Definitions (`@types/node`)

To get TypeScript's type checking and autocompletion benefits when working with Node.js's built-in modules (like `fs`, `http`, `path`), you'll need the type definitions for Node.js:

```
npm install --save-dev @types/node # or yarn add --dev @types/node
```

These definitions provide TypeScript with information about the types of objects, functions, and variables in Node.js, enabling accurate type checking and improved developer experience.

3. Express.js (`express`)

Express.js is a minimalist and flexible web framework for Node.js. It provides a solid foundation for building web servers, APIs, and other backend applications. Let's add it to our project:

```
npm install express # or yarn add express
```

4. Express.js Type Definitions (`@types/express`)

To leverage TypeScript's type checking when working with Express.js, install the type definitions for Express:

```
npm install --save-dev @types/express # or yarn add --dev @types/express
```

5. Other Dependencies (As Needed)

Depending on the specific requirements of your project, you might need to install additional dependencies:

- **Database Drivers:** If your backend interacts with a database, install the appropriate driver for your database (e.g., `mongoose` for MongoDB, pg for PostgreSQL).
- **Middleware:** Express.js supports a wide range of middleware for handling tasks like authentication, logging, body parsing, and more. Install the middleware you need (e.g., `cors`, `helmet`, `body-parser`, `passport`).
- **Utility Libraries:** You might find other utility libraries helpful, such as `lodash` for general-purpose functions, `winston` for logging, or `dotenv` for managing environment variables.

Key Points

- Install TypeScript and its type definitions for Node.js as development dependencies.
- Install Express.js as a dependency, along with its type definitions.
- Install other dependencies based on your project's specific needs.

With these dependencies installed, you have a solid foundation for building a robust and type-safe Node.js backend using TypeScript. Next, we'll explore how to configure TypeScript for Node.js development.

Configuring TypeScript

The `tsconfig.json` file is the heart of your TypeScript configuration. It provides instructions to the TypeScript compiler (`tsc`) on how to transpile your code into JavaScript and offers a range of options to tailor the build process to your specific Node.js environment.

Creating the `tsconfig.json` File

If you haven't already created a `tsconfig.json` file, the easiest way is to use the TypeScript compiler itself:

```
tsc --init
```

This will generate a basic `tsconfig.json` file in your project's root directory with sensible default options.

Essential Configuration Options

Here are some key options you'll want to configure within the `"compilerOptions"` section for Node.js development:

- **`module`:** Specifies the module system to use. For Node.js, the recommended choices are:
  - **CommonJS:** The traditional module system used by Node.js (prior to the introduction of ES Modules).
  - **ESNext (or ES2020, etc.):** Use this for the newer ES Modules (ESM) standard if you're targeting modern Node.js versions that support it.
- **`target`:** Specifies the version of JavaScript that TypeScript should generate as output. For Node.js, you'll typically choose:
  - **ES6 (or newer):** This enables you to use modern JavaScript features while still being compatible with a wide range of Node.js versions.
- **`outDir`:** Specifies the directory where the compiled JavaScript files will be placed. It's common to use a directory like `dist` or `build` to keep your source code (`src`) and compiled output separate.
- **`rootDir`:** Specifies the root directory of your TypeScript source files. This is usually the `src` directory.
- **`strict` (Highly Recommended):** Turning on strict mode enables all strict type-checking options, leading to more robust and predictable code.

Example `tsconfig.json` for Node.js

```
{ "compilerOptions": { "target": "ES2020", "module": "CommonJS", "outDir":
"./dist", "rootDir": "./src", "strict": true, "esModuleInterop": true } }
```

Additional Options

TypeScript offers a wealth of other configuration options to fine-tune your build process. Some you might consider include:

- **`allowJs`:** Allow JavaScript files to be compiled.
- **`noImplicitAny`:** Raise errors on implicitly typed any values.
- **`removeComments`:** Remove comments from the output.

- **`sourceMap`:** Generate source maps for debugging.

Key Points

- The `tsconfig.json` file controls how the TypeScript compiler behaves.
- Set the `module` and `target` options appropriately for your Node.js environment.
- Use `outDir` to specify the output directory and `rootDir` for your source directory.
- Enable `strict` mode for enhanced type checking.
- Explore other options to customize your build process.

By understanding and configuring the `tsconfig.json` file, you gain control over how TypeScript compiles your code, ensuring that it aligns with your project's requirements and produces optimized JavaScript output for your Node.js backend.

Building a Simple API

Express.js: The Web Framework

When it comes to building web applications and APIs with Node.js, Express.js reigns supreme. It's a minimalist, flexible, and unopinionated framework that provides just the right amount of structure and tools to get you started quickly without sacrificing control or performance.

Core Concepts

Express.js is designed around a few key concepts:

1. **Middleware:** Functions that have access to the request and response objects and can perform various tasks, such as parsing request bodies, handling authentication, logging, or modifying headers. Think of middleware as a series of filters or layers that your requests pass through before reaching their final destination.
2. **Routing:** The mechanism for defining how your application responds to client requests for specific endpoints (URLs) and HTTP methods (GET, POST, PUT, DELETE, etc.). Express.js provides a simple and intuitive API for defining routes and their associated handlers.
3. **Request and Response Objects:** The `request` object (`req`) contains information about the incoming request, such as the URL, headers, query parameters, and body. The `response` object (`res`) is used to send a response back to the client, including the status code, headers, and the response body.

Minimalist and Flexible

Express.js intentionally doesn't include a lot of built-in features. This keeps it lightweight and allows you to choose the libraries and tools that best fit your needs. You can add features like templating engines, database integrations, and authentication mechanisms as needed through middleware or additional libraries.

Example: A Basic Express.js Server

```
import express from "express"; import type { Request, Response } from
'express'; const app = express(); const port = 3000; app.get('/', (req:
Request, res: Response) => { res.send('Hello, TypeScript with Express!'); });
app.listen(port, () => { console.log(`Server running at
http://localhost:${port}/`); });
```

In this example:

1. We import the `express` module.
2. We create an Express.js application using `express()`.
3. We define a route handler for the root path (`/`) that sends a "Hello, TypeScript with Express!" message as the response.
4. We start the server to listen on port 3000.

Key Points

- Express.js is a minimalist web framework for Node.js.
- It uses middleware, routing, and request/response objects to handle HTTP requests.
- Its flexibility allows you to customize it to fit your specific needs.

Defining Routes and Controllers

In Express.js, routes determine how your application responds to client requests for specific endpoints (URLs) and HTTP methods (GET, POST, PUT, DELETE, etc.). Controllers, on the other hand, are classes or modules that group related route handlers and provide a logical structure for your application's business logic.

Basic Routing with Express.js

Express.js makes it simple to define routes and their corresponding handlers:

```
import express from "express"; import type { Request, Response } from
'express'; const app = express(); // GET request to the root path app.get("/",
(req: Request, res: Response) => { res.send("Hello from the root route!"); });
// POST request to /users app.post("/users", (req, res) => { // ... handle
user creation logic ... });
```

In this example, we define two routes:

- A GET route for the root path (`/`) that sends a simple greeting.
- A POST route for `/users` that presumably handles user creation.

Organizing Routes with Controllers

As your application grows, it's helpful to organize your routes into controllers. A controller is simply a class (or a module in CommonJS) that groups related route handlers:

```
// userController.ts (Using ES Modules) import { Request, Response } from
'express'; class UserController { getUsers(req: Request, res: Response) { //
... fetch and return user data ... } createUser(req: Request, res: Response) {
// ... handle user creation logic ... } } export default new UserController();

// index.ts import express from 'express'; import userController from
'./userController'; const app = express(); app.get("/users",
userController.getUsers); app.post("/users", userController.createUser);
```

In this example, we create a `UserController` class to handle routes related to users.

Decorators for Defining Controllers and Routes (Optional)

While not built into Express.js, you can use third-party libraries like `@decorators/express` or `routing-controllers` to leverage decorators for defining controllers and routes. This can lead to more concise and expressive code.

Example: Using Decorators

```
import { Controller, Get, Post } from '@decorators/express'; import { Request,
Response } from 'express'; import express from 'express';
@Controller('/users') class UserController { @Get('/') getUsers(req: Request,
res: Response) { // ... fetch and return user data ... } @Post('/')
createUser(req: Request, res: Response) { // ... handle user creation logic
... } } const app = express(); const userController = new UserController();
app.use(userController.router);
```

Key Points:

- Routes define how your application responds to specific URLs and HTTP methods.
- Controllers organize related route handlers into logical units.
- Decorators (if you choose to use them) provide a concise syntax for defining controllers and routes.
- By structuring your API with controllers and routes (or decorators), you create a more maintainable and scalable codebase.

This was a brief overview. For more comprehensive documentation and examples of the decorators used above, you can refer to the documentation for `@decorators/express` here: https://www.npmjs.com/package/@decorators/express

Handling Requests and Responses

Express.js provides a robust yet streamlined way to handle incoming requests and craft appropriate responses in your TypeScript Node.js backend. Let's delve into the mechanisms for accessing request data, shaping responses, and using middleware to customize the request/response cycle.

Request Handling

The `request` object (`req`) passed to your route handlers is packed with information about the incoming request:

- **`req.params`:** Access route parameters (dynamic segments in the URL).
  ```
  app.get('/users/:id', (req, res) => { const userId = req.params.id; //
  Access the 'id' parameter });
  ```
- **`req.query`:** Access query string parameters.
  ```
  app.get('/search', (req, res) => { const searchTerm = req.query.q; //
  Access the 'q' query parameter });
  ```
- **`req.body`:** Access the request body (usually for POST, PUT, or PATCH requests). Note: You'll need middleware like `express.json()` or `express.urlencoded()` to parse the body.
  ```
  app.use(express.json()); // Middleware to parse JSON bodies
  app.post('/users', (req, res) => { const newUser = req.body; // Access
  the parsed request body });
  ```
- **`req.headers`:** Access request headers.
  ```
  app.get('/', (req, res) => { const userAgent = req.headers['user-agent'];
  // Access the 'User-Agent' header });
  ```
- **`req.method`:** Access the HTTP method of the request.

Response Handling

The `response` object (`res`) is your tool for constructing the server's response:

- **`res.status(code)`:** Set the HTTP status code (e.g., `200` OK, `404 Not Found`, `500 Internal Server Error`).
- **`res.send(data)`:** Send a response body. This can be a string, an object (which will be automatically converted to JSON), a buffer, etc.
  ```
  app.get('/products/:id', (req, res) => { const product = findProductById(req.params.id); res.status(200).json(product); });
  ```
- **`res.json(data)`:** Send a JSON response. This is a shorthand for `res.status(200).json(data)`.
- **`res.redirect(url)`:** Redirect the client to a different URL.
- **`res.set(headers)`:** Set response headers.
  ```
  app.get('/', (req, res) => { res.set('Content-Type', 'text/plain'); res.send('Hello in plain text!'); });
  ```

Middleware

Middleware functions in Express.js are executed in a specific order. They can modify the request or response objects, end the request-response cycle by sending a response, or pass control to the next middleware function in the chain.

```
app.use((req, res, next) => { console.log("This is a middleware function.");
next(); // Move to the next middleware/route handler });
```

Common Middleware Use Cases

- **Logging:** Log incoming requests and responses.
- **Authentication:** Verify user credentials and protect routes.
- **Error Handling:** Catch and handle errors gracefully.
- **Body Parsing:** Parse request bodies (e.g., JSON or form data).
- **CORS:** Enable Cross-Origin Resource Sharing for your API.

By mastering request and response handling in Express.js, along with the concept of middleware, you can create versatile APIs that serve data in various formats, handle errors gracefully, and implement security measures effectively.

Type Safety in Node.js with TypeScript

Request and Response Types

One of the most significant advantages of using TypeScript with Node.js and Express.js is the ability to define strong types for your request and response objects. This enhances type safety, prevents errors, and improves the overall developer experience when building your backend APIs.

Defining Request Types

The Express.js `Request` object contains a wealth of information about the incoming request, including parameters, query strings, headers, and the request body. You can create interfaces or type aliases to define the structure of the data you expect in each of these areas.

```
// request.d.ts declare namespace Express { export interface Request { params:
{ id: string; } body: { name: string; email: string; } user?: User; //
Optional property to store authenticated user data } }
```

By doing so, you clearly define the expected shape of the request object for each route. If a route handler tries to access a property that doesn't exist or use it with the wrong type, TypeScript will raise a type error, helping you catch mistakes during development.

Defining Response Types

Similarly, you can define types for the response data that your API endpoints will send back to the client.

```
interface Product { id: number; name: string; price: number; } interface User
{ id: number; name: string; email: string; }
```

In this example, the `Product` and `User` interfaces represent the expected structure for product and user data. You can now use these types to annotate the return values of your route handlers:

```
app.get('/products/:id', (req, res) => { const product: Product = { id: 1,
name: 'Laptop', price: 999.99 }; // Type annotation res.json(product); });
app.get('/users/:id', (req, res) => { const user: User = { id: 123, name:
'Alice', email: 'alice@example.com' }; // Type annotation res.json(user); });
```

Benefits of Typed Requests and Responses

- **Early Error Detection:** TypeScript catches type-related errors during development, preventing them from causing runtime issues.
- **Improved Code Readability:** Type annotations make your code self-documenting. It's clear what data each route expects and what it will return.
- **Easier Refactoring:** If you change the structure of your request or response data, TypeScript can help you find and update all the places in your code that are affected.
- **Stronger Contracts:** Typed requests and responses establish clear contracts between your frontend and backend, reducing the chance of miscommunication and errors.

Important Note: In Express, you'll typically need to extend the default `Request` and `Response` interfaces to add your custom types. The specific method for doing this might vary depending on whether you're using CommonJS or ES Modules and whether you have the `skipLibCheck` compiler option enabled in your `tsconfig.json`.

By embracing the power of TypeScript's type system in your Node.js and Express.js applications, you'll create more robust, maintainable, and easier-to-understand APIs.

Middleware with TypeScript

In Express.js, middleware functions are the backbone of request processing. They intercept and handle incoming requests before they reach your route handlers. TypeScript brings its type-checking prowess to middleware, ensuring that you work with request and response objects safely and consistently.

Middleware Signature

In TypeScript, a middleware function is typically defined as follows:

```
import { Request, Response, NextFunction } from 'express'; type RequestHandler
= (req: Request, res: Response, next: NextFunction) => any; function
```

```
myMiddleware(req: Request, res: Response, next: NextFunction) { // Middleware logic }
```

- `RequestHandler` is a type provided by Express.js for request handler functions.
- The function takes three arguments:
    - `req`: An object representing the HTTP request.
    - `res`: An object representing the HTTP response.
    - `next`: A function to call to pass control to the next middleware function in the stack.
- The function can return any.

Adding TypeScript Types to Middleware

The key to type safety in middleware is to properly annotate the `req` and `res` objects. You can either use the default `Request` and `Response` types from Express.js or create custom interfaces to extend them with your own properties.

Example: Custom Interfaces for Typed Middleware

```
// Request interface for `/users/:id` route interface UserRequest extends Request { params: { id: string; } } // Middleware function function authenticateUser(req: UserRequest, res: Response, next: NextFunction) { const userId = req.params.id; // ... Authentication logic ... next(); // Pass control to the next middleware/route handler }
```

In this example, we define a `UserRequest` interface that extends the `Request` interface from Express.js. This custom interface adds a `params` property with an `id` of type `string`, allowing us to access the `id` parameter in a type-safe manner within the `authenticateUser` middleware.

Example: Middleware to Attach User Data to the Request

```
import { Request, Response, NextFunction } from 'express'; interface CustomRequest extends Request { user?: { id: number; name: string }; // Add user data to the request } function attachUserData(req: CustomRequest, res: Response, next: NextFunction) { // ... fetch user data from a database or authentication middleware ... // Attach the user data to the request object req.user = { id: 123, name: 'Alice' }; // Example data next(); // Move to the next middleware/route handler }
```

By extending the request interface, you enable access to the custom property (`user`) that your middleware attaches. **Key Points**

- Middleware functions are typed using the `Request`, `Response`, and `NextFunction` types from Express.js.
- You can create custom interfaces to extend the `Request` and `Response` types and add your own properties.
- TypeScript's type checking ensures that you use the correct types within your middleware functions, preventing errors and improving code reliability.

By adding types to your Express.js middleware, you gain the benefits of TypeScript's type safety and enhanced developer experience, making your backend code more robust and easier to maintain.

Error Handling

Errors are an inevitable part of any software application, and your Node.js backend is no exception. TypeScript provides you with powerful tools for defining custom error types, handling errors gracefully, and preventing them from crashing your application.

1. Defining Custom Error Types

In TypeScript, you can create custom error classes that extend the base `Error` class. This allows you to create specific error types that convey more meaningful information about the nature of the error.

```
class ApiError extends Error { statusCode: number; constructor(message: string, statusCode: number) { super(message); // Call the parent Error constructor this.statusCode = statusCode; this.name = 'ApiError'; } } class NotFoundError extends ApiError { constructor(message: string = 'Resource not found') { super(message, 404); // Set status code for "Not Found" this.name = 'NotFoundError'; } } class ValidationError extends ApiError { constructor(message: string) { super(message, 400); // Set status code for "Bad Request" this.name = 'ValidationError'; } }
```

In this example, we define two custom error types: `NotFoundError` and `ValidationError`, both extending the generic `ApiError`. This hierarchy provides a clear structure for your error types.

2. Throwing and Catching Errors

You can throw these custom errors in your code and catch them using `try...catch` blocks:

```
function getUserById(id: number): User { const user = findUser(id); if (!user) { throw new NotFoundError(`User with ID ${id} not found`); } return user; } try { const user = getUserById(123); } catch (error) { if (error instanceof NotFoundError) { // Handle not found error (e.g., send a 404 response) } else if (error instanceof ApiError) { // Handle generic API error } else { // Handle unexpected errors } }
```

3. Error Handling Middleware

Express.js allows you to define error-handling middleware that catches errors that occur during request processing.

```
app.use((err: Error, req: Request, res: Response, next: NextFunction) => { console.error(err); // Log the error for debugging if (err instanceof ApiError) { res.status(err.statusCode).json({ error: err.message }); } else { res.status(500).json({ error: 'Internal Server Error' }); } });
```

This middleware will be called whenever an error is thrown in your route handlers or other middleware functions. It logs the error and sends an appropriate JSON response to the client, including the status code and error message.

Best Practices

- **Use Custom Error Types:** Create specific error types that convey the nature of the error, making it easier to diagnose and handle.
- **Centralize Error Handling:** Define error-handling middleware to catch and process errors in a consistent way throughout your application.
- **Logging:** Log errors for debugging purposes, but avoid exposing sensitive details to the client.
- **User-Friendly Error Messages:** Provide clear and informative error messages to the client, helping them understand what went wrong.
- **Distinguish Between Client and Server Errors:** Use appropriate HTTP status codes (e.g., 4xx for client errors, 5xx for server errors) to indicate the type of error.

Key Points

- TypeScript allows you to define custom error classes that extend the `Error` class.
- Use `try...catch` blocks to handle errors gracefully.
- Create error-handling middleware in Express.js to catch and process errors centrally.

By implementing robust error handling with TypeScript, you create Node.js applications that are more reliable, resilient, and easier to debug.

Working with Databases

Connecting to MongoDB with Mongoose

MongoDB is a popular NoSQL database known for its flexibility and scalability. Mongoose, an Object Data Modeling (ODM) library for Node.js, provides a powerful and convenient way to interact with MongoDB databases, offering features like schema validation, data modeling, and query building. Let's explore how to use Mongoose with TypeScript to create a type-safe connection to your MongoDB database.

Installing Mongoose

First, make sure you have Mongoose installed as a project dependency:

```
npm install mongoose # or yarn add mongoose
```

Connecting to MongoDB

To connect to your MongoDB database, use the `mongoose.connect()` function:

```
import mongoose from 'mongoose'; async function connectToDatabase() { try {
await mongoose.connect('mongodb://localhost:27017/mydatabase');
console.log('Connected to MongoDB'); } catch (err) { console.error('Failed to
connect to MongoDB:', err); } } connectToDatabase();
```

Replace `'mongodb://localhost:27017/mydatabase'` with your actual MongoDB connection string. The `connect` function returns a promise, so we use `await` inside an `async` function to handle the result.

Defining Schemas and Models

In Mongoose, schemas define the structure of your documents (data records) within a collection. Models are then created from these schemas and provide an interface for interacting with the data.

```
import mongoose from 'mongoose'; interface User { name: string; email: string;
age: number; } const userSchema = new mongoose.Schema<User>({ name: { type:
String, required: true }, email: { type: String, required: true, unique: true
```

```
}, age: { type: Number, required: true }, }); const User =
mongoose.model<User>('User', userSchema); // Create User model
```

In this example:

1. We define a TypeScript `User` interface to represent the shape of our user data.
2. We create a Mongoose schema (`userSchema`) from the `User` interface. Each field in the schema has a corresponding type (e.g., `String`, `Number`) and can have additional options (e.g., `required`, `unique`).
3. We create a Mongoose model (`User`) based on the schema. This model gives us methods like `find`, `create`, `update`, and `delete` for interacting with user documents in the database.

Using the Model

```
async function createUser(user: User) { try { const newUser = new User(user);
await newUser.save(); console.log('User created:', newUser); } catch (err) {
console.error('Failed to create user:', err); } }
```

By passing a `User` object to the model's constructor and invoking the `save()` method, we ensure type safety throughout the database interaction process.

Key Points

- Use `mongoose.connect()` to connect to your MongoDB database.
- Define schemas using Mongoose to specify the structure of your documents.
- Create models from schemas to interact with data in your collections.
- TypeScript interfaces help ensure type safety when working with schemas and models.

By integrating Mongoose and TypeScript, you create a robust and type-safe foundation for your Node.js backend, allowing you to efficiently manage data in your MongoDB database.

Defining Data Models and Schemas

Mongoose provides a bridge between your TypeScript code and your MongoDB database. To ensure seamless integration and type safety, you'll utilize TypeScript interfaces to define the shape of your data and Mongoose schemas to map that structure to MongoDB documents.

TypeScript Interfaces: The Blueprint

Start by creating a TypeScript interface that defines the properties and their types for your data model. This interface acts as the blueprint for your data, ensuring consistency and predictability.

```
interface Product { name: string; description: string; price: number;
category: string; tags?: string[]; // Optional array of tags }
```

In this example, the `Product` interface describes a product with properties like `name`, `description`, `price`, `category`, and an optional `tags` array.

Mongoose Schema: The Bridge to MongoDB

Next, you create a Mongoose schema based on your TypeScript interface. The schema not only defines the structure of your documents but also allows you to specify additional validation rules, default values, and hooks.

```
import mongoose from 'mongoose'; import { Product } from
'./product.interface'; // Assuming you have an interface file const
productSchema = new mongoose.Schema<Product>({ name: { type: String, required:
true }, description: { type: String, required: true }, price: { type: Number,
required: true, min: 0 }, category: { type: String, required: true }, tags:
[String] // Optional array of strings });
```

Mongoose will enforce these rules whenever you try to save a product to the database.

Mongoose Model: Interacting with the Database

Finally, you create a Mongoose model from the schema. This model gives you methods for interacting with the database, such as `find`, `create`, `update`, and `delete`.

```
const Product = mongoose.model<Product>('Product', productSchema);
```

Type Safety in Action

```
const newProduct: Product = { name: 'Awesome Gadget', description: 'The best
gadget ever!', price: 199.99, category: 'electronics', }; const product = new
Product(newProduct); product.save().then((savedProduct) => {
console.log('Product saved:', savedProduct); });
```

In this example, TypeScript ensures that the `newProduct` object conforms to the `Product` interface before you save it to the database. If you try to create a product with missing or incorrect properties, TypeScript will raise a type error during development.

By combining TypeScript interfaces with Mongoose schemas, you establish a robust and type-safe connection between your TypeScript code and your MongoDB database. This approach simplifies data modeling, improves code readability, and helps prevent errors, ultimately leading to more reliable and maintainable Node.js applications.

Authentication and Authorization

Authentication and authorization are critical aspects of building secure and reliable backend applications. In this section, we'll delve into how to implement authentication middleware in your TypeScript Node.js project using Express.js, exploring common strategies like JSON Web Tokens (JWT) and session-based authentication.

Implementing Authentication Middleware

Authentication middleware acts as a gatekeeper, ensuring that only authorized users can access certain routes or resources within your API. It typically involves verifying the user's credentials (e.g., username and password) and establishing a session or issuing a token that can be used for subsequent requests.

JSON Web Tokens (JWT): Stateless Authentication

JWTs are a popular choice for authentication in modern web applications. They are self-contained tokens that include encoded information about the user, such as their ID and expiration time. Here's how you can use JWTs for authentication in your Node.js/Express.js backend:

1. **Install Dependencies:**
   ```
   npm install jsonwebtoken # or yarn add jsonwebtoken
   ```

2. **Create JWT Middleware:**
```
import { Request, Response, NextFunction } from "express"; import jwt
from "jsonwebtoken"; function authenticateJwt(req: Request, res:
Response, next: NextFunction) { const authHeader =
req.headers.authorization; const token = authHeader && authHeader.split('
')[1]; if (token == null) return res.sendStatus(401); // Unauthorized
jwt.verify(token, process.env.ACCESS_TOKEN_SECRET!, (err: any, user: any)
=> { if (err) return res.sendStatus(403); // Forbidden req.user = user;
next(); }); }
```
This middleware function checks for a valid JWT in the Authorization header, verifies it using a secret key (stored in an environment variable), and attaches the decoded user payload to the `req.user` object if successful.
3. **Apply Middleware to Protected Routes:**
```
app.get('/protected', authenticateJwt, (req, res) => { // Access the
authenticated user from req.user res.json({ message: 'Protected data' });
});
```

Session-Based Authentication: Maintaining State

Session-based authentication involves storing user data on the server-side and associating it with a session identifier (usually a cookie) sent to the client.

1. **Install Dependencies:**
```
npm install express-session # or yarn add express-session
```
2. **Create Session Middleware:**
```
import session from 'express-session'; app.use(session({ secret:
process.env.SESSION_SECRET!, resave: false, saveUninitialized: false,
}));
```
3. **Apply Middleware to Protected Routes**
```
function authenticateSession(req: Request, res: Response, next:
NextFunction) { if (!req.session.userId) { return
res.status(401).send('Unauthorized'); } next(); } app.get('/protected',
authenticateSession, (req, res) => { // ... });
```

Choosing an Authentication Strategy

Both JWT and session-based authentication have their pros and cons:

Feature	JWT	Session-Based
Statelessness	Yes (token contains all necessary data)	No (user data stored on the server)
Scalability	High (no server-side storage needed)	Lower (server needs to manage sessions)
Security	Potentially vulnerable to replay attacks if not implemented carefully	Potentially vulnerable to session hijacking or fixation if not secured properly
Implementation	Requires client-side storage of the token	Requires server-side session management

Use Cases	APIs, microservices, single-page applications (SPAs), mobile apps	Traditional web applications, where server-side state is beneficial

The best choice depends on your application's specific requirements. Consider factors like scalability, security needs, the type of application you're building, and the infrastructure you have in place.

Let me know if you'd like a more detailed explanation or code examples for a particular authentication strategy!

Protecting Routes

Now that you have authentication middleware in place, let's explore how to use it to protect specific routes in your Express.js application, ensuring that only authorized users can access certain resources or perform particular actions.

Applying Middleware to Routes

Express.js makes it easy to apply middleware functions to individual routes or groups of routes. You can use the `app.get()`, `app.post()`, `app.put()`, `app.delete()`, or other route methods, passing your authentication middleware as the first argument:

```
// Assuming you have the authenticateJwt middleware defined (from the previous example) app.get('/profile', authenticateJwt, (req, res) => { // This route is protected and accessible only to authenticated users res.json(req.user); });
```

In this example, the `authenticateJwt` middleware will be executed before the route handler for `/profile`. If the user is not authenticated, the middleware will send a 401 Unauthorized response, preventing access to the route.

Role-Based Access Control (RBAC)

You can further refine authorization by checking the user's role or permissions:

```
function authorize(allowedRoles: string[]) { return (req: Request, res: Response, next: NextFunction) => { const userRole = req.user?.role; // Assuming your user object has a 'role' property if (allowedRoles.includes(userRole)) { next(); // Allow access } else { res.status(403).send('Forbidden'); // Deny access } }; }
```

Now you can apply this middleware to protect routes based on roles:

```
app.post('/admin/users', authorize(['admin']), (req, res) => { // ... create a new user (only for admins) ... });
```

Protecting Multiple Routes

If you have multiple routes that require the same authorization checks, you can use Express.js routers to group them together:

```
const adminRouter = express.Router(); adminRouter.use(authorize(['admin'])); // Apply middleware to all routes in adminRouter adminRouter.get('/dashboard', (req, res) => { // ... admin dashboard ... }); adminRouter.post('/users',
```

```
(req, res) => { // ... create a new user ... }); app.use('/admin',
adminRouter);
```

Key Points

- Apply middleware functions to specific routes using the `app.METHOD()` methods or by using routers.
- Use the `next()` function in your middleware to pass control to the next middleware or route handler if the user is authorized.
- Check the user's role or permissions in your middleware to implement fine-grained access control.

By incorporating authentication and authorization middleware into your Express.js application, you can secure your APIs, protect sensitive data, and ensure that users can only access the resources they are permitted to use.

Advanced Topics

WebSockets with Socket.IO and TypeScript

In the world of web applications, **WebSockets** are a powerful technology that enables real-time, bidirectional communication between the client (browser) and the server. However, working with raw WebSockets can be cumbersome. Socket.IO, a popular library, simplifies real-time communication by providing a higher-level abstraction and handling many of the complexities of WebSockets for you. TypeScript, with its type system, adds an extra layer of safety to Socket.IO, ensuring that the data you send and receive is of the expected type.

A Brief Introduction to WebSockets and Socket.IO

- **WebSockets:** A protocol that establishes a persistent connection between a client and a server. This connection allows for real-time data exchange, making it ideal for applications like chat apps, collaborative tools, and live updates.
- **Socket.IO:** A library that builds on top of WebSockets, providing additional features like fallback mechanisms (to long polling or other techniques when WebSockets are not available), automatic reconnection, and a simple event-based API for sending and receiving data.

Typing Events and Data in Socket.IO

TypeScript provides type definitions for Socket.IO, allowing you to define interfaces for your events and their associated data payloads. This brings type safety to your real-time communication, catching errors early in development.

Example: Chat Application

```
// server.ts import { Server } from "socket.io"; const io = new Server(3000);
interface ChatMessage { username: string; message: string; }
io.on("connection", (socket) => { socket.on("chat message", (msg: ChatMessage)
=> { io.emit("chat message", msg); }); }); // client.ts const socket =
io('http://localhost:3000'); function sendMessage(message: string) {
socket.emit('chat message', { username: 'Alice', message }); }
```

By typing the events (`chat message`) and defining an interface for the data, TypeScript can verify if the messages sent by the client has the expected structure. This prevents you from sending or receiving malformed data.

Benefits of Using TypeScript with Socket.IO

- **Type Safety:** Catch type-related errors at compile time, preventing them from causing problems in production.
- **Improved Developer Experience:** Code editors can provide autocompletion and type hints for events and payloads, making development faster and easier.
- **Easier Maintenance:** Type definitions act as documentation, making your Socket.IO code easier to understand and maintain.

Key Points

- WebSockets are a protocol for real-time communication.
- Socket.IO is a library that simplifies WebSocket development.
- TypeScript provides type definitions for Socket.IO.
- You can define interfaces for events and data payloads to ensure type safety.

By incorporating TypeScript into your Socket.IO projects, you unlock a new level of robustness and maintainability. Type safety helps you catch errors early and makes your real-time communication code more reliable and easier to work with.

GraphQL APIs with TypeScript

GraphQL has emerged as a compelling alternative to traditional REST APIs for building modern web services. It offers a more flexible and efficient way for clients to request exactly the data they need, reducing over-fetching and under-fetching of data. When paired with TypeScript, you gain the added benefits of a strong type system, making your GraphQL API development more predictable and error-resistant.

A Brief Overview of GraphQL

Unlike REST APIs, which expose a fixed set of endpoints, GraphQL provides a single endpoint that clients can query with a flexible and expressive query language. This query language allows clients to specify the exact fields they need from nested objects, eliminating the need for multiple round trips to the server.

Here's a simple example of a GraphQL query:

```
query { me { id name email } }
```

This query requests the `id`, `name`, and `email` fields for the currently authenticated user (assuming the server has a `me` field defined).

TypeScript and GraphQL Schema Definition

A GraphQL schema defines the types of data available in your API and the operations (queries and mutations) that clients can perform. TypeScript excels at defining these schemas due to its strong type system and support for interfaces and custom types.

Example: Product Type

```
type Product = { id: ID! name: String! price: Float! category: String };
```

In this example, we define a `Product` type in TypeScript, which will be used to create the corresponding GraphQL type.

Example: Query Type

```
type Query = { product(id: ID!): Product products(category: String):
[Product!]! };
```

The `Query` type defines two possible queries: `product`, which takes an ID and returns a single `Product`, and `products`, which optionally takes a `category` and returns an array of `Product`.

Type Safety with TypeScript

TypeScript helps ensure type safety in your GraphQL API development:

- **Schema Validation:** TypeScript can validate your schema definitions, ensuring that they adhere to the GraphQL specification and that types are used consistently.
- **Type-Safe Resolvers:** You can define TypeScript functions (resolvers) for each field in your schema, and TypeScript will check that the types of the data you return match the types defined in the schema.
- **Autocompletion and Tooling:** TypeScript-aware editors can provide autocompletion, type hints, and validation for your GraphQL queries and schema definitions, improving your development experience.

Popular GraphQL Libraries for TypeScript

- **Apollo Server:** A popular library for building GraphQL servers with TypeScript.
- **TypeGraphQL:** A framework for building GraphQL APIs with TypeScript using decorators.
- **GraphQL Code Generator:** A tool that generates TypeScript types and hooks based on your GraphQL schema.

By combining GraphQL's flexible query language with TypeScript's type safety, you can build robust and scalable APIs that are both developer-friendly and easy to maintain. GraphQL's ability to fetch precise data, coupled with TypeScript's ability to catch errors early, makes this combination a powerful choice for modern web development.

Serverless Functions with TypeScript

Serverless functions, also known as Function-as-a-Service (FaaS), have become a game-changer in modern backend development. They allow you to run code in response to events without managing the underlying infrastructure. AWS Lambda is a prime example of a serverless platform, and TypeScript shines in this environment due to its enhanced developer experience and type safety benefits.

Understanding Serverless Functions

With serverless functions, you focus solely on writing your code, while the cloud provider (e.g., AWS) takes care of provisioning, scaling, and managing the servers. Functions are triggered by events like HTTP requests, database changes, or scheduled events. This event-driven model offers several advantages:

- **Reduced Operational Overhead:** You don't need to manage servers or infrastructure, freeing you to focus on building your application logic.
- **Automatic Scaling:** The cloud provider automatically scales your functions up or down based on demand, ensuring optimal performance and cost efficiency.
- **Pay-per-Use:** You only pay for the actual execution time of your functions, not for idle server time.

TypeScript and Serverless Functions: A Perfect Fit

TypeScript brings a wealth of benefits to serverless function development:

1. **Type Safety:** TypeScript's static typing helps prevent errors and ensures that your functions handle data correctly. This is especially important in serverless environments where functions are often triggered by events with varying data structures.
2. **Improved Developer Experience:** TypeScript-aware editors provide code completion, type hints, and refactoring tools that greatly enhance productivity when writing serverless functions.
3. **Easier Debugging:** The type information provided by TypeScript makes it easier to track down issues and understand the flow of data within your functions.
4. **Maintainability:** With clear type definitions, your serverless functions become more self-documenting and easier to maintain, especially as your project grows.

Building Serverless Functions with TypeScript

Here's a simplified example of an AWS Lambda function written in TypeScript:

```
import { APIGatewayProxyEvent, APIGatewayProxyResult } from 'aws-lambda';
export const handler = async ( event: APIGatewayProxyEvent ):
Promise<APIGatewayProxyResult> => { const name =
event.queryStringParameters?.name || 'World'; return { statusCode: 200, body:
`Hello, ${name}!`, }; };
```

In this example:

- We use TypeScript types (`APIGatewayProxyEvent` and `APIGatewayProxyResult`) to define the input and output shapes of the function.
- The function handles a GET request, extracts the `name` parameter from the query string (or uses "World" as a default), and returns a JSON response.

Deployment

You can deploy TypeScript Lambda functions using various tools like the Serverless Framework, AWS SAM, or the AWS CDK. These tools handle the bundling, packaging, and deployment of your code to the AWS Lambda environment. They also integrate with TypeScript, allowing you to write your functions in TypeScript and automatically compile them to JavaScript before deployment.

Key Points

- Serverless functions offer a scalable, cost-effective, and low-maintenance way to run backend code.
- TypeScript enhances serverless development by providing type safety, improved tooling, and better maintainability.
- You can use libraries like the Serverless Framework, AWS SAM, or AWS CDK to deploy TypeScript functions to AWS Lambda.

By embracing serverless functions and TypeScript, you can build scalable, reliable, and type-safe backend services without the hassle of managing infrastructure. This combination allows you to focus on writing high-quality code while leaving the operational concerns to the cloud provider.

Chapter Summary

In this chapter, we explored the exciting intersection of TypeScript and Node.js, discovering how to build powerful and type-safe backend applications. Here's a summary of the key points we covered:

- **Node.js: The JavaScript Runtime for the Server:** We introduced Node.js, the versatile runtime that brings JavaScript to the server-side, enabling the creation of web servers, APIs, real-time applications, and more. We discussed its event-driven, non-blocking architecture, which makes it efficient and scalable.

- **Why TypeScript is Ideal for Node.js:** We delved into the advantages of using TypeScript for Node.js development, highlighting its type safety for catching errors early, enhanced tooling support for increased productivity, scalability for managing complex projects, and maintainability through better code structure and documentation.
- **Setting Up a TypeScript Node.js Project:** We provided a step-by-step guide on initializing a new Node.js project and installing essential dependencies like TypeScript, Node.js types, Express.js, and relevant libraries for your specific project.
- **Building a Simple API:** We introduced Express.js as a minimalist web framework for Node.js and demonstrated how to define routes, organize them into controllers, and handle requests and responses using TypeScript. We also discussed the use of decorators for cleaner route definitions.
- **Type Safety in Node.js with TypeScript:** We explored how to define types for request and response objects, ensuring type safety throughout your API. We also covered how to create type-safe middleware functions that handle specific tasks within the request-response cycle.
- **Working with Databases:** We demonstrated how to connect to a MongoDB database using Mongoose, an ODM library, and how to define type-safe data models and schemas using TypeScript interfaces.
- **Authentication and Authorization:** We discussed strategies for implementing authentication middleware (like JWT or session-based authentication) and how to protect routes using middleware to ensure only authorized users can access specific resources.
- **Advanced Topics:** We briefly introduced more advanced concepts like WebSockets with Socket.IO, GraphQL APIs, and serverless functions, highlighting how TypeScript can be applied to these technologies for enhanced type safety and development experience.

By mastering these concepts, you have gained the knowledge and tools to build robust, scalable, and type-safe backend applications with TypeScript and Node.js. You can now leverage the strengths of both technologies to create efficient and reliable web services, APIs, and real-time applications.

In the next chapter, we'll shift our focus to asynchronous programming in TypeScript, exploring how to work with promises and the `async/await` syntax to handle asynchronous operations effectively.

Asynchronous TypeScript: Promises and Async/Await

Outline

- Understanding Asynchronous Code
  - What is Asynchronicity?
  - Why Asynchronicity Matters in JavaScript/TypeScript
  - Common Asynchronous Operations in Node.js
- Promises: Managing Asynchronous Operations
  - The Promise Object: States and Chaining
  - Creating and Resolving Promises
  - Promise.all and Promise.allSettled
  - Error Handling with Promises (Catch and Finally)
- Async/Await: A Cleaner Syntax for Promises
  - Async Functions
  - Await Expressions
  - Error Handling with Try...Catch
- Real-World Examples
  - Fetching Data from APIs
  - Reading/Writing Files
  - Working with Timeouts and Intervals
- Best Practices for Asynchronous TypeScript Code
  - Choosing Between Promises and Async/Await
  - Error Handling Strategies
  - Avoiding Callback Hell
  - Proper Use of Async/Await
- Chapter Summary

Understanding Asynchronous Code

What is Asynchronicity?

In the world of programming, asynchronicity refers to the ability to perform tasks concurrently without waiting for each task to finish before starting the next one. This is in contrast to synchronous code, which executes line by line, waiting for each operation to complete before moving on.

Think of it like this:

Synchronous Code (Like a Fast Food Drive-Thru):

1. You drive up to the window.
2. You place your order.
3. You wait for your food to be prepared.
4. You receive your food and drive away.

In this scenario, each step must be completed in order before you can move on to the next one. This is how synchronous code works.

Asynchronous Code (Like a Fine Dining Restaurant):

1. You arrive at the restaurant and are seated.

2. You place your order.
3. While your food is being prepared, you can chat with your friends, read a book, or enjoy a drink. (Other code can execute)
4. When your food is ready, the waiter brings it to your table.

In this case, the process of preparing your food (the asynchronous operation) happens in the background while you do other things. Once the food is ready, you're notified, and you can proceed with eating it.

Why Asynchronicity Matters

In the context of JavaScript and TypeScript, asynchronicity is crucial for several reasons:

- **Non-Blocking I/O:** Many operations, like network requests (fetching data from APIs), file input/output, and database queries, can take a significant amount of time. If JavaScript were purely synchronous, your entire application would freeze while waiting for these operations to complete. Asynchronicity allows these operations to happen in the background, keeping your application responsive.
- **Improved Performance:** By allowing tasks to run concurrently, asynchronous code can often achieve better performance, especially in scenarios where multiple tasks can be executed simultaneously.
- **User Experience:** In web applications, asynchronous operations are essential for creating a smooth user experience. For example, a webpage can continue to be interactive while it's fetching data in the background.

Common Scenarios for Asynchronous Code

- **Network Requests:** Fetching data from APIs or making AJAX calls.
- **File Operations:** Reading from or writing to files on the disk.
- **Timers:** Using `setTimeout` and `setInterval` to schedule tasks.
- **Database Operations:** Querying or updating databases.
- **User Interactions:** Handling events like button clicks, mouse movements, or keyboard input.

In the next sections, we'll explore how to work with asynchronous code in TypeScript using tools like Promises and the `async/await` syntax, which make it easier to manage and reason about these types of operations.

Why Asynchronicity Matters in JavaScript/TypeScript

JavaScript and TypeScript, by nature, are single-threaded languages. This means they can only execute one line of code at a time. However, modern applications often need to perform tasks that take time to complete, such as fetching data from a server or reading a file from disk. If JavaScript were strictly synchronous, these operations would block the execution of other code, leading to unresponsive and frustrating user experiences.

The Event Loop to the Rescue

To overcome this limitation, JavaScript employs an **event loop**. The event loop is a continuous cycle that monitors the call stack (where your code is executed) and the callback queue (where asynchronous tasks wait to be processed). Here's a simplified breakdown of how it works:

1. **Code Execution:** When you run your JavaScript code, it starts executing on the call stack.
2. **Asynchronous Tasks:** If an asynchronous operation is encountered (like a network request), it is offloaded to the browser or Node.js environment's built-in APIs.
3. **Callback Registration:** A callback function is associated with the asynchronous operation. This callback will be executed once the operation completes.

4. **Event Loop Monitoring:** While the asynchronous operation is being processed in the background, the event loop continues to run, checking the call stack and the callback queue.
5. **Callback Execution:** Once the asynchronous operation finishes, its callback function is placed in the callback queue.
6. **Call Stack Clearing:** When the call stack is empty, the event loop takes the first callback from the queue and puts it onto the call stack for execution.

This cycle repeats continuously, ensuring that long-running tasks don't block the main thread of execution.

Example: Blocking vs. Non-Blocking

```
// Blocking (Synchronous) Code const data = fs.readFileSync('./data.txt',
'utf-8'); // Blocks until file is read console.log(data); // Non-Blocking
(Asynchronous) Code fs.readFile('./data.txt', 'utf-8', (err, data) => { if
(err) throw err; console.log(data); }); console.log("This line is executed
immediately"); // Non-blocking
```

In the blocking example, the entire script execution is paused until the file is read. In the non-blocking example, the `readFile` operation is initiated, and the script continues executing. The callback function is called later when the file reading completes.

Key Points

- JavaScript is single-threaded, meaning it can only do one thing at a time.
- The event loop allows JavaScript to handle asynchronous operations without blocking the main thread.
- Asynchronous operations are crucial for creating responsive applications that don't freeze while waiting for tasks to complete.
- Understanding the event loop is essential for writing efficient and performant JavaScript/TypeScript code.

By embracing asynchronicity, you can write Node.js applications that handle multiple requests concurrently, perform background tasks without affecting the user interface, and deliver a smooth and responsive user experience.

Common Asynchronous Operations in Node.js

Node.js is designed to excel at handling asynchronous operations, making it ideal for building scalable and responsive server-side applications. Let's explore some of the most common scenarios where you'll encounter asynchronicity in your Node.js and TypeScript projects.

1. File Operations

The Node.js built-in `fs` (file system) module provides a wealth of functions for interacting with files and directories. Most of these functions have asynchronous versions that return promises or accept callback functions.

```
import fs from 'fs'; // Asynchronous file reading (using promises)
fs.promises.readFile('data.txt', 'utf-8') .then(data => { console.log(data);
}) .catch(err => { console.error('Error reading file:', err); }); //
Asynchronous file writing (using callbacks) fs.writeFile('output.txt', 'Hello,
world!', (err) => { if (err) throw err; console.log('File written
successfully'); });
```

2. Network Requests

Node.js offers various ways to make HTTP requests and fetch data from APIs. The built-in `http` and `https` modules provide low-level control, while libraries like `node-fetch` (or `fetch` if you're in a modern Node.js environment) offer a more convenient Promise-based API.

```
import fetch from 'node-fetch'; fetch('https://api.example.com/data')
.then(response => response.json()) .then(data => { console.log(data); })
.catch(err => { console.error('Error fetching data:', err); });
```

3. Database Queries

If your Node.js backend interacts with a database (like MongoDB, PostgreSQL, or MySQL), most database libraries provide asynchronous methods for querying and updating data. For example, Mongoose (for MongoDB) offers promise-based methods like `find`, `findOne`, `create`, `update`, and `delete`.

```
import mongoose from 'mongoose'; const User = mongoose.model('User',
userSchema); User.findOne({ email: 'john@example.com' }) .then(user => { //
Process the user data }) .catch(err => { // Handle errors });
```

4. Timers

The `setTimeout` and `setInterval` functions are used to schedule tasks to be executed in the future. They are inherently asynchronous because they don't block the execution of other code while waiting for the timer to expire.

```
setTimeout(() => { console.log('This will be logged after 2 seconds'); },
2000); // 2000 milliseconds = 2 seconds
```

Key Points

- Node.js is designed for asynchronous programming, leveraging an event loop to handle non-blocking I/O operations.
- Common asynchronous operations in Node.js include file operations, network requests, database queries, and timers.
- Most Node.js APIs provide asynchronous versions of their functions, often returning promises or accepting callback functions.

Understanding these common asynchronous operations and how to work with them is essential for building efficient, scalable, and responsive Node.js applications with TypeScript.

Promises: Managing Asynchronous Operations

The Promise Object: States and Chaining

In the world of asynchronous JavaScript and TypeScript, Promises have become the cornerstone of managing operations that take time to complete. They offer a structured and elegant way to handle the outcomes of such operations, whether they succeed or fail.

What is a Promise?

Think of a Promise as an IOU for a future value. It's an object that represents the eventual result of an asynchronous operation. When you initiate an asynchronous task, like fetching data from an API, you get a Promise in return. This Promise acts as a placeholder for the data that you'll eventually receive.

The Three States of a Promise

A Promise can be in one of three states:

1. **Pending:** The initial state. The operation is ongoing, and the outcome is not yet known.
2. **Fulfilled:** The operation completed successfully, and the Promise now holds the resulting value.
3. **Rejected:** The operation failed, and the Promise now holds a reason for the failure (usually an error object).

Chaining Promises with `.then()`

The real magic of Promises comes with their ability to be chained together using the `.then()` method. This allows you to create sequences of asynchronous operations that depend on each other.

```
fetch('/api/users') .then(response => response.json()) // Parse response as
JSON .then(users => { // Process the users data console.log(users); })
.catch(error => { // Handle errors console.error('Error fetching users:',
error); });
```

In this example:

1. The first `then` block parses the response from the initial API call into JSON format.
2. The second `then` block processes the extracted user data, and `catch` is used for handling errors.

Each `.then()` block receives the result of the previous operation as its argument. This allows you to build a chain of actions that are executed in order, even though each step is asynchronous.

Visualizing Promise Chains

Imagine a series of dominoes lined up. Each domino represents a `.then()` block in your Promise chain. When you initiate the first asynchronous operation, it's like tipping over the first domino. When that operation completes, it "tips over" the next domino (the next `.then()` block), and so on. If any domino (operation) fails, the chain is broken, and the `catch` block is triggered.

Key Points

- Promises are objects that represent the eventual results of asynchronous operations.
- They have three states: pending, fulfilled, and rejected.
- You can chain Promises using `.then()` to create sequences of asynchronous actions.
- `catch()` is used to handle errors that occur during the execution of Promises.
- Promise chains make asynchronous code more readable and easier to reason about.

By understanding Promises and their chaining mechanism, you'll be well-equipped to handle the asynchronous nature of Node.js and build applications that are responsive, efficient, and reliable.

Creating and Resolving Promises

Promises in TypeScript are created using the `Promise` constructor. This constructor takes an *executor* function as its argument. The executor is responsible for initiating the asynchronous operation and signaling its eventual success or failure.

Promise Constructor Syntax

```
const myPromise = new Promise<ValueType>((resolve, reject) => { //
Asynchronous operation // ... if (/* operation successful */) {
resolve(value); // Resolve with a value of type ValueType } else {
reject(error); // Reject with an error } });
```

Key points:

- **Generic Type:** The `Promise<ValueType>` indicates the type of value the Promise will resolve with.
- **Executor Function:** This function is executed immediately when the Promise is created.
- **`resolve(value)`:** Call this function within the executor to indicate that the asynchronous operation was successful and pass the resulting `value`.
- **`reject(error)`:** Call this function to indicate that the operation failed and provide an `error` object (or any other value) as the reason.

Example: A Simple Promise

```
const myPromise = new Promise<string>((resolve, reject) => { setTimeout(() =>
{ const success = Math.random() < 0.5; // Simulate success/failure if
(success) { resolve("Operation completed successfully!"); } else { reject(new
Error("Operation failed!")); } }, 2000); // Delay for 2 seconds to simulate an
asynchronous task });
```

In this example:

1. We create a Promise that resolves with a string if a random condition is met or rejects with an error otherwise.
2. The `setTimeout` function simulates an asynchronous operation that takes 2 seconds to complete.

Consuming the Promise

You use the `.then()` and `.catch()` methods to handle the outcome of the Promise:

```
myPromise.then((message) => { console.log(message); }).catch((error) => {
console.error(error); });
```

Important Considerations

- **Immutability:** Once a Promise is settled (fulfilled or rejected), its state cannot be changed.
- **Microtasks:** Promise callbacks (in `.then`, `.catch`, `.finally`) are executed as microtasks, meaning they are placed at the end of the current event loop tick, ensuring that they run after any synchronous code that might be in the call stack.
- **Error Handling:** Always include a `.catch()` handler to gracefully handle rejected promises. Unhandled rejections can lead to unexpected behavior in your application.

By understanding how to create and resolve Promises, you gain a fundamental tool for managing asynchronous operations in TypeScript. This opens the door to more advanced techniques like Promise chaining, error handling, and the `async/await` syntax, which we'll explore shortly.

Promise.all and Promise.allSettled

When working with asynchronous operations in TypeScript, you'll often encounter scenarios where you need to handle multiple promises simultaneously. `Promise.all` and `Promise.allSettled` are powerful methods that help you manage these situations gracefully.

`Promise.all`: All or Nothing

`Promise.all` takes an array (or any iterable) of promises as input and returns a new promise. This returned promise:

- **Resolves:** When *all* input promises have resolved, the returned promise resolves with an array containing the results of each input promise in the same order.
- **Rejects:** If *any* of the input promises is rejected, the returned promise is immediately rejected with the reason of the first rejected promise. The remaining promises are not awaited.

Use Cases for `Promise.all`:

- When you need the results of all promises to proceed.
- When the success of your operation depends on the successful completion of all individual tasks.
- When you want to perform multiple independent asynchronous operations concurrently and gather their results.

Example:

```
const promise1 = Promise.resolve(3); const promise2 = new
Promise<string>((resolve, reject) => { setTimeout(() => resolve("foo"), 1000);
}); const promise3 = Promise.resolve(42); Promise.all([promise1, promise2,
promise3]).then((values) => { console.log(values); // Output: [3, "foo", 42]
}).catch(error => { console.error('Error:', error); // Error of the first
rejected promise will be logged. });
```

- `Promise.all` is suitable here if you need the results of all these operations before you proceed. However, if any of these promises get rejected, the entire operation would fail, and the error handling block will be triggered.

`Promise.allSettled`: Get All Outcomes

`Promise.allSettled`, introduced in ES2020, also takes an array of promises. However, unlike `Promise.all`, the promise returned by `Promise.allSettled`:

- **Always Resolves:** It *always* resolves, even if some or all of the input promises are rejected.
- **Returns an Array of Objects:** It resolves with an array of objects, each describing the outcome of an individual promise. Each object has a `status` property ("fulfilled" or "rejected") and either a `value` property (if fulfilled) or a `reason` property (if rejected).

Use Cases for `Promise.allSettled`:

- When you want to know the outcome of each promise, regardless of whether it succeeded or failed.
- When the success of your operation doesn't depend on the success of every individual task.
- When you want to perform multiple independent asynchronous operations and collect information about each one's result.

Example:

```
const promise1 = Promise.resolve(3); const promise2 = Promise.reject("Error!"); const promise3 = new Promise((resolve, reject) => { setTimeout(() => resolve("foo"), 1000); }); Promise.allSettled([promise1, promise2, promise3]).then((results) => { console.log(results); // Output: [ // { status: 'fulfilled', value: 3 }, // { status: 'rejected', reason: 'Error!' }, // { status: 'fulfilled', value: 'foo' } // ] });
```

- `Promise.allSettled` is the best choice of concurrency method here because it always returns a result, and you can then decide how to proceed based on the outcome of each individual promise.

Choosing the Right Method

- If you need all promises to succeed for your overall operation to be considered successful, use `Promise.all`.
- If you want to know the outcome of each promise, even if some fail, and continue with your logic accordingly, use `Promise.allSettled`.

By understanding the differences between `Promise.all` and `Promise.allSettled`, you'll be equipped to choose the right tool for managing concurrent asynchronous operations in your TypeScript projects.

Error Handling with Promises: `.catch` and `.finally`

Promises provide a structured way to handle both successful outcomes and errors in asynchronous operations. Let's explore how to use the `.catch` and `.finally` methods to gracefully manage errors and perform cleanup tasks with Promises.

`.catch`: Handling Errors

The `.catch()` method is your safety net for dealing with rejected Promises. When a Promise is rejected (due to an error or a failed operation), the `catch` block is triggered, allowing you to gracefully handle the error.

```
fetch('/api/data') .then(response => response.json()) .then(data => { // Process the data }) .catch(error => { console.error('Error fetching data:', error); // Show an error message to the user // Take other corrective actions });
```

In this example, if the `fetch` operation fails (e.g., due to a network error), the `.catch` block will be called, logging the error and potentially taking additional steps to recover or inform the user.

`.finally`: Guaranteed Cleanup

The `.finally()` method, introduced in ES2018, is a way to perform cleanup tasks regardless of whether the Promise was fulfilled or rejected. This is useful for actions that need to happen unconditionally, such as hiding a loading indicator, closing a connection, or releasing resources.

```
fetch('/api/data') .then(response => response.json()) .then(data => { // Process the data }) .catch(error => { console.error('Error:', error); }) .finally(() => { // Hide loading indicator setIsLoading(false); });
```

In this modified example, the `.finally` block ensures that the `setIsLoading(false)` call is always executed, whether the data fetching succeeds or fails.

Chaining `.catch` and `.finally`

You can chain multiple `.catch` blocks to handle different types of errors:

```
fetch('/api/data') .then(response => { if (!response.ok) { throw new
Error(`Request failed with status ${response.status}`); } return
response.json(); }) .then(data => { /* ... */ }) .catch(NetworkError, err => {
/* ... */ }) .catch(ApiError, err => { /* ... */ }) .catch(err => { /* ...
general error handling ... */ }) .finally(() => { /* ... cleanup ... */ });
```

And you can also have multiple `finally` blocks, although this is less common:

```
somePromise .then(result => { /* ... */ }) .finally(() => { /* ... */ })
.then(result => { /* ... */ }) .finally(() => { /* ... */ });
```

Key Points

- Use `.catch` to handle rejected promises (errors).
- Use `.finally` to perform cleanup tasks, regardless of whether the promise succeeded or failed.
- You can chain multiple `.catch` blocks to handle different error types.
- You can have multiple `.finally` blocks, although this is less common.

By mastering error handling with `.catch` and `.finally`, you ensure that your asynchronous TypeScript code is robust, resilient, and provides a smooth experience even in the face of unexpected issues.

Async/Await: A Cleaner Syntax for Promises

Async Functions

Async functions, introduced in ES2017 (ES8), have revolutionized the way we write asynchronous code in JavaScript and TypeScript. They offer a cleaner and more intuitive syntax that makes working with promises feel almost like writing synchronous code.

What are Async Functions?

An async function is declared using the `async` keyword before the `function` keyword (or before the parentheses in arrow function syntax). It always returns a Promise, even if you don't explicitly return one. If the function returns a value that's not a Promise, it's automatically wrapped in a `Promise.resolve`.

Syntax:

```
async function myAsyncFunction(): Promise<number> { // ... return 42; // This
returns a Promise that resolves with the value 42 } const myAsyncArrowFunction
= async (): Promise<string> => { // ... return "Hello"; };
```

How Async Functions Work

When you call an async function, it starts executing its code. However, when it encounters an `await` keyword (which we'll discuss in the next section), the function pauses its execution and waits for the

Promise following the `await` to settle (either resolve or reject). Once the Promise settles, the async function resumes execution, using the result of the Promise.

Example: Fetching Data with `async/await`

```
async function fetchData(): Promise<any> { const response = await
fetch('https://api.example.com/data'); // Await the Promise const data = await
response.json(); // Await another Promise return data; } fetchData().then(data
=> { console.log(data); }).catch(error => { console.error('Error:', error);
});
```

In this example, `fetchData` is an async function that fetches data from an API. Notice how the `await` keyword makes the code read more like synchronous code. We wait for the `fetch` Promise to resolve, then wait for the `response.json()` Promise to resolve, and finally return the parsed data.

Why Use Async Functions?

- **Cleaner Syntax:** The `async/await` syntax is significantly cleaner and easier to read than traditional Promise chaining with `.then()` and `.catch()`.
- **Error Handling:** You can use standard `try...catch` blocks to handle errors in async functions, just like in synchronous code.
- **Better Control Flow:** The `await` keyword allows you to pause and wait for specific operations, giving you more control over the flow of your asynchronous code.

Important Points

- Async functions always return a Promise.
- Use `await` inside async functions to pause execution and wait for Promises to settle.
- You can use `try...catch` for error handling in async functions.

Async functions have become the preferred way to write asynchronous code in TypeScript (and JavaScript). By making asynchronous code look and behave more like synchronous code, they improve readability, maintainability, and overall developer experience. Next up, we'll dive into the details of the `await` keyword and how it works.

Await Expressions

The `await` keyword is the magical companion to `async` functions, allowing you to pause the execution of your asynchronous code until a Promise is resolved. This seemingly simple mechanism revolutionizes how you work with asynchronous operations, making your code read more like synchronous code and significantly improving readability.

How `await` Works

1. **Pausing Execution:** When you place `await` before a Promise, the `async` function's execution is temporarily paused at that point. The function essentially "waits" for the Promise to settle (either resolve or reject) before moving on.
2. **Resolving and Returning:** If the Promise resolves successfully, the value it resolves with is returned to the `await` expression. You can then assign this value to a variable or use it directly in your code.
3. **Rejecting and Throwing:** If the Promise is rejected, the `await` expression throws an error. You can catch this error using a `try...catch` block (which we'll cover in the next section).

Syntax

```
async function myAsyncFunction() { const result = await myPromise; // Pause and wait for myPromise to resolve // ... use the result }
```

Example: Fetching and Parsing JSON Data

```
async function fetchAndParseData(url: string): Promise<any> { const response = await fetch(url); // Wait for fetch to complete const data = await response.json(); // Wait for response.json() to complete return data; }
```

In this example, `await` is used twice:

1. To wait for the initial `fetch` request to complete.
2. To wait for the `response.json()` method to parse the response body as JSON.

Only after both Promises have resolved does the function proceed to return the parsed `data`.

Simplifying Promise Chaining

The `await` keyword significantly simplifies Promise chaining compared to the traditional `.then()` approach. Instead of nesting callbacks, you can write your code in a more linear and synchronous-looking style.

```
// Promise chaining fetch(url) .then(response => response.json()) .then(data => { // Process the data }) .catch(error => { // Handle errors }); // Async/await async function fetchData(url: string) { const response = await fetch(url); const data = await response.json(); // Process the data } fetchData(url).catch(error => { // Handle errors });
```

The `async/await` version is much cleaner and easier to read, making the flow of the asynchronous logic more apparent.

Key Points

- `await` can only be used inside `async` functions.
- It pauses the execution of the async function until the Promise is settled.
- It returns the resolved value or throws an error if the Promise is rejected.
- `await` dramatically simplifies Promise chaining and error handling.

By embracing async functions and the `await` keyword, you can transform your asynchronous TypeScript code into a more readable, maintainable, and enjoyable form. This powerful combination is a cornerstone of modern JavaScript and TypeScript development.

Error Handling with Try...Catch

Even with the cleaner syntax of `async/await`, errors can still occur during asynchronous operations. Fortunately, `try...catch` blocks offer a familiar and reliable way to handle these errors gracefully within your `async` functions.

The `try...catch` Structure

The structure of a `try...catch` block is simple:

```
try { // Code that might throw an error const result = await
someAsyncOperation(); } catch (error) { // Code to handle the error
console.error("Error:", error); }
```

1. **try Block:** This block contains the code you suspect might throw an error. In the context of `async/await`, this would typically be an `await` expression waiting for a Promise to resolve.
2. **catch Block:** If an error occurs within the `try` block, execution immediately jumps to the `catch` block. The `error` parameter (you can name it anything) will be assigned the error object, which you can then inspect and handle.

Example: Handling API Errors

```
async function fetchUserData(userId: number): Promise<User> { try { const
response = await fetch(`/api/users/${userId}`); if (!response.ok) { throw new
Error(`Failed to fetch user: ${response.statusText}`); // Throw error for
non-200 status } return await response.json(); } catch (error) {
console.error("Error fetching user data:", error); throw error; // Rethrow the
error for further handling } }
```

In this example:

1. The `fetchUserData` function attempts to fetch user data from an API.
2. If the response status is not ok (not 200), it throws an error.
3. If any other error occurs during the fetch or JSON parsing process, the `catch` block catches it, logs the error, and re-throws it (so it can be potentially handled by another `catch` block further up the call stack).

Using Error Types with `catch`

You can use TypeScript's type system to make your error handling more specific:

```
try { // ... } catch (error: unknown) { // Catch any type of error if (error
instanceof NetworkError) { // Handle network errors } else if (error
instanceof ApiError) { // Handle API errors } else { // Handle other types of
errors } }
```

In this example, we catch the error as type unknown and then use type guards (`instanceof`) to narrow down the type before handling it.

Benefits of `try...catch` in Async Functions

- **Clear Error Handling:** Makes error handling more explicit and easier to understand.
- **Error Isolation:** Allows you to handle errors locally within specific `async` functions, preventing them from propagating and crashing your entire application.
- **Type Safety:** TypeScript's type system helps you write more accurate error handling logic.
- **Seamless Integration with `async/await`:** `try...catch` works seamlessly with `async` functions and `await` expressions, making error handling in asynchronous code more intuitive.

Key Points

- Use `try...catch` blocks within `async` functions to handle errors gracefully.

- The `try` block contains the code that might throw an error.
- The `catch` block handles the error.
- Use type guards to handle specific error types if needed.

By mastering error handling with `try...catch` in async functions, you'll be equipped to build more robust and reliable Node.js applications in TypeScript. Your code will be better prepared to recover from unexpected errors, ensuring a smoother experience for your users.

Real-World Examples

Fetching Data from APIs

Asynchronous operations are at the heart of modern web development, and fetching data from APIs is a prime example. Let's dive into how to use TypeScript, along with tools like `fetch` or `axios`, to retrieve data from APIs and handle responses gracefully using Promises or `async/await`.

Fetching with the `fetch` API

The `fetch` API is a built-in feature of modern browsers and is also available in Node.js with the `node-fetch` package. It provides a simple and intuitive way to make network requests.

Example: Fetching JSON Data

```
interface Todo { userId: number; id: number; title: string; completed:
boolean; } async function fetchTodos(): Promise<Todo[]> { try { const response
= await fetch('https://jsonplaceholder.typicode.com/todos'); if (!response.ok)
{ // Check if the request was successful (status code 200-299) throw new
Error(`HTTP error! status: ${response.status}`); } const data = await
response.json(); return data; } catch (error) { console.error('Error fetching
todos:', error); throw error; // Re-throw the error to be handled by the
caller if needed } } // Usage fetchTodos() .then(todos => {
console.log(todos); }) .catch(error => { // Handle errors });
```

Explanation:

1. We define an interface Todo to model the data structure we expect from the API.
2. The `fetchTodos` function is declared as `async`, indicating that it returns a Promise that resolves with an array of Todo objects.
3. We use `await fetch()` to make the request and wait for the response.
4. We check if the response is successful using `response.ok`. If not, we throw an error.
5. We use `await response.json()` to parse the response body as JSON.
6. The parsed data is returned as a `Todo[]`.

Fetching with `axios`

Axios is a popular third-party library that simplifies making HTTP requests. It automatically parses JSON responses and offers additional features like request/response interception.

```
import axios from 'axios'; async function fetchPosts() { try { const response
= await axios.get('https://jsonplaceholder.typicode.com/posts'); return
```

```
response.data; } catch (error: any) { console.error('Error fetching posts:', error.message); // Access the specific error message property from axios throw error; } }
```

Key Points

- Use the `fetch` API or libraries like `axios` to make asynchronous HTTP requests.
- Define TypeScript interfaces to model the expected response data.
- Handle errors gracefully using `try...catch` blocks or `.catch()` in Promise chains.

By combining these techniques, you can seamlessly integrate external data into your Node.js applications while maintaining type safety and robustness.

Reading/Writing Files

Node.js provides the `fs` (file system) module for interacting with files and directories on your server. The `fs/promises` API (introduced in Node.js 10.0) offers a convenient way to perform file operations asynchronously using Promises, which integrate beautifully with TypeScript's `async/await` syntax.

1. Reading Files Asynchronously

```
import fs from 'fs/promises'; // Import the fs/promises API async function readFile(filePath: string): Promise<string> { try { const data = await fs.readFile(filePath, 'utf-8'); return data; } catch (error) { console.error(`Error reading file from ${filePath}:`, error); throw error; // Rethrow the error for handling elsewhere } } // Usage const filePath = 'data.txt'; readFile(filePath).then(data => { console.log(data); }).catch(error => { // Handle the error here });
```

In this example:

- We import the `fs/promises` API.
- The `readFile` function takes a `filePath` (string) and returns a Promise that resolves with the file contents as a string.
- We use `await` to pause execution until the `fs.readFile` Promise resolves.
- We handle potential errors using a `try...catch` block.

2. Writing Files Asynchronously

```
import fs from 'fs/promises'; async function writeFile(filePath: string, data: string): Promise<void> { try { await fs.writeFile(filePath, data, 'utf-8'); console.log(`File written to ${filePath}`); } catch (error) { console.error(`Error writing file to ${filePath}:`, error); throw error; // Rethrow the error for handling elsewhere } } // Usage: const filePathToWrite = 'output.txt'; const dataToWrite = 'Hello, from Node.js!'; writeFile(filePathToWrite, dataToWrite);
```

In this example:

- The `writeFile` function takes a `filePath` and the `data` to write as a string. It returns a Promise that resolves when the writing is complete.
- We use `await` to wait for the `fs.writeFile` operation to finish.
- Error handling is done similarly to the `readFile` example.

Key Points:

- Use the `fs/promises` API for Promise-based asynchronous file operations.
- Use `async/await` to write clean and readable asynchronous code.
- Always handle errors using `try...catch` to prevent your application from crashing.
- You can use similar patterns to work with other asynchronous `fs` operations like `appendFile`, `mkdir`, `readdir`, etc.

Important Considerations:

- **Encoding:** When reading or writing files, it's important to specify the correct encoding (e.g., 'utf-8') to ensure proper handling of characters.
- **Error Handling:** File operations can fail due to various reasons (e.g., file not found, permissions issues). Make sure to handle these errors gracefully to provide a good user experience.
- **File Paths:** Use absolute file paths whenever possible to avoid ambiguity and ensure that your code works correctly regardless of the current working directory.

By using the `fs/promises` API and `async/await`, you can write asynchronous file-handling code in Node.js that is both efficient and easy to read and maintain.

Working with Timeouts and Intervals

Timers are a fundamental tool in JavaScript for scheduling tasks to run in the future. Node.js provides the `setTimeout` and `setInterval` functions, which are inherently asynchronous. Let's explore how to use them effectively with TypeScript, along with how to integrate them with Promises and `async/await`.

`setTimeout`: Running a Task After a Delay

The `setTimeout` function schedules a callback function to be executed once after a specified delay (in milliseconds).

```
function greetAfterDelay(name: string, delayMs: number) { setTimeout(() => {
console.log(`Hello, ${name} (after ${delayMs} ms)!`); }, delayMs); }
greetAfterDelay("Alice", 2000); // Output (after 2 seconds): "Hello, Alice
(after 2000 ms)!"
```

`setInterval`: Repeating a Task

The `setInterval` function schedules a callback to be executed repeatedly at a specified interval (in milliseconds).

```
function countDown(from: number) { let currentCount = from; const intervalId =
setInterval(() => { console.log(currentCount); currentCount--; if
(currentCount < 0) { clearInterval(intervalId); // Stop the interval } },
1000); // 1000 milliseconds = 1 second } countDown(5); // Output: 5, 4, 3, 2,
1
```

Promises and Timers

You can create a Promise that resolves after a timeout using `setTimeout`:

```
function delay(ms: number): Promise<void> { return new Promise((resolve) => setTimeout(resolve, ms)); } async function delayedGreeting(name: string) { await delay(1000); console.log(`Hello, ${name}!`); } delayedGreeting("Bob"); // Output (after 1 second): "Hello, Bob!"
```

Here, the `delay` function returns a Promise that resolves after the specified number of milliseconds. In `delayedGreeting`, we `await` this Promise, effectively pausing execution until the delay is complete.

`async/await` with `setInterval` (Caution!)

While you can use `await` inside an `async` function to wait for a single interval iteration, be cautious when using `await` in a loop with `setInterval`. This can lead to unexpected behavior if the interval fires faster than the `await` can resolve.

Alternative: Recursive `setTimeout`

A safer way to achieve repeated tasks with `await` is to use a recursive `setTimeout` function:

```
async function repeatTask(task: () => Promise<void>, intervalMs: number) { await task(); setTimeout(() => repeatTask(task, intervalMs), intervalMs); } async function myTask() { // ... your task logic ... } repeatTask(myTask, 3000); // Repeat myTask every 3 seconds
```

Key Points

- `setTimeout` and `setInterval` are asynchronous functions for scheduling tasks.
- Use `setTimeout` to execute a task once after a delay.
- Use `setInterval` for repeating tasks at regular intervals (remember to clear the interval when done).
- You can create Promises that resolve after a timeout.
- Use `async/await` to write cleaner code with timers, but be careful with `setInterval`.
- Consider using recursive `setTimeout` for safer repeated tasks with `await`.

By mastering timers and integrating them with Promises and `async/await`, you can add time-based behavior to your Node.js applications while maintaining clean and predictable code.

Best Practices for Asynchronous TypeScript Code

Choosing Between Promises and Async/Await

Promises and `async/await` are both powerful tools for handling asynchronous operations in TypeScript. They are often interchangeable, but each has its strengths and weaknesses, making them more suitable for different scenarios. Let's weigh the options to help you choose the right approach for your code.

Promises: The Foundation

Promises provide a structured way to represent the eventual result of an asynchronous operation. They offer a chainable interface using `.then`, `.catch`, and `.finally`, allowing you to express sequential dependencies between asynchronous tasks.

Advantages of Promises:

- **Explicit Chaining:** Clearly shows the order in which asynchronous operations are executed.
- **Error Handling:** Easily handle errors using `.catch` and perform cleanup with `.finally`.
- **Widely Supported:** Available in all modern browsers and Node.js environments.

Disadvantages of Promises:

- **Callback Hell:** Deeply nested `.then` blocks can become difficult to read and maintain (though this can be mitigated with techniques like Promise.all).
- **Less Intuitive:** The syntax for error handling and complex chaining might be less intuitive than synchronous code.

Async/Await: The Streamlined Syntax

Async/await builds on top of Promises, providing a more concise and synchronous-looking syntax for writing asynchronous code.

Advantages of Async/Await:

- **Readability:** Code resembles synchronous code, making it easier to understand the flow of logic.
- **Error Handling:** Error handling using `try...catch` blocks feels familiar and intuitive.
- **Conciseness:** Eliminates the need for nested `.then` blocks, resulting in cleaner code.

Disadvantages of Async/Await:

- **Requires async Functions:** You can only use `await` inside functions marked with the `async` keyword.
- **Error Handling Gotchas:** It's easy to forget to handle errors with `try...catch`, which can lead to unhandled rejections.
- **Less Flexible (Potentially):** Might not be the best fit for scenarios that require very fine-grained control over Promise execution order.

When to Choose Promises

Consider using Promises directly when:

- **You need very precise control over the order of Promise execution.**
- **You're working with older browsers or Node.js versions that don't support `async/await`.**
- **You have a strong preference for the explicit chaining style.**

When to Choose Async/Await

Opt for async/await when:

- **Readability is a priority.** Async/await makes your code more concise and easier to follow.
- **You have linear, sequential asynchronous operations.** Async/await excels at expressing simple flows.
- **You're comfortable with error handling using `try...catch`.**

Real-World Considerations

- **Mixing and Matching:** In many cases, you can use a mix of Promises and async/await in your code. For example, you might use `async/await` at a higher level to handle the main flow of your logic, while still using Promise chaining within specific functions.
- **Library Compatibility:** Be mindful of the libraries and APIs you're using. Some might primarily use Promises, while others might be designed to work seamlessly with async/await. Choose the approach that aligns best with the libraries you're using.

Remember, there's no one-size-fits-all answer. The choice between Promises and async/await often depends on personal preference, the specific use case, and the complexity of your asynchronous code. By understanding their strengths and weaknesses, you can make an informed decision and write clean, efficient, and maintainable asynchronous TypeScript code.

Error Handling Strategies

Error handling is paramount in asynchronous TypeScript code, especially in Node.js applications where errors can arise from network requests, database interactions, file operations, and more. Let's dive into best practices for creating robust error-handling mechanisms that prevent crashes and provide meaningful feedback.

1. The Power of `try...catch`

The `try...catch` block is your first line of defense against errors in asynchronous code. When working with promises or `async/await`, always wrap your code in a `try...catch` block to catch any potential errors.

```
async function fetchData() { try { const response = await
fetch('https://api.example.com/data'); const data = await response.json(); //
... process the data } catch (error) { console.error("An error occurred:",
error); // ... handle the error (e.g., retry, show an error message to the
user) } }
```

In this example, the `try` block contains the code that could potentially throw an error (e.g., a network error during the fetch request). If an error occurs, it's immediately caught in the `catch` block, allowing you to log the error and take appropriate action.

2. Logging Errors: Gaining Insight into Failures

Logging errors is crucial for debugging and understanding what went wrong in your application. In Node.js, you can use libraries like `winston` or `bunyan` for more sophisticated logging, but even a simple `console.error` can be helpful.

```
catch (error) { console.error("An error occurred:", error); // ... additional
error handling ... }
```

Remember to include relevant information in your log messages, such as the time of the error, the location in your code where it occurred (e.g., file name, function name, line number), and any relevant details about the error itself.

3. Informative Error Messages: Guiding Users

When an error occurs, it's important to provide users with clear and informative error messages. Avoid vague messages like "Something went wrong" that don't offer any actionable guidance.

```
catch (error) { if (error instanceof ValidationError) { res.status(400).json({
error: error.message }); // Specific validation error } else if (error
instanceof NotFoundError) { res.status(404).json({ error: "Resource not found"
}); } else { res.status(500).json({ error: "Internal server error" }); //
Generic error for unexpected issues } }
```

In this example, we differentiate between different types of errors (e.g., validation errors, not found errors) and provide tailored error messages for each scenario.

4. Error Handling Middleware (Express.js)

In Express.js, you can create dedicated error-handling middleware that sits at the end of your middleware chain and catches any unhandled errors. This provides a central place to manage errors and ensures that they are handled consistently across your application.

```
app.use((err: Error, req: Request, res: Response, next: NextFunction) => {
console.error(err); res.status(500).json({ error: "Internal server error" });
});
```

Additional Tips

- **Use Custom Error Classes:** (as discussed in a previous section) to create specific error types that convey more information about the nature of the error.
- **Retry Logic:** Consider implementing retry mechanisms for transient errors (e.g., network issues) to improve the resilience of your application.
- **Monitoring and Alerting:** For production environments, integrate error logging with monitoring and alerting tools to proactively detect and address issues.

By following these best practices and incorporating a robust error-handling strategy into your TypeScript Node.js code, you'll create applications that are not only more reliable and easier to debug but also provide a better experience for your users.

Avoiding Callback Hell

In the early days of asynchronous JavaScript, handling multiple sequential or dependent asynchronous operations often led to a dreaded phenomenon known as “callback hell.” This refers to a situation where your code becomes a deeply nested pyramid of callbacks, making it difficult to read, understand, and maintain.

The Callback Hell Trap

Let's imagine a scenario where you need to fetch data from multiple APIs in sequence. With a callback-based approach, it might look something like this:

```
fetch('/api/user/123', (userError, userData) => { if (userError) { // Handle
user fetch error } else { fetch(`/api/orders/${userData.id}`, (orderError,
orderData) => { if (orderError) { // Handle order fetch error } else {
fetch(`/api/products/${orderData.productId}`, (productError, productData) => {
if (productError) { // Handle product fetch error } else { // Finally, do
something with the data } }); } }); } });
```

As you can see, this code quickly becomes a tangled mess of nested callbacks, making it hard to follow the logic and even harder to debug.

Promises to the Rescue

Promises offer a more structured way to handle asynchronous operations and avoid callback hell. By chaining `.then()` methods, you can express the sequence of operations in a more linear and readable manner.

```
fetch('/api/user/123') .then(response => response.json()) .then(userData =>
fetch(`/api/orders/${userData.id}`)) .then(response => response.json())
.then(orderData => fetch(`/api/products/${orderData.productId}`))
.then(response => response.json()) .then(productData => { // Finally, do
something with the data }) .catch(error => { // Handle errors });
```

- Here you can see, all the promises are now chained in a linear way making it much easier to read and maintain.

`async/await`: The Elegance of Synchronous-Like Code

Async/await takes this improvement a step further. By using the `await` keyword, you can pause the execution of an `async` function until a Promise is resolved, making your code look remarkably like synchronous code.

```
async function fetchData() { try { const userResponse = await
fetch('/api/user/123'); const userData = await userResponse.json(); const
orderResponse = await fetch(`/api/orders/${userData.id}`); const orderData =
await orderResponse.json(); const productResponse = await
fetch(`/api/products/${orderData.productId}`); const productData = await
productResponse.json(); // Do something with the data } catch (error) { //
Handle errors } }
```

- The above code makes it super easy to understand the flow of logic of this async code by removing all the callbacks and writing it as a synchronous code.

Key Points

- Callback hell is a common issue in asynchronous JavaScript code with deeply nested callbacks.
- Promises and `async/await` provide cleaner and more structured ways to handle asynchronous operations.
- Promise chaining using `.then()` creates a more linear flow of code.
- `async/await` makes asynchronous code look and behave like synchronous code.
- Error handling with `try...catch` in async/await is more concise and familiar.

By adopting Promises and async/await, you can transform your asynchronous TypeScript code into a more elegant, readable, and maintainable form, liberating you from the clutches of callback hell.

Proper Use of Async/Await

While `async/await` offers a more elegant way to write asynchronous code, it's important to understand its nuances and use it judiciously. Let's explore when `await` is appropriate and when it might be best to use alternative approaches.

When to Use `await`

- **Sequential Operations:** `await` shines when you have a series of asynchronous operations that need to be executed in a specific order. The linear, sequential nature of `await` makes the code easier to read and reason about.
- **Dependent Operations:** When the result of one asynchronous operation is needed before the next one can start, `await` is the perfect tool to express this dependency clearly.
- **Error Handling:** `await` integrates seamlessly with `try...catch` blocks, making error handling in asynchronous code as straightforward as in synchronous code.

Example: Sequential Data Fetching

```
async function fetchUserProfile(userId: string) { const profileResponse =
await fetch(`/api/users/${userId}`); const profileData = await
profileResponse.json(); const postsResponse = await
fetch(`/api/users/${userId}/posts`); const postsData = await
postsResponse.json(); return { profile: profileData, posts: postsData }; }
```

In this example, we need to fetch the user profile before we can fetch their posts. The `await` keyword ensures that we wait for each fetch to complete before moving on to the next one.

When to Avoid `await` (or Use it Sparingly)

- **Independent Operations:** If you have multiple asynchronous operations that can run independently and their order doesn't matter, using `Promise.all` might be more efficient than multiple `await` statements.
- **Top-Level Code:** Avoid using `await` at the top level of your code (outside of an `async` function), as it can block the execution of other code in your application.
- **Performance Considerations:** While `await` is convenient, excessive use can potentially introduce minor performance overhead. If you have a large number of independent asynchronous operations, consider using `Promise.all` to parallelize them, or explore more advanced techniques like asynchronous iterators.

Optimizing Asynchronous Code with TypeScript

Here are some tips for optimizing asynchronous code in TypeScript:

- **Promise.all for Parallelism:** Use `Promise.all` to run multiple independent promises concurrently.
- **Async Iterators:** Explore asynchronous iterators for more efficient handling of streams of data.
- **Batching:** If you need to make multiple requests to an API, consider batching them together to reduce network overhead.
- **Caching:** Cache results of expensive or slow asynchronous operations to avoid redundant calculations.
- **Debouncing and Throttling:** Limit the rate at which events (like user input or scrolling) trigger asynchronous operations to prevent performance issues.

Key Points

- Use `await` for sequential and dependent asynchronous operations.
- Consider `Promise.all` for independent operations to potentially improve performance.
- Avoid `await` at the top level of your code.
- Be mindful of the potential performance impact of excessive use of `await`.
- Explore alternative techniques like asynchronous iterators for more advanced scenarios.

By understanding the nuances of `async/await` and following best practices, you can write asynchronous TypeScript code that is not only clean and readable but also efficient and performant.

Chapter Summary

In this chapter, we explored the asynchronous world of TypeScript, where tasks can be performed concurrently without blocking the main thread of execution. Here's a recap of what we covered:

- **Understanding Asynchronous Code:**
  - We defined asynchronicity as the ability to perform tasks concurrently without waiting for each task to finish before starting the next.
  - We discussed how JavaScript's single-threaded nature and the event loop make asynchronous operations essential for building responsive applications.
  - We identified common asynchronous operations in Node.js, such as file operations, network requests, database queries, and timers.
- **Promises: Managing Asynchronous Operations:**
  - We introduced Promises as objects that represent the eventual results of asynchronous operations, explaining their three possible states: pending, fulfilled, and rejected.
  - We showed how to create and resolve Promises using the `Promise` constructor, the `resolve` and `reject` functions, and how to chain them with `.then()`.
  - We discussed `Promise.all` and `Promise.allSettled` for handling multiple Promises concurrently, highlighting their differences in behavior.
  - We explored error handling with Promises using `.catch` to handle rejections and `.finally` to perform cleanup tasks.
- **Async/Await: A Cleaner Syntax for Promises:**
  - We introduced `async` functions as a way to write asynchronous code that looks more like synchronous code.
  - We explained how to use the `await` keyword to pause execution until a Promise is resolved, simplifying Promise chaining.
  - We demonstrated how to handle errors in `async` functions using `try...catch` blocks.
- **Real-World Examples:**
  - We provided practical examples of using `fetch` and `axios` to make asynchronous requests to APIs and how to handle responses with Promises or `async/await`.
  - We showed how to perform asynchronous file operations using Node.js's `fs/promises` API and `async/await`.
  - We demonstrated how to work with timers (`setTimeout` and `setInterval`) in asynchronous code.
- **Best Practices for Asynchronous TypeScript Code:**
  - We discussed when to choose Promises or `async/await` based on code complexity and readability requirements.
  - We emphasized the importance of error handling in asynchronous code, using `try...catch`, logging errors, and providing informative messages.
  - We explained how to avoid callback hell and how to use `async/await` effectively.

By mastering asynchronous programming techniques with TypeScript, you are now equipped to handle real-world scenarios like data fetching, file operations, and more, creating efficient and responsive Node.js applications. With a solid understanding of Promises, `async/await`, and error handling, you can confidently tackle the challenges of asynchronous programming and build robust and reliable backend systems.

Testing Your TypeScript Code: Ensuring Quality

Outline

- Introduction to Testing
    - The Importance of Testing
    - Types of Tests (Unit, Integration, End-to-End)
- Test Runners and Frameworks
    - Jest: A Popular Choice for TypeScript
    - Mocha: A Flexible Alternative
- Writing Your First Test
    - Anatomy of a Test
    - Assertions with Jest
    - Mocking Dependencies
- Testing React Components
    - React Testing Library (RTL): Testing from the User's Perspective
    - Jest with React Testing Library
    - Snapshot Testing
- Testing Node.js Applications
    - Testing API Endpoints with Supertest
    - Testing Database Interactions
- Continuous Integration (CI)
    - Integrating Testing into Your Workflow
    - Popular CI Tools
- Best Practices for Testing TypeScript Code
    - Test Coverage
    - Test-Driven Development (TDD)
    - Maintainable Tests
- Chapter Summary

Introduction to Testing

The Importance of Testing

Testing is a fundamental practice in software development, regardless of the language or framework you use. In the realm of TypeScript, where type safety provides a certain level of confidence, testing remains crucial for ensuring the overall quality, reliability, and maintainability of your code.

Why Testing is Essential

- **Early Bug Detection:** Tests act as a safety net, catching errors and bugs before they reach your users. By writing tests that exercise different parts of your code, you can identify and fix issues early in the development cycle, when they are typically less expensive and easier to resolve.
- **Preventing Regressions:** As you modify and evolve your codebase, tests help prevent regressions – unintended side effects or the reintroduction of previously fixed bugs. Running your test suite after every change gives you confidence that existing functionality hasn't been broken inadvertently.
- **Improving Code Design:** The process of writing tests often forces you to think more carefully about how your code should be structured and organized. This can lead to better design decisions and more modular code that is easier to understand and maintain.

- **Documentation Through Examples:** Well-written tests can serve as executable documentation, illustrating how different parts of your code should be used and what outputs are expected. This is particularly valuable for complex or subtle edge cases.
- **Confidence and Peace of Mind:** A comprehensive test suite gives you and your team confidence that your code is working as intended. This allows you to make changes and deploy new features with greater assurance, knowing that your tests are there to catch any issues before they affect your users.

Testing TypeScript: Beyond Type Safety

While TypeScript's static type system helps catch a wide range of errors related to type mismatches, it doesn't guarantee the absence of logical errors. Your code might be perfectly type-safe, but it could still contain bugs due to incorrect calculations, faulty logic, or unexpected edge cases.

This is where testing comes in. By writing tests that verify the correctness of your code's behavior, you can uncover these logical errors and ensure that your TypeScript applications function as expected.

Key Points

- Testing is essential for catching bugs early, preventing regressions, and improving code design.
- Tests act as a safety net and provide confidence in the quality of your codebase.
- TypeScript's type safety doesn't eliminate the need for testing, as it doesn't catch logical errors.
- A comprehensive test suite helps you build reliable, maintainable, and trustworthy applications.

In the following sections, we'll dive into different types of tests, popular testing frameworks for TypeScript, and best practices for writing effective tests.

Types of Tests (Unit, Integration, End-to-End)

In the world of software testing, there are various levels at which you can validate the functionality and correctness of your code. Understanding these different types of tests and their purposes is crucial for creating a comprehensive testing strategy.

Unit Tests

What: Unit tests focus on the smallest testable parts of your code—individual functions, classes, or modules. They isolate these units and verify that they work correctly in isolation, given specific inputs and expected outputs.

Purpose:

- Catch errors early in the development cycle.
- Ensure that individual units of code work as expected.
- Facilitate refactoring by providing confidence that changes don't break existing functionality.

When to Use:

- For testing the core logic of functions and methods.
- For verifying that classes and objects behave as intended.
- For testing utility functions or helper modules.

Integration Tests

What: Integration tests assess how different units of code work together. They verify that the interactions between components, modules, or services are functioning correctly.

Purpose:

- Catch errors that arise from the combination of multiple units.
- Ensure that data flows correctly between different parts of the application.
- Verify that the overall system behavior is as expected.

When to Use:

- For testing interactions between components (e.g., parent-child communication).
- For testing communication between modules or services.
- For testing how your application interacts with external APIs or databases.

End-to-End (E2E) Tests

What: End-to-end tests simulate real user scenarios and verify that the entire application works as expected from start to finish. They typically involve interacting with the user interface, making API requests, and checking the resulting behavior.

Purpose:

- Catch issues that might not be apparent in unit or integration tests, such as UI glitches or complex interactions.
- Ensure that the application behaves correctly from the user's perspective.
- Validate the application in a production-like environment.

When to Use:

- For testing critical user flows (e.g., signup, login, checkout).
- For verifying that the frontend and backend components work together seamlessly.
- For testing in a realistic environment (e.g., with a real database and network interactions).

The Testing Pyramid

The different types of tests are often visualized as a pyramid:

```
  E2E Tests
Integration Tests
  Unit Tests
```

This illustrates the ideal distribution of tests:

- **Unit Tests:** The base of the pyramid, with the largest number of tests. They are fast to run and provide granular feedback on individual components.
- **Integration Tests:** A smaller layer that focuses on the interactions between units.
- **E2E Tests:** The smallest layer, covering critical user flows. They are slower and more complex to write but provide the highest level of confidence in the overall application.

Key Points

- A balanced combination of unit, integration, and E2E tests provides comprehensive coverage of your application.
- Start with unit tests to establish a solid foundation.
- Add integration tests to verify how different parts of your code work together.
- Use E2E tests to validate critical user flows and overall application behavior.

By strategically employing different types of tests, you can ensure that your TypeScript code is thoroughly tested, reducing the risk of bugs, improving code quality, and instilling confidence in the reliability of your applications.

Test Runners and Frameworks

Jest: A Popular Choice for TypeScript

In the realm of TypeScript testing, Jest stands out as a versatile and powerful framework that simplifies the process of writing and running tests. Developed by Facebook, Jest is renowned for its comprehensive features, ease of use, and smooth integration with TypeScript projects.

Key Features

- **Built-in Test Runner:** Jest comes with a built-in test runner that automatically discovers and executes your test files. No need to set up additional tools for running your tests.
- **Assertion Library:** It includes a rich assertion library (using `expect`) with a wide range of matchers for verifying the behavior of your code.
- **Mocking Capabilities:** Jest's mocking features allow you to easily replace external dependencies (like API calls or database interactions) with controlled substitutes, making your tests more focused and reliable.
- **Simple Syntax:** Jest's syntax is clean, intuitive, and easy to learn, even for developers new to testing.
- **Fast Execution and Parallelization:** Jest is designed for speed. It can run tests in parallel, significantly reducing the overall execution time of your test suite.
- **Snapshot Testing:** Jest's snapshot testing lets you capture the rendered output of your React components and compare it against a stored snapshot, making it easy to detect unexpected changes in your UI.
- **Code Coverage Reporting:** Jest can automatically generate reports that show how much of your code is covered by tests, helping you identify areas that need more testing.

Installing Jest

To install Jest and its TypeScript support in your project, run the following command:

```
npm install --save-dev jest ts-jest @types/jest # or yarn add --dev jest
ts-jest @types/jest
```

Creating a Basic Test File

Jest expects your test files to have a specific naming convention. They should either end in `.test.ts` or `.spec.ts`. Let's create a simple test file called `sum.test.ts`:

```
// sum.test.ts function sum(a: number, b: number): number { return a + b; }
test('adds 1 + 2 to equal 3', () => { expect(sum(1, 2)).toBe(3); });
```

- Here you can see the `sum` function and its unit test case.

Running Tests

You can run your tests using the following command:

```
npm test # or yarn test
```

Jest will automatically find all files matching the test naming convention and execute the tests within them.

Configuring Jest

While Jest works well with its default configuration in most cases, you can customize it further. Create a `jest.config.js` file at the root of your project:

```
// jest.config.js module.exports = { // ... your Jest configuration ...
preset: 'ts-jest', // Use ts-jest for TypeScript support };
```

Key Points

- Jest is a powerful and popular testing framework for TypeScript.
- It provides a built-in test runner, assertion library, mocking, snapshot testing, and code coverage.
- Install Jest and its TypeScript support using npm `install --save-dev jest ts-jest @types/jest`.
- Name your test files with the `.test.ts` or `.spec.ts` extension.
- Run tests using `npm test` (or `yarn test`).
- Customize Jest configuration using `jest.config.js`.

With Jest as your testing ally, you'll be well-equipped to write comprehensive tests for your TypeScript code, ensuring its quality, reliability, and maintainability.

Mocha: A Flexible Alternative

While Jest is a popular all-in-one solution for testing TypeScript code, Mocha offers a compelling alternative, especially for those who prefer a more customizable and modular approach.

Flexibility and Choice

The key differentiator of Mocha is its flexibility. Unlike Jest, which comes bundled with its own assertion and mocking libraries, Mocha allows you to choose your preferred tools for these tasks.

Here are some popular choices for combining with Mocha:

- **Assertion Libraries:**
  - **Chai:** Offers a variety of assertion styles (expect, should, assert) to suit different preferences.
  - **Expect.js:** Provides a BDD-style (Behavior Driven Development) interface for writing expressive assertions.
- **Mocking Libraries:**
  - **Sinon.JS:** A powerful library for creating spies, stubs, and mocks to control the behavior of dependencies in your tests.

Benefits of Mocha's Flexibility

- **Customization:** You have the freedom to choose the assertion and mocking libraries that best fit your project's style and requirements.
- **Modularity:** Mocha's modular nature allows you to pick and choose the features you need, keeping your testing stack lean and efficient.
- **Integration:** Mocha integrates well with other testing tools and libraries, giving you a wide range of options for building your testing infrastructure.

Example: Using Mocha with Chai and Sinon.JS

```
import { expect } from 'chai'; import { spy } from 'sinon';
describe('MyFunction', () => { it('should do something', () => { const mySpy =
spy(); // Create a Sinon spy myFunction(mySpy);
expect(mySpy.calledOnce).to.be.true; // ... other assertions ... }); });
```

Who Should Consider Mocha

Mocha is a good option if you:

- **Value flexibility:** You prefer to have the freedom to choose your own testing tools and libraries.
- **Have complex testing needs:** Your project might have unique testing requirements that are better addressed by specialized libraries that integrate with Mocha.
- **Want a minimal footprint:** Mocha itself is a relatively lightweight library, making it suitable for projects where bundle size is a concern.

Key Points

- Mocha is a flexible and customizable testing framework.
- It allows you to choose your own assertion and mocking libraries.
- It integrates well with other testing tools and libraries.
- It's a good choice for projects with complex testing needs or a desire for customization.

Both Jest and Mocha are excellent choices for TypeScript testing, and the best one for you depends on your personal preferences and the specific requirements of your project.

Writing Your First Test

Anatomy of a Test

In Jest, test cases follow a clear and intuitive structure, making them easy to read, understand, and maintain. Let's break down the anatomy of a typical test case.

1. The `describe` Block: Grouping Tests

The `describe` block is used to group related tests together. It provides a descriptive label for a set of tests, making your test output more organized and easier to navigate.

```
describe("Math Utilities", () => { // Test cases for the MathUtils module go
here });
```

In this example, we create a `describe` block called "Math Utilities" to group tests related to a hypothetical module of mathematical functions.

2. The `test` (or `it`) Block: Defining a Test Case

Inside the `describe` block, you define individual test cases using the `test` or `it` function. Both functions are interchangeable and serve the same purpose. They take two arguments:

1. **Test Name (string):** A descriptive name for your test that explains what you're testing. Aim for clear and concise names that accurately reflect the behavior you expect.
2. **Test Function:** A function that contains the actual code to execute your test. This is where you'll call the function or method you're testing, set up any necessary data or mocks, and make assertions to verify the results.

```
describe("Math Utilities", () => { test("addition works correctly", () =>
{ // Test case for addition function }); it("subtraction works
correctly", () => { // Test case for subtraction function }); });
```

In this example, we have two test cases: one for testing the `addition` function and another for testing the `subtraction` function.

3. Assertions: Verifying Expected Behavior

Assertions are the heart of your test cases. They are statements that check whether the actual result of your code matches the expected result. Jest provides a rich set of assertion methods that you can use to check equality, truthiness, object properties, exceptions, and more.

```
test('adds 1 + 2 to equal 3', () => { expect(sum(1, 2)).toBe(3); // Assertion
using Jest's `expect` and `toBe` matcher });
```

In this basic example, the `expect(sum(1, 2)).toBe(3)` assertion checks if the result of calling the `sum` function with arguments 1 and 2 is equal to 3. If the assertion passes, the test passes; if it fails, Jest will report an error.

Key Points

- Use `describe` blocks to group related tests together.
- Define individual test cases using `test` or `it` blocks.
- Use descriptive names for your tests.
- Write assertions within your test functions to verify the expected behavior of your code.
- Jest provides a wide range of assertion methods to cover various scenarios.

By following this structured approach, you'll create well-organized and easy-to-follow test suites that ensure the quality and reliability of your TypeScript code.

Assertions with Jest

Assertions are the heart of your unit tests. They are statements that express what you *expect* the result of a specific piece of code to be. Jest provides a rich set of assertion methods that allow you to check for equality, truthiness, object properties, exceptions, and much more.

The `expect` Function

At the core of Jest's assertion library is the `expect` function. You pass the actual value you want to test into `expect`, and then chain it with a matcher function that performs the desired comparison.

```
expect(someValue).toBe(someOtherValue); // Checks strict equality
```

Common Matchers

Jest offers a wide variety of matchers to cover different scenarios. Here are some of the most frequently used ones:

- **`toBe(value)`:** Checks for strict equality (===) between the actual value and the expected `value`.
- **`toEqual(value)`:** Checks for deep equality between objects or arrays. It recursively checks that all nested properties and elements are the same.
- **`toBeTruthy()`:** Checks if the value is considered truthy (e.g., not `null`, `undefined`, `0`, `''`, `false`).
- **`toBeFalsy()`:** Checks if the value is considered falsy (e.g., `null`, `undefined`, `0`, `''`, `false`).
- **`toBeGreaterThan(number)`:** Checks if the value is greater than `number`.
- **`toBeLessThan(number)`:** Checks if the value is less than `number`.
- **`toContain(item)`:** Checks if an array or iterable contains `item`.

- **`toHaveProperty(keyPath, value?)`:** Checks if an object has a property at `keyPath`, optionally with the specified `value`.
- **`toThrow(error?)`:** Checks if a function throws an error, optionally matching the error or error message.
- **`toBeInstanceOf(class)`:** Checks if a value is an instance of a specific `class`.

Examples

```
// Testing a function that returns a string
expect(greet("Alice")).toBe("Hello, Alice!"); // Testing an array expect([1,
2, 3]).toContain(2); // Testing an object expect({ name: "Bob", age: 30
}).toHaveProperty("age", 30); // Testing for errors expect(() => divide(10,
0)).toThrow("Division by zero");
```

Asynchronous Assertions

For testing asynchronous code (e.g., Promises), Jest provides `.resolves` and `.rejects` matchers. They ensure that your code behaves as expected when dealing with asynchronous results:

```
test('fetches data successfully', async () => { const data = await
fetchData(); expect(data).resolves.toEqual({ id: 1, name: 'John Doe' }); });
test('fetch fails with an error', async () => {
expect(fetchDataWithInvalidUrl()).rejects.toThrow('Invalid URL'); });
```

- In these examples, `resolves` and `rejects` are matchers that wait for the promises from `fetchData` to be either resolved or rejected to complete before running the assertions.

Key Points

- Use Jest's `expect` function to make assertions.
- Choose the appropriate matcher for your specific test case.
- Use `.resolves` and `.rejects` for asynchronous assertions.

Jest's assertion library is comprehensive and intuitive, allowing you to write clear and expressive tests that thoroughly validate the behavior of your TypeScript code.

Mocking Dependencies

In the real world, your TypeScript code often interacts with external dependencies like databases, APIs, or other modules. When writing unit tests, however, it's crucial to isolate the code you're testing from these dependencies. This is where mocking comes in handy.

What is Mocking?

Mocking involves replacing a real dependency with a fake (mock) implementation in your tests. This allows you to:

- **Isolate the Unit Under Test:** Focus your tests on the specific function, class, or module you're testing without worrying about external factors.
- **Control Behavior:** Dictate how the mock dependency should behave in your tests, simulating different scenarios and responses.
- **Simplify Setup:** Avoid complex setup or interactions with real resources (like databases or networks) during testing.

- **Speed Up Tests:** Mock dependencies often execute much faster than real ones, making your tests run quickly.

Mocking with Jest

Jest provides excellent mocking capabilities out of the box. There are several ways to create and use mocks in Jest:

1. **`jest.fn()`:** Creates a simple mock function that you can use to track calls, parameters, and return values.

   ```
   const mockFn = jest.fn(); myFunction(mockFn); // Call the function with the mock expect(mockFn).toHaveBeenCalledTimes(1); // Check if the mock was called
   ```

2. **`jest.spyOn()`:** Creates a mock function that spies on an existing method on an object. You can use it to track calls, modify the implementation, or restore the original implementation later.

   ```
   const video = { play() { // ... } }; const spy = jest.spyOn(video, 'play'); // Spy on the play method video.play(); expect(spy).toHaveBeenCalled(); // Check if the method was called
   ```

3. **`jest.mock()`:** Mocks an entire module by creating a module factory for that module. By default it will automatically mock all of the functions (and classes) in the module for you.

   ```
   import axios from 'axios'; jest.mock('axios'); // Mocking the axios module test('should fetch users', async () => { const users = [{name: 'Bob'}]; const resp = {data: users}; (axios.get as jest.Mock).mockResolvedValue(resp); // or you could use the following depending on your use case: axios.get = jest.fn().mockResolvedValue(resp); const data = await fetchData(); expect(axios.get).toBeCalledWith('/users'); expect(data).toEqual(users); });
   ```

Example: Mocking an API Call

```
import { fetchData } from './api'; // Your module with an API call import axios from 'axios'; jest.mock('axios'); // Mock axios test('fetches data from API', async () => { // Set up the mock response (axios.get as jest.Mock).mockResolvedValue({ data: { message: "Success!" } }); const data = await fetchData(); expect(data).toEqual({ message: "Success!" }); });
```

In this example, we mock the `axios.get` function to return a specific response instead of making a real network request. This allows us to test the `fetchData` function in isolation, ensuring that it handles the response correctly.

Key Points

- Mocking involves replacing real dependencies with fake implementations.
- Jest provides a powerful mocking system that allows you to create and use mocks easily.
- Mocking is essential for isolating units of code and controlling their behavior in tests.

- By mocking dependencies, you can write faster and more reliable tests that focus on the core logic of your code.

By incorporating mocking into your TypeScript testing workflow, you'll create a more controlled and reliable testing environment, leading to higher quality and more maintainable code.

Testing React Components

React Testing Library (RTL): Testing from the User's Perspective

React Testing Library (RTL) has gained immense popularity in the React community due to its philosophy of testing components from the user's perspective. Instead of focusing on the internal implementation details of your components, RTL encourages you to test how users would interact with them, leading to more robust and meaningful tests.

The Guiding Principle

RTL's primary guiding principle is:

The more your tests resemble the way your software is used, the more confidence they can give you.

This means that your tests should interact with your components in the same way a real user would. This involves:

- **Querying the DOM:** RTL provides a set of utility functions (`screen.getBy...`, `screen.queryBy...`, `screen.findBy...`) to find elements in the rendered DOM based on text content, labels, roles, and other attributes that users would typically use to interact with the UI.
- **User Events:** RTL provides functions (`fireEvent`, `userEvent`) to simulate user interactions like clicking buttons, typing into input fields, and selecting options.
- **Avoiding Implementation Details:** RTL discourages direct access to component instances or internal state. This ensures that your tests focus on the component's observable behavior rather than its internal workings, making your tests less brittle and more resilient to changes.

Benefits of RTL

- **Confidence:** By testing how users interact with your components, you gain confidence that your application will work as expected in the real world.
- **Maintainability:** RTL tests are less likely to break when you refactor your components' internal implementation, as long as the user-facing behavior remains the same.
- **Accessibility:** RTL encourages you to write tests that verify the accessibility of your components, ensuring that they are usable by everyone, including people with disabilities.

Example: Testing a Button Component (using RTL)

```
import React from "react"; import { render, screen, fireEvent } from
"@testing-library/react"; import Button from "./Button"; // Your Button
component import { ButtonProps } from "./types/components"; test("Button
renders with correct label and calls onClick when clicked", () => { const
onClickMock = jest.fn(); render(<Button label="Click Me" onClick={onClickMock}
/>); const buttonElement = screen.getByRole('button', {name: /Click Me/i}); //
Find the button by its role and name
expect(buttonElement).toBeInTheDocument(); fireEvent.click(buttonElement);
```

```
expect(onClickMock).toHaveBeenCalledTimes(1); // Check if onClick was called
});
```

Key Points

- React Testing Library focuses on testing components from the user's perspective.
- Use query functions to find elements in the DOM based on how a user would interact with them.
- Simulate user interactions using `fireEvent` or `userEvent`.
- Avoid testing implementation details and focus on observable behavior.

By adopting the user-centric testing approach of React Testing Library, you'll write more meaningful and reliable tests for your TypeScript React components, leading to a higher quality user experience.

Jest with React Testing Library

Jest and React Testing Library (RTL) work hand-in-hand to form a formidable testing duo for your TypeScript React applications. Jest provides the testing framework (test runner, assertions, mocks), while RTL focuses on testing components from the user's perspective. Let's see how to combine their strengths to write comprehensive tests.

Example: Testing a `Counter` Component

```
// Counter.tsx import React, { useState } from 'react'; interface CounterProps
{ initialCount?: number; } function Counter({ initialCount = 0 }:
CounterProps) { const [count, setCount] = useState(initialCount); const
increment = () => setCount(count + 1); const decrement = () => setCount(count
- 1); return ( <div> <span>{count}</span> <button
onClick={decrement}>-</button> <button onClick={increment}>+</button> </div>
); } export default Counter;
```

```
// Counter.test.tsx import React from 'react'; import { render, screen,
fireEvent } from '@testing-library/react'; import '@testing-library/jest-dom';
// Import Jest DOM matchers import Counter from './Counter'; test('renders
initial count', () => { render(<Counter initialCount={5} />); const
countElement = screen.getByText('5'); // Use RTL to find the element
expect(countElement).toBeInTheDocument(); // Jest assertion });
test('increments count when button is clicked', async () => { render(<Counter
/>); const incrementButton = screen.getByText('+');
fireEvent.click(incrementButton); // Simulate click using RTL const
countElement = await screen.findByText('1'); // Wait for the count to update
expect(countElement).toBeInTheDocument(); });
```

Explanation:

1. **Import:** We import `render`, `screen`, and `fireEvent` from RTL and the `@testing-library/jest-dom` package to provide additional Jest matchers for DOM elements.
2. **`render(<Counter ... />)`:** We render the `Counter` component with optional props.

3. **`screen.getByText/getByRole`:** We use RTL's `screen.getByText` query to find elements in the rendered DOM by their text content, and also `screen.getByRole` to find elements by their role (e.g., 'button').
4. **`expect(...).toBeInTheDocument()`:** We use Jest assertions to verify that the elements are present in the DOM.
5. **`fireEvent.click()`:** We simulate a user clicking the increment button using RTL's `fireEvent` function.
6. **`screen.findByText()`:** In the second test, we use `screen.findByText` because the count update is asynchronous (due to React's state update mechanism). `findByText` waits for the element to appear and then returns a promise.

Key Points and Best Practices

- **User-Centric Testing:** Test how a user would interact with the component, not its internal implementation details.
- **Use Queries:** Rely on RTL's query functions (`getBy...`, `queryBy...`, `findBy...`) to find elements in a way that simulates how users would find them.
- **Simulate Interactions:** Use `fireEvent` (or the more advanced `userEvent`) to simulate user actions like clicking, typing, or selecting.
- **Avoid Implementation Details:** Don't directly access component instances or internal state in your tests.
- **Test Accessibility:** Ensure your tests cover accessibility aspects by using queries like `getByRole`.
- **Use Jest's Matchers:** Leverage Jest's rich set of matchers (e.g., `toBeInTheDocument`, `toHaveClass`, `toHaveTextContent`) to write expressive assertions.

By combining Jest and React Testing Library, you can create a comprehensive and effective testing strategy for your React components. Your tests will be more reliable, easier to maintain, and focus on delivering a great user experience.

Snapshot Testing

Snapshot testing is a unique approach to testing React components that focuses on verifying the rendered output (the UI structure) rather than the specific behavior. It's like taking a picture of your component's UI and then comparing that picture against a previously saved reference snapshot. If the snapshots don't match, it signals a potential change in your UI that you may not have intended.

How Snapshot Testing Works

1. **Initial Snapshot:** When you run a snapshot test for the first time, Jest automatically generates a snapshot file that captures the rendered output of your component. This snapshot file is typically stored alongside your test file.
2. **Subsequent Runs:** On subsequent test runs, Jest compares the newly rendered output with the stored snapshot. If the output has changed, the test fails, alerting you to a potential issue.
3. **Reviewing Changes:** You then review the changes and decide whether they are intentional or not. If the changes are expected (e.g., you intentionally updated the UI), you can update the snapshot to reflect the new state. If the changes are unexpected, it indicates a potential bug that needs to be addressed.

Example: Snapshot Test with React Testing Library

```
import React from "react"; import { render } from "@testing-library/react";
import MyComponent from "./MyComponent"; test("MyComponent renders correctly",
```

```
() => { const { container } = render(<MyComponent />);
expect(container).toMatchSnapshot(); // Generate or compare against a snapshot
});
```

In this example, `toMatchSnapshot` is a Jest matcher that handles the snapshot comparison. If it's the first run, a snapshot file will be created. In subsequent runs, the test will fail if the rendered output of `MyComponent` differs from the stored snapshot.

Benefits of Snapshot Testing

- **Quick Feedback:** Snapshot tests are a fast way to catch unexpected changes in your UI.
- **Visual Regression Testing:** They act as a visual regression test, ensuring that your UI hasn't changed unintentionally.
- **Easy to Update:** If you intentionally change your UI, you can simply update the snapshot with a single command (`jest -u`).
- **Comprehensive Coverage:** Snapshot tests can cover a large portion of your UI without requiring you to write extensive assertions for each element.

Limitations of Snapshot Testing

- **False Positives:** Trivial changes (like whitespace or reordering of attributes) can cause snapshot tests to fail, even if the UI looks the same to the user.
- **Readability:** Snapshot files are large and not always easy to read or understand.
- **Over-Reliance:** Snapshot tests should not be your only form of testing. They are best used in conjunction with other types of tests (like unit tests and integration tests) to ensure the overall correctness of your components.

When to Use Snapshot Testing

Snapshot testing is most valuable for:

- **UI Components:** Ensuring that visual elements render as expected.
- **Regression Testing:** Catching unintended changes in the UI after refactoring or updates.
- **Complex Output:** Quickly testing components that have large or complex output that would be tedious to write detailed assertions for.

By understanding the benefits and limitations of snapshot testing and using it strategically, you can add a valuable layer of protection against regressions and unintended UI changes in your TypeScript React applications.

Testing Node.js Applications

Testing API Endpoints with Supertest

Supertest is a powerful library designed to simplify the testing of Node.js HTTP servers, making it an ideal companion for your Express.js or other Node.js-based APIs. It provides a high-level interface for sending requests to your server and making assertions about the responses, all within the comfort of your testing environment.

Why Supertest?

- **Seamless Integration:** Supertest works seamlessly with popular testing frameworks like Jest and Mocha.
- **Intuitive API:** Its fluent API makes it easy to write expressive tests for your API endpoints.

- **End-to-End Testing:** It allows you to test your entire request-response cycle, including middleware, routing, and error handling.
- **No Need for a Running Server:** Supertest can create a test instance of your Express app, eliminating the need to spin up a separate server for testing.

Installing Supertest

If you haven't already, install Supertest as a development dependency:

```
npm install --save-dev supertest # or yarn add --dev supertest
```

Example: Testing a GET Endpoint

Let's say you have an Express.js route that fetches a list of users:

```
// server.ts app.get('/users', (req, res) => { // ... (fetch users from
database) ... res.json(users); });
```

Here's how you can test this endpoint using Supertest:

```
// user.test.ts import request from 'supertest'; import app from './server';
// Import your Express app describe('GET /users', () => { it('should return a
list of users', async () => { const response = await request(app)
.get('/users') .expect(200) // Expect a 200 OK status code
.expect('Content-Type', /json/); // Expect JSON response
expect(response.body).toHaveLength(3); // Assert the number of users
expect(response.body[0]).toHaveProperty('name'); // Assert the structure of a
user object }); });
```

Explanation:

1. **Import:** We import `supertest` and your Express app (app).
2. **`request(app)`:** We create a Supertest agent that will make requests to your app.
3. **`.get('/users')`:** We specify the HTTP method (GET) and the endpoint (`/users`).
4. **`.expect(200)`:** We expect a 200 OK status code in the response.
5. **`.expect('Content-Type', /json/)`:** We expect the response to be in JSON format.
6. **`expect(response.body)`:** We use Jest's `expect` and matchers to make assertions about the response body.

Testing Other HTTP Methods and Scenarios

You can use similar patterns to test POST, PUT, DELETE, and other HTTP methods. Supertest also allows you to set request headers, send request bodies, and simulate authentication or error scenarios.

Key Points

- Supertest is a powerful tool for testing Node.js HTTP servers.
- It seamlessly integrates with Jest and other testing frameworks.
- It provides a simple and expressive API for sending requests and making assertions.
- Use Supertest to test your entire request-response cycle, including middleware and error handling.

By integrating Supertest into your testing workflow, you'll create more comprehensive and reliable tests for your Node.js and TypeScript APIs, ensuring that they behave as expected and deliver a seamless experience to your users.

Testing Database Interactions

Testing code that interacts with databases is essential for ensuring that your application can reliably store, retrieve, and modify data. However, it also presents some unique challenges compared to testing pure logic or UI components. Let's discuss some strategies for testing database interactions in your TypeScript Node.js backend.

Strategies for Testing Database Interactions

1. **Real Database Testing (Integration Testing):**
   - **Benefits:** Offers the most realistic testing scenario, ensuring that your code works correctly with the actual database you'll use in production.
   - **Drawbacks:** Can be slower and more complex to set up, especially if your database has complex dependencies or requires specific configurations.
   - **Setup:** Spin up a dedicated test database instance (e.g., a Docker container or a separate test environment) and seed it with test data. Ensure that your tests clean up the database after each test run.
   - **Example (Mongoose):**
     ```
     beforeAll(async () => { await
     mongoose.connect('mongodb://localhost:27017/testdb'); // Connect to
     test database }); afterAll(async () => { await
     mongoose.connection.close(); // Close the connection after tests });
     test('creates a new user', async () => { const user = new User({
     name: 'John Doe', email: 'john@example.com' }); await user.save();
     const retrievedUser = await User.findOne({ email: 'john@example.com'
     }); expect(retrievedUser).not.toBeNull(); // Assert that user was
     created });
     ```
2. **In-Memory Database Testing:**
   - **Benefits:** Faster and easier to set up than real database testing, as you don't need to manage external database connections.
   - **Drawbacks:** Might not fully reflect the behavior of your actual database, especially if you rely on specific features or edge cases.
   - **Setup:** Use libraries like `mongodb-memory-server` (for MongoDB) to create an in-memory instance of your database for testing.
3. **Mocking Database Interactions:**
   - **Benefits:** Allows you to isolate the code you're testing from the database, making tests faster and more focused.
   - **Drawbacks:** Might not catch all potential errors that could arise from real database interactions.
   - **Setup:** Use mocking libraries (like Jest's built-in mocking or Sinon.JS) to create mock objects for your database client or repository. Define the behavior of the mock objects to return specific results or throw errors as needed for your tests.

Choosing the Right Approach

The best testing strategy often involves a combination of these approaches:

- **Unit Tests:** Focus on mocking database interactions to test the logic of your functions and classes in isolation.
- **Integration Tests:** Use a real or in-memory database to test the interaction between your code and the database.

- **E2E Tests:** (if applicable) Test your entire application flow, including database interactions, in a realistic environment.

Key Points

- **Test Data Setup:** Before each test, ensure your database is in a known state. Seed your database with test data, and clean it up after each test to avoid interference between tests.
- **Transactions:** If your database supports transactions, consider wrapping your test cases in transactions so that any changes made during the test are rolled back, leaving the database in its original state.
- **Focus on the Right Level:** Choose the appropriate testing level (unit, integration, or E2E) based on what you're trying to test.
- **Clear Assertions:** Write clear and specific assertions that verify the expected results of your database interactions.

By implementing a well-rounded testing strategy that includes testing database interactions, you'll create more reliable and trustworthy Node.js backends in TypeScript.

Continuous Integration (CI)

Integrating Testing into Your Workflow

Continuous Integration (CI) is a development practice that involves frequently integrating code changes from multiple developers into a shared repository (like GitHub). After each integration, automated builds and tests are run to verify that the new code doesn't introduce errors or break existing functionality.

How CI Works

The basic CI workflow looks like this:

1. **Code Changes:** Developers work on their local branches, making changes and writing tests.
2. **Commit and Push:** Developers commit their changes to their local branch and push it to the shared repository (e.g., GitHub).
3. **Trigger:** The push to the repository triggers the CI pipeline.
4. **Build:** The CI server (e.g., Jenkins, CircleCI, Travis CI) checks out the latest code, installs dependencies, and builds the project (e.g., compiles TypeScript to JavaScript).
5. **Test:** The CI server runs the automated test suite to ensure that all tests pass.
6. **Feedback:** The CI server reports the results of the build and tests back to the team, typically through email notifications, chat messages, or a dashboard.
7. **Repeat:** This cycle repeats for every code change that is pushed to the repository.

Benefits of CI for Early Bug Detection

- **Rapid Feedback:** CI provides immediate feedback on the quality of your code. If a test fails, you're notified quickly, allowing you to fix the issue before it gets merged into the main branch. This helps catch bugs early in the development cycle when they're easier and less expensive to fix.
- **Reduced Risk:** By continuously integrating and testing, you reduce the risk of introducing large-scale bugs or compatibility issues when merging code from different developers.
- **Improved Code Quality:** CI encourages developers to write tests for their code and to ensure that their changes don't break existing tests. This leads to a higher overall quality of the codebase.
- **Faster Development:** By automating repetitive tasks like building and testing, CI frees up developers to focus on writing new features and fixing issues, resulting in faster development cycles.

Ensuring Code Quality

CI plays a vital role in ensuring the quality of your TypeScript code:

- **Type Checking:** The build step in your CI pipeline will typically include compiling your TypeScript code. This step can catch type-related errors before they reach production.
- **Linting:** You can integrate linting tools like ESLint into your CI pipeline to enforce code style guidelines and catch potential issues.
- **Testing:** The testing step is the most critical aspect of CI for code quality. A comprehensive test suite covering unit, integration, and (optionally) end-to-end tests provides a high level of confidence in the correctness of your code.

Key Points

- Continuous Integration (CI) is a practice of integrating code changes frequently and running automated builds and tests.
- CI helps catch bugs early, prevents regressions, improves code quality, and speeds up development.
- Integrate TypeScript compilation, linting, and testing into your CI pipeline.
- Choose a suitable CI tool (like Jenkins, CircleCI, Travis CI, or GitHub Actions) to automate your workflow.

By embracing Continuous Integration, you can create a reliable and efficient development process that helps you deliver high-quality TypeScript applications with confidence.

Popular CI Tools

Continuous Integration (CI) tools are the backbone of modern software development, automating the process of building, testing, and deploying your code. Here are some of the most popular CI tools that work seamlessly with TypeScript and can help you streamline your testing workflow:

1. **Jenkins:** A venerable open-source automation server with a vast ecosystem of plugins. It's highly flexible and customizable, making it suitable for a wide range of projects.
2. **CircleCI:** A cloud-based CI/CD (Continuous Integration/Continuous Deployment) platform known for its ease of use and fast feedback loops. It integrates well with popular version control systems like GitHub and Bitbucket.
3. **Travis CI:** Another cloud-based CI/CD platform, popular among open-source projects. It's easy to set up and offers seamless integration with GitHub.
4. **GitHub Actions:** A CI/CD platform that is tightly integrated with GitHub. It allows you to automate workflows directly within your GitHub repositories, making it convenient for projects hosted on GitHub.

Choosing a CI Tool

The best CI tool for you depends on various factors, including:

- **Project Size and Complexity:** For smaller projects, simpler tools like Travis CI or GitHub Actions might suffice. For larger and more complex projects, the flexibility of Jenkins or the features of CircleCI might be more suitable.
- **Hosting:** If your code is hosted on GitHub, GitHub Actions might be the most convenient option. If you have more complex infrastructure requirements, Jenkins or self-hosted solutions might be preferable.
- **Budget:** Some CI tools offer free plans for open-source or small projects, while others have paid plans with more features and resources.
- **Ease of Use and Configuration:** Consider the learning curve and the amount of configuration required for each tool. Some tools, like CircleCI and GitHub Actions, aim for simplicity, while others, like Jenkins, offer more customization but might require more setup.

Key Points

- CI tools automate your build, test, and deployment processes.
- Choose a CI tool that fits your project's size, complexity, hosting, budget, and ease-of-use requirements.
- Consider popular options like Jenkins, CircleCI, Travis CI, and GitHub Actions.
- Integrate your TypeScript testing framework (like Jest) into your CI pipeline for automated testing.

By incorporating a CI tool into your workflow, you can catch errors early, improve code quality, and streamline your development process, ultimately leading to more reliable and maintainable TypeScript applications.

Best Practices for Testing TypeScript Code

Test Coverage

Test coverage is a metric that indicates how much of your codebase is actually executed during your tests. It's usually expressed as a percentage, where a higher percentage means more of your code has been tested. While test coverage doesn't guarantee the absence of bugs, it's a valuable indicator of how thorough your tests are and can help you identify areas of your code that might need more attention.

How Test Coverage is Measured

Test coverage tools typically analyze your code and your test suite to determine:

- **Line Coverage:** The percentage of lines of code that have been executed during tests.
- **Statement Coverage:** The percentage of statements (individual instructions) that have been executed.
- **Branch Coverage:** The percentage of conditional branches (if-else statements, loops) that have been taken.
- **Function Coverage:** The percentage of functions that have been called.

The goal is to achieve high coverage across all these dimensions. However, it's important to remember that 100% coverage doesn't necessarily mean your code is bug-free. It's possible to write tests that execute every line of code but still miss some edge cases or logical errors.

Tools for Measuring Test Coverage

Jest, the testing framework we discussed earlier, comes with built-in code coverage reporting. To generate a coverage report, simply run your tests with the `--coverage` flag:

```
npm test -- --coverage # or yarn test --coverage
```

Jest will output a detailed report in the terminal and generate an HTML report in the `coverage` directory. This report provides a visual overview of your test coverage, highlighting which lines, statements, branches, and functions are covered or missed by your tests.

Other Coverage Tools

- **Istanbul:** A popular JavaScript code coverage tool that can be used with various testing frameworks, including Jest and Mocha.
- **nyc:** A command-line interface for Istanbul that simplifies its usage and provides additional features.

Aiming for High Coverage

While there's no magic number for the ideal test coverage percentage, many projects strive for at least 80% coverage. However, the target coverage depends on your project's specific needs and risk tolerance. Some critical parts of your application (like security-sensitive modules or complex business logic) might warrant higher coverage than less critical areas.

Techniques for Improving Coverage

- **Write More Tests:** The most obvious way to improve coverage is to write more tests, especially for areas of your code that are not well-tested.
- **Refactor Your Code:** Sometimes, refactoring your code into smaller, more focused functions can make it easier to test and improve coverage.
- **Use a Mocking Library:** Mocking libraries like Jest's built-in mocking or Sinon.JS can help you isolate units of code and make them easier to test.
- **Analyze Coverage Reports:** Use the coverage reports generated by Jest or other tools to identify areas of your code that lack test coverage.

Remember: Test coverage is a useful metric, but it's not the only measure of code quality. Focus on writing meaningful tests that verify the correct behavior of your code, and use coverage reports as a guide to identify areas that might need more attention.

Test-Driven Development (TDD)

Test-Driven Development (TDD) is a software development methodology that flips the traditional coding process on its head. Instead of writing your code first and then adding tests later, you start by writing tests that describe the desired behavior of your code. Only then do you write the minimum amount of code necessary to make those tests pass. This iterative cycle of writing tests, failing tests, writing code, and refactoring leads to a more robust, reliable, and well-designed codebase.

The TDD Cycle: Red, Green, Refactor

TDD is often described as a "Red-Green-Refactor" cycle:

1. **Red:** Write a failing test. This test should describe a specific behavior or functionality that you want to implement. Since the code doesn't exist yet, the test will naturally fail.
2. **Green:** Write the simplest possible code that makes the test pass. The goal here is not to create perfect code but to get the test to pass with the minimal effort.
3. **Refactor:** Once the test is passing, you can refactor your code to improve its design, structure, or readability. The safety net of the passing test ensures that your refactoring doesn't introduce new bugs.

You then repeat this cycle for the next piece of functionality you want to add, continuously building your codebase one test at a time.

Benefits of TDD

- **Improved Code Design:** By writing tests first, you're forced to think more carefully about how your code will be used and how it should be structured to make it testable. This often leads to better design decisions and more modular code.
- **Higher Test Coverage:** TDD naturally results in high test coverage because you write tests before the code. This means that almost every line of code is tested, giving you greater confidence in the correctness of your application.
- **Faster Feedback:** Running tests frequently throughout development provides rapid feedback on the impact of your changes. This allows you to catch errors quickly and fix them before they become bigger problems.
- **Reduced Debugging Time:** With a comprehensive test suite, you can easily pinpoint the source of errors and spend less time on manual debugging.

- **Living Documentation:** Tests act as living documentation for your code. They describe how your code should behave, making it easier for you and others to understand it.
- **Refactoring Confidence:** The safety net of tests allows you to refactor your code with confidence, knowing that you'll be alerted if any changes break existing functionality.

Example: TDD in Action (Jest)

Let's say you want to write a function called `calculateDiscount` that takes a product price and a discount percentage and returns the discounted price.

1. **Red (Failing Test):**
```
test('calculateDiscount applies discount correctly', () => { const price
= 100; const discountPercentage = 20; const expectedDiscountedPrice = 80;
const actualDiscountedPrice = calculateDiscount(price,
discountPercentage);
expect(actualDiscountedPrice).toBe(expectedDiscountedPrice); });
```
2. **Green (Passing Test):**
```
function calculateDiscount(price: number, discountPercentage: number):
number { return price - (price * discountPercentage) / 100; }
```
3. **Refactor (Optional):** If needed, you can now refactor the `calculateDiscount` function to improve its readability or performance, knowing that the test will catch any regressions.

Key Points

- TDD is a development methodology where you write tests before the code.
- The TDD cycle involves writing a failing test, making it pass, and then refactoring.
- TDD leads to better code design, higher test coverage, faster feedback, reduced debugging time, and increased confidence in your code.

While TDD might require a shift in your development mindset, its benefits for code quality and long-term maintainability are significant. By embracing the "test-first" approach, you'll create TypeScript applications that are more robust, reliable, and easier to evolve over time.

Maintainable Tests

Writing tests is only half the battle. The other half is ensuring that your tests are maintainable – that they can evolve alongside your codebase without becoming a burden to update or understand. Let's explore some best practices for writing maintainable tests in TypeScript.

1. Keep Tests Small and Focused

Each test case should ideally focus on a single, specific behavior or scenario. Avoid creating large tests that try to cover too much functionality. Smaller tests are easier to understand, debug, and update when your code changes.

- **One Assertion per Test (Generally):** While not a strict rule, a good guideline is to have only one main assertion per test case. This makes it clear what the test is verifying and simplifies debugging if the test fails.
- **Test One Thing Well:** Resist the temptation to cram multiple assertions into a single test. Break down complex behaviors into multiple smaller tests that each focus on a specific aspect.

2. Use Descriptive Test Names

The names of your tests are crucial for understanding their purpose. Choose descriptive names that accurately describe the behavior being tested. A good test name should:

- **Clearly State the Expected Behavior:** For example, instead of "it should work," use "it should return the sum of two numbers" or "it should render a button with the correct label."
- **Be Concise:** Avoid overly long or verbose names.
- **Follow a Consistent Convention:** Establish a consistent naming convention for your tests (e.g., "should" or "when" prefix).

3. Avoid Overly Complex Assertions

While Jest offers a wide range of matchers, strive for clarity and simplicity in your assertions. Avoid nesting multiple matchers or creating complex conditions within a single assertion. If an assertion becomes too complicated, consider breaking it down into multiple smaller assertions.

```
// Avoid this:
expect(myObject).toHaveProperty("nested.deeply.value").toEqual(42); // Prefer
this: const nestedObject = myObject.nested.deeply;
expect(nestedObject).toHaveProperty("value");
expect(nestedObject.value).toEqual(42);
```

4. Organize Your Tests

Use `describe` blocks to group related tests and create a logical structure for your test suite. This makes it easier to navigate your tests and find specific cases. Consider using nested `describe` blocks for more complex test suites.

5. Refactor Your Tests

Just like your production code, your tests can benefit from refactoring. As your codebase evolves, review and refactor your tests to keep them clean, concise, and up-to-date. Eliminate redundant tests, extract common setup code, and ensure that your tests accurately reflect the current behavior of your code.

6. Use TypeScript to Your Advantage

Leverage TypeScript's type system to ensure type safety in your tests. Define types for your test data, mock objects, and function arguments. This will help you catch errors early and prevent regressions caused by type mismatches.

Key Points

- Write small, focused tests that each have a clear purpose.
- Use descriptive names for your tests that accurately describe the expected behavior.
- Keep your assertions simple and avoid excessive nesting.
- Organize your tests using `describe` blocks for better structure.
- Refactor your tests regularly to keep them maintainable.
- Leverage TypeScript's type system to ensure type safety in your tests.

By adhering to these best practices, you'll build a robust and maintainable test suite that gives you confidence in your TypeScript code, helps you catch bugs early, and enables you to evolve your codebase with ease.

Chapter Summary

In this chapter, we delved into the essential practice of testing your TypeScript code to guarantee its quality, reliability, and maintainability. We explored:

- **The Importance of Testing:** We emphasized the critical role of testing in catching bugs early, preventing regressions, improving code design, and providing documentation through examples. We stressed that even with TypeScript's type safety, testing is crucial for uncovering logical errors.
- **Types of Tests:** We introduced the three main categories of tests: unit tests (for testing individual units of code), integration tests (for testing interactions between components or modules), and end-to-end (E2E) tests (for simulating user interactions and testing the entire application). We discussed the purpose and appropriate use cases for each type.
- **Test Runners and Frameworks:**
  - We highlighted **Jest** as a popular all-in-one testing framework for TypeScript, praising its built-in test runner, assertion library, mocking capabilities, simplicity, speed, snapshot testing, and code coverage reporting. We walked through the process of installing Jest and creating a basic test.
  - We briefly mentioned **Mocha** as a flexible alternative that allows you to choose your own assertion and mocking libraries.
- **Writing Your First Test:**
  - We dissected the anatomy of a test case, explaining the use of `describe` blocks for grouping tests, `test` (or `it`) blocks for defining individual test cases, and assertions for verifying expected behavior.
  - We demonstrated how to use Jest's assertion library with its `expect` function and various matchers to write clear and expressive tests.
  - We explained the concept of mocking and how Jest's mocking features can be used to isolate the code under test and control the behavior of its dependencies.
- **Testing React Components:**
  - We introduced **React Testing Library** (RTL) as a user-centric approach to testing React components, emphasizing the importance of testing behavior over implementation details.
  - We showed how to use Jest with RTL to write comprehensive tests for rendering, user interactions, and state changes in React components.
  - We discussed **snapshot testing**, its benefits (quick feedback, visual regression testing) and limitations (false positives, readability challenges), and when to use it effectively.
- **Testing Node.js Applications:**
  - We introduced **Supertest** as a library for testing Node.js HTTP servers, demonstrating how to use it to send requests to API endpoints and assert responses.
  - We discussed strategies for testing database interactions, including using real databases, in-memory databases, or mocking database interactions, each with its own advantages and trade-offs.
- **Continuous Integration (CI):**
  - We explained the concept of CI, where code changes are frequently integrated and automatically tested to catch errors early and ensure code quality.
  - We mentioned popular CI tools like Jenkins, CircleCI, Travis CI, and GitHub Actions that you can integrate with your TypeScript projects.
- **Best Practices for Testing:**
  - We discussed the importance of test coverage and how to measure it using tools like Jest's built-in coverage reports.
  - We introduced Test-Driven Development (TDD) as a test-first methodology that promotes better code design.
  - We provided guidance on writing maintainable tests, emphasizing the importance of small, focused tests, descriptive names, and avoiding overly complex assertions.

By incorporating testing into your TypeScript development workflow and adhering to these best practices, you can build more reliable, maintainable, and high-quality applications. Testing is an investment that pays off in the long run by reducing bugs, improving code design, and instilling confidence in your codebase.

In the next chapter, we'll shift our focus to the tooling ecosystem that surrounds TypeScript, exploring how to leverage various tools to streamline your development workflow and boost productivity.

Tooling: Streamlining Your TypeScript Workflow

Outline

- Linting
  - Introduction to Linters
  - ESLint: The Standard Linter for TypeScript
- Formatting
  - Code Formatters (Prettier)
  - Integrating Prettier with Your Editor
- Build Tools
  - Webpack: Bundling for the Web
  - Parcel: Zero-Configuration Bundling
  - Rollup: Library-Focused Bundling
- IDE Extensions
  - Visual Studio Code: The TypeScript Powerhouse
  - Other Popular Editors and IDEs
- Additional Tools and Libraries
  - TypeDoc: Generating Documentation
  - ts-node: Running TypeScript Directly
- Tips for Optimizing Your Workflow
- Chapter Summary

Linting: Catching Errors Early and Enforcing Consistency

Introduction to Linters: Your Automated Code Inspector

Linters are tools that analyze your code statically (without executing it) to identify potential errors, bugs, stylistic issues, and deviations from established coding standards. Think of them as vigilant code inspectors that meticulously examine your code, flagging anything that might be amiss.

The Role of Linters

1. **Error Detection:** Linters can catch a wide range of errors, including syntax errors, typos, unused variables, unreachable code, and even potential logical errors. By catching these issues early in development, you can prevent them from causing problems later on.
2. **Enforcing Code Style:** Linters help enforce a consistent code style across your project. This is particularly important when working in teams, as it ensures that everyone adheres to the same formatting and naming conventions, making the code more readable and easier to understand.
3. **Bug Prevention:** By following best practices and adhering to coding standards, linters help you avoid common pitfalls that can lead to bugs. For example, a linter might warn you about using a deprecated function or accessing a variable before it has been initialized.
4. **Automated Code Review:** Think of linters as an automated code review process. They perform checks that would otherwise require manual inspection, saving you time and effort.
5. **Continuous Improvement:** Linters can encourage you to adopt better coding practices and learn from your mistakes. They can also be configured to evolve along with your project, enforcing new rules as your codebase grows and changes.

Example: Common Linting Errors

Here are a few examples of issues that linters can catch in your TypeScript code:

- **Syntax errors:** Missing semicolons, typos in variable or function names, incorrect use of keywords, etc.
- **Type errors:** Assigning a value of the wrong type to a variable, calling a function with incorrect arguments, etc.
- **Unused variables or imports:** Variables or imports that are declared but not used.
- **Unreachable code:** Code that can never be executed (e.g., after a `return` statement).
- **Potentially confusing comparisons:** Using loose equality (==) instead of strict equality (===), comparing values of different types, etc.
- **Code style violations:** Inconsistent indentation, incorrect use of whitespace, non-descriptive variable names, etc.

Key Points

- Linters are tools that analyze your code statically to find errors, bugs, and style issues.
- They help maintain code quality, consistency, and prevent bugs.
- Linters can be customized to enforce specific coding standards.
- They can be integrated into your editor or IDE for real-time feedback.
- They can be part of your continuous integration (CI) pipeline to catch errors early in development.

By incorporating linters into your TypeScript workflow, you'll create a more robust and reliable development process, catch errors early, and produce cleaner, more maintainable code.

ESLint: The Standard Linter for TypeScript

ESLint is the undisputed champion of JavaScript linting, and with the help of some additional packages, it extends its watchful eye to TypeScript projects as well. It's a versatile and highly configurable tool that can significantly improve your code quality, consistency, and adherence to best practices.

Installing ESLint for TypeScript

To bring the power of ESLint to your TypeScript project, follow these steps:

1. **Install ESLint:**
   ```
   npm install --save-dev eslint # or yarn add --dev eslint
   ```
2. **Install TypeScript Parser and Plugin:**
   Since ESLint doesn't understand TypeScript syntax natively, you need to install a parser and a plugin:
   ```
   npm install --save-dev @typescript-eslint/parser
   @typescript-eslint/eslint-plugin # or yarn add --dev
   @typescript-eslint/parser @typescript-eslint/eslint-plugin
   ```
   - **`@typescript-eslint/parser`:** This parser allows ESLint to understand TypeScript syntax.
   - **`@typescript-eslint/eslint-plugin`:** This plugin provides TypeScript-specific linting rules.
3. **Create ESLint Configuration File:**
   Create a file named `.eslintrc.json` (or `.eslintrc.js` or `.eslintrc.yaml`) in your project's root directory to configure ESLint.

Popular ESLint Configurations

- **`eslint:recommended`:** A set of core ESLint rules that are generally considered good practices for JavaScript code.
- **`plugin:@typescript-eslint/recommended`:** A set of recommended rules from the TypeScript ESLint plugin. These rules are tailored for TypeScript code and leverage type information to catch potential issues.

Here's a basic ESLint configuration that combines both of these sets:

```
{ "root": true, "parser": "@typescript-eslint/parser", "plugins":
["@typescript-eslint"], "extends": [ "eslint:recommended",
"plugin:@typescript-eslint/recommended" ] }
```

By default, this configuation won't let you use `console.log()` statements in your code. So we need to override that rule in this configuration.

```
{ "root": true, "parser": "@typescript-eslint/parser", "plugins":
["@typescript-eslint"], "extends": [ "eslint:recommended",
"plugin:@typescript-eslint/recommended" ], "rules": {
"@typescript-eslint/no-console": "off" } }
```

Customizing ESLint Rules

You can customize your ESLint configuration to fit your project's specific coding conventions. The `"rules"` section of your configuration file allows you to enable, disable, or modify individual rules.

```
{ // ... (other config options) "rules": { "indent": ["error", 2], // Enforce
2-space indentation "semi": ["error", "always"], // Require semicolons
"@typescript-eslint/no-unused-vars": "error" // Disallow unused variables } }
```

You can find a comprehensive list of ESLint rules in the official documentation: https://eslint.org/docs/rules/

Key Points

- ESLint is the standard linter for TypeScript.
- You need to install `@typescript-eslint/parser` and `@typescript-eslint/eslint-plugin` to use ESLint with TypeScript.
- Use popular configurations like `eslint:recommended` and `plugin:@typescript-eslint/recommended` as a starting point.
- Customize rules in the `.eslintrc.json` file to match your project's coding style.

By harnessing the power of ESLint and its TypeScript plugin, you can automate code quality checks, catch potential errors early, and enforce consistent coding practices throughout your project, leading to cleaner, more maintainable, and less error-prone code.

Formatting: Keeping Your Code Beautiful

Code Formatters (Prettier)

While linters focus on catching errors and enforcing style guidelines, code formatters take a different approach. They automatically format your code to adhere to a consistent style, freeing you from the tedious task of manual formatting and ensuring a polished look across your codebase.

Introducing Prettier

Prettier is an opinionated code formatter that has gained immense popularity due to its simplicity, effectiveness, and support for a wide range of languages, including TypeScript. It takes your code and reformats it according to a set of predefined rules, ensuring a consistent style throughout your project.

Benefits of Using a Code Formatter

- **Consistency:** Prettier eliminates the endless debates about tabs vs. spaces, line length, quote styles, etc. It automatically formats your code based on its own rules, ensuring a uniform style across the entire codebase.
- **Readability:** Consistent formatting makes code easier to read and understand. By removing stylistic distractions, Prettier helps you focus on the logic and structure of your code.
- **Time Savings:** Manual formatting is a time-consuming and often tedious task. Prettier automates this process, saving you valuable development time.
- **Reduced Cognitive Load:** When code is consistently formatted, you don't have to mentally parse different styles, freeing up cognitive resources to focus on the actual problem you're solving.
- **Reduced Code Review Friction:** By eliminating style disagreements, Prettier helps streamline code reviews and reduce conflicts.

How Prettier Works

Prettier takes your TypeScript code (or any other supported language) as input and reformats it based on its own set of rules. These rules cover aspects like indentation, line wrapping, spacing around operators, and more. Prettier is opinionated, meaning it has its own preferences for how code should be formatted. However, you can customize some of its behavior through configuration options.

Example: Prettier in Action

```
// Before formatting function add(a , b) { return a+b ; } // After formatting
with Prettier function add(a, b) { return a + b; }
```

Key Points

- Prettier is a code formatter that automatically formats your code for consistency and readability.
- It saves you time and reduces the mental burden of manual formatting.
- Prettier is opinionated but allows for some customization through configuration options.
- It integrates well with most popular code editors and can be set up to format your code on save.

By embracing Prettier in your TypeScript workflow, you can free yourself from the drudgery of manual formatting and ensure that your code always looks its best. This leads to a more consistent and maintainable codebase, allowing you to focus on what truly matters: writing clean, efficient, and reliable TypeScript code.

Integrating Prettier with Your Editor: Effortless Code Formatting

Integrating Prettier with your code editor allows you to automatically format your TypeScript code as you work, saving you time and ensuring consistent style across your projects. Let's focus on Visual Studio Code (VS Code), a popular editor with excellent Prettier support.

1. Install the Prettier Extension

- Open VS Code's Extensions Marketplace (Ctrl+Shift+X or Cmd+Shift+X).
- Search for "Prettier - Code Formatter".
- Click "Install" to add the extension to your VS Code.

2. Basic Configuration (Optional)

In most cases, Prettier will work out of the box with sensible defaults. However, if you want to customize its behavior, you can create a `.prettierrc` configuration file (JSON, YAML, or TOML format) in your project's root directory. Here's an example:

```
{ "semi": true, // Use semicolons "singleQuote": true, // Use single quotes
"tabWidth": 2 // Use 2 spaces for indentation }
```

3. Automatic Formatting on Save

The most convenient way to use Prettier is to set it up to format your code automatically whenever you save a file. Here's how to do it in VS Code:

- Go to **File > Preferences > Settings** (or use the shortcut Ctrl+, or Cmd+,).
- Search for "format on save."
- Make sure the "Editor: Format On Save" option is checked.
- Set "Editor: Default Formatter" to "Prettier - Code Formatter" (if it's not already the default).

Now, every time you save a TypeScript file, Prettier will automatically reformat it according to your configuration.

4. Formatting with Keyboard Shortcuts

If you prefer manual control over formatting, you can use keyboard shortcuts:

- **Format Document:** Shift + Alt + F (Windows) or Shift + Option + F (macOS)
- **Format Selection:** Ctrl + K, Ctrl + F (Windows) or Cmd + K, Cmd + F (macOS)

5. Overriding Prettier Defaults (Optional)

If you need to deviate from Prettier's default rules for a specific section of code, you can use special comments to disable formatting:

```
// prettier-ignore const uglyCode = ' this will not be formatted ';
```

Additional Tips

- **Project-Level Configuration:** If you want to share the same Prettier configuration across multiple projects, consider creating a global `.prettierrc` file in your home directory.
- **EditorConfig Integration:** You can also use EditorConfig files (`.editorconfig`) to define basic formatting rules (like indentation style) and let Prettier handle the rest.
- **Command Line Interface:** Prettier also has a command-line interface (CLI) that you can use to format files directly from your terminal.

Key Points

- Prettier is a powerful code formatter for TypeScript.
- Integrate it with your editor (like VS Code) for automatic formatting on save.
- Use keyboard shortcuts for manual formatting.
- Customize Prettier's behavior using a `.prettierrc` file.

By integrating Prettier into your workflow, you can ensure that your TypeScript code is always beautifully formatted, consistent, and easy to read, allowing you to focus on writing high-quality code.

Build Tools: Preparing Your Code for Production

Webpack: Bundling for the Web

In the world of modern web development, bundlers play a crucial role in packaging your code and its dependencies into optimized files ready for deployment. Webpack, a powerful and versatile module bundler, stands out as a popular choice for TypeScript projects. It offers a wide array of features for transforming, optimizing, and managing your code, making it an indispensable tool in your TypeScript workflow.

What is Webpack?

Webpack is essentially a code transformation and optimization tool. It takes your source code, which may consist of multiple modules and files, and bundles it into a smaller set of files that can be efficiently loaded by web browsers. It also handles tasks like:

- **Module Resolution:** Resolving the relationships between different modules in your project.
- **Code Transformation:** Applying loaders to transform files (e.g., transpiling TypeScript to JavaScript, converting SCSS to CSS).
- **Code Splitting:** Splitting your code into smaller chunks that can be loaded on demand, improving initial page load performance.
- **Minification and Optimization:** Reducing the size of your JavaScript and CSS files through techniques like minification and tree shaking.
- **Asset Management:** Handling assets like images, fonts, and videos.

Core Concepts

To effectively use webpack, it's important to understand its key concepts:

- **Entry Point:** The starting point of your application, usually a JavaScript or TypeScript file. Webpack begins by analyzing this file and its dependencies.
- **Output:** The bundled file (or files) that webpack generates. You can configure the output filename and directory.
- **Loaders:** Transformations applied to your code. For example, you'll need a TypeScript loader (`ts-loader`) to transpile your TypeScript code into JavaScript.
- **Plugins:** Additional functionality that extends webpack's capabilities. You can use plugins for tasks like code splitting, asset optimization, or generating reports.

Basic Webpack Configuration for TypeScript

Here's a simplified example of a `webpack.config.js` file for a TypeScript project:

```
const path = require('path'); module.exports = { mode: 'development', // or
'production' entry: './src/index.ts', // Your main TypeScript file output: {
filename: 'bundle.js', path: path.resolve(__dirname, 'dist') }, module: {
rules: [ { test: /\.tsx?$/, // Match TypeScript and TSX files use:
'ts-loader', // Use ts-loader to transpile TypeScript exclude: /node_modules/
} ] }, resolve: { extensions: ['.tsx', '.ts', '.js'] // Allow importing
TypeScript files without extensions } };
```

This configuration tells webpack to:

1. Start at the `src/index.ts` file.
2. Use `ts-loader` to process any TypeScript or TSX files it encounters.
3. Output the bundled JavaScript file as `bundle.js` in the `dist` folder.

Running Webpack

To run webpack and generate the bundle, simply execute:

```
npx webpack # or yarn webpack
```

Beyond the Basics

Webpack offers a vast array of configuration options and plugins to customize your build process. You can set up hot module replacement (HMR) for live reloading during development, split your code into chunks for lazy loading, optimize your assets, and much more.

Key Points

- Webpack is a powerful module bundler for TypeScript projects.
- It bundles your code and dependencies into optimized files for the browser.
- Key concepts include entry points, output, loaders, and plugins.
- Create a `webpack.config.js` file to configure webpack.
- Use `ts-loader` to transpile TypeScript code.

By mastering webpack, you'll gain a powerful tool for building, optimizing, and managing your TypeScript projects for the web. The investment in learning webpack pays off handsomely with improved performance, streamlined development workflows, and the ability to create complex and sophisticated web applications.

Parcel: Zero-Configuration Bundling

If you're looking for a simpler and more streamlined way to bundle your TypeScript code, Parcel might be the perfect fit. Parcel is a zero-configuration bundler that aims to make web development fast and easy. Unlike Webpack, which often requires extensive configuration, Parcel works out of the box with minimal setup.

Benefits of Parcel

- **Zero Configuration:** The most significant advantage of Parcel is its lack of required configuration. It automatically handles most common tasks like transpiling TypeScript, transforming CSS, and bundling assets.
- **Fast Development:** Parcel's development server provides hot module replacement (HMR), which allows for instant updates to your browser without full page reloads, significantly improving development speed.
- **Simplified Setup:** Getting started with Parcel is incredibly easy. You can often set up a TypeScript project with just a few commands.
- **Asset Management:** Parcel automatically handles the bundling and optimization of various assets like images, fonts, and videos.

Using Parcel with TypeScript

Here's a quick guide to get started:

1. **Install Parcel:**
   ```
   npm install -g parcel-bundler # Install Parcel globally # or npm install --save-dev parcel-bundler # Install as dev dependency
   ```
2. **Create a TypeScript File:**
   Create an `index.html` file and a `index.ts` (or `index.tsx`) file:
   ```
   <!DOCTYPE html> <html> <body> <script src="./index.ts"></script> </body> </html>
   ```
   ```
   // index.ts console.log("Hello from TypeScript!");
   ```
3. **Start the Development Server:**
   ```
   parcel index.html
   ```
   Parcel will start a development server, automatically compile your TypeScript code, and open your default browser to display the result.

Configuration (Optional)

While Parcel excels at zero-configuration, you can still customize it if needed by creating a `package.json` file with a "scripts" section:

```
// package.json "scripts": { "start": "parcel index.html", "build": "parcel build index.html" }
```

or by creating a `.parcelrc` file. Refer to Parcel's documentation for details on available configuration options:

https://parceljs.org/

Key Points

- Parcel is a zero-configuration bundler that simplifies web development.
- It automatically handles TypeScript compilation and asset management.
- It's a great choice for projects that value simplicity and speed.

If you're looking for a streamlined and beginner-friendly way to build TypeScript projects, give Parcel a try. It might be the perfect tool to accelerate your development workflow.

Rollup: Library-Focused Bundling

While Webpack shines in building full-fledged web applications, Rollup is a bundler that specifically excels at creating libraries. Its focus on library-specific optimizations makes it a preferred choice for developers who want to produce small, efficient, and highly performant libraries.

Strengths of Rollup

1. **Tree-Shaking:** Rollup's tree-shaking algorithm is known for its effectiveness. It statically analyzes your code and eliminates unused exports, resulting in leaner bundle sizes. This is especially crucial for libraries, where consumers often only use a subset of the exported features.
2. **Small Output:** Rollup excels at producing small output bundles due to its tree-shaking capabilities and its focus on static module analysis. This is important for libraries, as it reduces the overhead for users who import the library.
3. **Compatibility:** Rollup has excellent support for modern JavaScript features (ES modules) and can also generate code in various formats (CommonJS, UMD, etc.) to ensure compatibility with different environments.
4. **Plugin Ecosystem:** While Rollup might not have as extensive a plugin ecosystem as Webpack, it offers a curated selection of plugins specifically designed for library creation. This includes plugins for code splitting, minification, and other optimizations.
5. **Ease of Use:** Rollup's configuration is often simpler and more straightforward than Webpack's, especially for smaller library projects.

When to Choose Rollup

Consider Rollup as your bundler of choice when:

- **You're Building a Library:** Rollup's strengths in tree-shaking and producing small bundles are particularly beneficial for libraries that need to be efficient and have minimal impact on the consumer's project.
- **Performance Matters:** If your library's performance is critical, Rollup's focus on optimization can help you achieve the smallest possible bundle size.
- **Modern JavaScript:** If you're primarily using modern JavaScript features (like ES modules) and don't require extensive customization or asset handling, Rollup's streamlined approach might be preferable.

Key Points

- Rollup is a module bundler that specializes in creating libraries.
- It excels at tree-shaking and generating small, efficient bundles.
- Choose Rollup when building libraries where performance and bundle size are important considerations.
- It has excellent support for ES Modules and various output formats.

By choosing the right tool for the job, you can optimize your TypeScript development workflow and create libraries that are not only powerful and type-safe but also efficient and easy to integrate into other projects.

IDE Extensions: Supercharging Your Editor

Visual Studio Code: The TypeScript Powerhouse

Visual Studio Code (VS Code), developed by Microsoft, has emerged as a dominant force in the world of code editors. Its combination of speed, flexibility, and extensive customization options has made it a favorite among developers across various languages and platforms. However, VS Code truly shines when it comes to TypeScript development, thanks to its exceptional built-in support and a rich ecosystem of extensions.

Built-in TypeScript Support

VS Code's deep understanding of TypeScript is baked right into its core. This means that without installing any additional extensions, you get a host of features that make working with TypeScript a breeze:

- **Real-time Type Checking and Error Highlighting:** As you type, VS Code continuously checks your code against TypeScript's type system, highlighting any errors with squiggly lines and providing helpful error messages. This immediate feedback helps you catch and fix issues early on, saving you time and frustration later.
- **Intelligent Code Completion (IntelliSense):** VS Code's IntelliSense engine leverages TypeScript's type definitions to provide smart suggestions for code completion. It suggests relevant variables, functions, classes, modules, and even entire code snippets based on the context of your code. This not only speeds up development but also helps you discover the available APIs and types in your project.
- **Refactoring Tools:** VS Code offers powerful refactoring tools that are aware of TypeScript's type system. You can safely rename variables, functions, or classes, extract code into new functions or components, move code around, and perform other refactorings with confidence, knowing that TypeScript will help you update all references correctly.
- **Debugging:** VS Code's built-in debugger seamlessly integrates with TypeScript. You can set breakpoints, inspect variables, step through your code, and even debug asynchronous operations, making it easier to diagnose and fix problems in your TypeScript applications.

Integration with Linters and Formatters

VS Code makes it effortless to integrate with popular TypeScript linters (like ESLint) and formatters (like Prettier). You can configure them to run automatically on save or on demand, ensuring that your code adheres to consistent style guidelines and is free of common errors.

Vast Ecosystem of TypeScript Extensions

VS Code's true power lies in its vast marketplace of extensions. You can find extensions for virtually every aspect of TypeScript development, including:

- **Snippet Packs:** Collections of pre-written code snippets for common TypeScript patterns.

- **Testing Frameworks:** Integration with Jest, Mocha, or other testing frameworks to streamline your testing workflow.
- **Code Navigation:** Tools for easily navigating between files, symbols, and references in your project.
- **Code Visualization:** Extensions that visualize your code's structure and dependencies.
- **Themes and Customization:** A plethora of themes and customization options to personalize your VS Code experience.

Key Points

- Visual Studio Code provides excellent built-in support for TypeScript development.
- Real-time type checking, code completion, refactoring tools, and debugging capabilities are readily available.
- VS Code integrates seamlessly with linters and formatters.
- The extensive marketplace of TypeScript extensions allows you to customize and enhance your development workflow.

By choosing Visual Studio Code as your editor for TypeScript projects, you'll gain access to a powerful and comprehensive toolset that will significantly boost your productivity, code quality, and overall developer experience.

Other Popular Editors and IDEs

While Visual Studio Code reigns supreme for TypeScript development, it's not the only option. Several other code editors and IDEs offer excellent TypeScript support through plugins or built-in features. Let's explore a few popular choices and how to equip them for your TypeScript journey.

1. Sublime Text: Lightweight and Customizable

Sublime Text is a favorite among developers who value speed, simplicity, and a minimalist interface. While it doesn't have built-in TypeScript support, its extensive plugin ecosystem fills the gap:

- **TypeScript Plugin:** Install the official TypeScript plugin for syntax highlighting, code completion, and basic type checking.
- **LSP (Language Server Protocol):** For enhanced TypeScript features like code navigation, refactoring, and diagnostics, consider setting up an LSP server (e.g., TypeScript Language Server) and a corresponding Sublime Text LSP plugin.

Strengths:

- Fast and lightweight
- Highly customizable with plugins
- Powerful editing features

2. WebStorm: The JavaScript IDE

WebStorm, developed by JetBrains, is a full-fledged IDE designed specifically for web development. It boasts out-of-the-box TypeScript support, including intelligent code completion, refactoring, debugging, and seamless integration with popular frameworks like Angular and React.

Strengths:

- Comprehensive TypeScript support
- Powerful refactoring and debugging tools
- Deep integration with web frameworks
- Rich set of built-in tools for web development

3. Atom: Hackable and Open Source

Atom, a free and open-source editor from GitHub, is known for its hackability and customization. With the TypeScript and Atom TypeScript packages installed, you gain a solid foundation for TypeScript development.

Strengths:

- Highly customizable
- Open-source and community-driven
- Integrated with GitHub

Setting Up Other Editors

For Sublime Text and Atom:

1. Install the TypeScript plugin or packages.
2. Optionally, set up an LSP server and plugin for enhanced features.
3. Configure the editor to automatically compile TypeScript files (usually through a build system like webpack or Parcel).

For WebStorm:

- TypeScript support is built-in, so you generally don't need to install additional plugins.
- Explore the IDE's settings to customize TypeScript features and code style.

Key Points

- VS Code is the most popular choice for TypeScript development due to its built-in support and rich ecosystem.
- Sublime Text, WebStorm, and Atom are also excellent alternatives with varying strengths.
- Regardless of your chosen editor, install the necessary plugins or packages to enable TypeScript support.
- Explore and customize your editor's settings to create an efficient and personalized TypeScript workflow.

Remember, the best editor for you depends on your individual preferences and workflow. Experiment with different options and find the one that makes you the most productive and comfortable while working with TypeScript.

Additional Tools and Libraries

TypeDoc: Generating Documentation

Documentation is a cornerstone of good software development. It provides essential information about how your code works, making it easier for you and other developers to understand, use, and maintain it. In the TypeScript world, **TypeDoc** is a valuable tool that automates the process of generating documentation from your source code.

What is TypeDoc?

TypeDoc is a documentation generator that specializes in TypeScript projects. It parses your TypeScript source files, extracts type information, and interprets special comments to create comprehensive HTML documentation. This documentation typically includes:

- **Modules:** Descriptions of your modules and their purpose.

- **Classes:** Details about classes, their constructors, properties, and methods, including their types and any comments you've written.
- **Interfaces:** Definitions of interfaces, their properties, and methods, along with their types.
- **Functions:** Descriptions of functions, their parameters (with types), return types, and any associated comments.
- **Types:** Information about type aliases, enums, and other custom types you've defined.

How TypeDoc Works

TypeDoc leverages the type information inherent in TypeScript, as well as special JSDoc-style comments you add to your code. Here's a simplified example:

```
/** * Calculates the sum of two numbers. * @param a - The first number. *
@param b - The second number. * @returns The sum of the two numbers. */
function add(a: number, b: number): number { return a + b; }
```

TypeDoc will then parse this code and generate documentation that includes the description of the function, the parameter names and types, and the return type. **Installing and Using TypeDoc**

1. **Installation:**
   `npm install --save-dev typedoc # or yarn add --dev typedoc`
2. **Configuration (Optional):** You can customize TypeDoc's behavior using a configuration file (`typedoc.json`) or command-line options.
3. **Generating Documentation:** Run TypeDoc from your project's root directory:
   `npx typedoc # Use this if you installed typedoc as a dev dependency # or typedoc # Use this if you installed typedoc globally`
   TypeDoc will generate an HTML documentation site in the `docs` folder by default (you can customize this).

Benefits of TypeDoc

- **Automated Documentation:** Saves you the time and effort of writing documentation manually.
- **Always Up-to-Date:** Your documentation stays synchronized with your code.
- **Enhanced Collaboration:** Clear and comprehensive documentation makes it easier for other developers to understand and contribute to your project.
- **Improved Code Readability:** Encourages you to write well-documented code with clear comments.

Key Points

- TypeDoc automatically generates documentation from TypeScript source code.
- It uses type information and JSDoc-style comments to create detailed documentation.
- It's a valuable tool for improving code readability, maintainability, and collaboration.

By incorporating TypeDoc into your TypeScript workflow, you'll create a living documentation resource that accurately reflects the structure and functionality of your code. This investment in documentation pays off by making your codebase more accessible and easier to understand for both yourself and other developers.

ts-node: Running TypeScript Directly

Traditionally, running TypeScript code requires a compilation step where your `.ts` files are transformed into JavaScript (`js`) files. This can sometimes feel like an extra hurdle, especially for quick scripts or during development when you want to see your changes immediately. `ts-node` comes to the rescue, allowing you to execute TypeScript files directly without the need for manual compilation.

What is `ts-node`?

`ts-node` is a handy tool that combines the TypeScript compiler (`tsc`) and the Node.js runtime environment. It essentially does the following on the fly:

1. Reads your TypeScript code.
2. Compiles it into JavaScript (in memory).
3. Executes the generated JavaScript in Node.js.

This means you can simply run your `.ts` files like you would run `.js` files, with just a small twist in the command you use.

Installing `ts-node`

To install `ts-node`, use your package manager:

```
npm install -g ts-node # Install globally # or npm install --save-dev ts-node
# Install as a dev dependency
```

Using `ts-node`

Once installed, you can run a TypeScript file (`script.ts`) directly using:

```
ts-node script.ts
```

Benefits of `ts-node`

- **Rapid Development:** Speeds up your development cycle by eliminating the need for manual compilation. You see the results of your changes immediately.
- **Scripting and Prototyping:** Ideal for quickly writing and running TypeScript scripts or creating prototypes.
- **Simplified Workflow:** You don't have to constantly switch between compiling and running your code.
- **REPL (Read-Eval-Print Loop):** `ts-node` provides an interactive REPL environment where you can experiment with TypeScript code snippets on the fly.

Example: A Simple Script

```
// script.ts import fs from 'fs'; async function main() { const data = await
fs.promises.readFile('data.txt', 'utf-8'); console.log(data); } main();
```

- Run this script directly with `ts-node` instead of Node.js with a compiled version of `script.ts`.

Considerations

- **Performance:** While `ts-node` is convenient for development, it might not be the most performant option for production environments due to the on-the-fly compilation overhead. For production, it's recommended to pre-compile your TypeScript code.
- **Type Checking:** `ts-node` can be configured to skip type checking to improve performance. However, this means potential errors might not be caught until runtime.
- **Configuration:** You can customize `ts-node`'s behavior using a `ts-node` section in your `tsconfig.json` file.
- **Alternatives:** For larger projects, build tools like Webpack or Parcel might offer a more integrated and optimized solution for both development and production.

Key Points

- `ts-node` allows you to run TypeScript files directly without pre-compilation.
- It's useful for scripting, prototyping, and fast development cycles.
- Consider using it during development and pre-compiling your code for production.
- Be mindful of potential performance and type-checking trade-offs.

By incorporating `ts-node` into your TypeScript toolkit, you gain a valuable tool for boosting productivity and streamlining your development workflow, especially in scenarios where you want to experiment, iterate quickly, or avoid the overhead of a separate compilation step.

Tips for Optimizing Your Workflow

Optimizing your TypeScript workflow can save you time, reduce errors, and make your development process more enjoyable. Here are some practical tips to streamline your workflow and maximize your efficiency:

1. **Configure Your Editor for Automatic Type Checking, Linting, and Formatting:**
   - **Type Checking:** Enable TypeScript's built-in type checking in your editor to get immediate feedback on potential errors as you type.
   - **Linting:** Install and configure ESLint to catch code style issues, potential errors, and enforce best practices. Set up your editor to lint your code on save or on demand.
   - **Formatting:** Integrate Prettier with your editor to automatically format your code on save. This eliminates the need for manual formatting and ensures consistent style across your project.
2. **Embrace Build Tools (Webpack, Parcel, Rollup):**
   - **Automation:** Build tools like Webpack, Parcel, or Rollup automate repetitive tasks like bundling, minification, and optimization, saving you time and effort.
   - **Hot Module Replacement (HMR):** If your build tool supports it, enable HMR during development. This will instantly update your browser whenever you make changes to your code, significantly speeding up your iteration cycle.
3. **Leverage TypeScript-Specific Tools:**
   - **TypeDoc:** Generate documentation automatically from your TypeScript source code, saving you time and ensuring your documentation is always up-to-date.
   - **`ts-node`:** Use `ts-node` for running TypeScript scripts or prototyping ideas without the need for explicit compilation.
4. **Explore the TypeScript Ecosystem:**
   - **Libraries:** The TypeScript ecosystem is rich with libraries and frameworks that can simplify common tasks. For example, use `io-ts` for runtime type validation or `fp-ts` for functional programming in TypeScript.
   - **Community:** The TypeScript community is vibrant and active. Participate in forums, online discussions, and conferences to learn from other developers and stay up-to-date with the latest trends and best practices.
5. **Stay Up-to-Date:**
   - **TypeScript:** New TypeScript versions often introduce exciting features and improvements. Keep an eye on the release notes and update your projects to leverage the latest capabilities.
   - **Libraries and Tools:** Similarly, keep your project dependencies up-to-date to take advantage of bug fixes, performance enhancements, and new features.

Additional Tips

- **Use a Monorepo (Optional):** For large projects with multiple packages or modules, consider using a monorepo (a single repository for all your code). This can simplify dependency management and development workflows.
- **Implement a CI/CD Pipeline:** Set up a continuous integration and continuous delivery (CI/CD) pipeline to automate testing, building, and deployment of your TypeScript projects.
- **Code Reviews:** Conduct regular code reviews to ensure that your code follows best practices, is well-documented, and is easy to understand.

By adopting these tips and incorporating the right tools into your TypeScript workflow, you'll transform your development experience, boost productivity, and create high-quality, maintainable code with ease.

Chapter Summary

In this chapter, we explored the essential tools and techniques that empower you to optimize your TypeScript development workflow. We covered:

- **Linting (ESLint):** We introduced linters as automated code inspectors that catch errors, enforce style guidelines, and prevent bugs. We dove into ESLint, the most popular linter for TypeScript, covering its installation, configuration with recommended rule sets, and customization to fit your project's specific needs.
- **Formatting (Prettier):** We discovered Prettier, a powerful code formatter that automatically beautifies your code according to consistent rules. We discussed how to integrate Prettier with your code editor for effortless and automatic code formatting.
- **Build Tools:** We explored build tools that are essential for preparing your TypeScript code for production:
  - **Webpack:** A versatile module bundler for web applications, capable of handling module resolution, code transformation, optimization, and asset management.
  - **Parcel:** A zero-configuration bundler that prioritizes simplicity and speed, ideal for projects that don't require extensive customization.
  - **Rollup:** A bundler specifically designed for creating libraries, known for its efficient tree-shaking and ability to produce small bundles.
- **IDE Extensions:** We highlighted Visual Studio Code (VS Code) as the leading IDE for TypeScript development, thanks to its built-in TypeScript support, intelligent code completion, refactoring tools, debugging capabilities, and vast ecosystem of extensions. We also briefly mentioned other popular editors like Sublime Text, WebStorm, and Atom, outlining how to set them up for TypeScript.
- **Additional Tools:** We introduced TypeDoc, a documentation generator for TypeScript, and `ts-node`, a tool for running TypeScript code directly without compilation.
- **Optimizing Your Workflow:** We provided practical tips for streamlining your TypeScript development process, including configuring your editor, using build tools, leveraging TypeScript-specific tools, exploring other libraries in the ecosystem, and staying up-to-date with the latest TypeScript features and tooling updates.

By mastering these tools and techniques, you've equipped yourself to build a highly efficient and productive TypeScript development workflow. With automated error checking, consistent code formatting, streamlined builds, and powerful editor integrations, you'll be able to focus more on writing quality code and less on manual tasks, ultimately leading to better TypeScript projects.

Section IV:
Beyond the Basics

Advanced Type Manipulation: Conditional Types and More

Outline

- Introduction
  - TypeScript's Type System: A Powerful Tool
  - Beyond Basic Types
- Conditional Types
  - The `extends` Keyword in Type Context
  - The Ternary Operator for Types
  - Inferring and Distributing Conditional Types
  - Practical Examples of Conditional Types
- Mapped Types
  - Modifying Existing Types
  - Readonly, Optional, and Required Modifiers
  - Proxying Properties
  - Practical Examples of Mapped Types
- Template Literal Types
  - Type-Level String Manipulation
  - Creating String Unions with Template Literals
  - Practical Examples of Template Literal Types
- Keyof and Typeof
  - keyof: Obtaining Keys of an Object Type
  - typeof: Getting the Type of a Value
  - Combining keyof and typeof for Dynamic Access
- Advanced Tips and Tricks
  - Type Guards and Assertions in Advanced Scenarios
  - Utility Types for Type Manipulation
- Chapter Summary

Introduction

TypeScript's Type System: A Powerful Tool

As we've journeyed through the core concepts of TypeScript, you've witnessed the robustness and flexibility of its type system. We've covered the fundamental building blocks like numbers, strings, arrays, and interfaces, but the true power of TypeScript lies in its ability to go far beyond these basics.

The TypeScript type system is not just about catching simple type errors. It's a rich and expressive language for describing the shape, structure, and behavior of your data. It's a tool that empowers you to create more reliable, maintainable, and scalable applications.

Advanced Type Manipulation: Unleashing TypeScript's Potential

In this chapter, we'll delve into the world of advanced type manipulation, where you'll learn techniques to create complex types that precisely model your data and application logic. We'll explore concepts like:

- **Conditional Types:** Type-level "if-else" statements that allow you to create types that adapt based on specific conditions.
- **Mapped Types:** A way to transform existing types by systematically modifying their properties.
- **Template Literal Types:** A powerful tool for type-level string manipulation.
- **`keyof` and `typeof`:** Operators that allow you to extract keys from objects and get the types of values at compile time.
- **Utility Types:** Built-in TypeScript types that simplify common type transformations.

By mastering these advanced techniques, you'll be able to:

- **Express Complex Relationships:** Model intricate relationships between different types of data.
- **Create Reusable Types:** Build generic types that can be adapted to various use cases.
- **Enforce Type Safety:** Ensure that your code handles data correctly and consistently.
- **Write More Expressive Code:** Create types that precisely capture the intent of your code, making it more self-documenting and easier to understand.

The techniques we'll cover in this chapter are not just academic exercises; they are practical tools that you can apply to real-world problems to build more robust and reliable TypeScript applications.

Beyond Basic Types

In previous chapters, we laid the foundation with TypeScript's core types like numbers, strings, booleans, and interfaces. Now, it's time to venture into the more advanced realms of the TypeScript type system. This chapter will empower you with tools and techniques to manipulate types with precision, allowing you to express complex relationships, create reusable type definitions, and build a bulletproof type safety net for your applications.

Conditional Types: Type-Level Decision Making

Conditional types are a bit like "if" statements for your types. They allow you to define a type that changes based on certain conditions, providing a powerful way to model type-level logic.

Mapped Types: Transforming Types with Ease

Mapped types let you create new types by applying modifications to the properties of existing types. This is incredibly handy for creating variations of interfaces, removing or adding optional modifiers, or performing other transformations.

Template Literal Types: String Manipulation on Steroids

Template literal types take the power of template literals (those backtick-enclosed strings) and apply it to types. You can create dynamic types based on string patterns, opening up a world of possibilities for type-level string manipulations.

`keyof` and `typeof`: Reflection at Compile Time

The `keyof` and `typeof` operators provide a form of "reflection" for your types. `keyof` gives you a union of the keys (property names) of a type, while `typeof` lets you get the type of a value. Combining these operators allows you to dynamically access object properties while maintaining type safety.

Utility Types: Your Type Manipulation Toolbox

TypeScript comes with a set of built-in utility types that provide convenient shortcuts for common type transformations. We'll explore handy tools like `Partial`, `Pick`, `Omit`, `Record`, and others that can streamline your type manipulations.

Advanced Type Guards and Assertions

We'll dive deeper into type guards and type assertions, discussing how to use them in more complex scenarios involving the advanced types we've covered.

The Power of Advanced Types

With these advanced type manipulation techniques, you'll be able to:

- **Express Complex Relationships:** Model intricate relationships between different types of data, capturing the nuances of your domain.
- **Create Reusable Types:** Build generic and adaptable types that can be used in various contexts, promoting code reuse and reducing duplication.
- **Enforce Stricter Type Safety:** Create more precise type definitions that catch potential errors early in the development process.
- **Write More Expressive Code:** Craft types that accurately reflect the intent of your code, making it more self-documenting and easier to understand.

This chapter marks a significant step up in your TypeScript journey. The concepts might seem a bit mind-bending at first, but with practice and exploration, you'll unlock a new level of mastery over TypeScript's type system, empowering you to write safer, more elegant, and more maintainable code. So, buckle up and get ready to dive into the exciting world of advanced type manipulation!

Conditional Types

The `extends` Keyword in Type Context

At the heart of TypeScript's advanced type system lies the concept of conditional types. These unique types act like if-else statements at the type level, allowing you to define types that depend on the fulfillment of a condition. The core building block of a conditional type is the `extends` keyword, but in this case, it's used in a type context rather than for class inheritance.

Syntax

```
T extends U ? X : Y
```

This translates to: "If type T extends type U, then the type is X, otherwise the type is Y."

Basic Example

Let's start with a simple example:

```
type IsNumber<T> = T extends number ? true : false; type A = IsNumber<number>;
// A is true type B = IsNumber<string>; // B is false
```

In this code:

1. We define a type alias `IsNumber<T>`, which is a conditional type.
2. The condition T `extends number` checks if the type argument T extends (or is assignable to) the `number` type.
3. If T extends `number`, the conditional type resolves to `true`; otherwise, it resolves to `false`.

4. We create two type aliases A and B to test the IsNumber type with different type arguments.

How It Works

Think of conditional types as a decision tree for types. TypeScript evaluates the condition (T extends number) and chooses the appropriate branch (true or false) based on whether the condition holds true or not. The type of the result is then determined by the type in the chosen branch.

More Examples

```
type IsString<T> = T extends string ? true : false; type A = IsString<string>;
// A is true type B = IsString<number>; // B is false type NonNullable<T> = T
extends null | undefined ? never : T; type C = NonNullable<string | null>; //
C is string type D = NonNullable<number>; // D is number
```

Key Points

- Conditional types act like type-level if-else statements.
- The extends keyword is used to check if a type is assignable to another type.
- The result of a conditional type is either the "true" type or the "false" type, depending on the outcome of the condition.

By understanding the extends keyword in the context of conditional types, you're taking your first steps towards mastering type-level logic. Next, we'll explore how to create more complex conditional types using the ternary operator and how to leverage the infer keyword for even greater flexibility.

The Ternary Operator for Types

While the extends keyword is great for basic conditional types, TypeScript takes it a step further by allowing you to use the familiar ternary operator (condition ? trueType : falseType) at the type level. This gives you a concise and expressive way to create types that dynamically adapt based on boolean conditions.

Syntax

```
SomeType extends OtherType ? TrueType : FalseType;
```

Just like the regular ternary operator in JavaScript, this syntax translates to: "If SomeType extends OtherType, then the resulting type is TrueType; otherwise, it's FalseType."

Example: Making Properties Optional

Let's say you want to create a type that is identical to an existing interface, but with all properties made optional. You can use a conditional type with the ternary operator to achieve this:

```
interface Person { name: string; age: number; } type PartialPerson = { [P in
keyof Person]?: Person[P]; };
```

In this example, we utilize Mapped Types (to be discussed in detail later) and the ternary operator to iterate over all properties of the Person interface, and make them optional using the ? symbol.

Type Inference and Conditional Types

TypeScript's type inference engine works seamlessly with conditional types, making them even more powerful. It can often deduce the types involved, saving you from writing explicit type annotations.

```
type Stringify<T> = T extends string ? string : string; // This is not optimal, as it always returns a string type NameOrId<T> = T extends { name: string } ? string : number; let a = 'Alice'; // type of `a` inferred as string let b = 5; // type of `b` inferred as number let c: Stringify<typeof a> = identity(a); // type of `c` inferred as string, regardless of the parameter being passed into `identity` let d: NameOrId<typeof a> = identity(a); // type of `d` inferred as string let e: NameOrId<typeof b> = identity(b); // type of `e` inferred as number
```

Advantages of Conditional Types

- **Dynamic Type Creation:** You can create types that change based on runtime conditions.
- **Type-level Logic:** Express complex logic at the type level, leading to more sophisticated and reusable types.
- **Conciseness:** The ternary operator provides a concise way to define conditional types.
- **Improved Type Inference:** TypeScript's type inference works well with conditional types, reducing the need for explicit annotations.

Use Cases

Conditional types have a wide range of applications, including:

- **Making properties optional:** As demonstrated above.
- **Creating union types based on conditions:** You can build union types that include or exclude specific types based on a condition.
- **Extracting types from other types:** You can extract specific property types or return types from functions.
- **Type Narrowing:** Conditional types can be used to create custom type guards that refine types based on runtime checks.

By mastering conditional types and the ternary operator, you unlock a new level of expressiveness and flexibility in your TypeScript code. You can create types that adapt to different situations, leading to safer, more reliable, and more maintainable applications.

Inferring and Distributing Conditional Types

Conditional types become even more powerful when combined with the `infer` keyword and distributed over union types. Let's delve into these advanced techniques that enable you to perform intricate type manipulations and create more flexible and expressive TypeScript code.

The `infer` Keyword: Capturing Types Dynamically

The `infer` keyword within a conditional type allows you to declare a type variable (usually denoted by a single uppercase letter) that can "capture" a type from the condition. Think of it as a way to extract a type from a more complex type expression.

Example: Extracting an Element Type from an Array

```
type ArrayElement<ArrayType> = ArrayType extends Array<infer ElementType> ? ElementType : never; type A = ArrayElement<number[]>; // A is number type B =
```

```
ArrayElement<string[]>; // B is string type C = ArrayElement<boolean>; // C is never
```

In this example, the `ArrayElement` type uses `infer` to capture the element type of the `ArrayType` if it's an array. If it's not an array, the type resolves to `never`. This is a common pattern for extracting element types from arrays.

Distributing Conditional Types Over Unions

TypeScript allows you to distribute a conditional type over a union type. This means that the conditional type is applied to each member of the union individually, and the results are combined into a new union type.

Example: Making Properties of a Union Type Optional

```
type MakeOptional<T> = { [K in keyof T]?: T[K] }; type Person = { name: string; age: number; }; type PartialPerson = MakeOptional<Person>; // { name?: string; age?: number; }
```

Here, `MakeOptional<T>` distributes over the `keyof Person` union type. For each key, it creates a new optional property in the resulting `PartialPerson` type.

Example: Extracting String Literal Types from a Union

```
type StringFromUnion<T> = T extends string ? T : never; type Union = "a" | "b" | 1 | 2; type Result = StringFromUnion<Union>; // Result is "a" | "b"
```

In this example, `StringFromUnion<T>` filters out any non-string members from the `Union` type, resulting in a new type `Result` that only includes string literals.

Key Points

- `infer` allows you to capture and reuse types within conditional types.
- Conditional types can be distributed over union types.
- This combination enables powerful type transformations like making properties optional, filtering types, and more.
- Type inference often works seamlessly with `infer` and distributed conditional types.

By mastering these advanced techniques, you unlock a new level of control and flexibility in your TypeScript type manipulations. You can create sophisticated type definitions that accurately model your data and application logic, leading to more robust and maintainable code.

Practical Examples of Conditional Types

Conditional types, with their type-level logic, are incredibly versatile. Let's dive into some practical examples to illustrate how you can use them to solve common problems and streamline your TypeScript code.

1. Extracting a Property Type from an Object Type

Suppose you have an interface representing a `Person` and you want to create a type alias specifically for the type of the `name` property. You can use a conditional type to achieve this:

```
interface Person { name: string; age: number; } type NameType = Person extends { name: infer Name } ? Name : never; // Usage: const personName: NameType = "Alice"; // Valid // const personAge: NameType = 30; // Error: Type 'number' is not assignable to type 'NameType'
```

In the above example, the type alias `NameType` will be inferred as a string, as the `Person` interface contains a `name` property of type string.

2. Removing Types from a Union

You can use conditional types to filter out specific types from a union:

```
type NonNullable<T> = T extends null | undefined ? never : T; type A = NonNullable<string | null>; // A is string type B = NonNullable<number | undefined>; // B is number
```

The `NonNullable` type filters out null and undefined types from a union type.

3. Creating Conditional Return Types for Functions

Conditional types allow you to create functions whose return types depend on the type of their arguments:

```
type Stringify<T> = T extends { toString(): string } ? string : unknown; function stringifyValue<T>(value: T): Stringify<T> { if (typeof value === 'string') { return value; // string } else if (typeof value === 'number' || typeof value === 'boolean') { return value.toString(); // string } else if (value && typeof value.toString === 'function') { return value.toString(); // string } else { return String(value); // string } } const str1 = stringifyValue("hello"); // string const str2 = stringifyValue(42); // string const str3 = stringifyValue(true); // string const str4 = stringifyValue([1, 2, 3]); // string (because arrays have a toString() method)
```

4. Building Complex Type Guards

While the `typeof` and `instanceof` operators are great for basic type guards, you can use conditional types to create more sophisticated type guards.

```
interface User { id: number; name: string; isAdmin?: boolean; } function isAdmin(user: User): user is User & { isAdmin: true } { return user.isAdmin === true; } // Usage: const user: User = { id: 1, name: "Alice", isAdmin: true }; if (isAdmin(user)) { console.log(user.isAdmin); // TypeScript knows 'isAdmin' is definitely true here }
```

By combining these techniques, you can create powerful and flexible functions that operate seamlessly on different types, making your TypeScript code more concise, reusable, and robust.

Mapped Types

Modifying Existing Types

In the realm of advanced TypeScript, mapped types are your key to elegantly transforming existing types into new ones. They allow you to create variations of interfaces or object types by systematically modifying their properties. This powerful feature promotes code reusability and enables you to tailor types to specific needs without writing repetitive boilerplate.

How Mapped Types Work

Think of mapped types as a way to iterate over the keys (property names) of an existing type and apply a set of transformations to each property, resulting in a new type with modified properties.

Syntax

```
type NewType = { [Property in keyof ExistingType]: ModifiedProperty; };
```

Let's break down the syntax:

- **`NewType`:** The name of the new type you're creating.
- **`Property`:** A placeholder that represents each key (property name) in the `ExistingType`.
- **`keyof ExistingType`:** This is a special TypeScript operator that creates a union type of all the keys in `ExistingType`.
- **`in`:** The keyword used to iterate over the keys in the union.
- **`ModifiedProperty`:** The type expression that determines how each property in the new type will be transformed.

Example: Making All Properties Optional

```
interface Person { name: string; age: number; email: string; } type
PartialPerson = { [P in keyof Person]?: Person[P]; };
```

In this example:

1. We define an interface `Person` with three required properties.
2. We create a mapped type `PartialPerson` by iterating over each property P in `Person`.
3. The `?:` modifier makes each property optional in the new `PartialPerson` type.
4. `Person[P]` is a lookup type that retrieves the type of the corresponding property in the `Person` interface.

Example: Mapping from Number to String

```
type NumberToString = { [K in keyof Record<number, string>]: string; }; const
numStringMap: NumberToString = { 1: "one", 2: "two", 3: "three", };
```

In this example:

1. We created a new type, `NumberToString` which will map to keys of type number to a string value.
2. We used the `Record<Keys, Type>` utility type in the above example. It constructs an object type whose property keys are Keys and whose property values are Type. This utility can be used to map the properties of a type to another type.

Key Points

- Mapped types allow you to create new types by modifying existing types.
- They iterate over the keys of the original type and apply transformations to create a new object type.
- You can make properties optional (`?:`), readonly (`readonly`), or apply other transformations.

Mapped types are a versatile tool for type transformations in TypeScript. They promote code reuse, reduce boilerplate, and allow you to create types that precisely match the needs of your application.

Readonly, Optional, and Required Modifiers

Mapped types in TypeScript give you the power to not only transform the types of properties but also modify their attributes, such as whether they are readonly or optional. Let's explore how to use the `readonly`, ? (optional), and - (remove) modifiers to fine-tune your types.

Adding or Removing `readonly`

The `readonly` modifier prevents a property from being reassigned after its initial value is set. You can add or remove the `readonly` modifier in a mapped type by prefixing it with a + (add) or - (remove) symbol, respectively.

```
interface Point { x: number; y: number; } type ReadonlyPoint = { +readonly [P in keyof Point]: Point[P]; // Make all properties readonly }; type WritablePoint = { -readonly [P in keyof Point]: Point[P]; // Make all properties writable };
```

Adding or Removing `?` (Optional)

The ? modifier marks a property as optional, meaning it might not be present on an object of that type. You can add or remove the optional modifier in a mapped type using the + and - prefixes:

```
interface Person { name: string; age: number; email?: string; // Already optional } type AllOptionalPerson = { [P in keyof Person]?: Person[P]; // Make all properties optional }; type RequiredEmailPerson = { [P in keyof Person]-?: Person[P]; // Make all properties required, including 'email' }; type Partial<T> = { [P in keyof T]?: T[P]; }; type Required<T> = { [P in keyof T]-?: T[P]; };
```

In the example above, we've demonstrated the usage of the built-in mapped types `Partial` and `Required` which add or remove the optional modifier to properties respectively.

Important Notes

- **Default Behavior:** If you don't specify a + or - prefix, the mapped type modifier is treated as + (add).
- **Combining Modifiers:** You can combine multiple modifiers. For example, `+readonly` adds the `readonly` modifier, while `-?` removes the optional modifier.

By mastering these modifiers in mapped types, you gain precise control over the mutability and optionality of properties, allowing you to tailor your TypeScript types to perfectly fit your application's requirements.

Proxying Properties

Mapped types, as we've seen, are excellent for transforming existing types. A particularly interesting use case is creating "proxy" types—types that mirror the structure of another type while allowing you to modify or augment its properties in a controlled manner.

What is a Proxy Type?

In TypeScript, a proxy type is a type that has the same properties as another type (the "base" type), but with some or all of those properties modified in some way. For example, you might want to create a proxy type that makes all properties of the base type readonly, or you might want to add a new property to the proxy type.

Creating Proxy Types with Mapped Types

To create a proxy type, you use a mapped type to iterate over the keys of the base type and define how each property should be transformed in the proxy type.

Example: Adding a Prefix to Property Names

```
interface Person { name: string; age: number; } type PrefixedPerson = { [P in keyof Person as `user${Capitalize<P>}`]: Person[P] }; // Usage const user: PrefixedPerson = { userName: "Alice", userAge: 30 }; //console.log(user.name); // Error: Property 'name' does not exist on type 'PrefixedPerson'
```

In this example, `PrefixedPerson` is a proxy type that mirrors the `Person` interface, but with each property name prefixed with "user" (and the first letter capitalized).

Example: Making All Properties Optional and Readonly

```
type ReadonlyPartial<T> = { +readonly [P in keyof T]?: T[P]; }; type PartialPerson = ReadonlyPartial<Person>; // { readonly name?: string; readonly age?: number; }
```

This example creates a proxy type `ReadonlyPartial<T>` that makes all properties of the base type T both readonly and optional. We then apply this to `Person` to create `PartialPerson`.

Use Cases for Proxy Types

- **Immutable Data:** Create readonly versions of types to ensure data integrity.
- **Partial Updates:** Generate types for partial updates of objects (e.g., in PATCH requests).
- **Computed Properties:** Add derived or computed properties to a type without modifying the original.
- **Data Transformation:** Map properties from one type to another (e.g., renaming properties for API compatibility).

Key Points

- Proxy types mirror the structure of a base type while modifying or adding properties.
- Use mapped types to create proxy types by iterating over the keys of the base type.
- Proxy types are a powerful tool for creating type-safe transformations and variations of existing types.

By mastering proxy types, you gain the ability to customize and extend your TypeScript types in a controlled and flexible manner, making your code more adaptable to various use cases.

Practical Examples of Mapped Types

Mapped types are incredibly versatile tools for transforming existing types into new ones that better suit your needs. Let's dive into concrete examples to illustrate how you can use mapped types to achieve common type manipulations.

1. Making All Properties Readonly

You can create a readonly version of an existing type using the `readonly` modifier within a mapped type:

```
interface User { id: number; name: string; email: string; } type ReadonlyUser = { readonly [P in keyof User]: User[P]; }; const user: User = { id: 1, name: "Alice", email: "alice@example.com" }; const readonlyUser: ReadonlyUser = user; //readonlyUser.name = "Bob"; // Error: Cannot assign to 'name' because it is a read-only property.
```

In this example, `ReadonlyUser` mirrors the structure of the `User` interface but makes all its properties readonly. Any attempt to modify properties on a `ReadonlyUser` object will result in a type error.

2. Making All Properties Optional

Similarly, you can make all properties of a type optional using the ? modifier:

```
type PartialUser = { [P in keyof User]?: User[P]; }; const partialUser: PartialUser = { name: "Bob" }; // Valid, other properties are optional
```

Here, `PartialUser` is a mapped type that makes all properties of `User` optional. You can create a `PartialUser` object without specifying all the properties.

3. Creating a Partial Type with a Subset of Properties

You can use mapped types to create a new type that includes only a subset of the properties of an existing type:

```
type UserNameAndEmail = { [P in keyof User as P extends "name" | "email" ? P : never]: User[P]; }; // Or, using Pick built-in mapped type type UserNameAndEmail2 = Pick<User, 'name' | 'email'>; const userSubset: UserNameAndEmail = { name: "Alice", email: "alice@example.com" };
```

This creates a new type that only has two of the properties from the original `User` interface.

4. Picking or Omitting Specific Properties

TypeScript provides built-in utility types, `Pick` and `Omit`, for easily picking or omitting properties from an existing type:

```
// Pick<Type, Keys> type UserInfo = Pick<User, "name" | "email">; // { name: string; email: string; } // Omit<Type, Keys> type UserWithoutID = Omit<User, "id">; // { name: string; email: string; }
```

These examples illustrate how to pick a subset of properties (`UserInfo`) and omit specific properties (`UserWithoutID`) from the `User` interface.

Key Points

- Mapped types can create modified versions of existing types.
- Use `readonly`, ?, and - modifiers to control property attributes.
- Create partial types or types with specific subsets of properties.
- Leverage built-in utility types like `Pick` and `Omit` for concise type transformations.

By mastering mapped types and their modifiers, you gain a powerful tool for customizing and refining your TypeScript types, making your code more flexible, expressive, and type-safe.

Template Literal Types

Type-Level String Manipulation

Template literal types are a relatively new but exciting feature in TypeScript (introduced in version 4.1). They bring the power of template literals—those versatile backtick-enclosed strings you use for interpolation and multi-line strings in JavaScript—to the type level. This allows you to perform string manipulations and create dynamic types based on string patterns, opening up a world of possibilities for type-level string validation and manipulation.

How Template Literal Types Work

Template literal types have the same syntax as template literals in JavaScript, but they're used in type positions rather than to represent actual string values. The key idea is that they can be combined with string literal types (e.g., `"hello"`) and type parameters to create new string literal types or string unions.

Syntax

```
type MyTemplateLiteralType = `prefix-${string}-${number}`;
```

In this example:

- We use backticks (`) to define a template literal type.
- The template can contain string literals (e.g., `"prefix-"`), type placeholders (e.g., `string`, `number`), and expressions within `${...}`.
- When the template is evaluated, the type placeholders are replaced with the actual types, and the expressions are resolved to their resulting types.

Creating String Unions

One of the most common uses of template literal types is to create string unions. By using type parameters and conditional types, you can dynamically generate unions based on string patterns.

Example: Creating Event Name Types

```
type EventName<T extends string> = `on${Capitalize<T>}`; type ButtonClickEvent
= EventName<"click">; // "onClick" type InputChangeEvent =
EventName<"change">; // "onChange"
```

In this example:

1. We define a generic type `EventName<T>`, where T is a string type parameter.
2. The template literal type on`${Capitalize<T>}` capitalizes the first letter of T and prepends “on” to it.
3. We use this type to create two specific event names: `ButtonClickEvent` and `InputChangeEvent`.

Type Safety with Template Literal Types

TypeScript's compiler can enforce that you only use valid string literal types. This can be especially useful for things like event names, API endpoints, or command names, where you have a predefined set of valid strings.

Example: Validating API Endpoints

```
type ApiEndpoint = `/users` | `/products`; // Allowed endpoint types function fetchData(endpoint: ApiEndpoint) { // ... fetch data from the specified endpoint ... } fetchData('/users'); // Valid fetchData('/orders'); // Error: Argument of type '/orders' is not assignable to parameter of type 'ApiEndpoint'.
```

By using template literal types, you bring the power of string manipulation to the type level, creating more expressive and type-safe TypeScript code.

Creating String Unions with Template Literals

One of the most powerful features of template literal types is their ability to dynamically create string unions. This allows you to define a set of valid string values based on patterns, ensuring that your code only accepts strings that conform to those patterns.

Basic Syntax

```
type MyStringUnion = `prefix-${string}-suffix`;
```

In this basic example, `MyStringUnion` is a type that represents any string starting with "prefix-", followed by any string, and ending with "-suffix". For instance, "prefix-hello-suffix" and "prefix-world-suffix" are both valid values of this type.

Using Type Parameters

To make this even more flexible, you can use type parameters to create string unions that are based on other types:

```
type EventName<T extends string> = `on${Capitalize<T>}`; type ButtonEvents = EventName<"click" | "hover">; // "onClick" | "onHover"
```

Here, `EventName<T>` is a generic type that takes a string type T and returns a string that starts with "on" followed by the capitalized version of T. The `ButtonEvents` type then uses this to create a union of two valid event names for a button: "onClick" and "onHover."

Example: Validating CSS Class Names

```
type Size = "small" | "medium" | "large"; type Color = "primary" | "secondary" | "warning"; type ButtonClass = `btn-${Size}-${Color}`; let btnClass: ButtonClass = "btn-medium-primary"; // Valid let invalidClass: ButtonClass = "btn-xlarge-success"; // Error: Type '"btn-xlarge-success"' is not assignable to type 'ButtonClass'.
```

This allows you to define a type `ButtonClass` that represents all valid combinations of size and color class names for a button element in your CSS.

Example: File Paths

```
type FileExtension = "jpg" | "png" | "gif"; type ImagePath =
`/images/${string}.${FileExtension}`; let imagePath: ImagePath =
"/images/logo.png"; // Valid let invalidPath: ImagePath =
"/images/document.pdf"; // Error
```

You can even create types for valid file paths as shown above.

Key Points

- Template literal types can create string unions based on patterns.
- Use type parameters to create flexible string unions derived from other types.
- This technique enhances type safety by ensuring that only valid strings are used.
- Template literal types are great for defining valid event names, API endpoints, file paths, and more.

By mastering template literal types and their ability to create string unions, you can add a powerful tool to your TypeScript toolkit, enabling you to express and enforce string-based constraints in your code. This leads to a higher level of type safety and more predictable behavior in your TypeScript applications.

Practical Examples of Template Literal Types

Template literal types are not just theoretical constructs; they have practical applications in various areas of TypeScript development. Let's dive into some real-world scenarios where template literal types can improve your code's type safety and expressiveness.

1. Generating Type-Safe API Endpoint URLs

```
type UserApiEndpoint = `/api/users/${number}`; type PostApiEndpoint =
`/api/posts/${number}`; type CommentApiEndpoint =
`/api/posts/${number}/comments/${number}`; type ApiEndpoint = UserApiEndpoint
| PostApiEndpoint | CommentApiEndpoint; function fetchData(endpoint:
ApiEndpoint) { // ... fetch data from the specified endpoint ... }
fetchData("/api/users/123"); // Valid fetchData("/api/posts/456"); // Valid
fetchData("/api/posts/456/comments/789"); // Valid fetchData("/api/invalid");
// Error: Type '"api/invalid"' is not assignable to type 'ApiEndpoint'
```

By defining this type, we ensure that only valid endpoints can be passed to this function.

2. Creating Types for CSS Class Names

```
type ButtonSize = "small" | "medium" | "large"; type ButtonVariant = "primary"
| "secondary"; type ButtonClassName = `btn-${ButtonSize} ${ButtonVariant}`;
type ButtonProps = { children: React.ReactNode, className?: ButtonClassName;
onClick: () => void; }; function Button({ children, className, onClick }:
ButtonProps): JSX.Element { return <button className={className}
onClick={onClick}>{children}</button>; };
```

In this example, `ButtonClassName` is a template literal type that represents all valid combinations of button size and variant classes. TypeScript will prevent you from accidentally using invalid class names, ensuring consistency in your styling.

3. Defining Valid Routes for a Router

```
type ValidRoute = "/home" | "/about" | "/contact" | `/product/${string}`;
function navigateTo(route: ValidRoute) { // ... navigation logic ... }
navigateTo("/home"); // Valid navigateTo("/product/123"); // Valid
navigateTo("/invalid"); // Error
```

Here, `ValidRoute` defines the valid routes for your application. TypeScript will then check that you only navigate to allowed routes, preventing errors due to typos or invalid URLs.

Key Points

- Template literal types offer a flexible way to define string-based types with type safety.
- They are especially useful for creating string unions based on patterns.
- Use cases include API endpoint URLs, CSS class names, command names, file paths, and more.
- They can be combined with other TypeScript features like generics and conditional types to create even more powerful type definitions.

By embracing template literal types, you can leverage the power of string manipulation at the type level, creating more robust, expressive, and type-safe TypeScript code for various scenarios.

Keyof and Typeof

TypeScript offers two special operators, `keyof` and `typeof`, that give you the ability to inspect and manipulate types at compile time. They open up a whole new realm of possibilities for building type-safe and flexible code.

keyof: Obtaining Keys of an Object Type

The `keyof` operator is like a key to the hidden world of object types. It allows you to extract the keys (property names) of an object type (interface, type alias, or class) and transform them into a union type. This means you can create types that represent the valid keys of an object, leading to more type-safe code when accessing properties.

Syntax

```
keyof ObjectType
```

Example: Interface Keys

```
interface Person { name: string; age: number; } type PersonKeys = keyof
Person; // "name" | "age"
```

In this example, `PersonKeys` is a union type consisting of the string literals `"name"` and `"age"`, which are the keys of the `Person` interface.

Example: Type Alias Keys

```
type Coordinates = { x: number; y: number }; type CoordinateKeys = keyof
Coordinates; // "x" | "y"
```

The same principle applies to type aliases. `CoordinateKeys` is a union type of the keys `"x"` and `"y"` from the `Coordinates` type alias.

Using keyof in Practice

- **Type-Safe Property Access:**
  ```
  function getProperty<T, K extends keyof T>(obj: T, key: K): T[K] { return obj[key]; } const person: Person = { name: "Alice", age: 30 }; const name = getProperty(person, "name"); // Type of name is string
  ```
  The `getProperty` function ensures that you only try to access valid properties on the object `obj`. TypeScript infers the return type based on the provided key and the object's type.
- **Constraining Generic Types:**
  ```
  function updateProperty<T, K extends keyof T>(obj: T, key: K, value: T[K]): void { obj[key] = value; }
  ```
  The `updateProperty` function enforces that you provide a valid key and a value of the correct type for that key.

Key Points

- The `keyof` operator extracts the keys of an object type as a union type.
- Use `keyof` to create types that represent valid keys for an object.
- Combine `keyof` with generics to write type-safe functions that operate on objects with varying structures.

By mastering the `keyof` operator, you gain a powerful tool for working with object types in a more type-safe and flexible manner, ensuring that you only access valid properties and improving the robustness of your TypeScript code.

typeof: Getting the Type of a Value

While the `keyof` operator focuses on object keys, the `typeof` operator in TypeScript allows you to peek into the world of values and determine their types at compile time. It's a versatile tool that can be used to create flexible functions, type guards, and other advanced type manipulations.

Understanding `typeof`

In JavaScript, the `typeof` operator is used at runtime to determine the type of a value. It returns a string representation of the type (e.g., `"string"`, `"number"`, `"boolean"`, `"object"`, etc.).

In TypeScript, `typeof` takes on a dual role. It can be used at runtime just like in JavaScript, but it can also be used as a *type operator* at compile time to extract the type of a variable or expression.

Syntax

```
typeof variableName
```

Example: Type Inference with `typeof`

```
let value = "Hello, world!"; // TypeScript infers the type of value as string
type ValueType = typeof value;
```

In this example, `ValueType` is inferred as the literal type `"Hello, world!"`. This means `ValueType` is not just any string; it's specifically a string with the value "Hello, world!".

`typeof` as a Type Guard

One of the most common use cases for `typeof` in TypeScript is creating type guards. We've already seen how `typeof` can be used in `if` statements to narrow down types within union types.

```
function logValue(value: string | number) { if (typeof value === "string") { // value is now narrowed to string } else { // value is now narrowed to number } }
```

`typeof` for Creating Type-Safe Functions

Let's see how you can leverage `typeof` to create a function that works with different types of input:

```
function doubleValue(value: unknown): unknown { // unknown type allows any input if (typeof value === "number") { return value * 2; } else if (typeof value === "string") { return value + value; } else { return value; } }
```

Here, the `doubleValue` function can handle both numbers (by doubling them) and strings (by concatenating them). The `typeof` operator is used to determine the type of the input and execute the appropriate logic.

Key Points

- In TypeScript, `typeof` can be used as a type operator at compile time to get the type of a value.
- This is different from JavaScript's `typeof`, which operates at runtime.
- You can use `typeof` to create type guards that narrow down the types of variables.
- Combine `typeof` with conditional types and function overloads to create functions that work with different types of input in a type-safe manner.

By understanding how to use `typeof` effectively, you gain a powerful tool for building flexible and type-safe TypeScript code.

Combining keyof and typeof for Dynamic Access

The real magic happens when you combine the `keyof` and `typeof` operators. Together, they provide a way to dynamically access object properties while maintaining the full benefits of TypeScript's type safety. This is particularly useful for creating generic functions that can operate on objects with different structures.

Dynamic Access with Type Safety

Let's illustrate with a practical example:

```
function getProperty<T, K extends keyof T>(obj: T, key: K): T[K] { return obj[key]; // Type-safe property access } interface Person { name: string; age: number; } const person: Person = { name: "Alice", age: 30 }; const name = getProperty(person, "name"); // Type of name is string const age = getProperty(person, "age"); // Type of age is number // getProperty(person, "address"); // Error: Argument of type '"address"' is not assignable to parameter of type '"name" | "age"'
```

In this example:

1. **`getProperty` Function:** We define a generic function `getProperty` that takes two type parameters:
   - T: Represents the type of the object.

   - K: Represents the type of the key, which is constrained to be one of the keys of the object type T using `K extends keyof T`.
2. **Type-Safe Access:** Inside the function, we use `obj[key]` to access the property dynamically. However, thanks to the constraint on K, TypeScript ensures that `key` can only be a valid property name for the object `obj`. It also infers the correct return type based on the property's type within the object type T.
3. **Usage:** We can safely use `getProperty` to access the `name` and `age` properties of the `person` object, as they are valid keys of the `Person` interface.

Benefits

- **Flexibility:** This technique allows you to write generic functions that can operate on objects with different structures without sacrificing type safety.
- **Dynamic Access:** You can access properties using variables or expressions, making your code more dynamic.
- **Type Safety:** TypeScript ensures that you only access properties that exist on the object and that the types are used correctly.

Use Cases

This pattern is often used in scenarios where:

- You're building utility functions that need to work with various object types.
- You're interacting with data from external sources (e.g., APIs) where the structure of the objects might not be fully known in advance.
- You need to dynamically access object properties based on user input or other runtime conditions.

Key Points

- Combine `keyof` and `typeof` to dynamically access object properties in a type-safe way.
- Use generic type parameters and constraints to ensure type safety.
- This technique is particularly useful for creating reusable functions that operate on objects with different structures.

By mastering this powerful combination of `keyof` and `typeof`, you open up new possibilities for creating flexible and type-safe TypeScript code that can handle dynamic data structures with confidence.

Advanced Tips and Tricks

Type Guards and Assertions in Advanced Scenarios

As we venture into the realm of advanced type manipulation, the synergy between type guards and type assertions becomes even more crucial for maintaining type safety and writing expressive code. Let's explore how to use these tools effectively in complex scenarios involving conditional types, mapped types, and template literal types.

1. Type Guards with Conditional Types

Conditional types often involve checking whether a type satisfies certain conditions. Type guards can be used within the `true` branch of a conditional type to narrow down the type further.

```
type ExtractProperty<T, U> = T extends { [key: string]: U } ? U : never;
function getPropertyValue<T, U>(obj: T, key: keyof T): ExtractProperty<T, U> {
if (typeof obj[key] === "number") { return obj[key] as ExtractProperty<T, U>;
```

```
// Type assertion after narrowing } else { throw new Error(`Property ${key} is not of type number`); } }
```

In this example, `ExtractProperty<T, U>` is a type that finds if the object T has a property of type U. Then we're narrowing down the type of the value obtained at `obj[key]`, then we use type assertion (`as`) to tell the compiler that the value is indeed of the type `ExtractProperty<T, U>`.

2. Type Guards with Mapped Types

When working with mapped types, you might need to apply type guards to the properties of the original type to determine how to transform them in the mapped type.

```
type FilterByValueType<T, U> = { [K in keyof T as T[K] extends U ? K : never]: T[K]; }; interface Person { name: string; age: number; email: string; } type StringProps = FilterByValueType<Person, string>; // { name: string; email: string; }
```

The type `FilterByValueType` iterates through the keys of an object T, returning a new object type that only includes properties whose values extend or are of the type U.

3. Type Guards with Template Literal Types

Type guards can help you discriminate between members of a string union created with template literal types:

```
type Action = 'create' | 'update' | 'delete'; function handleAction(action: Action) { if (action === 'create' || action === 'update') { // Perform logic for create or update actions } else { // Perform logic for delete action } }
```

The type guard `action === 'create' || action === 'update'` narrows the type of `action` to `'create' | 'update'` within the corresponding block, allowing for more specific operations.

4. Leveraging Type Inference

In many cases, TypeScript's type inference can be used to simplify your code when working with type guards and conditional types. Consider this example:

```
function processValue<T>(value: T) { if (typeof value === 'string') { // TypeScript infers that value is of type 'string' in this block } }
```

TypeScript automatically infers the narrower type within the `if` block, eliminating the need for explicit type assertions.

Key Points

- Combine type guards with conditional and mapped types to refine types and perform safe operations.
- Use type assertions cautiously after narrowing types to inform the compiler about specific types.
- Leverage type inference to reduce the need for explicit type annotations.
- Be mindful of edge cases and potential type errors when working with complex type manipulations.

By mastering these advanced techniques, you'll be able to write more sophisticated and robust TypeScript code that takes full advantage of the type system's power to ensure safety, flexibility, and clarity.

Utility Types for Type Manipulation

TypeScript comes equipped with a handy set of built-in utility types that can significantly simplify common type transformations. Think of them as pre-made tools in your TypeScript toolbox, ready to streamline your code and save you from writing repetitive type definitions.

Let's explore some of the most useful utility types:

1. **`Partial<Type>`:** Creates a type where all properties of Type are optional.
   ```
   interface User { id: number; name: string; email: string; } type PartialUser = Partial<User>; // { id?: number; name?: string; email?: string; }
   ```
   Useful when dealing with partial updates to an object.
2. **`Required<Type>`:** Creates a type where all properties of Type are required.
   ```
   type RequiredUser = Required<User>; // { id: number; name: string; email: string; }
   ```
   Useful for ensuring all properties are present.
3. **`Readonly<Type>`:** Creates a type where all properties of Type are readonly.
   ```
   type ReadonlyUser = Readonly<User>;
   ```
   Enforces immutability of objects.
4. **`Pick<Type, Keys>`:** Creates a type by picking a set of specific properties (`Keys`) from Type.
   ```
   type UserName = Pick<User, "id" | "name">; // { id: number; name: string; }
   ```
   Useful for extracting a subset of properties.
5. **`Omit<Type, Keys>`:** Creates a type by excluding a set of properties (`Keys`) from Type.
   ```
   type UserWithoutEmail = Omit<User, "email">; // { id: number; name: string; }
   ```
6. **`Record<Keys, Type>`:** Constructs an object type whose property keys are `Keys` and whose property values are `Type`.
   ```
   type DaysOfWeek = Record<"Monday" | "Tuesday" | "Wednesday" | "Thursday" | "Friday" | "Saturday" | "Sunday", number>;
   ```
7. **`Exclude<UnionType, ExcludedMembers>`:** Creates a new type by excluding specific members from a union type.
   ```
   type T0 = Exclude<"a" | "b" | "c", "a">; // "b" | "c"
   ```
8. **`Extract<UnionType, Union>`:** Creates a type by extracting members of a `UnionType` that are assignable to `Union`.
   ```
   type T0 = Extract<"a" | "b" | "c", "a" | "f">; // "a"
   ```
9. **`ReturnType<Type>`:** Extracts the return type of a function type.
   ```
   type T0 = ReturnType<() => string>; // string
   ```

Key Points

- Utility types are built-in type transformers provided by TypeScript.
- They simplify common type manipulations, making your code more concise.
- Use utility types whenever possible to avoid reinventing the wheel and to keep your type definitions clear and focused.

By becoming familiar with these utility types and incorporating them into your workflow, you'll be able to write cleaner, more efficient, and more type-safe TypeScript code with ease.

Chapter Summary

In this chapter, we delved into the realm of advanced type manipulation in TypeScript, expanding your toolkit for creating expressive and powerful type definitions. Here's a recap of what we covered:

- **TypeScript's Type System: A Powerful Tool:** We reiterated the immense power and flexibility of TypeScript's type system, emphasizing its ability to go far beyond basic types.
- **Beyond Basic Types:** We provided a glimpse into the advanced type features covered in this chapter, including conditional types, mapped types, template literal types, `keyof`, `typeof`, and utility types.
- **Conditional Types:** We explored conditional types as type-level if-else statements, allowing you to create types that adapt based on specific conditions. We demonstrated how to use the `extends` keyword and the ternary operator to create conditional types, and how the `infer` keyword can be used to capture types dynamically.
- **Mapped Types:** We learned how to transform existing types into new ones using mapped types. We covered the `readonly`, ? (optional), and `-` (required) modifiers for manipulating property attributes. We also discussed how to create proxy types that mirror the structure of other types while modifying or adding properties.
- **Template Literal Types:** We introduced template literal types as a way to perform string manipulation at the type level. We showed how to create string unions based on string literal templates and discussed their practical use cases for generating type-safe API endpoint URLs, CSS class names, and routes.
- **`keyof` and `typeof`:** We explored the `keyof` operator for obtaining keys of an object type and the `typeof` operator for getting the type of a value at compile time. We demonstrated how to combine them to dynamically access object properties in a type-safe manner.
- **Advanced Tips and Tricks:** We discussed how to use type guards and type assertions effectively in complex scenarios involving the advanced types we covered. We also introduced several utility types (`Partial`, `Pick`, `Omit`, `Record`, `Exclude`, `Extract`, and `ReturnType`) that simplify common type transformations.

By mastering these advanced techniques, you've unlocked a new level of control over TypeScript's type system. You can now create complex and reusable type definitions that accurately model your data and application logic, leading to more robust, maintainable, and expressive code.

Integrating TypeScript with Existing Projects

Outline

- Introduction
    - The Challenge of Adoption
    - Gradual Typing: A Key Strategy
- Incremental Adoption Strategies
    - Starting with Configuration (tsconfig.json)
    - Adding TypeScript to Individual Files
    - Dealing with JavaScript Dependencies
    - Using Type Definitions (DefinitelyTyped)
- Refactoring JavaScript to TypeScript
    - Adding Type Annotations
    - Gradual Refactoring Techniques
    - Common Challenges and Solutions
- Tools to Aid Migration
    - TypeScript Compiler Options
    - Codemods and Automated Refactoring
- Case Studies
    - Integrating TypeScript with a React project
    - Integrating TypeScript with a Node.js project
- Chapter Summary

Introduction

The Challenge of Adoption

Integrating TypeScript into an existing JavaScript project is a transformative journey that offers significant benefits but also presents challenges. It's not just a matter of changing file extensions; it's a shift in mindset and a commitment to a more structured and disciplined approach to JavaScript development. Let's delve into the common obstacles you might encounter and strategies for navigating them.

1. Resistance to Change

It's natural for teams to be resistant to change, especially when it involves learning a new language and potentially rewriting existing code. Some developers might perceive TypeScript as adding unnecessary complexity or slowing down development. Others might be comfortable with JavaScript's dynamic nature and feel that TypeScript's type system is too restrictive.

To overcome this resistance, it's essential to:

- **Communicate the Benefits:** Clearly articulate the advantages of TypeScript, such as improved code quality, reduced bugs, enhanced developer experience, and better long-term maintainability. Emphasize how TypeScript can actually *speed up* development by catching errors early and providing better tooling support.
- **Start Small and Incrementally:** Don't try to convert the entire codebase overnight. Begin with a gradual approach, adding TypeScript to specific modules or components and demonstrating the benefits before expanding its usage.
- **Provide Training and Resources:** Offer resources like tutorials, documentation, or workshops to help your team members learn TypeScript and feel comfortable using it.

2. The Learning Curve

TypeScript, while based on JavaScript, has its own syntax, type system, and tooling. There's a learning curve involved in mastering these concepts, especially for developers who are accustomed to JavaScript's dynamic nature.

To ease the learning process:

- **Focus on the Fundamentals:** Start with the basics of TypeScript's type system (primitives, arrays, interfaces, functions). Once these concepts are understood, the more advanced features become easier to grasp.
- **Gradual Learning:** Don't try to learn everything at once. Focus on the concepts you need for the immediate task at hand and gradually expand your knowledge as you go.
- **Pair Programming:** Encourage pair programming sessions where experienced TypeScript developers can mentor and guide those who are new to the language.

3. Incremental Migration

Migrating a large JavaScript codebase to TypeScript can seem daunting. However, TypeScript's design allows for incremental adoption. You can start by adding type annotations to a few files, gradually increasing coverage over time.

This approach allows you to:

- **Minimize Disruption:** You can continue developing and shipping your application while gradually introducing TypeScript.
- **Identify Pain Points:** As you convert parts of your codebase, you'll identify areas that might require more attention or refactoring to become type-safe.
- **Build Confidence:** As you see the benefits of TypeScript in action, it's easier to gain buy-in from your team and justify further adoption.

The Need for a Careful Approach

While TypeScript offers many advantages, it's not a magic bullet. Introducing it into an existing project requires a thoughtful and planned approach. By acknowledging the potential challenges, addressing resistance, and adopting a gradual migration strategy, you can successfully integrate TypeScript into your JavaScript codebase and reap its rewards in terms of code quality, developer productivity, and long-term maintainability.

Gradual Typing: A Key Strategy

One of the most significant advantages of TypeScript is its support for **gradual typing**. This approach recognizes that migrating a large existing JavaScript codebase to TypeScript can be a daunting task. Instead of requiring a complete overhaul, TypeScript allows you to adopt it incrementally, starting with loose type checking and gradually increasing the strictness as you become more comfortable with the language.

How Gradual Typing Works

1. **JavaScript is Valid TypeScript:** Every valid JavaScript file is also a valid TypeScript file. This means you can start by simply renaming your `.js` files to `.ts` without any immediate changes to your code.
2. **Optional Type Annotations:** TypeScript doesn't force you to add type annotations everywhere from the beginning. You can start by adding types to a few critical variables, functions, or classes, leaving the rest untyped.

3. **Type Inference:** TypeScript's powerful type inference engine can often deduce types based on the context, even in files without explicit annotations. This helps you get some type safety benefits even before you add full annotations.
4. **Gradual Strictness:** TypeScript offers various compiler options that control the level of type checking. You can start with looser options like `allowJs` (allow JavaScript files) and `noImplicitAny` (disallow implicit any types) and gradually enable stricter options like `strictNullChecks` and `strictFunctionTypes` as your codebase becomes more type-safe.

Why Gradual Typing is Beneficial

- **Reduced Friction:** It allows you to adopt TypeScript without a complete rewrite of your codebase, minimizing disruption to your development process.
- **Learning Curve:** You can start with the basics of TypeScript and gradually learn the more advanced features as you go.
- **Team Adoption:** It's easier to get buy-in from your team when they see that adopting TypeScript doesn't require a complete overhaul.
- **Incremental Improvement:** You can focus on adding types to the most critical parts of your code first, reaping the benefits of type safety in those areas while gradually expanding coverage.

Example: Gradual Migration

1. **Rename Files:** Start by renaming your `.js` files to `.ts`. TypeScript will treat them as valid TypeScript files, even without any type annotations.
2. **Add Basic Annotations:** Begin by adding basic type annotations to key variables and functions, like specifying that a variable holds a `string` or a function takes a `number` as an argument.
3. **Use Interfaces:** Define interfaces for objects to provide structure and clarity.
4. **Enable Stricter Options:** As you become more comfortable with TypeScript, gradually enable stricter compiler options like `strictNullChecks` and `noImplicitAny` to catch potential errors earlier.
5. **Refactor and Add More Types:** Continue adding type annotations to your code, refactoring it as needed to improve type safety and maintainability.

Key Points

- Gradual typing allows for a smooth transition from JavaScript to TypeScript.
- You can start with loose type checking and progressively add more type annotations.
- TypeScript's type inference helps deduce types even in untyped code.
- Use compiler options to control the strictness of type checking.

By embracing the gradual typing approach, you can seamlessly integrate TypeScript into your existing projects, enhancing code quality and maintainability without sacrificing productivity or causing major disruptions to your workflow.

Incremental Adoption Strategies

Starting with Configuration (`tsconfig.json`)

Embarking on the journey of integrating TypeScript into an existing JavaScript project doesn't have to be an all-or-nothing endeavor. The key to a smooth transition lies in gradual adoption, starting with the configuration of your TypeScript compiler. The `tsconfig.json` file is your control center for this process, offering options to fine-tune how TypeScript interacts with your existing codebase.

Creating the `tsconfig.json` File

If you don't have a `tsconfig.json` file in your project's root directory, you can easily generate one using the TypeScript compiler:

```
tsc --init
```

This command will create a `tsconfig.json` file with sensible default options, providing a good starting point for your configuration.

Essential Configuration Options

Let's delve into some key options that are particularly relevant when gradually adopting TypeScript:

- **`allowJs`:** Set this to `true` to allow JavaScript files (`.js` files) to coexist alongside your TypeScript files (`.ts` files). This is crucial for incremental adoption, as you can gradually convert files to TypeScript without breaking your existing JavaScript code.
- **`checkJs`:** When `allowJs` is enabled, setting `checkJs` to `true` will instruct TypeScript to perform type checking on your JavaScript files as well. This can help catch potential errors even in code that hasn't been explicitly converted to TypeScript.
- **`noImplicitAny`:** By default, TypeScript allows variables to be implicitly typed as `any` if their type cannot be inferred. Enabling `noImplicitAny` will raise an error in such cases, encouraging you to add explicit type annotations and improving type safety.
- **`strict`:** This is a master switch for enabling a set of stricter type-checking options. When you're first starting with TypeScript, you might want to leave this disabled or set it to `false` to allow for a more relaxed typing experience. As you gain confidence, you can gradually enable `strict` mode to enforce stricter rules and catch more potential errors.

Example Configuration for Gradual Adoption

```
{ "compilerOptions": { "allowJs": true, // Allow JavaScript files "checkJs":
false, // Start with JS type checking off, gradually turn it on later
"noImplicitAny": true, // Disallow implicit 'any' types "strict": false //
Start with strict mode off, gradually enable it }, "include": ["src/**/*"] //
Include all files in the src directory }
```

This configuration allows for a gentle introduction of TypeScript:

1. JavaScript files are allowed within the TypeScript project.
2. Initially, the code will run as is (without TypeScript's intervention).
3. any type is not allowed to be used implicitly.
4. Once you are confident enough, you may uncomment `"checkJs": true` and then `"strict": true` for strict type checking.

Key Points

- Use `tsconfig.json` to control TypeScript's behavior.
- Enable `allowJs` to allow JavaScript files in your project.
- Consider enabling `checkJs` to get type checking feedback on your JavaScript code.
- Start with `noImplicitAny` and gradually enable `strict` mode for stricter type checking.

By starting with a well-thought-out configuration, you lay the foundation for a successful and gradual migration to TypeScript, ensuring a smooth transition and minimizing disruption to your existing workflow.

Adding TypeScript to Individual Files

One of the most powerful aspects of adopting TypeScript is that you don't have to convert your entire JavaScript project at once. You can gradually introduce TypeScript into your codebase, file by file, allowing for a smoother transition and minimizing disruption to your workflow.

Renaming Files: A Simple First Step

The most basic step in adopting TypeScript is to change the file extension from `.js` to `.ts` (or `.tsx` if you're working with React components that use JSX). This signals to TypeScript that the file should be treated as TypeScript code and enables type checking.

```
# Before
my-project/
├── src/
|   └── myComponent.js

# After
my-project/
├── src/
|   └── myComponent.ts
```

Keep in mind that just changing the file extension to .ts does not mean the code is magically converted into TypeScript. You need to make the necessary changes to make it compatible.

Incremental Type Annotations

Once you've renamed your files, you can start adding TypeScript type annotations incrementally. You don't have to annotate every variable or function right away. Focus on the most critical parts of your code or areas where you're likely to encounter type-related errors.

```
// myComponent.ts function greet(name: string): string { // Type annotations
added return "Hello, " + name + "!"; }
```

TypeScript's type inference can still help you even if you don't annotate everything. For example, in the above code, it can infer the type of the parameter and return values for the functions.

Leveraging Type Inference

TypeScript's type inference engine plays a crucial role in gradual adoption. Even if you haven't added explicit types to every variable or function, TypeScript can often infer their types based on how they are used. This gives you some degree of type safety even in partially converted files.

```
// myComponent.ts (before adding types) function processData(data) { return
data.map(item => item * 2); }
```

In this example, TypeScript can infer that `data` is likely an array of numbers because it's being used with the `map` method, which is typically applied to arrays.

Gradual Progression

As you become more comfortable with TypeScript, you can gradually add more type annotations to your code. Start with basic types like `string`, `number`, and `boolean`, then move on to more complex types like arrays, objects, functions, and interfaces.

Key Points

- Rename `.js` files to `.ts` (or `.tsx`) to start using TypeScript.
- Add type annotations incrementally, starting with the most critical parts of your code.
- Leverage TypeScript's type inference to get some type safety benefits even in partially converted files.
- Gradually increase the strictness of your type checking by enabling more compiler options as you gain confidence.

By adopting this incremental approach, you can smoothly transition your project to TypeScript, making it more robust, maintainable, and enjoyable to work with.

Dealing with JavaScript Dependencies

As you integrate TypeScript into your existing JavaScript projects, you'll inevitably encounter dependencies that were written in JavaScript and don't include TypeScript type definitions. Fortunately, TypeScript provides several ways to bridge this gap and ensure type safety when working with JavaScript libraries.

1. DefinitelyTyped: The Community's Type Repository

DefinitelyTyped is a massive community-driven repository that hosts high-quality type definitions (declaration files) for thousands of popular JavaScript libraries and frameworks. These declaration files, typically named `@types/library-name`, provide TypeScript with the necessary type information to understand and work with JavaScript libraries.

Installing Type Definitions from DefinitelyTyped

You can install type definitions from DefinitelyTyped using npm or yarn:

```
npm install --save-dev @types/lodash # Install types for Lodash # or yarn add
--dev @types/express # Install types for Express.js
```

Once installed, TypeScript will automatically discover these type definitions and use them to provide type checking and code completion for the corresponding library.

2. Creating Your Own Declaration Files (`.d.ts`)

If type definitions for a specific library are not available on DefinitelyTyped, you can create your own declaration files. These files have the `.d.ts` extension and typically live alongside your TypeScript code.

```
// lodash.d.ts declare module "lodash" { export function camelCase(str:
string): string; // ... other Lodash function declarations ... }
```

In this example, we create a `lodash.d.ts` file that declares the `camelCase` function from Lodash, along with its parameters and return type. TypeScript will now understand how to use this function in a type-safe way.

Note: Writing your own declaration files requires a deeper understanding of TypeScript types and the library you're working with. It's generally recommended to search for existing type definitions on DefinitelyTyped first before resorting to creating your own.

3. Ambient Modules:

For smaller libraries or quick fixes, you can use an ambient module declaration to tell TypeScript that a module exists without providing explicit type definitions:

```
declare module 'my-untyped-library';
```

This allows you to use the library in your TypeScript code, but without any type checking for its functions or variables. Use ambient modules sparingly, as they bypass TypeScript's safety net.

4. Partial Type Definitions:

Sometimes, you might not need to fully type a library. You can create partial declaration files that only define the types for the parts of the library you actually use.

Key Points

- DefinitelyTyped is your first stop for finding type definitions for JavaScript libraries.
- You can create your own declaration files (`.d.ts`) for libraries without existing type definitions.
- Use ambient modules sparingly when you only need to tell TypeScript that a module exists.
- Consider partial type definitions if you only need to type specific parts of a library.

By effectively managing your JavaScript dependencies with type definitions, you can enjoy the benefits of TypeScript's type safety even when working with code that wasn't originally written in TypeScript. This ensures a smoother integration process and reduces the risk of errors in your projects.

Using Type Definitions (DefinitelyTyped)

While TypeScript's type system is powerful, it can't magically infer types for every JavaScript library out there. That's where DefinitelyTyped swoops in to save the day.

What is DefinitelyTyped?

DefinitelyTyped is a massive open-source repository hosted on GitHub (https://github.com/DefinitelyTyped/DefinitelyTyped) that houses high-quality type definitions for a vast number of JavaScript libraries and frameworks. These definitions, often contributed by community members, enable TypeScript to understand the structure and APIs of these libraries, providing you with type checking, autocompletion, and a seamless development experience.

Finding Type Definitions

The easiest way to find type definitions for a library is to search for it on the DefinitelyTyped website or on npm. Type definitions for a library named "my-library" will typically be packaged as `@types/my-library`.

Installing Type Definitions

Installing type definitions from DefinitelyTyped is a breeze with your package manager:

```
npm install --save-dev @types/my-library # or yarn add --dev @types/my-library
```

How Type Definitions Work

When you install a `@types` package, TypeScript automatically includes it in your project's type checking process. It essentially acts as a bridge between your TypeScript code and the JavaScript library, providing TypeScript with the necessary type information to understand how to interact with the library's functions, classes, and objects.

Example: Type Definitions for Lodash

```
import _ from "lodash"; // Assuming you have Lodash installed const myArray =
[1, 2, 3, 4, 5]; const sorted = _.sortBy(myArray); // TypeScript understands
the 'sortBy' method and its return type
```

In this example, because you have installed `@types/lodash`, TypeScript knows that the `sortBy` function from Lodash takes an array as input and returns a sorted array. This allows it to provide accurate type checking and code completion as you work with Lodash in your TypeScript code.

Key Points

- DefinitelyTyped is a central repository for TypeScript type definitions.
- Type definitions are typically named `@types/library-name`.
- Install type definitions using `npm install --save-dev @types/library-name` or `yarn add --dev @types/library-name`.
- TypeScript automatically uses type definitions to provide type checking and IntelliSense for JavaScript libraries.

DefinitelyTyped is a testament to the power of the TypeScript community. By leveraging the vast collection of type definitions in this repository, you can seamlessly integrate countless JavaScript libraries into your TypeScript projects, enjoying the benefits of type safety, autocompletion, and a smoother development experience.

Refactoring JavaScript to TypeScript

Adding Type Annotations

Now that you've embraced the benefits of TypeScript and configured your project for gradual adoption, it's time to start the exciting journey of adding type annotations to your existing JavaScript code. This is a gradual process where you'll incrementally introduce types, making your code safer, more predictable, and easier to maintain. Let's break it down step by step.

1. Start with Basic Types

Begin by annotating variables, constants, and function parameters with basic types like `string`, `number`, and `boolean`. This is a simple yet impactful first step towards establishing a type system for your code.

```
// Before (JavaScript) let name = "Alice"; let age = 30; let isActive = true;
function greet(name) { console.log("Hello, " + name + "!"); }
```

```
// After (TypeScript) let name: string = "Alice"; let age: number = 30; let
isActive: boolean = true; function greet(name: string) { console.log("Hello, "
+ name + "!"); }
```

2. Tackle Arrays and Objects

Next, move on to annotating arrays and objects. Use array types like `number[]` or `string[]` for arrays containing a single type of element. For objects, use interfaces or inline type annotations to specify the expected properties and their types.

```
// Arrays let numbers: number[] = [1, 2, 3]; let names: string[] = ["Alice",
"Bob", "Charlie"]; // Objects interface Person { name: string; age: number; }
let person: Person = { name: "Alice", age: 30 };
```

3. Annotate Function Return Types

Add type annotations to specify the return types of your functions. This ensures that functions always return values of the expected type, preventing surprises and making your code more predictable.

```
function calculateAge(birthYear: number): number { const currentYear = new Date().getFullYear(); return currentYear - birthYear; }
```

4. Create and Use Interfaces

Interfaces are your blueprint for defining the shape of objects. Create interfaces to represent the structure of your data models and use them to type variables, function parameters, and return values.

```
interface Product { id: number; name: string; price: number; } function getProduct(productId: number): Product { // ... (fetch product data) ... }
```

5. Refactor Gradually

Don't feel obligated to add types to every line of code all at once. Take a gradual approach, focusing on the most critical parts of your codebase first. As you become more comfortable with TypeScript, you can gradually add more type annotations and refactor your code to improve its type safety.

Tips for Gradual Refactoring

- **Start Small:** Begin with individual files or modules.
- **Prioritize Public APIs:** Add types to functions and classes that are exposed to other parts of your codebase.
- **Use any Strategically:** When you're unsure of a type, use the any type as a placeholder. You can refine it later when you have a better understanding of the code.
- **Lean on Type Inference:** Let TypeScript's type inference engine help you fill in the gaps. It can often deduce types based on the context of your code.
- **Refactor Iteratively:** Break down complex refactorings into smaller, more manageable steps.
- **Write Tests:** If you have existing tests, make sure they still pass after adding type annotations.

By taking a step-by-step approach and leveraging TypeScript's gradual typing features, you can smoothly transition your JavaScript projects to TypeScript, reaping the benefits of type safety without sacrificing productivity or causing major disruptions to your workflow.

Gradual Refactoring Techniques

Refactoring a JavaScript codebase to TypeScript doesn't have to be an overwhelming task. You can adopt a gradual approach, making incremental changes that slowly introduce types and improve the type safety of your code. Here are some strategies to guide your refactoring journey:

1. Prioritize Critical or Frequently Used Code

Start by identifying the most critical or frequently used parts of your codebase. These might be modules that are essential for core functionality or areas where you've encountered bugs or issues related to type mismatches. By focusing on these areas first, you can quickly realize the benefits of TypeScript and demonstrate its value to your team.

2. Focus on Public APIs

Prioritize adding types to the public interfaces of your modules, classes, and functions. These are the parts of your code that are used by other modules or components, so ensuring type safety here will have a ripple effect throughout your project. This approach also helps you gradually build up a library of typed components and utilities that you can reuse in other parts of your codebase.

3. Use any Strategically (As a Temporary Measure)

The any type is a double-edged sword. While it provides flexibility, it also defeats the purpose of type checking. However, when you're first migrating to TypeScript and unsure of a particular type, any can serve as a temporary placeholder.

```
function processData(data: any) { // Use 'any' as a placeholder // ... }
```

As you refactor the code and gain a better understanding of its structure, you can gradually replace any with more specific types, improving type safety over time.

4. Leverage TypeScript's Tooling

Modern code editors and IDEs (like Visual Studio Code) offer excellent TypeScript support. They can often infer types automatically based on how values are used in your code. Take advantage of these features to speed up the refactoring process. Some editors even have automated refactorings that can help you add type annotations more easily.

Example: Automatic Type Declaration

```
const person = { name: "Alice", age: 30 }; // VS Code might suggest: //const
person: { name: string; age: number; } = { name: "Alice", age: 30 };
```

Additional Tips

- **Break Down Large Tasks:** Divide your refactoring into smaller, manageable tasks. Don't try to convert everything at once.
- **Use Interfaces and Type Aliases:** Define reusable interfaces or type aliases to represent complex data structures, improving code organization and readability.
- **Write Tests:** If you have existing tests, run them regularly as you refactor to catch any regressions or unexpected behavior caused by your changes.
- **Be Patient:** Migrating a large codebase to TypeScript takes time. Don't rush the process. Focus on steady progress and celebrate small victories along the way.

By following these gradual refactoring techniques and utilizing the power of TypeScript's tooling, you can smoothly transition your JavaScript projects to TypeScript and unlock the full potential of type safety for your codebase.

Common Challenges and Solutions

The journey from JavaScript to TypeScript can be incredibly rewarding, but it's not always smooth sailing. Let's tackle some common obstacles you might encounter during the migration process and explore effective strategies for overcoming them.

1. Dealing with Complex or Dynamically Typed JavaScript Code

Challenge: Legacy JavaScript codebases often lack clear type annotations and rely heavily on dynamic typing. This can make it difficult to infer types accurately or refactor code safely.

Solutions:

- **Start with Interfaces:** Begin by defining interfaces that represent the expected shape of objects and functions in your code. This will help guide your type annotations and provide structure.
- **Gradual Typing:** Don't try to add types to everything at once. Start with the most critical or frequently used parts of your code and gradually expand coverage.
- **any as a Temporary Crutch:** Use the any type as a temporary placeholder when you're unsure of a specific type. This allows you to keep moving forward without getting bogged down in complex type definitions.

- **Type Assertions (with Caution):** If you're confident about the type of a value but TypeScript can't infer it, you can use type assertions (`as` or angle bracket syntax) to override the inferred type. However, use assertions sparingly and carefully, as they can potentially introduce runtime errors if used incorrectly.
- **JSDoc Comments:** If your JavaScript code already has JSDoc comments that describe types, you can leverage these comments to help TypeScript infer types.

2. Resolving Type Conflicts Between Dependencies

Challenge: When you have multiple JavaScript libraries in your project, their type definitions might not always play well together. This can lead to conflicts and errors that can be tricky to resolve.

Solutions:

- **Check for Updated Type Definitions:** Ensure you're using the latest versions of type definitions from DefinitelyTyped (`@types/*`). Newer versions often fix compatibility issues.
- **Module Augmentation:** If a type definition is missing or incomplete, you can use TypeScript's module augmentation feature to extend the existing definitions.
- **Custom Type Definitions:** As a last resort, you might need to create your own declaration files (`.d.ts`) to define or override types for specific libraries.
- **Peer Dependencies:** If your project has peer dependencies (dependencies that need to be installed by the user of your library), ensure that your type definitions are compatible with the versions of those dependencies that your users might have installed.

3. Managing the Build Process

Challenge: When you have a mix of JavaScript and TypeScript files in your project, your build process might require some adjustments to ensure that everything compiles correctly and that the right output is generated.

Solutions:

- **Build Tools:** Use a build tool like webpack, Parcel, or Rollup to manage your build process. These tools can handle tasks like transpiling TypeScript to JavaScript, bundling modules, and resolving dependencies.
- **Configuration:** Configure your build tool to include both your TypeScript and JavaScript files in the compilation process. You might need to adjust loader configurations or module resolution settings to ensure that everything works together smoothly.
- **Incremental Builds:** Consider using incremental build tools (like `tsc --watch`) or hot module replacement (HMR) features in your bundler to speed up the development cycle.

Additional Tips

- **Start with a Clean Slate (Optional):** If possible, create a new branch or a separate environment for experimenting with TypeScript integration. This allows you to make changes without impacting your main codebase.
- **Communicate with Your Team:** Keep your team informed about the migration process and the benefits of TypeScript. This can help address any concerns and build momentum for the transition.
- **Celebrate Small Wins:** TypeScript migration can be a long journey. Celebrate milestones and successes along the way to keep morale high and encourage progress.

By anticipating these challenges and employing the right strategies, you can successfully navigate the integration of TypeScript into your existing projects. This will unlock a world of type safety, improved tooling, and enhanced developer experience, ultimately leading to better code quality and more robust applications.

Tools to Aid Migration

Transitioning from JavaScript to TypeScript doesn't have to be a manual, painstaking process. TypeScript itself, along with some clever compiler options, can become your helpful assistant in this journey. Let's explore these options and how they can make your migration smoother.

TypeScript Compiler Options

The `tsconfig.json` file, where you define TypeScript's behavior, offers a range of compiler options that are particularly handy when integrating TypeScript into existing JavaScript projects.

1. `allowJs`: JavaScript's Welcome Mat

By default, TypeScript only compiles files with the `.ts` extension. Enabling the `allowJs` option lets you include JavaScript files (`.js`) in your project as well. This means you can gradually convert your files to TypeScript without having to do it all at once.

```
{ "compilerOptions": { "allowJs": true, // ... other options ... } }
```

2. `checkJs`: Enforcing Types in JavaScript

While `allowJs` merely allows JavaScript files, `checkJs` takes it a step further. It activates TypeScript's type checker for your `.js` files. This can be immensely helpful for identifying potential type-related issues in your existing JavaScript code, even before you start adding explicit type annotations.

```
{ "compilerOptions": { "allowJs": true, "checkJs": true, // Enable type
checking for JavaScript files // ... } }
```

However, be prepared for a potentially large number of errors initially, especially if your JavaScript code is dynamically typed or not very strict. It's often best to start with `checkJs` disabled and gradually enable it for specific files or directories as you add type annotations.

3. `noImplicitAny`: Banishing the "Any" Menace

In TypeScript, the any type is like a wildcard – it can represent any value. While convenient in some cases, overusing any can undermine TypeScript's type safety. The `noImplicitAny` option prevents TypeScript from silently inferring the any type when it cannot determine a more specific type.

```
{ "compilerOptions": { "noImplicitAny": true, // ... } }
```

With this option enabled, TypeScript will raise errors when it encounters variables or functions with implicit any types, forcing you to be more explicit about your types.

4. `strict`: The Path to TypeScript Enlightenment

The `strict` mode is a powerful setting that enables several stricter type-checking rules. These rules help you catch more potential errors and write more robust code. However, enabling `strict` mode all at once can be overwhelming if you're starting with a large JavaScript codebase.

The recommended approach is to gradually increase the strictness of your TypeScript configuration as you become more familiar with the language. You can start by enabling `noImplicitAny` and then gradually enable other strict options like `strictNullChecks` and `strictFunctionTypes`.

Key Points

- Use `allowJs` to include JavaScript files in your TypeScript project.
- Enable `checkJs` to get type checking feedback on your JavaScript code.
- Use `noImplicitAny` to encourage explicit type annotations and improve type safety.
- Gradually enable `strict` mode to enforce stricter type checking rules and catch more potential errors.

By strategically using these TypeScript compiler options, you can tailor the migration process to your project's specific needs and smoothly transition your codebase to TypeScript's type-safe embrace.

Codemods and Automated Refactoring

While you can certainly refactor your JavaScript code to TypeScript manually, certain tools can help automate parts of the process, saving you time and effort. **Codemods** are one such tool.

What are Codemods?

Codemods are scripts or transformations that automatically modify your source code. They can be used to perform various refactoring tasks, such as:

- **Adding Type Annotations:** Some codemods can analyze your JavaScript code and automatically add basic type annotations based on inferred types or common patterns.
- **Converting Module Systems:** If you're transitioning from CommonJS (`require`/`module.exports`) to ES Modules (`import`/`export`), codemods can help you update your import and export statements.
- **Renaming Variables:** You can use codemods to rename variables or functions across your entire codebase.
- **Updating API Usage:** When libraries or frameworks you depend on change their APIs, codemods can automate the process of updating your code to use the new APIs.

Popular Codemod Tools

- **jscodeshift:** A toolkit from Facebook for creating and running codemods. It provides a powerful API for traversing and transforming your code's Abstract Syntax Tree (AST).
- **ts-migrate (from AirBnB):** A tool specifically designed for migrating JavaScript codebases to TypeScript. It provides a variety of codemods for adding types, fixing errors, and refactoring code.
- **Custom Codemods:** You can create your own custom codemods to automate specific refactoring tasks unique to your project.

How to Use Codemods

1. **Install the Tool:** Install the codemod tool of your choice (e.g., jscodeshift, ts-migrate).
2. **Find or Create a Codemod:** Look for a pre-existing codemod that performs the refactoring you need, or create your own using the tool's API.
3. **Run the Codemod:** Execute the codemod against your JavaScript codebase. It will automatically apply the transformations to your files.
4. **Review Changes:** Carefully review the changes made by the codemod to ensure they are correct and don't introduce any unintended issues.
5. **Test Thoroughly:** Run your tests after applying the codemod to make sure your code still works as expected.

Important Considerations

- **Complexity:** Codemods are not a silver bullet. Complex codebases might require additional manual refactoring after applying codemods.

- **Backup:** Always create a backup of your code before running codemods, as they modify your source files directly.
- **Testing:** Thoroughly test your code after applying codemods to catch any potential errors or regressions.

Key Points

- Codemods automate refactoring tasks, making TypeScript migration easier.
- Popular tools include jscodeshift and ts-migrate.
- Use codemods with caution, as they directly modify your source code.

Codemods can be a valuable asset in your TypeScript migration journey, automating tedious tasks and helping you adopt TypeScript more quickly and efficiently. However, remember that they are just tools, and their effectiveness depends on the complexity of your codebase and the quality of the codemod itself.

Case Studies

Integrating TypeScript with a React project

Project Background

Imagine a mid-sized e-commerce application built with React. The codebase has grown organically over time, and the lack of type safety has become a major pain point. The team struggles with runtime errors, difficult refactoring, and onboarding new developers takes longer than expected. The decision is made to gradually migrate the project to TypeScript.

Challenges Encountered

1. **Large Codebase:** The sheer size of the codebase (over 10,000 lines of JavaScript) makes it impossible to convert everything to TypeScript at once.
2. **Dynamic Typing:** Much of the existing code relies on dynamic typing and lacks clear type annotations, making it difficult for TypeScript's inference to work effectively.
3. **External Dependencies:** The project uses several third-party libraries, some of which don't have up-to-date TypeScript type definitions.
4. **Resistance to Change:** Some team members are hesitant about adopting TypeScript, citing concerns about the learning curve and potential disruption to the development process.

Solutions Applied

1. **Gradual Migration:** The team adopts a gradual typing approach, starting with core components and modules that are critical for business logic or prone to errors. They prioritize adding types to public APIs first to maximize the benefits of type safety for consumers of those modules.
2. **`tsconfig.json` Configuration:** They create a `tsconfig.json` file with the following settings:
   ```
   { "compilerOptions": { "allowJs": true, // Allow JavaScript files
   "checkJs": false, // Gradually enable this for type checking in JS files
   "noImplicitAny": true, // Enforce explicit type annotations "strict":
   false // Start with loose type checking, gradually increase strictness }
   }
   ```
3. **DefinitelyTyped and Custom Type Definitions:** They leverage type definitions from DefinitelyTyped for popular libraries like React and Redux. For libraries without existing type definitions, they either create their own or use the any type as a temporary workaround.
4. **Refactoring and Type Annotations:** They systematically refactor their JavaScript code, adding type annotations to variables, functions, props, and state. They create interfaces and type aliases to model their data and ensure type consistency.

5. **Tooling:** They integrate ESLint with the `@typescript-eslint/parser` and `@typescript-eslint/eslint-plugin` to catch errors and enforce code style. They also adopt Prettier for automatic code formatting.
6. **Testing:** They write new unit and integration tests for their TypeScript code and update existing tests to ensure they continue to pass after adding type annotations.
7. **Education and Communication:** They invest in training resources to help team members learn TypeScript. They regularly communicate the progress of the migration and the benefits they're seeing in terms of reduced bugs and improved maintainability.

Results

After several months of incremental migration, the team successfully converted a significant portion of their codebase to TypeScript. They observed the following benefits:

- **Reduced Runtime Errors:** TypeScript caught numerous type-related errors during development, preventing them from reaching production.
- **Increased Confidence in Refactoring:** They were able to confidently refactor code, knowing that TypeScript would alert them to any potential issues.
- **Improved Code Readability:** Type annotations made the code more self-documenting and easier for new developers to understand.
- **Faster Onboarding:** New team members could get up to speed more quickly due to the improved type safety and documentation.

Lessons Learned

- **Gradual Migration is Key:** Don't rush the process. Start small and incrementally add types to your code.
- **Invest in Education:** Provide resources and support for your team to learn TypeScript effectively.
- **Use Tools:** Leverage linters, formatters, and IDE features to automate tasks and catch errors early.
- **Celebrate Success:** Acknowledge and celebrate milestones in your migration to keep the team motivated.

This case study demonstrates that even large, complex JavaScript projects can be successfully migrated to TypeScript with a thoughtful and incremental approach. By prioritizing type safety, investing in education, and leveraging the right tools, you can transform your legacy codebase into a more robust, maintainable, and enjoyable codebase.

Integrating TypeScript with a Node.js project

Project Background

Consider a Node.js backend application built using Express.js to serve a REST API. The project has been in production for a while, and while it functions correctly, the team has been experiencing issues with:

- **Unexpected Errors:** Runtime errors due to incorrect data types or missing properties are becoming more frequent, especially as the API evolves and new features are added.
- **Slow Development:** The lack of type information makes refactoring and understanding the codebase more difficult, slowing down development and increasing the risk of introducing bugs.
- **Onboarding Challenges:** New developers struggle to get up to speed quickly due to the lack of clear documentation and the implicit nature of JavaScript's types.

The team decides to gradually integrate TypeScript into the project to address these issues.

Challenges Encountered

1. **Existing JavaScript Codebase:** The entire backend is written in JavaScript, with no type annotations or interfaces.
2. **Third-Party Dependencies:** The project relies on several external libraries and modules that don't have TypeScript type definitions.
3. **Maintaining Backwards Compatibility:** The team needs to ensure that the transition to TypeScript doesn't break the existing functionality of the API.

Solutions Applied

1. **Gradual Migration:** The team starts by renaming files from `.js` to `.ts` and adding basic type annotations to core modules and controllers. They prioritize typing the request and response objects for API endpoints.
2. **`tsconfig.json` Configuration:** They create a `tsconfig.json` file to configure the TypeScript compiler. They enable `allowJs` to include JavaScript files and `noImplicitAny` to enforce explicit type annotations. They initially leave `strict` mode disabled to allow for a smoother transition.
3. **DefinitelyTyped:** They leverage the DefinitelyTyped repository to find type definitions for most of their dependencies. For a few libraries without existing definitions, they create their own declaration files (`.d.ts`) with partial type information.
4. **Refactoring with Type Safety:** They refactor their code incrementally, adding types to functions, variables, and data models. They introduce interfaces to define the structure of their request and response payloads. They also use type guards and assertions to safely work with data coming from external sources.
5. **Tooling:** The team adopts ESLint and Prettier to ensure code quality and consistency as they introduce TypeScript. They also leverage VS Code's TypeScript support for enhanced code completion and error checking.
6. **Testing:** They write new tests for the TypeScript code they add and update existing tests to ensure continued functionality.

Results

As the team progressively adopts TypeScript, they observe several positive outcomes:

- **Reduced Errors:** TypeScript's type checker catches many errors early in development, preventing them from reaching production.
- **Increased Confidence:** The team gains more confidence in refactoring and making changes, knowing that TypeScript will flag any type-related issues.
- **Improved Code Quality:** The addition of types makes the code more self-documenting and easier for new developers to understand.
- **Faster Onboarding:** New team members can quickly grasp the structure and types of the codebase, leading to faster onboarding and increased productivity.
- **Enhanced Collaboration:** The type definitions act as a shared language, improving communication among team members and reducing misunderstandings.

Lessons Learned

- **Gradual Adoption:** The key to success was the incremental approach. Starting small and building on their understanding of TypeScript allowed the team to avoid overwhelming challenges.
- **Flexibility:** While aiming for type safety, the team also used the `any` type strategically as a temporary measure when faced with complex or untyped dependencies.
- **Community Resources:** DefinitelyTyped proved invaluable for finding type definitions for most of their dependencies.
- **Tooling is Key:** ESLint, Prettier, and VS Code's TypeScript support were instrumental in ensuring code quality, consistency, and efficient development.

This case study demonstrates that even in the context of a backend Node.js project with an existing JavaScript codebase, TypeScript can be seamlessly integrated to enhance type safety, improve code quality, and boost developer productivity.

Chapter Summary

In this chapter, we explored the process of integrating TypeScript into existing JavaScript projects, a common and often challenging task. We delved into:

- **The Challenge of Adoption:** We acknowledged the hurdles of introducing TypeScript into a codebase, including potential resistance, the learning curve, and the need for an incremental approach.
- **Gradual Typing:** We highlighted the power of gradual typing, where you can start with minimal type annotations and gradually increase TypeScript's strictness as you refactor your code.
- **Incremental Adoption Strategies:**
    - We discussed how to start by configuring TypeScript with a `tsconfig.json` file, using options like `allowJs`, `checkJs`, `noImplicitAny`, and `strict` to control the level of type checking.
    - We explained how to add TypeScript to individual files, leveraging type inference to get initial benefits even without full type annotations.
    - We explored strategies for dealing with JavaScript dependencies, including using type definitions from DefinitelyTyped and creating custom declaration files.
- **Refactoring JavaScript to TypeScript:**
    - We provided a step-by-step guide on adding type annotations, starting with basic types and progressing to more complex types like arrays, objects, functions, and interfaces.
    - We discussed gradual refactoring techniques, such as prioritizing critical code, focusing on public APIs, using `any` strategically, and leveraging TypeScript's tooling for automatic type inference.
    - We addressed common challenges like dealing with complex or dynamic code, resolving type conflicts, and managing the build process.
- **Tools to Aid Migration:**
    - We discussed helpful TypeScript compiler options like `allowJs`, `checkJs`, `noImplicitAny`, and `strict`.
    - We mentioned codemods and automated refactoring tools as potential aids in the migration process.
- **Case Studies:** (Optional) We illustrated real-world examples of integrating TypeScript into React and Node.js projects, highlighting challenges and solutions.

By following the guidance in this chapter and adopting a patient and incremental approach, you can successfully integrate TypeScript into your existing projects, reaping the benefits of improved type safety, code quality, and developer experience. Remember, the journey to a fully typed codebase takes time and effort, but the rewards are well worth it.

TypeScript Best Practices: Writing Clean and Maintainable Code

Outline

- Project Organization
  - Structuring Your Codebase
  - Modularization
  - File and Folder Naming Conventions
- Coding Style
  - Type Annotations: When and How
  - Naming Conventions for Variables, Functions, and Classes
  - Comments and Documentation
- Error Handling
  - Robust Error Handling with Try...Catch and Custom Errors
  - Logging Best Practices
  - Input Validation
- Performance Considerations
  - Type-Checking Overhead
  - Avoiding Overuse of any
  - Efficient Data Structures
- Refactoring and Maintenance
  - Refactoring with Confidence
  - Maintaining Type Definitions
  - Code Reviews
- Beyond the Basics: Advanced Best Practices (Optional)
  - Type Narrowing Techniques
  - Advanced Generic Patterns
  - Utilizing Utility Types
- Chapter Summary

Project Organization

A well-organized codebase is not just about aesthetics; it's the foundation for maintainability, scalability, and developer productivity. In TypeScript, as in any software project, a clear and logical structure is crucial for keeping your codebase manageable and ensuring that new features can be added seamlessly without introducing unintended side effects.

Why Project Organization Matters

- **Easier Navigation:** A well-structured project makes it easy to find the code you're looking for, reducing the time spent on searching and context-switching.
- **Improved Understandability:** Clear organization helps you (and your teammates) quickly grasp the overall architecture of the project and the relationships between different modules.
- **Reduced Complexity:** By breaking down your code into smaller, focused modules, you reduce cognitive load and make each piece easier to reason about.
- **Enhanced Maintainability:** Changes and updates can be made more confidently and with less risk of breaking unrelated parts of the codebase.
- **Scalability:** A well-structured project is easier to scale as your application grows and evolves.

Structuring Your Codebase

Let's explore some common architectural approaches you can use to organize your TypeScript projects:

1. **Domain-Driven Design (DDD):**
   In DDD, you structure your code around the business domain and its concepts (e.g., users, products, orders). This approach aligns your code with the real-world concepts it represents, making it more intuitive and easier to maintain.
   - **Example:** You might have modules like `users`, `products`, and `orders`, each containing the TypeScript code related to those specific domain concepts.
2. **Feature-Based Organization:**
   This approach involves grouping code by features or functionality. Each feature is self-contained within its own module or directory, making it easier to understand, test, and maintain.
   - **Example:** A social media app might have modules like `authentication`, `feed`, `profile`, and `notifications`, each handling a distinct feature.
3. **Layered Architecture:**
   Layered architecture divides your application into distinct layers, each responsible for a specific concern. Common layers include:
   - **Presentation Layer (UI):** Handles user interface logic and interaction.
   - **Business Logic Layer:** Encapsulates the core business rules and processes.
   - **Data Access Layer:** Handles interaction with databases or external data sources.
   - **Example:** In a Node.js backend, you might have folders like `controllers` (presentation), `services` (business logic), and `models` (data access).

Examples of Project Structure

Example 1: Node.js Backend (Layered Architecture)

```
my-backend/
├── src/
│   ├── controllers/   # REST API controllers
│   ├── services/      # Business logic
│   ├── models/        # Database models (e.g., Mongoose schemas)
│   ├── middleware/    # Custom middleware
│   └── index.ts       # Entry point
├── tests/
├── tsconfig.json
└── package.json
```

Example 2: React Frontend (Feature-Based)

```
my-frontend/
├── src/
│   ├── components/    # Reusable components
│   ├── features/      # Features (e.g., authentication, profile)
│   ├── pages/         # Top-level pages or routes
│   ├── store/         # Redux store (if applicable)
│   └── index.tsx      # Main entry point
├── tests/
├── tsconfig.json
└── package.json
```

Key Points

- A well-organized codebase is essential for maintainability and scalability.

- Consider using architectural approaches like Domain-Driven Design, feature-based organization, or layered architecture.
- Structure your code using folders and modules to group related functionality.
- Define clear boundaries between modules and minimize dependencies.

Remember, there's no single "right" way to organize a TypeScript project. The best approach depends on the size and complexity of your project, your team's preferences, and the specific requirements of your application. The key is to choose a structure that makes your code easy to navigate, understand, and evolve over time.

Modularization

In the world of software development, complexity is the enemy of maintainability. As your projects grow, the lines of code multiply, interdependencies become tangled, and managing the codebase becomes a herculean task. This is where modularization comes to the rescue. By breaking down your code into smaller, self-contained modules, you create a structure that is easier to understand, test, maintain, and scale.

Benefits of Modularization

1. **Encapsulation and Organization:** Modules create clear boundaries around specific functionality. Each module focuses on a single responsibility, making it easier to grasp its purpose and internal workings. This encapsulation also helps prevent unintended side effects and reduces the risk of one part of your codebase interfering with another.
2. **Reusability:** When code is organized into modules, you can easily reuse those modules in different parts of your application or even across multiple projects. This promotes a DRY (Don't Repeat Yourself) approach, saving you time and effort in the long run.
3. **Maintainability:** Modules make your codebase more maintainable by isolating changes to specific areas. If you need to fix a bug or add a new feature, you can often do so within the relevant module without affecting other parts of your code.
4. **Collaboration:** In team environments, modularization allows different developers to work on separate modules independently, minimizing conflicts and improving collaboration.
5. **Testing:** Modules are easier to test in isolation, allowing you to write more focused and granular tests that verify the functionality of each module independently.

TypeScript's Module System

TypeScript, embracing the ECMAScript module standard, provides keywords to manage the relationships between modules:

- **`export`:** Use the `export` keyword to make variables, functions, classes, interfaces, or types within a module available for use in other modules. You can have multiple named exports (`export const x = 5;`) or a single default export (`export default class MyClass {}`).
- **`import`:** Use the `import` keyword to bring in exported members from other modules. You can import specific named exports (`import { function1, class2 } from './myModule';`), the default export (`import myModule from './myModule';`), or even the entire module as a namespace (`import * as myModule from './myModule';`).

Example: Modular Code

```
// mathUtils.ts export const PI = 3.14159; export function
calculateArea(radius: number): number { return PI * radius * radius; }
```

```
// app.ts import { PI, calculateArea } from './mathUtils'; console.log(PI);
const area = calculateArea(5); console.log(area);
```

Key Points

- Modules are the foundation of code organization in TypeScript.
- Use `export` to make members of a module accessible to other modules.
- Use `import` to bring in exported members from other modules.
- Organize your code into logical modules based on functionality or domain concepts.
- Define clear interfaces for communication between modules.
- Strive for low coupling and high cohesion within your modules.

By adopting a modular approach and utilizing TypeScript's module system, you'll be well on your way to building scalable, maintainable, and well-organized applications.

File and Folder Naming Conventions

In the world of TypeScript (and software development in general), choosing meaningful and consistent names for your files and folders is not just a matter of aesthetics. It's a crucial practice that enhances the readability and maintainability of your codebase, making it easier for you and your team to navigate, understand, and work with your project.

General Guidelines

- **Be Descriptive:** Choose names that accurately reflect the content or purpose of the file or folder. Avoid vague or generic names like `utils.ts` or `helpers.ts`. Instead, be more specific: `stringUtils.ts`, `httpHelpers.ts`, `userModels.ts`.
- **Use Lowercase:** Stick to lowercase letters for both file and folder names. This avoids potential issues with case sensitivity across different operating systems.
- **Kebab Case or Snake Case:** There are two main conventions for separating words in filenames:
    - **Kebab Case:** Uses hyphens to separate words (e.g., `user-profile.ts`, `api-client.ts`).
    - **Snake Case:** Uses underscores to separate words (e.g., `user_profile.ts`, `api_client.ts`).
- Choose one convention and use it consistently throughout your project.
- **File Extensions:**
    - **`.ts`:** Use for TypeScript files that don't contain JSX.
    - **`.tsx`:** Use for TypeScript files that contain JSX (React components).
    - **`.d.ts`:** Use for TypeScript declaration files (type definitions).

Examples of Good Naming Conventions

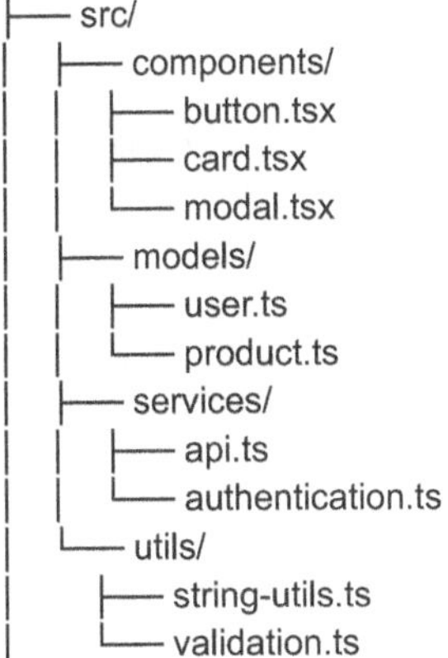

```
├── src/
│   ├── components/
│   │   ├── button.tsx
│   │   ├── card.tsx
│   │   └── modal.tsx
│   ├── models/
│   │   ├── user.ts
│   │   └── product.ts
│   ├── services/
│   │   ├── api.ts
│   │   └── authentication.ts
│   └── utils/
│       ├── string-utils.ts
│       └── validation.ts
│
```

The Importance of Consistency

Consistency in naming conventions is key. When everyone on your team follows the same guidelines, it creates a predictable and intuitive structure. This makes it easier for new developers to onboard and reduces the mental overhead of navigating the codebase.

Benefits of Clear Naming

- **Discoverability:** You can quickly locate the module you need based on its descriptive name.
- **Context:** The name itself gives you a clue about the module's purpose and functionality.
- **Maintainability:** When you need to update or refactor a module, it's easy to find the relevant files.
- **Team Collaboration:** Consistent naming conventions facilitate communication and collaboration among team members.

Key Points

- Use descriptive names for files and folders.
- Stick to lowercase letters.
- Choose either kebab case or snake case and use it consistently.
- Use the correct file extensions (.ts, .tsx, .d.ts).

By following these simple naming conventions, you'll create a more organized, readable, and maintainable codebase. Remember, clear and consistent naming is a small investment that pays off in the long run, saving you and your team valuable time and effort.

Coding Style

Type Annotations: When and How

Type annotations are the essence of TypeScript. They are the glue that binds your code to a type system, providing structure, guidance, and safety. However, knowing when and how to use them is an art that balances readability, conciseness, and type safety. Let's dive into the nuances of type annotations in TypeScript.

When to Use Type Annotations

1. **Clarity and Self-Documentation:** When a variable, function, or parameter's type isn't immediately obvious, an explicit type annotation can enhance code readability. It acts as a clear signpost, communicating the expected data types and making the code more self-explanatory.
   ```
   let age: number; // Clearly indicates that 'age' should hold a number function greet(name: string): string { // Specifies parameter and return types return `Hello, ${name}!`; }
   ```
2. **Complex Types:** For complex types like interfaces, type aliases, or functions with multiple parameters, type annotations are crucial for both readability and type safety. They ensure that you and other developers understand how to interact with your code correctly.
   ```
   interface User { id: number; name: string; isActive: boolean; } type Callback = (data: string) => void;
   ```
3. **Public APIs:** When you're building libraries or modules that will be used by other developers, it's good practice to explicitly annotate all public APIs with types. This provides a clear contract for how your code should be used.
4. **Error Prevention:** TypeScript's type checker uses type annotations to identify potential errors during development. By adding types, you can catch mismatched types, incorrect function calls, and other issues before they cause problems in your application.

When to Rely on Type Inference

TypeScript's type inference is a powerful feature that can often deduce the types of variables and expressions based on their values or how they are used. This means you don't always have to write explicit type annotations.

```
let message = "Hello"; // TypeScript infers type 'string' let count = 10; // TypeScript infers type 'number' let isActive = true; // TypeScript infers type 'boolean'
```

In these simple cases, TypeScript correctly infers the types, so explicit annotations are not needed. However, it is often good practice to explicitly provide the return type of a function.

Guidelines for Adding Types

1. **Variables and Constants:**
    - If the type is obvious from the initial value, you can often omit the type annotation.
    - For variables that might be reassigned to a different type, consider using a union type (e.g., `string | number`).
    - Always annotate constants (`const`) with their types.
2. **Functions:**
    - Always annotate the parameters and the return type.
    - If a function doesn't return a value, use the `void` type.
3. **Objects:**
    - Use interfaces or inline type annotations to specify the expected properties and their types.
    - Mark properties as optional (with ?) if they might not always be present.

Balancing Act: Readability vs. Verbosity

TypeScript encourages a "gradual typing" approach where you can add types incrementally. Don't feel obligated to annotate every single variable and function in your code. Strike a balance between readability and conciseness. Use type annotations when they clarify intent and improve type safety, but don't overdo it to the point of making your code overly verbose.

Key Points

- Type annotations improve code readability and catch errors early on.
- Use type inference when the type is clear, but be explicit when it's not.
- Prioritize adding types to public APIs and areas prone to errors.
- Balance readability and conciseness in your type annotations.

By thoughtfully applying type annotations, you'll harness the full power of TypeScript's type system, creating code that is both expressive and robust.

Naming Conventions for Variables, Functions, and Classes

Naming is a cornerstone of clean and maintainable code. In TypeScript, following established conventions for naming variables, functions, and classes ensures clarity, predictability, and a smooth experience for both you and your fellow developers.

PascalCase for Classes and Interfaces

Classes and interfaces represent blueprints for objects and define the structure of your code. Using PascalCase (also known as UpperCamelCase) for their names makes them easily distinguishable:

```
class UserProfile { // ... } interface Product { // ... }
```

In this convention, each word in the name starts with a capital letter, with no spaces or separators between them. This creates a visual cue that these are structural elements of your code.

camelCase for Variables, Functions, and Methods

Variables, functions, and methods represent values, actions, or operations within your code. They should be named using camelCase (also known as lowerCamelCase).

```
let firstName = "John"; function calculateTotal(price: number, quantity: number): number { // ... } class Customer { getFirstName(): string { // ... } }
```

In camelCase, the first word is lowercase, and subsequent words start with a capital letter. This convention is widely used in JavaScript and helps differentiate variables and functions from classes.

UPPER_CASE for Constants

Constants are values that should not be changed throughout your code. To make them visually stand out, use all uppercase letters with underscores to separate words:

```
const MAX_ATTEMPTS = 3; const API_URL = "https://api.example.com";
```

Why Consistent Naming Matters

Consistent naming conventions bring numerous benefits:

- **Readability:** When code follows established conventions, it becomes much easier to read and understand. Developers can quickly identify what a particular identifier represents based on its name and capitalization style.
- **Predictability:** Consistent naming creates a sense of predictability in your code. Developers know what to expect when they encounter a new identifier, reducing cognitive load and making it easier to navigate the codebase.
- **Maintainability:** Consistently named code is easier to refactor and modify. You can quickly locate and update all references to a variable or function based on its predictable naming pattern.
- **Collaboration:** When working in teams, consistent naming ensures that everyone uses the same style, preventing confusion and disagreements.

Beyond Conventions: Choosing Meaningful Names

While following conventions is important, it's equally crucial to choose descriptive and meaningful names for your identifiers. A good name should convey the purpose or meaning of the variable, function, or class.

```
// Avoid generic names: let data = ...; function doSomething(input) { // ... } // Prefer descriptive names: let userData = ...; function calculateDiscount(originalPrice) { // ... }
```

Key Points

- Use PascalCase for classes and interfaces.
- Use camelCase for variables, functions, and methods.
- Use UPPER_CASE for constants.
- Choose descriptive and meaningful names that reflect the purpose of the identifier.

By adhering to naming conventions and choosing clear, informative names, you'll create TypeScript code that is not only functional but also a joy to read, understand, and maintain.

Comments and Documentation

In the world of TypeScript, where types provide a certain level of self-documentation, comments still play a crucial role in making your code truly understandable and maintainable. Well-written comments and documentation guide you and your team through the intricacies of your code, clarify intent, explain complex logic, and illuminate potential pitfalls.

The Power of Clarity

While TypeScript's type annotations provide valuable information about the structure of your code, they don't always reveal the why behind the how. Comments bridge this gap by providing explanations, insights, and context that types alone can't convey.

Here's why comments are essential:

- **Understanding Intent:** Comments explain the purpose of a piece of code, the reasoning behind a particular approach, or the expected behavior. This helps developers quickly grasp the "why" behind the code, making it easier to modify or debug.
- **Documenting Assumptions:** Comments can clarify assumptions that the code makes about its inputs, dependencies, or the environment it runs in. This prevents misunderstandings and ensures that future developers (including your future self!) don't make incorrect assumptions.
- **Explaining Complex Logic:** Some algorithms or calculations might not be immediately obvious. Comments can provide a step-by-step explanation, making the code more approachable and easier to maintain.
- **Highlighting Potential Issues:** Comments can warn about potential pitfalls, edge cases, or performance considerations, helping developers avoid mistakes or optimize their code.

JSDoc: A Standard for Documentation

TypeScript embraces JSDoc, a standard for adding documentation comments to JavaScript and TypeScript code. JSDoc comments are special blocks that start with `/**` and end with `*/`. Within these blocks, you can use tags to provide structured information about your code.

Common JSDoc Tags

- **`@param`:** Describes a function parameter, including its name, type, and a description of its purpose.
- **`@returns`:** Describes the return value of a function, including its type and a description of its meaning.
- **`@throws`:** Documents the types of errors a function might throw.
- **`@description`:** Provides a general description of the function, class, or variable.
- **`@example`:** Demonstrates how to use the code with example usage.

Example: JSDoc-Style Comments

```
/** * Calculates the area of a rectangle. * * @param width - The width of the rectangle. * @param height - The height of the rectangle. * @returns The calculated area. */ function calculateArea(width: number, height: number): number { return width * height; }
```

Tips for Writing Effective Comments

- **Be Concise and Clear:** Aim for comments that are easy to read and understand. Avoid overly verbose explanations or unnecessary repetition of the code's logic.
- **Focus on the Why, Not the How:** Explain the purpose or intention behind the code, not just what it does.

- **Keep Comments Up-to-Date:** Ensure that your comments reflect the current state of the code. Outdated comments can be misleading and confusing.
- **Use a Consistent Style:** Adopt a consistent style for your comments, whether it's JSDoc-style or a simpler format.

Generating Documentation with TypeDoc

You can use the TypeDoc tool (covered in Chapter 15) to automatically generate HTML documentation from your JSDoc comments. This creates a browsable reference for your code, making it easy for other developers to understand how to use your modules and classes.

Key Points

- Comments are essential for making your TypeScript code understandable and maintainable.
- Use JSDoc-style comments for structured documentation.
- Write clear, concise comments that explain the *why* behind your code.
- Keep comments up-to-date and use a consistent style.
- Consider using TypeDoc to generate HTML documentation from your comments.

By embracing the practice of writing clear and informative comments, you'll enhance the readability, maintainability, and overall quality of your TypeScript projects.

Error Handling

Errors are an inevitable part of software development. They can occur due to unexpected input, network failures, database issues, or even bugs in your own code. In TypeScript, robust error handling is essential for creating reliable and user-friendly applications. Let's explore best practices for managing errors effectively, ensuring that your code doesn't crash and that users receive informative feedback when things go wrong.

Robust Error Handling with Try...Catch and Custom Errors

1. `try...catch` Blocks: Your Safety Net

The `try...catch` statement is your fundamental tool for handling errors in TypeScript. It allows you to isolate code that might throw errors and provide specific actions to take when an error occurs.

Basic Syntax

```
try { // Code that might throw an error } catch (error) { // Code to handle the error }
```

- **`try` Block:** This block contains the code you suspect might throw an error.
- **`catch` Block:** If an error occurs within the `try` block, execution immediately jumps to the `catch` block. The `error` object (you can name it anything) provides details about the error, including the error message and stack trace.

Example: Division by Zero

```
function divide(x: number, y: number): number { if (y === 0) { throw new Error("Division by zero!"); // Throw an error } return x / y; } try { const result = divide(10, 0); } catch (error) { console.error("Error:", error.message); // "Error: Division by zero!" }
```

2. Custom Error Classes: Clarity and Specificity

TypeScript allows you to define your own custom error classes that extend the base `Error` class. This gives you the ability to create error types that convey more specific information about the nature of the error.

Example: NetworkError and DatabaseError

```
class NetworkError extends Error { constructor(message: string) {
super(message); this.name = "NetworkError"; } } class DatabaseError extends
Error { constructor(message: string) { super(message); this.name =
"DatabaseError"; } }
```

By creating these custom error classes, you can differentiate between network-related errors and database errors, allowing for more targeted error handling.

3. Logging Errors: Gaining Insights

Logging errors is crucial for debugging and understanding what went wrong. Always log errors with relevant details:

- **Timestamp:** Include the date and time of the error.
- **Context:** Log the file name, function name, and line number where the error occurred.
- **Error Message:** Include the error message and stack trace (if available).
- **Additional Details:** Log any relevant data that might help you diagnose the problem (e.g., user input, request parameters, database query).

Use a logging library like Winston or Bunyan for structured logging in production environments.

4. Informative Error Messages to Users

Provide users with clear and actionable error messages. Explain the issue in plain language and suggest possible solutions. Avoid revealing sensitive details about your system's inner workings.

```
try { // ... } catch (error: unknown) { if (error instanceof NetworkError) {
// Handle network error (e.g., show a "Retry" button) } else if (error
instanceof DatabaseError) { // Handle database error } else { // Log the error
and show a generic error message to the user console.error(error); // Send a
500 Internal Server Error response (if applicable) } }
```

By combining `try...catch` blocks, custom error classes, informative logging, and user-friendly messages, you'll build resilient TypeScript applications that can gracefully handle errors, providing a better experience for both developers and users.

Logging Best Practices

Logging is an indispensable tool in your Node.js and TypeScript arsenal. It provides valuable insights into your application's behavior, aids in debugging, helps monitor performance, and even assists in detecting security issues. Let's dive into best practices to make your logging effective, informative, and manageable.

1. Logging Levels: Categorizing Information

Using logging levels is a fundamental practice. It allows you to categorize your log messages based on their severity or importance. Common log levels include:

- **`error`:** Critical errors that might cause the application to crash or fail.
- **`warn`:** Warnings about potential issues that might not be fatal but should be addressed.
- **`info`:** General information about the application's operation, such as successful requests or state changes.
- **`debug`:** Detailed information for debugging purposes, typically only enabled in development environments.
- **`trace`:** Very granular logging, often used for tracing the flow of execution in intricate scenarios.

By using different levels, you can easily filter and analyze your logs based on their relevance. For example, in production, you might only want to see errors and warnings, while in development, you might enable debug or trace logging for more detailed insights.

2. Structured Logging: Making Sense of Data

Structured logging involves formatting your log messages in a consistent and machine-readable format (often JSON). This makes it easier to parse and analyze logs using tools like ELK Stack (Elasticsearch, Logstash, Kibana) or other log aggregation services.

```
logger.error({ message: "Database connection failed", error: errorObject });
```

In this example, the error message is logged as a JSON object with both a human-readable message and an error object containing details about the error.

3. Logging Context: Where and When

Provide context in your log messages to help you understand where and when an event occurred. This typically includes the timestamp, the file name, the function name, and the line number.

Example: Using Winston Logger

```
import winston from 'winston'; const logger = winston.createLogger({ level:
'info', // Set the default logging level format: winston.format.json(),
transports: [ new winston.transports.Console(), // Add other transports for
file logging, etc. ], }); // Logging with context logger.error('Error
message', { timestamp: new Date(), filename: __filename, functionName:
'myFunction' });
```

4. Log Rotation: Managing Log Files

If you're writing logs to files, implement log rotation strategies to prevent log files from growing indefinitely. Log rotation involves archiving or deleting old log files periodically to free up disk space.

5. Performance Considerations

- **Avoid Excessive Logging:** Too much logging can impact performance, especially if you're writing to files or external services. Log only essential information, and use log levels to control the amount of detail based on the environment (development, testing, production).
- **Asynchronous Logging:** For high-performance applications, consider using asynchronous logging to avoid blocking the main thread.

6. Security Best Practices

- **Sanitize Sensitive Data:** Never log sensitive information like passwords, credit card numbers, or personal data directly. Use proper masking or anonymization techniques to protect this data.

- **Secure Log Storage:** If you store logs in files or databases, ensure they are protected from unauthorized access.

7. Logging Libraries

Consider using logging libraries like:

- **Winston:** A versatile logger with support for multiple transports (console, files, databases) and custom formatting.
- **Bunyan:** A fast and efficient JSON logger designed for production environments.
- **Pino:** A high-performance JSON logger with a focus on minimal overhead.

By adopting these best practices and utilizing logging libraries, you'll create a powerful logging infrastructure for your TypeScript Node.js applications. Your logs will become invaluable assets for debugging, monitoring, and understanding the behavior of your code in the wild.

Input Validation

In the wild west of web development, user input is the most unpredictable and potentially dangerous element your backend will encounter. Input validation is your sheriff, standing guard against malicious attacks, data corruption, and unexpected errors. It's a crucial practice for building secure, reliable, and robust Node.js applications with TypeScript.

The Importance of Input Validation

1. **Security:** Malicious users can exploit vulnerabilities in your application by injecting harmful code or data into input fields. Input validation is your first line of defense against attacks like SQL injection, cross-site scripting (XSS), and command injection.
2. **Data Integrity:** Unvalidated input can lead to inconsistent or corrupted data in your database or other data stores. This can cause errors, crashes, and unpredictable behavior in your application.
3. **Error Prevention:** By validating input early on, you can prevent errors from propagating further into your application. This makes debugging easier and improves the overall stability of your code.

Input Validation Techniques

TypeScript provides various techniques for validating user input:

1. Type Guards: Leverage TypeScript's type system to check if input data matches the expected types. For example:

```
function createUser(name: string, age: number) { if (typeof name !== 'string'
|| typeof age !== 'number') { throw new Error('Invalid input types'); } // ...
}
```

2. Regular Expressions: Regular expressions are powerful tools for pattern matching. Use them to validate email addresses, phone numbers, passwords, or any input that needs to conform to a specific format.

```
function isValidEmail(email: string): boolean { const emailRegex =
/^[^\s@]+@[^\s@]+\.[^\s@]+$/; return emailRegex.test(email); }
```

3. Custom Validation Functions: Write your own validation functions to enforce custom rules. For example, you might have a function that checks if a username is unique in your database.

4. Libraries: Several libraries can streamline input validation in TypeScript:

- **io-ts:** A library for runtime type validation based on codecs that describe the shape of your data. It provides a powerful and flexible way to validate complex data structures.
- **zod:** Another library for schema-based validation that offers a concise and intuitive API for defining and validating data schemas.
- **class-validator:** A decorator-based validation library that works seamlessly with TypeScript classes.

Example: Validating User Input with zod

```
import { z } from "zod"; const createUserSchema = z.object({ name:
z.string().min(3, "Name must be at least 3 characters"), email:
z.string().email("Invalid email address"), age: z.number().min(18, "Age must
be 18 or older"), }); function createUser(userData: unknown) { const result =
createUserSchema.safeParse(userData); // Validate the input data if
(!result.success) { throw new ValidationError(result.error.message); } // ...
(process the validated user data) }
```

By following best practices and utilizing appropriate validation techniques, you can significantly enhance the security and robustness of your TypeScript Node.js applications, protecting them from malicious attacks, data corruption, and unexpected errors.

Performance Considerations

TypeScript's superpower is its type system, which brings a wealth of benefits to your development process and the quality of your code. However, it's important to acknowledge that this power comes with a small cost in terms of performance overhead. Let's explore this aspect and discuss strategies for mitigating it when necessary.

Type-Checking Overhead

TypeScript's compiler performs static type checking at compile time. This means it analyzes your code and verifies that types are used consistently and correctly. This process naturally adds some overhead to the compilation time compared to plain JavaScript, which doesn't have this type-checking step.

However, in most cases, this overhead is negligible and doesn't significantly impact the overall development or runtime performance of your application. Modern computers and build tools are highly efficient, and TypeScript's type checking is generally fast enough to not cause noticeable delays.

When Performance Matters

There are scenarios where performance becomes a critical factor, and the type-checking overhead might become more noticeable:

- **Extremely Large Codebases:** In massive projects with hundreds of thousands of lines of TypeScript code, the compilation time might increase noticeably.
- **Continuous Integration (CI) Pipelines:** If you have a CI pipeline that runs tests and builds frequently, the added compilation time due to TypeScript could impact the overall speed of your feedback loop.
- **Resource-Constrained Environments:** In environments with limited resources (e.g., low-powered devices or servers), the additional processing required for type checking might be a concern.

Strategies for Mitigating Overhead

If you encounter performance issues related to TypeScript's type checking, here are some strategies to consider:

- **Incremental Builds:** Use tools like `tsc --watch` or configure your build system (e.g., webpack) to perform incremental builds. This means that only the files that have changed will be re-compiled, saving time.
- **Caching:** Leverage caching mechanisms provided by your build tool to store the results of type checking and avoid repeating the process for unchanged files.
- **Parallelism:** If you have a multi-core machine, explore options for running the TypeScript compiler in parallel to utilize multiple cores and potentially speed up compilation.
- **Focus on Bottlenecks:** Profile your build process to identify the specific parts that are consuming the most time. Optimize those areas first to achieve the biggest impact on performance.
- **Use any Sparingly:** While the any type can be tempting for quick fixes, it circumvents type checking and can lead to runtime errors. Try to use more specific types or the `unknown` type whenever possible.

Key Points

- TypeScript's type checking does introduce some overhead during compilation.
- In most cases, this overhead is minimal and doesn't significantly impact performance.
- For large projects or performance-critical scenarios, consider using incremental builds, caching, and parallelism to mitigate overhead.

Remember, the benefits of TypeScript's type safety often far outweigh the minor performance cost. By making informed decisions and applying the appropriate optimizations when needed, you can enjoy the best of both worlds: type safety and performance.

Avoiding Overuse of any

The any type in TypeScript is a bit like a double-edged sword. It offers flexibility by allowing a variable to hold a value of any type, but it comes at a cost: it sacrifices the type safety that TypeScript is designed to provide. Think of it as a temporary escape hatch that lets you bypass the type system's checks, but it's important to use it sparingly and strategically.

The Dangers of any

- **Loss of Type Safety:** When you use any, TypeScript essentially stops checking the type of that variable or its values. This means you lose the benefits of early error detection, refactoring safety, and code clarity.
- **Runtime Errors:** Code that relies heavily on any can be more prone to runtime errors. Since TypeScript isn't checking types, it won't catch mismatches between expected and actual types, which can lead to unexpected behavior or crashes.
- **Reduced Maintainability:** Code with excessive use of any can become difficult to understand and maintain. Without explicit type information, it's harder to reason about how the code works and how it interacts with other parts of the system.
- **Defeating the Purpose of TypeScript:** If you use any everywhere, you might as well be writing plain JavaScript. You're essentially bypassing the very feature that makes TypeScript so valuable: its type system.

When to Use any (and When Not To)

There are legitimate use cases for the any type, but they are relatively limited:

- **Legacy JavaScript Code:** When migrating a JavaScript codebase to TypeScript, you might use any as a temporary placeholder for parts of the code that haven't been fully typed yet. This allows you to gradually add types without having to rewrite everything at once.
- **Dynamic Data from External Sources:** If you're receiving data from an external API or a source where the structure isn't strictly defined, you might use any initially while you figure out the appropriate types. However, strive to define more specific types as soon as possible.
- **Libraries Without Type Definitions:** If you're using a JavaScript library that doesn't have TypeScript type definitions, you might need to use any to interact with it. Consider searching for type definitions on DefinitelyTyped or contributing your own if they don't exist.

Alternatives to any

In most cases, there are better alternatives to any:

- **unknown:** The unknown type is similar to any in that it can hold values of any type. However, unlike any, you need to perform type checks (using type guards or type assertions) before you can use a value of type unknown. This adds a layer of safety and encourages you to narrow down the type as soon as possible.
- **Union Types:** If a value can be one of several known types, use a union type (e.g., `string | number`). This allows for flexibility while still maintaining type safety.
- **Interfaces or Type Aliases:** Define clear interfaces or type aliases to describe the structure of your objects and functions. This will help you avoid the need for any altogether in many cases.

Key Points

- Avoid overusing any, as it undermines TypeScript's type safety benefits.
- Use any sparingly, such as when dealing with legacy code, dynamic data, or libraries without type definitions.
- Prefer more specific types (unknown, union types, interfaces) whenever possible.

By minimizing the use of any and embracing TypeScript's type system, you can create code that is more reliable, predictable, and maintainable. Remember, the goal of TypeScript is to catch errors early in development, and overusing any defeats that purpose.

Efficient Data Structures

In the pursuit of high-performance TypeScript applications, the choice of data structures can be a pivotal factor. Different data structures excel in different scenarios, offering varying trade-offs between time and space complexity. Understanding these trade-offs and choosing the right data structure for the task at hand can significantly impact your code's efficiency.

Time Complexity: A Key Metric

Time complexity is a measure of how the runtime of an algorithm or operation grows with the size of the input data. It's usually expressed using Big O notation (e.g., O(1), O(n), O(log n), O(n^2)), where 'n' represents the size of the input.

- **O(1) (Constant Time):** The best-case scenario, where the operation takes a constant amount of time regardless of the input size.
- **O(n) (Linear Time):** The operation time grows linearly with the input size.
- **O(log n) (Logarithmic Time):** The operation time grows logarithmically with the input size (e.g., binary search).
- **O(n^2) (Quadratic Time):** The operation time grows with the square of the input size (e.g., nested loops).

Common Data Structures and Their Time Complexities

Let's look at some common data structures in TypeScript and their typical time complexities for key operations:

Data Structure	Access	Search	Insertion	Deletion
Array	O(1)	O(n)	O(1)	O(n)
Set	O(1)	O(1)	O(1)	O(1)
Map	O(1)	O(1)	O(1)	O(1)

Note: These are average or typical time complexities. The actual performance might vary depending on the specific implementation and the nature of your data.

Choosing the Right Data Structure

- **Arrays:** Excellent for random access (getting an element at a specific index), but inefficient for searching and deleting elements, especially in large arrays.
- **Sets:** Ideal for storing unique values and checking if a value exists in the set. They offer fast insertion, deletion, and membership testing.
- **Maps:** Similar to sets, but they store key-value pairs. Great for looking up values based on keys.

Example: Finding Unique Values

If you need to find unique values in an array, a set is usually a better choice than an array:

```
const numbers = [1, 2, 2, 3, 4, 4, 5]; // Using a set for efficient uniqueness
check const uniqueNumbers = new Set(numbers); // Using an array (less
efficient) const uniqueNumbersArray = numbers.filter((value, index, self) =>
self.indexOf(value) === index);
```

Both methods return an array of unique numbers but the one using a Set has less time complexity and is faster. **Example: Storing User Data**

If you need to store and retrieve user data by their ID, a map is the most efficient choice:

```
const usersById = new Map<number, User>(); // Add a user usersById.set(123, {
name: "Alice", email: "alice@example.com" }); // Retrieve a user const user =
usersById.get(123);
```

Key Points

- Choose the right data structure based on your specific use case and the operations you'll be performing most frequently.
- Consider the time complexity of different operations on each data structure.
- Use arrays for sequential access and simple storage.
- Use sets for storing unique values and checking for membership.
- Use maps for fast key-value lookups.

By understanding the performance characteristics of different data structures and using them strategically, you can optimize your TypeScript code for efficiency and build high-performance applications.

Refactoring and Maintenance

Refactoring with Confidence

Refactoring is an essential practice in software development. It's the process of restructuring existing code to improve its design, readability, or maintainability without changing its external behavior. In JavaScript projects, refactoring can be a risky endeavor due to the dynamic nature of the language. However, TypeScript's type system acts as a powerful safety net, significantly reducing the risk of introducing bugs during refactoring.

Type-Guided Refactoring

When you refactor TypeScript code, the compiler becomes your watchful guardian. If your changes inadvertently break type contracts or introduce inconsistencies, the compiler will raise an error, pinpointing exactly where the issue occurred. This immediate feedback loop allows you to catch and fix errors early on, before they cause problems in production.

Examples of Type-Safe Refactoring

1. **Renaming Variables and Functions:** When you rename a variable or function, TypeScript will automatically update all references to that identifier throughout your codebase, ensuring that the change is propagated consistently and preventing broken references.
2. **Changing Function Signatures:** If you modify the parameters or return type of a function, TypeScript will alert you to any places in your code where the function is called with incompatible arguments or where its return value is used incorrectly. This helps you avoid introducing subtle bugs that might not be immediately apparent.
3. **Modifying Interfaces:** If you change the structure of an interface (e.g., by adding, removing, or renaming properties), TypeScript will flag any code that is no longer compatible with the updated interface. This ensures that all objects that implement the interface are updated accordingly.
4. **Extracting or Moving Code:** When you extract a piece of code into a separate function or move it to a different module, TypeScript's type checking can help you ensure that the extracted or moved code is still used correctly in its new context.

Example: Refactoring a Function with Type Safety

```
// Before function calculateArea(length, width) { return length * width; }

// After function calculateArea(length: number, width: number): number { //
Add types return length * width; } // In another file const area: string =
calculateArea("10", 5); // TypeScript Error
```

Here the compiler would have shown an error as we cannot assign the result from `calculateArea` to the `area` variable that is of type string. **Key Benefits of Type-Guided Refactoring**

- **Reduced Risk:** TypeScript's type checker acts as a safety net, significantly reducing the risk of introducing bugs during refactoring.
- **Early Error Detection:** Type-related errors are caught during compilation, preventing them from causing problems at runtime.
- **Increased Confidence:** You can refactor your code with greater confidence, knowing that TypeScript will alert you to any inconsistencies or breaking changes.
- **Improved Maintainability:** Refactoring is less daunting and more straightforward in TypeScript, leading to cleaner and more maintainable code over time.

Key Points

- TypeScript's type system enables type-safe refactoring.
- The compiler helps you catch errors and inconsistencies that might arise from changes to types.

- Use refactoring tools in your IDE to automate repetitive tasks and ensure consistency.
- Write tests to verify that your refactored code still behaves as expected.

By embracing TypeScript's type-guided refactoring, you can refactor your code with confidence, knowing that the compiler is watching your back and helping you maintain the integrity of your codebase.

Maintaining Type Definitions

Type definitions are the backbone of TypeScript projects, providing the essential information that the compiler uses to check types and ensure code safety. However, type definitions are not static artifacts. As your codebase evolves, you'll inevitably make changes to the structure of your data, the interfaces of your modules, or the types of your variables and functions. To maintain the integrity of your TypeScript project, it's crucial to keep your type definitions in sync with these changes.

Why Up-to-Date Type Definitions Matter

- **Type Safety:** If your type definitions don't match the actual structure of your code, TypeScript won't be able to catch potential errors. For example, if you add a new property to an interface but forget to update the places where that interface is used, TypeScript won't be able to detect if that property is missing or being accessed incorrectly.
- **Developer Experience:** Out-of-date type definitions can lead to confusing error messages, incorrect code suggestions, and a generally frustrating development experience. When your types are accurate, TypeScript can provide more helpful feedback and guidance.
- **Refactoring Safety:** Refactoring becomes much riskier if your type definitions are out of sync. TypeScript won't be able to alert you to potential breaking changes, and you might introduce subtle bugs that are difficult to track down.

When to Update Type Definitions

- **Changing Data Structures:** If you modify an interface or type alias that represents a data structure (e.g., by adding, removing, or renaming properties), make sure to update all the places in your code where that type is used.
- **Modifying Function Signatures:** If you change the parameters or return type of a function, update its type definition to reflect the new signature. This will help TypeScript catch errors if the function is called incorrectly.
- **Updating Dependencies:** When you update a third-party library, check if the corresponding type definitions (`@types/*`) also need to be updated. In some cases, the library might have made changes that are incompatible with the older type definitions.

Tools and Techniques for Maintaining Type Definitions

- **IDE Support:** Most modern code editors and IDEs (like Visual Studio Code) provide tools for refactoring TypeScript code. When you rename a symbol or change a type definition, the IDE can automatically update all references to that symbol throughout your project.
- **Linters:** Linters like ESLint can help you catch inconsistencies between your type definitions and your actual code usage. Configure your linter to enforce rules related to types and imports to catch potential issues early on.
- **Code Reviews:** During code reviews, pay special attention to type definitions. Ensure that changes to interfaces, functions, or classes are accompanied by corresponding updates to their type definitions.
- **Tests:** Write tests that exercise your code with different types of data to ensure that your type definitions accurately reflect the expected behavior.

Key Points

- Maintaining up-to-date type definitions is crucial for type safety, developer experience, and refactoring confidence.
- Update type definitions whenever you change data structures, function signatures, or dependencies.
- Leverage tools like IDEs and linters to help you catch inconsistencies.
- Make type definitions a part of your code review process.
- Write tests to verify that your types are correct and your code works as expected.

By diligently maintaining your type definitions, you'll ensure that your TypeScript projects remain well-organized, easy to understand, and resistant to errors, providing a solid foundation for building reliable and maintainable applications.

Code Reviews

In the world of software development, code reviews play a pivotal role in maintaining code quality, catching potential issues, and ensuring that best practices are followed. When it comes to TypeScript projects, code reviews become even more valuable thanks to the rich type information provided by TypeScript's type system. Let's delve into the significance of code reviews and how TypeScript enhances this process.

Why Code Reviews Matter

1. **Error Detection:** A fresh pair of eyes can often spot errors, bugs, or potential issues that the original author might have overlooked. Code reviews provide a valuable opportunity for catching mistakes early on, before they make their way into production.
2. **Knowledge Sharing:** Code reviews are a learning opportunity for both the reviewer and the author. Reviewers can learn new techniques or approaches, while authors receive feedback and suggestions for improvement. This fosters a culture of continuous learning and knowledge sharing within the team.
3. **Enforcing Standards:** Code reviews help ensure that the codebase adheres to established coding standards and best practices. This includes consistent formatting, naming conventions, appropriate use of language features, and adherence to architectural patterns.
4. **Mentoring and Collaboration:** Code reviews provide a platform for senior developers to mentor junior developers, guiding them on best practices and helping them grow their skills. It's also an opportunity for team members to collaborate and share ideas, leading to better solutions and a more cohesive team.

TypeScript's Role in Code Reviews

TypeScript's type annotations significantly enhance the code review process. Here's how:

1. **Clarity of Intent:** Type annotations make the code more self-documenting. Reviewers can quickly understand the expected types of variables, function parameters, and return values, reducing the need for excessive comments or explanations.
2. **Early Feedback on Type Errors:** TypeScript's type checker often catches potential errors even before the code is run. During code review, you can focus on higher-level issues like design, architecture, and performance, as the type checker has already taken care of many potential type-related problems.
3. **Refactoring Discussions:** When discussing potential refactorings during a code review, type annotations can help clarify the impact of changes on the rest of the codebase. This can lead to more informed decisions and less risk of introducing unexpected side effects.
4. **Streamlined Review Process:** Overall, TypeScript's type information streamlines the code review process by making the code more transparent and easier to understand. This allows reviewers to focus on the core logic and provide more meaningful feedback.

Tips for Effective TypeScript Code Reviews

- **Focus on the Big Picture:** While type errors are important to catch, don't get bogged down in nitpicking minor stylistic issues. Focus on the overall design, functionality, and maintainability of the code.
- **Explain Type-Related Suggestions:** If you suggest changes to types, provide clear explanations for why those changes are necessary.
- **Use Tooling:** Leverage your IDE's code review tools to navigate through code, view type information, and track changes.
- **Encourage Discussion:** Code reviews should be a collaborative process. Encourage open communication and respectful discussion to foster a positive learning environment.

Key Points

- Code reviews are essential for maintaining code quality and ensuring best practices.
- TypeScript's type annotations make code reviews more efficient by clarifying the code's intent and structure.
- Focus on the big picture, explain type-related suggestions, use tooling, and encourage open communication during code reviews.

By incorporating TypeScript into your code review process, you can unlock a new level of collaboration and code quality assurance, leading to more robust, maintainable, and reliable TypeScript applications.

Beyond the Basics: Advanced Best Practices

Type Narrowing Techniques

As you delve deeper into TypeScript, you'll encounter scenarios where you need to work with values that could be of multiple types (union types). To safely interact with these values, TypeScript provides several powerful techniques for narrowing down their types. This process, called type narrowing, lets you confidently access properties or methods specific to a particular type within the union.

1. Type Guards: Explicit Checks for Specific Types

Type guards are expressions that perform runtime checks to determine the type of a value. TypeScript recognizes certain patterns as type guards, allowing it to narrow down the type within the guarded block of code.

- **`typeof` operator:** Used to check against primitive types (string, number, boolean, etc.).
```
if (typeof value === "string") { // TypeScript knows value is a string
here }
```
- **`instanceof` operator:** Used to check if a value is an instance of a specific class.
```
if (value instanceof MyClass) { // TypeScript knows value is of type
MyClass here }
```
- **in operator:** Used to check if a property exists on an object.
```
if ("propertyName" in myObject) { // TypeScript knows myObject has the
property 'propertyName' }
```
- **Custom type guards:** You can define your own type guards using functions that return a type predicate (e.g., `pet is Fish`).
```
function isFish(pet: Fish | Bird): pet is Fish { return (pet as
Fish).swim !== undefined; }
```

2. Discriminated Unions: Tagging for Easy Identification

Discriminated unions are a pattern where you include a common property (often called a discriminant or tag) in each member of a union. This property allows you to distinguish between the different types within the union during runtime.

```
interface Circle { kind: "circle"; radius: number; } interface Square { kind: "square"; sideLength: number; } type Shape = Circle | Square;
```

In this example, the `kind` property acts as the discriminant. You can use a type guard (e.g., a `switch` statement on `shape.kind`) to determine the specific type of a Shape value.

3. Control Flow Analysis: TypeScript's Deductive Reasoning

TypeScript's compiler is intelligent enough to analyze your code's control flow (e.g., `if` statements, `switch` statements, assignments) and automatically narrow down types based on the conditions and checks you perform.

```
function processValue(x: string | number) { if (typeof x === "string") { // TypeScript knows x is a string in this block } else { // TypeScript knows x is a number in this block } }
```

In this example, TypeScript automatically infers the narrower type of x within each branch of the `if` statement based on the `typeof` check.

Best Practices

- **Prioritize Type Guards:** Whenever possible, use explicit type guards for clarity and maintainability. They make your intentions explicit and help other developers understand your code.
- **Use Discriminated Unions:** For complex union types, consider using discriminated unions for easier type narrowing.
- **Leverage Control Flow Analysis:** Let TypeScript's compiler do the work for you. Write your code in a way that allows it to infer the correct types based on control flow.

By mastering these type narrowing techniques, you'll be equipped to handle complex type scenarios in your TypeScript code. You'll be able to work with values of different types confidently, ensuring that your code remains type-safe and free of errors.

Advanced Generic Patterns

While the basic usage of generics in TypeScript can be immensely powerful, there are more advanced patterns that can truly unlock the full potential of this feature. Let's delve into some of these techniques to create even more flexible, reusable, and type-safe code.

1. Generic Utility Functions: Building Blocks for Type Manipulation

Generic utility functions are functions that operate on a wide variety of types, providing reusable logic for common tasks like mapping, filtering, or combining data.

Example: `UnwrapPromise`

```
type UnwrapPromise<T> = T extends Promise<infer U> ? U : T; // Usage type PromiseResult = UnwrapPromise<Promise<string>>; // string type NumberResult = UnwrapPromise<number>; // number
```

This `UnwrapPromise<T>` type extracts the type that a Promise resolves to (if T is a Promise), or returns T itself if it's not a Promise. This can be used in various scenarios where you need to work with the result of a Promise without knowing its specific type in advance.

Example: `ExcludeNullUndefined`

```
type ExcludeNullUndefined<T> = Exclude<T, null | undefined>; // Usage type
StringWithoutNull = ExcludeNullUndefined<string | null>; // string
```

This `ExcludeNullUndefined<T>` type removes `null` and `undefined` from a union type, ensuring that the resulting type is non-nullable.

2. Complex Type Constraints: Ensuring Compatibility

You can use complex type constraints to enforce stricter requirements on the types that can be used with your generic functions or classes. This involves combining multiple type conditions using the `extends` keyword and other type operators.

Example: `IsEqual` Function

```
function isEqual<T, U extends T>(a: T, b: U): boolean { return a === b; }
```

In this example, the `isEqual` function requires that the second argument (b) be assignable to the first argument (a). This ensures type compatibility and prevents errors when comparing values of different types.

3. Conditional Types with Generics: Dynamic Type Selection

You can combine conditional types with generics to create types that adapt based on specific conditions.

Example: `ReturnType<T>` Utility Type

```
type ReturnType<T extends (...args: any) => any> = T extends (...args: any) =>
infer R ? R : any; function greet(name: string): string { return `Hello,
${name}!`; } type Greeting = ReturnType<typeof greet>; // string
```

- Here the `ReturnType<T>` type accepts a function type T and returns the return type of T.

Example: `InstanceType<T>` Utility Type

```
type InstanceType<T extends new (...args: any) => any> = T extends new
(...args: any) => infer R ? R : any;
```

This utility type takes a constructor function and returns the type of the instance that the constructor creates.

Key Points

- Advanced generic patterns offer greater flexibility and type safety.
- You can create generic utility functions for common type transformations.
- Complex type constraints help enforce stricter type requirements.
- Combining conditional types with generics allows for dynamic type selection.
- Explore TypeScript's built-in utility types for additional type manipulation options.

By delving into these advanced generic patterns, you'll gain a deeper understanding of TypeScript's type system and its capabilities. You'll be able to create more sophisticated and reusable types, leading to cleaner, more expressive, and more reliable TypeScript code.

Utilizing Utility Types

TypeScript's built-in utility types are like handy shortcuts for common type transformations. They provide a concise and expressive way to manipulate existing types, reducing boilerplate code and improving the readability and reusability of your type definitions.

Let's delve into some practical examples of how you can leverage these utility types:

1. `Partial<Type>`: Making All Properties Optional

Imagine you have a `User` interface with required properties:

```
interface User { id: number; name: string; email: string; }
```

Now, you need a type for updating user data, where not all fields might be provided. Instead of creating a new interface with all optional properties, you can use `Partial<User>`:

```
function updateUser(user: Partial<User>) { // ... update user logic ... }
updateUser({ name: 'New Name' }); // Valid, only updating the name
```

2. `Pick<Type, Keys>`: Selecting Specific Properties

If you only need a subset of properties from an existing type, use `Pick`:

```
type UserInfo = Pick<User, 'id' | 'name'>; // { id: number; name: string; }
```

This creates a new type `UserInfo` that includes only the `id` and `name` properties from `User`.

3. `Omit<Type, Keys>`: Excluding Specific Properties

Conversely, `Omit` allows you to create a new type by excluding certain properties:

```
type UserWithoutEmail = Omit<User, 'email'>; // { id: number; name: string; }
```

Here, `UserWithoutEmail` has the same properties as `User` except for `email`.

4. `Record<Keys, Type>`: Creating Dictionaries

The `Record` utility type lets you create a type that maps a set of keys to a specific type of value:

```
type WeekdaySchedule = Record<"Monday" | "Tuesday" | "Wednesday" | "Thursday"
| "Friday", string>; const mySchedule: WeekdaySchedule = { Monday: "Work",
Tuesday: "Gym", Wednesday: "Study", Thursday: "Rest", Friday: "Weekend!", };
```

In this example, `WeekdaySchedule` is a type where the keys are weekdays and the values are strings representing your schedule for each day.

5. `Exclude`, `Extract`, and `ReturnType`

Other utility types like `Exclude`, `Extract`, and `ReturnType` can be used for more specific type manipulations:

- **`Exclude<Type, Union>`:** Removes types from a union.
- **`Extract<Type, Union>`:** Extracts types from a union that match another union.
- **`ReturnType<Type>`:** Obtains the return type of a function type.

Key Points

- Utility types are your shortcuts for common type transformations.
- Use `Partial` for optional properties, `Pick` for selecting properties, and `Omit` for excluding properties.
- `Record` is helpful for defining dictionary-like types.
- Explore other utility types like `Exclude`, `Extract`, and `ReturnType` for more specialized needs.

By leveraging these utility types, you can create cleaner, more concise, and more reusable type definitions in your TypeScript projects. They encapsulate common patterns, reducing boilerplate code and making your type system more expressive.

Chapter Summary

In this chapter, we delved into best practices for writing clean, maintainable, and efficient TypeScript code. We covered the following key areas:

- **Project Organization:** We discussed the importance of structuring your codebase for maintainability, exploring approaches like Domain-Driven Design (DDD), feature-based organization, and layered architecture. We provided examples of how to use folders and modules effectively to create a clear and logical project structure.
- **Coding Style:** We emphasized the importance of type annotations for clarity and error prevention, while also encouraging the use of type inference where appropriate. We recommended naming conventions for variables, functions, and classes, and discussed the importance of clear and concise comments and documentation.
- **Error Handling:** We explored best practices for robust error handling in TypeScript, including using `try...catch` blocks, creating custom error classes, logging errors with detailed information, and providing informative error messages to users.
- **Performance Considerations:** We acknowledged the potential overhead of TypeScript's type checking and discussed strategies for mitigating it, such as incremental builds, caching, and parallelism. We also cautioned against overusing the any type and emphasized the importance of choosing efficient data structures.
- **Refactoring and Maintenance:** We highlighted how TypeScript's type system acts as a safety net during refactoring, helping you catch errors and maintain code integrity. We stressed the importance of keeping type definitions up-to-date and using code reviews to enforce best practices and ensure code quality.
- **Beyond the Basics:** We briefly touched upon advanced best practices like type narrowing techniques, advanced generic patterns, and utilizing TypeScript's built-in utility types for more sophisticated type manipulation.

By following these best practices and incorporating them into your TypeScript development workflow, you'll be well-equipped to create code that is not only functional but also clean, maintainable, efficient, and reliable. The combination of TypeScript's powerful type system and a disciplined approach to code organization and style will empower you to build high-quality applications that are a pleasure to work on and evolve over time.

TypeScript Community and Resources: Staying Up-to-Date

Outline

- The Vibrant TypeScript Community
- Official Resources
- Community Forums and Discussion Groups
- Conferences and Meetups
- Online Learning Platforms
- Chapter Summary

The Vibrant TypeScript Community

TypeScript isn't just a language; it's a thriving ecosystem with a passionate and supportive community of developers. Whether you're a beginner stumbling over your first type definitions or a seasoned pro tackling complex architectural challenges, the TypeScript community is your invaluable resource for learning, troubleshooting, and staying on the cutting edge of TypeScript's evolution.

Why the Community Matters

- **Learning Together:** The TypeScript community is a treasure trove of knowledge and experience. You'll find countless tutorials, blog posts, Stack Overflow answers, and open-source projects that can accelerate your learning journey. Don't hesitate to ask questions and learn from the collective wisdom of others.
- **Troubleshooting and Support:** Encountered a perplexing type error? Stuck on a tricky refactoring problem? The community is there to help. Online forums, discussion groups, and chat channels are filled with fellow TypeScript enthusiasts eager to share their expertise and help you overcome obstacles.
- **Staying Up-to-Date:** TypeScript is a rapidly evolving language, with new features and best practices emerging regularly. The community is your source for the latest news, updates, and discussions about the future of TypeScript. Engage with other developers to learn about new patterns, libraries, and tools that can enhance your TypeScript projects.

The Collaborative Spirit

One of the most remarkable aspects of the TypeScript community is its collaborative and supportive nature. You'll find experienced developers mentoring newcomers, passionate individuals creating and sharing open-source libraries, and everyone contributing to the overall growth of the TypeScript ecosystem.

Whether you're contributing to DefinitelyTyped by adding type definitions for libraries, answering questions on Stack Overflow, or simply participating in online discussions, your involvement in the community can make a real difference.

Getting Involved

Here are some ways to tap into the power of the TypeScript community:

- **Online Forums and Discussion Groups:**
  - Stack Overflow: Search for answers using the "typescript" tag or ask your own questions.

    - TypeScript Subreddit: Join discussions, share articles, and connect with other TypeScript enthusiasts.
    - TypeScript Discord Server: Engage in real-time conversations with other TypeScript developers.
- **Blogs and Newsletters:**
    - Follow the official TypeScript blog for updates and news.
    - Subscribe to TypeScript newsletters and blogs (like TypeScript Weekly) to receive curated content.
- **Conferences and Meetups:** Attend TypeScript conferences or local meetups to network with other developers and learn from experts.
- **Open Source Projects:** Contribute to TypeScript projects on GitHub or other platforms to sharpen your skills and give back to the community.

Remember, the TypeScript community is not just a resource; it's a network of passionate developers who are eager to share their knowledge and help others succeed. By actively participating, you can accelerate your learning, find solutions to challenges, and become an integral part of the vibrant TypeScript ecosystem.

Official Resources

The TypeScript team at Microsoft has created an abundance of official resources designed to help you learn, explore, and master the language. Let's dive into the most essential ones.

TypeScript Website: Your Central Hub

The official TypeScript website (https://www.typescriptlang.org/) is your gateway to the TypeScript universe. It serves as a comprehensive resource hub, offering everything you need to get started and stay up-to-date:

- **Download:** Find the latest version of TypeScript and instructions for installing it on your system.
- **Documentation:** Access in-depth documentation, tutorials, and guides that cover all aspects of TypeScript, from basic syntax to advanced type manipulation.
- **Playground:** Experiment with TypeScript code directly in your browser using the interactive TypeScript Playground. This is an excellent tool for testing code snippets, exploring new features, and sharing examples with others.
- **Community:** Find links to community forums, discussion groups, social media channels, and other resources where you can connect with fellow TypeScript developers and learn from their experiences.

TypeScript Handbook: Your Learning Companion

The TypeScript Handbook (https://www.typescriptlang.org/docs/handbook/intro.html) is the official guide to the language. It's a comprehensive and well-structured resource that takes you on a journey from the fundamentals of TypeScript to its most advanced features.

The handbook is organized into sections, each covering a specific aspect of the language:

- **Basic Types:** Covers primitive types, arrays, tuples, enums, and more.
- **Functions:** Explains function declarations, types, and how to work with them effectively.
- **Interfaces:** Introduces interfaces and their role in defining the shape of objects.
- **Classes:** Delves into classes, inheritance, and other object-oriented concepts.
- **Advanced Types:** Explores advanced type manipulation techniques like generics, conditional types, mapped types, and more.

Whether you're a beginner just starting or an experienced developer seeking to deepen your knowledge, the TypeScript Handbook is an invaluable resource that should always be within reach.

TypeScript Playground: Your Interactive Sandbox

The TypeScript Playground (https://www.typescriptlang.org/play) is a browser-based environment where you can write, compile, and run TypeScript code instantly. It's a fantastic tool for:

- **Experimentation:** Quickly test out new language features or try different approaches without having to set up a full project.
- **Learning:** Follow along with tutorials or examples from the handbook and see the results in real-time.
- **Sharing:** Easily share code snippets with others by creating a link to your playground code.

By taking advantage of these official resources, you'll have a solid foundation for learning and mastering TypeScript. The TypeScript website, handbook, and playground offer a wealth of information, examples, and interactive tools to guide you on your TypeScript journey.

Community Forums and Discussion Groups

The TypeScript community is vast and active, with numerous online spaces where you can connect with fellow developers, ask questions, share your knowledge, and stay up-to-date with the latest trends. Let's explore some of the most popular community forums and discussion groups.

Stack Overflow: The Q&A Powerhouse

Stack Overflow - https://stackoverflow.com/ is the undisputed champion of programming Q&A sites. It's a treasure trove of information, with countless questions and answers covering almost every imaginable TypeScript topic. Whether you're stuck on a specific error message or want to learn about a new feature, chances are someone has already asked and answered a similar question on Stack Overflow.

How to Use Stack Overflow Effectively

1. **Search:** Before asking a new question, use the search bar to look for existing solutions. Be specific in your keywords to narrow down the results.
2. **Use the "typescript" Tag:** Include the "typescript" tag in your searches to filter for TypeScript-related questions. If you're asking a new question, make sure to include this tag as well so that TypeScript experts can easily find and answer it.
3. **Provide Context:** When asking a question, provide as much context as possible, including code snippets, error messages, and relevant details about your environment. This will help others understand your problem and provide accurate solutions.
4. **Be Respectful:** The Stack Overflow community values well-formatted, clear, and respectful questions. Take the time to craft your questions thoughtfully to get the best possible responses.

TypeScript Subreddit: The Community Hub

The TypeScript subreddit (such as /r/typescript - https://www.reddit.com/r/typescript/) is a vibrant community where TypeScript enthusiasts gather to discuss the language, share articles and resources, and help each other out. It's a great place to:

- **Ask Questions:** Get help with TypeScript-related problems, big or small.
- **Discuss Features:** Share your thoughts and opinions about new TypeScript features or language proposals.
- **Discover Resources:** Find helpful tutorials, blog posts, libraries, and tools recommended by other developers.

- **Connect with Other Developers:** Meet like-minded people who share your passion for TypeScript.

TypeScript Discord Server: Real-Time Chat and Collaboration

The TypeScript Discord server offers a more real-time way to interact with the TypeScript community. It's a chat platform with channels dedicated to different topics, such as:

- **#help:** Ask questions and get assistance from other developers.
- **#general:** Discuss TypeScript topics in a casual setting.
- **#libraries:** Share and discover new TypeScript libraries and tools.
- **#off-topic:** Chat about non-TypeScript related topics (for when you need a break from typing).

The Discord server is a great place to get quick feedback, engage in conversations, and build relationships with other TypeScript enthusiasts.

Key Points

- The TypeScript community is a valuable resource for learning, troubleshooting, and staying up-to-date.
- Stack Overflow is your go-to platform for finding answers to specific questions.
- The TypeScript subreddit and Discord server offer spaces for discussion, sharing resources, and connecting with other developers.

By actively participating in these online communities, you'll accelerate your learning, find solutions to challenges, and become an integral part of the vibrant TypeScript ecosystem.

Conferences and Meetups

While online resources provide a wealth of information, there's something uniquely valuable about engaging with the TypeScript community in person. Conferences and meetups offer opportunities to learn directly from experts, network with fellow developers, and immerse yourself in the latest trends and innovations in the TypeScript ecosystem.

TypeScript Conferences: Deep Dives into the Language

TypeScript conferences are typically large-scale events that bring together TypeScript experts, thought leaders, and enthusiasts from around the world. These conferences feature:

- **Keynote Presentations:** Inspiring talks by industry leaders on the future of TypeScript and its applications.
- **Technical Sessions:** Deep dives into specific TypeScript features, best practices, and real-world use cases.
- **Workshops:** Hands-on sessions where you can learn new skills and techniques directly from experienced developers.
- **Networking Opportunities:** Connect with other TypeScript developers, share ideas, and build valuable relationships.

Notable TypeScript Conferences:

- **TSConf:** The premier TypeScript conference, featuring talks, workshops, and networking events.
- **International JavaScript Conference:** While not exclusively focused on TypeScript, this major conference often includes a significant number of TypeScript-related talks and workshops.
- **Various Tech Conferences:** Many general tech conferences like JSConf, React Conf, and QCon often include TypeScript-related content.

Finding Upcoming Conferences:

- **TypeScript Website:** The TypeScript website often lists upcoming conferences and events.
- **Conference Websites:** Check the websites of major tech conferences to see if they have TypeScript-related tracks.
- **Social Media:** Follow TypeScript and JavaScript-related hashtags on social media to discover new conferences.

Local TypeScript Meetups: Connecting with Your Community

TypeScript meetups are smaller, more informal gatherings of TypeScript enthusiasts in your local area. They often feature:

- **Lightning Talks:** Short presentations on specific topics by community members.
- **Coding Workshops:** Hands-on sessions to practice TypeScript skills.
- **Networking and Discussions:** Opportunities to meet other local developers, exchange ideas, and ask questions.

Finding Local Meetups:

- **Meetup.com:** Search for "TypeScript" on Meetup.com to find groups in your area.
- **Social Media:** Check social media groups or local developer communities for TypeScript meetups.

Key Points

- Conferences and meetups are excellent opportunities to learn, network, and stay up-to-date with TypeScript.
- TypeScript conferences offer deep dives into the language and its ecosystem.
- Local meetups provide a more intimate setting for connecting with other TypeScript developers in your area.
- Both conferences and meetups offer valuable opportunities for learning, networking, and staying engaged with the TypeScript community.

By actively participating in TypeScript conferences and meetups, you'll accelerate your growth as a TypeScript developer, gain valuable insights, and build lasting connections with like-minded individuals.

Online Learning Platforms

The internet is a vast repository of knowledge, and online learning platforms offer structured and accessible ways to master TypeScript. Here are some popular platforms where you can find high-quality TypeScript courses and tutorials:

1. **Frontend Masters:**
   This platform specializes in in-depth, expert-led courses on frontend technologies. Their TypeScript courses cover a wide range of topics, from the basics to advanced concepts, and are taught by experienced professionals.
2. **Udemy:**
   Udemy offers a massive selection of TypeScript courses at various price points. You'll find courses for beginners, intermediate learners, and even specialized courses on topics like TypeScript with React or Node.js. Look for courses with high ratings and reviews to ensure quality.
3. **Pluralsight:**
   Pluralsight is a subscription-based platform with a broad catalog of technical courses, including several on TypeScript. Their courses are known for their high production value and comprehensive coverage of topics.
4. **Coursera:**
   Coursera partners with universities and institutions to offer online courses, including some focused

on TypeScript. These courses often provide a more academic approach to learning TypeScript and might be part of broader programs or specializations.

5. **Egghead.io:**
   Egghead.io focuses on bite-sized video lessons on various programming topics, including TypeScript. Their lessons are concise, practical, and ideal for learning specific concepts or techniques.

Choosing the Right Platform

The best platform for you depends on your learning style, budget, and specific goals. Here are some factors to consider:

- **Course Format:** Some platforms offer video-based courses, while others focus on interactive lessons or text-based tutorials. Choose a format that aligns with your preferred learning style.
- **Level:** Consider your current TypeScript knowledge and choose courses that match your level (beginner, intermediate, or advanced).
- **Instructors:** Research the instructors and look for those with experience and expertise in TypeScript.
- **Cost:** Online learning platforms offer courses at various price points, including free and subscription-based options. Choose a platform that fits your budget.

Key Points

- Online learning platforms offer a wealth of TypeScript courses and tutorials.
- Consider your learning style, level, and budget when choosing a platform.
- Look for courses with high ratings, positive reviews, and experienced instructors.

By leveraging these online resources, you can take your TypeScript skills to the next level and build a strong foundation for your web development career. Whether you prefer structured courses or bite-sized lessons, you'll find the perfect learning path to master TypeScript.

Chapter Summary

In this chapter, we delved into the vibrant TypeScript community and the wealth of resources available to help you learn, troubleshoot, and stay at the forefront of TypeScript development. We covered the following key points:

- **The Vibrant Community:** We emphasized the importance of the TypeScript community for learning, support, and staying up-to-date. We highlighted its collaborative and supportive nature.
- **Official Resources:** We explored the official TypeScript resources provided by Microsoft:
  - **TypeScript Website:** The central hub for downloads, documentation, tutorials, the playground, and community links.
  - **TypeScript Handbook:** The comprehensive guide to the language, covering basic to advanced concepts.
  - **TypeScript Playground:** The interactive online environment for writing and testing TypeScript code.
- **Community Forums and Discussion Groups:** We highlighted online platforms where you can connect with fellow developers:
  - **Stack Overflow:** The go-to Q&A site for TypeScript questions and answers.
  - **TypeScript Subreddit:** A forum for discussions, articles, and resources.
  - **TypeScript Discord Server:** A real-time chat platform for interacting with the community.
- **Conferences and Meetups:** We explored TypeScript conferences (like TSConf) and local meetups as excellent opportunities to learn from experts, network with other developers, and stay informed about the latest developments in the TypeScript world.

- **Online Learning Platforms:** We listed popular online platforms like Frontend Masters, Udemy, Pluralsight, Coursera, and Egghead.io that offer TypeScript courses and tutorials.

By actively participating in the TypeScript community and utilizing the wide range of available resources, you'll be well-equipped to continue your learning journey, overcome challenges, and stay at the forefront of TypeScript development. The vibrant community and rich ecosystem of resources ensure that you'll never be alone on your TypeScript adventure.

Appendices

Appendix A: TypeScript Configuration Options

The `tsconfig.json` file is the heart of configuring your TypeScript projects. It allows you to fine-tune how the TypeScript compiler (tsc) behaves and tailors the build process to your specific needs. In this appendix, we'll delve into the essential and commonly used compiler options, empowering you to craft the perfect configuration for your projects.

Understanding the Structure

The `tsconfig.json` file is a JSON object that typically contains two main sections:

1. `compilerOptions`: Contains settings that control how TypeScript compiles your code.
2. Other Options: Includes settings for managing files, excluding directories, and more.

Essential Compiler Options

Target (`target`)

Specifies the version of JavaScript that TypeScript should generate as output. Common options include:

- **ES5:** The most widely supported version, ensuring compatibility with older browsers and environments.
- **ES6 (or ES2015):** Enables modern JavaScript features like arrow functions, classes, and template literals.
- **`ESNext`:** Targets the latest JavaScript features, including those not yet finalized.

Module (`module`)

Determines the module system to use in your project. The main options are:

- **`CommonJS`:** The standard module system for Node.js.
- **`ESNext` (or `ES2020`, etc.):** Use this for the newer ES Modules (ESM) standard, which is becoming the default in modern JavaScript environments.

outDir (`outDir`)

Specifies the directory where the compiled JavaScript files should be placed. It's a good practice to keep your source code and output separate, so a common value is `"./dist"` or `"./build"`.

rootDir (`rootDir`)

Specifies the root directory of your TypeScript source files. This is usually set to `"./src"`.

Strict Mode (`strict`)

Enabling strict mode turns on a set of stricter type-checking options that help you catch more potential errors and write more robust code.

Here are some of the key strict mode options:

- **`strictNullChecks`:** Requires explicit null and undefined checks.
- **`noImplicitAny`:** Disallows implicit any types.
- **`strictFunctionTypes`:** Enforces stricter contravariance for function parameters.
- **`strictBindCallApply`:** Disallows incorrect usage of `bind`, `call`, and `apply` on functions.

While strict mode might initially lead to more compiler errors, it ultimately helps you write safer and more predictable code.

allowJs (`allowJs`)

Set this to `true` if you want to include JavaScript files (`.js`) in your TypeScript project. This is useful during gradual migration from JavaScript to TypeScript.

checkJs (`checkJs`)

When `allowJs` is enabled, setting `checkJs` to `true` will make TypeScript perform type checking on your JavaScript files as well. This can help catch potential errors even in code that hasn't been explicitly converted to TypeScript.

Other Useful Options

- **`esModuleInterop`:** Enables interoperability between CommonJS and ES Modules when importing or exporting.
- **`skipLibCheck`:** Skips type checking of declaration files (e.g., `.d.ts` files from `node_modules`).
- **`forceConsistentCasingInFileNames`:** Helps avoid issues with case-sensitive file systems.
- `**include**`: Specifies the files or directories that should be included in the compilation process.
- `**exclude**`: Specifies the files or directories that should be excluded from the compilation process.
- **types:** Specifies the type declaration files (`.d.ts`) to include in the compilation scope.

Using the TypeScript Compiler (tsc)

Once you've configured your `tsconfig.json`, you can use the TypeScript compiler (`tsc`) to compile your code:

```
tsc // Compiles all TypeScript files in the project tsc myFile.ts // Compiles
a specific file
```

You can find a comprehensive list of all TypeScript compiler options in the official documentation: https://www.typescriptlang.org/docs/handbook/compiler-options.html

By understanding and customizing these configuration options, you can tailor TypeScript to your specific project needs, creating a build process that is efficient, type-safe, and optimized for your chosen environment.

Appendix B: TypeScript Compiler (tsc) Reference

The TypeScript compiler (`tsc`) is your trusty sidekick for transforming TypeScript code into JavaScript. It's a command-line tool that you can use to compile your code, check for errors, generate type declarations, and more. In this appendix, we'll provide a reference guide to some of the most common and useful `tsc` commands and options, empowering you to take full control of your TypeScript compilation process.

Basic Usage

- **`tsc`:** Compiles all TypeScript files in your project based on the configuration in your `tsconfig.json` file (or the default configuration if no `tsconfig.json` is present).
- **`tsc <filename>`:** Compiles a specific TypeScript file.

Compiler Options

Watch Mode (`--watch` or `-w`)

Watches for changes in your TypeScript files and automatically recompiles them whenever you save. This is extremely useful during development, as it provides immediate feedback on type errors and updates your JavaScript output without manual intervention.

```
tsc --watch # or tsc -w
```

Project Mode (`--project` or `-p`)

Specifies the path to your `tsconfig.json` file. If you have multiple TypeScript projects or custom configurations, you can use this option to tell `tsc` which configuration to use.

```
tsc --project ./tsconfig.app.json # or tsc -p tsconfig.app.json
```

No Emit (`--noEmit`)

Performs type checking but does not generate any output JavaScript files. This is useful if you only want to check for type errors without actually compiling your code.

```
tsc --noEmit
```

Emit Declaration Files (`--declaration` or `-d`)

Generates `.d.ts` declaration files alongside your compiled JavaScript. These files contain type information about your code and are essential for making your modules or libraries usable in other TypeScript projects.

```
tsc --declaration # or tsc -d
```

Other Useful Options

- **`--target` or `-t`:** Specifies the JavaScript version to target (e.g., `--target ES6`).
- **`--module` or `-m`:** Specifies the module system to use (e.g., `--module CommonJS`).
- **`--outDir`:** Specifies the output directory for compiled JavaScript files.
- **`--rootDir`:** Specifies the root directory of your TypeScript source files.

- **`--strict`:** Enables all strict type-checking options.
- **`--noImplicitAny`:** Disallows implicit any types.
- **`--removeComments`:** Removes comments from the generated JavaScript.
- **`--sourceMap`:** Generates source maps for debugging.

Advanced Usage

Build Scripts (`package.json`)

You can add scripts to your `package.json` file to streamline common tasks:

```
{ "scripts": { "build": "tsc", "build:watch": "tsc --watch", "start": "node dist/index.js" } }
```

Now you can run `npm run build` to compile your code, `npm run build:watch` to start the watch mode, and `npm start` to run your compiled code.

Integrating with Build Tools

For larger projects, you'll typically integrate `tsc` into your build process using tools like webpack, Parcel, or Rollup. These tools can automate the compilation of your TypeScript code as part of the overall build process.

Additional Notes

- Refer to the official TypeScript documentation for a complete list of compiler options and their descriptions: https://www.typescriptlang.org/docs/handbook/compiler-options.html
- Many code editors and IDEs have built-in support for running `tsc` and managing your TypeScript projects. Explore the settings in your editor to find these features.

By mastering the `tsc` compiler and its options, you gain full control over the TypeScript compilation process, allowing you to customize the output, catch errors early, and optimize your workflow for maximum productivity.

Conclusion

Congratulations! You've reached the end of "TypeScript Made Easy," but your journey into the world of TypeScript is just beginning. By mastering the core types, exploring advanced concepts like generics and decorators, diving into real-world applications with React and Node.js, and adopting best practices, you've laid a solid foundation for building robust, scalable, and maintainable TypeScript applications.

What You've Learned

- **Why TypeScript Matters:** You've seen how TypeScript enhances JavaScript by adding static types, improving code readability, catching errors early, and empowering you with better tooling and developer experience.
- **Core Types:** You've become familiar with TypeScript's fundamental types, including numbers, strings, booleans, arrays, tuples, and more.
- **Functions and Classes:** You've mastered the art of writing type-safe functions and classes, leveraging features like interfaces, type aliases, generics, and decorators.
- **Real-World Applications:** You've explored how TypeScript can be applied to build modern user interfaces with React and robust backends with Node.js. You've learned how to handle asynchronous operations, test your code thoroughly, and optimize your workflow with the right tools.
- **Advanced Concepts:** You've ventured into advanced type manipulation techniques, using conditional types, mapped types, and template literal types to express complex relationships and create highly reusable code.
- **Community and Resources:** You've discovered the vibrant TypeScript community and the wealth of resources available to help you continue your learning journey.

Your TypeScript Toolkit

You now have a comprehensive toolkit at your disposal:

- **Type System:** A robust system for defining and enforcing types in your code.
- **Interfaces and Classes:** Tools for creating organized and reusable code structures.
- **Generics:** A mechanism for writing flexible and type-safe code that can work with various data types.
- **Modules:** A way to structure your projects into reusable and maintainable units.
- **Advanced Type Manipulation:** Techniques for creating complex and expressive types.
- **Tooling and Libraries:** A wealth of tools and libraries to streamline your workflow and boost productivity.
- **A Supportive Community:** A vibrant community of developers ready to help and share knowledge.

The Path Ahead

TypeScript is a constantly evolving language, and the possibilities are endless. As you continue your journey, you'll discover even more advanced techniques, libraries, and frameworks that can elevate your TypeScript skills to new heights. Don't be afraid to experiment, explore, and push the boundaries of what you can achieve with TypeScript.

Remember, the key to mastering TypeScript is practice and continuous learning. Embrace the TypeScript mindset of type safety and use it to build applications that are not only functional but also reliable, maintainable, and enjoyable to work with.

---

www.ingramcontent.com/pod-product-compliance
Lightning Source LLC
LaVergne TN
LVHW081751050326
832903LV00027B/1902

* 9 7 9 8 3 2 6 7 3 6 3 3 8 *